America Through European Eyes

EDITED BY
AURELIAN CRAIUTU & JEFFREY C. ISAAC

AMERICA THROUGH EUROPEAN EYES

British and French Reflections on the New World
from the Eighteenth Century to the Present

The Pennsylvania State University Press
University Park, Pennsylvania

LIBRARY OF CONGRESS
CATALOGING-IN-PUBLICATION DATA

America through European eyes : British and French reflections on
the new world from the eighteenth century to the present / edited
by Aurelian Craiutu and Jeffrey C. Isaac.
p.   cm.
Includes bibliographical references and index.
Summary: "A collection of essays that discuss representative
eighteenth- and nineteenth-century French and English views of
American democracy and society, and offer a critical assessment of
various narrative constructions of American life, society, and
culture"—Provided by publisher.
ISBN 978-0-271-03391-4 (pbk: alk. paper)

1. United States—Foreign public opinion, British—History.
2. United States—Foreign public opinion, French—History.
3. Democracy—United States—Public opinion—History.
4. Public opinion—Great Britain—History.
5. Public opinion—France—History.
I. Craiutu, Aurelian.
II. Isaac, Jeffrey C., 1957– .

E169.1.A4719128 2009
303.3'80941—dc22
2008033412

The Pennsylvania State University Press is a member of the
Association of American University Presses.

It is the policy of The Pennsylvania State University Press
to use acid-free paper. This book is printed on stock
that meets the minimum
requirements of American National Standard for
Information Sciences—Permanence of Paper for
Printed Library Material, ANSI Z39.48-1992.

Contents

Acknowledgments

The chapters of this book were originally presented at an international conference, "America Seen through Foreign Eyes," organized at Indiana University, Bloomington, March 24–26, 2005. We would like to express our gratitude to all those who accepted our invitation and agreed to contribute to this volume. The completion of this project would not have been possible without the generous financial help provided by Indiana University's College of Arts and Sciences Arts and Humanities Institute (directed by Andrea Ciccarelli), Former Dean Kumble Subbaswamy, the West European Studies Institute, the Department of Political Science, and the Office of International Scholars at Indiana University.

We want to express our deepest gratitude to Margot Morgan, who served as a research assistant for Aurelian Craiutu on this project, and who has played an important editing role at key stages of this project. We would also like to thank Scott Feickert, Fern Bennett, and the late Rochelle Picou for their invaluable help. Alan Levine provided useful comments on a previous draft of the book's introduction, and Andrei Markovits, Fritz Breithaupt, Jonathan Elmer, and Oana Panaite were extremely generous to share with us their insights on the topics discussed in this book.

In recent years, the study of political theory at Indiana University, Bloomington, has evolved from an expanding graduate program into a vibrant intellectual community. We would like to thank our many colleagues, faculty and graduate students alike, for their participation in our regular Political Theory Lunch and in our conference, and for enriching our scholarly lives.

Finally, we would like to express our deepest gratitude to Sandy Thatcher and the two anonymous referees who provided extremely useful suggestions for revising the entire manuscript. Special thanks are also due to Joohyung Kim, who provided the index to this volume, and to the Penn State University Press staff and our copyeditor, Sue Breckenridge, for their expert editorial assistance.

A. C. & J. I.

Le pays singulier, où l'homme n'est mû que par trois
idées: l'argent, la liberté et Dieu.
—*Stendhal*

INTRODUCTION

Europeans in Search of America

Aurelian Craiutu and Jeffrey C. Isaac

In America I Saw More than America
—*Tocqueville*

Ever since its discovery by the Europeans, America[1] has captivated the imagination of people around the world, as a geographic space and as a site of human possibility. As the United States became a major political actor on the world scene and acquired over time a powerful symbolic status, Europeans often saw in America, to use Tocqueville's famous words, much "more than America."[2] In America, they perceived the "image of democracy itself, its inclinations, character, prejudices, and passions."[3] During the past two and a half centuries, admirers and critics alike have put forward an amazingly diverse array of interpretations ranging from celebrations of America as the land of freedom and the "City upon a Hill" to accusations of America as a police state that condones deep-seated injustices and plays the role of an arrogant imperial power.[4]

---

1. The use of the word *America* requires the usual caveats. Most of the time, the concept exclusively stands for the United States and does not designate the entire New World or the entire North American continent. While there might be many (methodological) reasons for working with a simplified meaning of the concept, we wanted to go *beyond* the conventional meaning of America, without seeking, however, to "deconstruct" or "overcome" America. True to our commitment to intellectual diversity, we have included two chapters (by Bradatan and Nesbitt) that discuss specifically the larger meaning of America as standing for the New World.

2. Alexis de Tocqueville, *Democracy in America,* trans. Delba Winthrop and Harvey C. Mansfield (Chicago: University of Chicago Press, 2000), 13.

3. Tocqueville, *Democracy in America,* 13.

4. Durand Echeverria's classic book, *Mirage in the West: A History of the French Image of American*

With the benefit of hindsight, it is difficult to deny that the twentieth century was, in almost all respects, an "American century" in which America's political and economic supremacy and symbolic status among other nations was consolidated. The United States stood firmly against both fascism and communism, and assumed responsibility for protecting the values of Western civilization that were threatened by the rise of totalitarian doctrines. Yet America's rise to prominence has paradoxically been accompanied by a certain uneasiness among its more ambivalent friends as well as its critics. While giving America its due credit for resisting European imperial aggressions, commentators have often feared that the growing Americanization of the world might come to have a nefarious influence on the human soul, as well as on the bodies, of the many peoples across the world who stood in the way of America's self-understood project of expanding the sphere of "liberty."

The end of the cold war almost two decades ago seemed to herald an "end of ideology," and to bolster America's image or self-image as the defender of freedom, by promoting the United States to the rank of the world's only superpower. Nonetheless, it did not take commentators long to realize that America's political, military, economic, and cultural hegemony was bound to generate unintended and troubling consequences, and that these would seriously challenge the political supremacy of the United States and its globalizing vision of democracy in the twenty-first century. After the shocking and tragic events of September 11, 2001, the generous rhetoric of *"We are all Americans"*[5] signaled for a brief

---

Society to 1815 (Princeton: Princeton University Press, 1957) is an indispensable point of departure for anyone interested in this topic; Echeverria's book also contains a useful bibliographical note (283–85). Other works addressing related questions are Philippe Roger, *The American Enemy: The History of French Anti-Americanism*, trans. Sharon Bowman (Chicago: University of Chicago Press, 2005); Andrei S. Markovits, *Uncouth Nation: Why Europe Dislikes America* (Princeton: Princeton University Press, 2007); James W. Ceaser, *Reconstructing America: The Symbol of America in Modern Thought* (New Haven: Yale University Press, 1997); Stephen Brooks, *America through Foreign Eyes* (Oxford: Oxford University Press, 2002); Jacques Portes, *Fascination and Misgivings: The United States in French Opinion, 1870–1914* (Cambridge: Cambridge University Press, 2000); Karen Ordahl Kopperman, ed., *America in European Consciousness: 1493–1750* (Chapel Hill: University of North Carolina Press, 1995); Peter Conrad, *Imagining America* (New York: Oxford University Press, 1980); Thomas K. Murphy, *The Changing Image of America in Europe, 1780–1830* (Lanham, Md.: Lexington Books, 2001); and Claus Offe, *Reflections on America: Tocqueville, Weber, and Adorno in the United States* (London: Polity, 2005). Also worth consulting are Halvden Koht, *The American Spirit in Europe* (Philadelphia: University of Pennsylvania Press, 1949); Sigmund Skard, *The American Myth and the European Mind* (New York: Harper & Row, 1949); and Allan Nevins, *America through British Eyes* (New York: Oxford University Press, 1948). The French intellectuals' attitudes toward America are discussed by Jean-Philippe Mathy, *Extrême-Occident: French Intellectuals and America* (Chicago: University of Chicago Press, 1993); Jean-Claude Lamberti, "Le modèle américain en France de 1789 à nos jours," *Commentaire* 10, no. 39 (1987): 490–98; and Reiji Matsumoto, "From Model to Menace: French Intellectuals and American Civilization," *Japanese Journal of American Studies* 15 (2004): 163–85. For a recent account, see Bernard-Henri Lévy, *American Vertigo: Traveling America in the Footsteps of Tocqueville* (New York: Random House, 2006).

5. The title of an op-ed published in the French newspaper *Le Monde* on September 12, 2001.

moment that the world—and especially the European world—felt a deep solidarity with a free country under attack by violent fundamentalist extremists. Yet in many quarters the genuine sympathy for America disappeared almost as quickly as it had surfaced, replaced by a growing aversion to U.S. foreign policy and, for some, an outright aversion to "America" itself, as a political and economic power and as a society, indeed as the modern society par excellence. While no doubt fueled in large part by the aggressively moralistic "Bush Doctrine," and by the Bush Administration's so-called "preventive" war in Iraq, for many it was not simply what America was doing but what it *was* that came under suspicion and sometimes under rhetorical attack. Commentators continue to debate the extent to which this criticism of the United States represented a troubling and perhaps virulent form of "anti-Americanism."[6] But there can be no denying that "America" is (yet again?) a source of symbolic and political controversy, and its exemplary status, and indeed its value as a "democratic republic," has been placed into question.

Regardless of whether or not America's current foreign policy should be regarded as a form of imperial overreach, the rise of new discourses of suspicion toward the United States, and indeed of new forms of what many supporters and critics alike have come to regard as "anti-Americanism," cannot—and should not—leave us indifferent. For the rhetorical contest over "America" condenses and shapes many of the central dynamics of contemporary geopolitical contestation. And yet, surprisingly and indeed ironically, as the symbolic contest for the "real" image of America goes on, for many citizens around the globe, American society continues to be an unknown (cultural and political) universe, a true *terra incognita*. The remark once made by Johan Huizinga—"we know much too little about America"[7]—remains as valid today as when it was uttered a century ago. This is especially true among many of America's critics around the world, who often rely on myths and preconceptions of American society that are vicarious expressions of their dissatisfaction with their own societies. This intellectual tendency to project hopes and fears onto "America" has abetted a disquieting

6. For more information, see, for example, this volume's concluding chapter by Jeffrey C. Isaac ("Conclusion: America Between Past and Future"). Also see Andrei Markovits, *European Anti-Americanism (and Anti-Semitism): Ever Present though Always Denied*, Working Series Paper 108 (Cambridge, Mass.: Minda de Gunzburg Center for European Studies, Harvard University, 2004); Markovits, *Uncouth Nation*; Jean-François Revel, *Anti-Americanism* (London: Encounter Books, 2004); Paul Hollander, *Anti-Americanism: Critiques at Home and Abroad, 1965–1990* (New York: Oxford University Press, 1992); Peter J. Katzenstein and Robert O. Keohane, eds., *Anti-Americanisms in World Politics* (Ithaca: Cornell University Press, 2006); Brendon O'Connor, ed., *Anti-Americanism: History, Causes, and Themes*, 4 vols. (Oxford: Greenwood, 2007); James C. Ceaser, "A Genealogy of Anti-Americanism," *Public Interest* 152 (Summer 2003): 3–18.

7. Johan Huizinga, *America: A Dutch Historian's Vision, from Afar and Near* (New York: Harper & Row, 1972), 3.

confusion of facts, images, and representations, and it makes it difficult, if not impossible, to disentangle the "real" from the "imagined" America. In one sense this is hardly an issue distinctive to America, for as we well know, all societies involve symbols and "social imaginaries," and indeed the modern nation-state is grounded not in any "real" substrate but in an "imagined community," to use Benedict Anderson's well-known phrase. Nonetheless, if all social forms are equally symbolic, this does not mean that all symbols are equally important. And, for reasons that have everything to do with the historical evolution of the United States in relation to Europe, and with the current structure of world politics, and especially with the global reach of American economic, political, and cultural power, "America" has become a particularly potent symbol, whose understanding—and misunderstanding—carries particularly significant consequences.

That is precisely why it is both timely and important to study the origins and the evolution of the image of America in the eyes of European travelers and commentators. It is our hope that by revisiting some classic accounts of American society and politics, we can shed some light on the genealogy and the coherence of current controversies about "America," and thereby help, in a small way, to make possible more productive debates both about what the United States does and what it is.[8]

Our book examines the representations of America in the writings of modern French and English travelers. We have chosen to limit our focus to British and French commentators mainly because their societies have historically had the most intense contact with America. Obviously, Spain's "discovery" of "the New World," and its colonization of part of it, was historically formative, as were the early activities of the Dutch and Portuguese. And obviously over the course of time, and as it expanded westward, the United States became a true "melting pot" of nations and ethnicities. The narratives produced by these complex encounters are all no doubt important, and the narrative of American history, and of the history of "America" as a symbol, has a place for all of these discourses. Nonetheless, from the Seven Years' War and the American Revolution to the Louisiana Purchase to the First and Second World Wars, the complex relations with Britain and France have exerted a powerful influence on the fate of America.

In choosing to present accounts of the opinions on America expressed by lesser-known French figures such as Gustave de Beaumont, Michel Chevalier, Jean-Jacques Ampère, Guillaume-Tell Poussin, Victor Jacquemont, Édouard Laboulaye, and Duvergier de Hauranne, we wanted not only to go beyond the often-cited Alexis de Tocqueville, but also to demonstrate the *faux pas* commit-

8. Huizinga, *America,* 4.

ted by recent critics of French politics who have mistakenly argued that France has been America's oldest enemy.[9] Not only is this false—France is the only major West European country never to have been at war with the United States—but, what is more, there were many perceptive French travelers to the United States who left valuable accounts of their travels that revealed original aspects of America that are worth reconsidering today. Although these French writers often complained that the Americans were "uncultivated," we should not assume that the whole range of French attitudes toward America was exhausted by the lamentations of their most skeptical Cassandras. The famous Statue of Liberty—a global symbol of America as a haven of liberty—was indeed a gift of France to America, and the thinker who first came up with the idea behind F. Bartholdi's project was none other than Édouard Laboulaye, a major liberal politician during the Second Empire and himself an enlightened disciple of Tocqueville.

More broadly, we have sought to underscore the complexity of European experiences *of* America as well as the complexity of European reflections *on* America. The writers discussed in this volume invite us to rediscover the diversity of America. Needless to say, what Gustave de Beaumont discerned in America differed from Frances Trollope's more critical view of American mores. Bryce and Chesterton were both Englishmen, but their accounts of America were remarkably different in their emphases, hopes, and fears. One might argue, by looking at the range of accounts offered by French and English commentators featured below, that each of them discovered, so to speak, their own America, and that in almost all cases, their perceptions of America were highly selective, filtered through preexisting conceptual lenses. Yet the accounts authored by these writers combined perceptive discussions of America with original meditations on the nature of modernity, the character of democracy, and the destiny of their own countries. For most of them, America was a starting point *sui generis*, or, to put it differently, a bridge between what they saw in Europe and what they aspired to change there. This attitude is best illustrated by the famous statement

---

9. See, for example, John J. Miller and Mark Molesky, *Our Oldest Enemy: A History of America's Disastrous Relationship with France* (New York: Doubleday, 2004). For an equally immoderate account of America, see Emmanuel Todd, *Après Empire* (Paris: Gallimard, 2003). Todd's book was reviewed by Henri Astier in the *Times Literary Supplement*, January 10, 2003, 3–4. A balanced interpretation of Franco-American relations can be found in Joseph Klaits and Michael H. Haltzel, eds., *Liberty/Liberté: The American and French Experiences* (Washington, D.C.: Woodrow Wilson Center Press; Baltimore: Johns Hopkins University Press, 1991). The book contains, among other interesting contributions, two useful chapters on the building and significance of the Statue of Liberty and the political writings of Édouard Laboulaye. For general surveys, see Jean-Baptiste Duroselle, *La France et les États-Unis des origines à nos jours* (Paris: Seuil, 1976); Henry Blumenthal, *American and French Culture, 1800–1900* (Baton Rouge: Louisiana State University Press, 1975); and Blumenthal, *A Reappraisal of Franco-American Relations, 1830–1871* (Chapel Hill: University of North Carolina Press, 1959).

made by Tocqueville in the introduction to *Democracy in America*. "I did not go to America to satisfy curiosity, however legitimate; I sought there lessons from which we might profit. . . . I admit that I saw in America more than America; it was the shape of democracy itself which I sought, its inclinations, character, prejudices, and passion; I wanted to understand it so as at least to know what we have to fear or hope therefrom."[10]

The essays in this book discuss a range of texts, including novels, letters, comparative histories, and philosophical treatises. Almost all of them represent reflections based on actual experience of America and are in some sense travel narratives. While one should be wary of relying too heavily on a genre that is impressionistic and often lacks historical sophistication, travel notes combine, arguably better than any other genre, the mundane need for practical details and information with the thirst for deeper knowledge and the spirit of adventure in love with exotic landscapes.[11] Travel is not only a fascinating way to appreciate America's peculiar physiognomy, but it also presents a unique opportunity for drawing comparisons and rethinking the legitimacy of claims to universal truth made on behalf of American civilization. The foreign travelers' uncanny eye for details, their insights into how everyday manners function as pillars of democracy in America, their sometimes unexpected affinity with and empathy for the non-familiar, as well as their unique propensity for comparison and hyperbole help us appreciate better America's vibrant dynamism and originality as well as some of the less attractive features of the American political landscape.

The writers discussed in this volume are important figures who played a sig-

10. Tocqueville, *Democracy in America*, 13. Two decades before Tocqueville, Madame de Staël wrote: "There is a people who will one day be very great, I mean the Americans. . . . What is there more honorable for mankind than this new world which has established itself without the prejudices of the old; this new world where religion is in all its fervor without needing the support of the state to maintain it, where the law commands by the respect it inspires, without being enforced by any military power?" (Madame de Staël, *Considerations on the Principal Events of the French Revolution,* ed. Aurelian Craiutu [1818; Indianapolis: Liberty Fund, 2008], 707). A century and a half ago, the German-born American politician Carl Schurz referred to his adoptive country as "the great representative of the reformatory age, the great champion of the dignity of human nature, the great repository of the last hopes of suffering mankind" (*Speeches, Correspondence, and Political Papers of Carl Schurz,* selected and edited by Frederic Bancroft, vol. 1 [New York: G. P. Putnam's Sons, 1913], 51). His words were echoed fifty years ago by another European friend of America, Jacques Maritain. "What the world expects from America," he wrote, "is that she keep alive, in human history, a fraternal recognition of the dignity of man" (Maritain, *Reflections on America* [New York: Charles Scribner's Sons, 1958], 199).

11. Perhaps the most distinguished representative of the tradition focusing on the "primitive" and exotic America was Chateaubriand, who visited America in 1791. For an account of his visit, see Chateaubriand, *Travels in America,* trans. Richard Switzer (Lexington: University of Kentucky Press, 1969). Other French travelers who visited America shortly after Chateaubriand spent less time on describing the exotic part of America and focused instead on the interplay between nature, culture, and politics. Two such interesting accounts of America can be found in Édouard de Montulé, *Travels in America, 1816–1817* (Bloomington: Indiana University Press, 1951), and Achille Murat, *A Moral and Political Sketch of the United States of North America* (London: Effingham Wilson, 1833).

nificant role in the cultural and political debates in their own countries. The ten chapters of our book present their views of America, place their writings in the historical, political, and cultural contexts of their times, and highlight the ways in which their insights and judgments have been part of a broader transatlantic discourse about the role of the United States with important resonances in both France and England. This discourse represents an interesting moment in modern intellectual history, and at the same time it sheds light on themes and issues of enduring significance that still reverberate in current controversies. It goes without saying that the writers profiled here were partial and flawed even if perceptive observers. Not all of their remarks were fair or accurate; some of their critiques were exaggerated, while others were based on superficial observations. Without a doubt, each of the writers analyzed here attained only provisional success in their attempt to understand the unique profile of America. Nonetheless these commentaries, taken together, constitute a remarkable and illuminating dialogue about "American exceptionalism" and the vices and virtues that flow from it.

By examining the ways in which the image of America was constructed in the writings of modern French and English writers, our volume demonstrates that both the idealization and the criticism of America were to some extent a projection of French and English aspirations and anxieties and an attempt to account for—and come to terms with—Europe's progressive loss of status and influence.[12] As Alan Levine, Jeremy Jennings, and Richard Boyd point out in their contributions to this volume, for many European critics of America the stakes were (and remain) very high, involving nothing less than the preservation of their own societies from the influence of American culture and democracy. Yet these societies are themselves complex entities in the throes of modernization, and only with great difficulty can they be reduced to some essential "national character." In the same way, French and English interpretations of America do not constitute a homogeneous bloc and, as Alan Levine shows in the opening chapter, it would be inappropriate to reduce the complex set of French and British narratives about America to a simplistic opposition between pro-Americans and anti-Americans, or even between promodernity and antimodernity. Various themes and images recur over time and are often arranged in new configurations. The chapters of this book selectively trace the transformation of these themes and demonstrate how America has moved from representing a pastoral Arcadia and Europe's past to symbolizing Europe's future and the land of incessant change, mobility, impersonality, and progress—in short, the apotheosis

---

12. This idea looms large in Alan Levine's opening chapter in this volume, "The Idea of America in the History of European Political Thought: 1492–9/11."

of modern society. They also show how European thinkers have sometimes missed the mark in blaming America for problems that should properly be laid at the feet of modernity itself.

The book consists of four parts. Alan Levine's opening essay, which constitutes Part 1, offers a historical survey of the multifarious ways in which America has been interpreted by Europeans since its discovery by Christopher Columbus in 1492. Levine's purpose is twofold: to illuminate the ways in which America was perceived by the political thinkers of Europe, and to examine the symbolic functions that America served for Europe over the centuries. Beginning with the "discovery" of America, Levine examines what theorists from the Old World thought about America and how they reacted to events in America at each stage of its unique development.

Levine identifies four major periods in the interpretation of America. The first period centers on the theorists of the Spanish Renaissance who first tried to explain the strange New World by incorporating it into the traditional Christian-Aristotelian worldview. The second centers on Enlightenment thinkers' attempts to explain America as the home of "natural man," the third encompasses eighteenth- and nineteenth-century European reactions to the experiment associated with the new American republic, and the fourth period centers on the twentieth-century view, widespread throughout Europe, of America as the epitome of the technological and consumerist society. Levine traces the evolution of America as a symbol and argues that America remains one of the most powerful symbols in the world, articulating European aspirations and anxieties about the Enlightenment, liberalism, and modernity itself. That is why, Levine concludes, European critiques of America often reveal more about Europe's own problems, hopes, and fears than about America's distinctiveness.

Part 2, "America and the Enlightenment," includes three essays examining the French *philosophes'* interpretation of America, Berkeley's educational project for the island of Bermuda, and the issues of race and slavery in the Americas through the lenses of Victor Schoelcher.

Costica Bradatan's "Notes on Bishop Berkeley's New World" takes up the larger meaning of "America" and focuses on George Berkeley's 1725 essay *A Proposal for the better Supplying of Churches in our Foreign Plantations, and for Converting the Savage Americans, to Christianity, By a College to be erected in the Summer Islands, otherwise called The Isles of Bermuda.* Despite the fact that he had never traveled to the islands of Bermuda, Berkeley offered in his *Proposal* an extremely detailed description of their natural landscapes and projected various details about their inhabitants, praising the purity of their morals and the innocence of their manners. The islands were thus in effect idealized settings for his boldest educational project. Bradatan discusses Berkeley's project from three complementary perspectives: from the point of view of the tradition of the quest for the "earthly paradise," which was the basis for the first voyages of discovery and colonization of America; from the point of view of utopianism, by placing Berkeley's project in the tradition of the educational utopias, from Plato to More, some of which left their distinct imprint on the establishment of the first colleges in the New World; and, finally, from the perspective of the project's messianic tones, with special reference to Berkeley's famous verses announcing that "Westward the Course of Empire takes its Way." As such, George Berkeley's project to build a theology and fine arts college in the islands of Bermuda is analyzed as a paradigmatic case of symbolic reconstruction and idealization of the New World, as the quest for the "earthly paradise" within the larger utopian and eschatological tradition. Bradatan shows that in designing his educational project, Berkeley was, consciously or unconsciously, under the strong influence of these ancient notions and patterns of thought and mapped out his encounter with the New World using a repertoire of old phantasms, hopes of universal renewal and dreams of spiritual salvation. Berkeley's American project, Bradatan argues, is hardly understandable without taking seriously into account its messianic elements, something that Berkeley seems to have shared with many of the early American colonists themselves.

Guillaume Ansart's "From Voltaire to Raynal and Diderot's *Histoire des deux Indes:* The French *Philosophes* and Colonial America" examines the image of America in the ideological milieu of the *philosophes* by focusing on the North American chapters of Raynal and Diderot's *Histoire des deux Indes* (1780). The *Histoire des deux Indes* contains a detailed treatment of the colonies and their history from their origins to the eve of the rebellion. The influence of religion on the development of the colonies receives extensive attention and, in many instances, Pennsylvania and the Quakers appear in contrast with Puritan New England. Raynal and Diderot emphasize the fact that the Quakers did not engage in theological dogmatism but instead preferred to encourage the practice of a "natural" morality inspired by the simplicity of early Christians. This tendency toward universalism greatly appealed to the *philosophes,* and the *Histoire des deux Indes* underscores the positive social effects of religion in Pennsylvania: tolerance, freedom, and equality lead to a climate of peace and social harmony, which in turn leads to prosperity. To the benign universalism of Quaker morality Raynal's book opposes the dogmatic severity of Puritanism, with its strict application of Old Testament norms to all aspects of everyday life.

The other significant opposition running through the North American chapters of the *Histoire des deux Indes* is the difference in cultural and political traditions between the northern and southern colonies. According to Raynal and Diderot, freedom and religious tolerance were not as deeply rooted in the South as in the

North, nor was the spirit of commerce and industry as developed. In this context, they underlined the positive consequences of Puritanism such as the orderly, rational organization of the New England colony from its inception, the republican spirit, and the development of commerce and industry. In the end, Ansart concludes, the *Histoire des deux Indes* hesitates between two distinct visions of colonial America: a return to an idealized communal past and a model for a new future of progress, freedom, and enlightened trade.

Nick Nesbitt's "On the Political Efficacy of Idealism: Tocqueville, Schoelcher, and the Abolition of Slavery" takes up the issue of slavery in the New World and examines the French debate on abolition in the period preceding 1848, which is presented as a conflict between realists and idealists. According to Nesbitt, though each camp stood opposed to the institution of chattel slavery in France's American colonies, it was the uncompromising political idealism of Victor Schoelcher that actually carried the day and brought an immediate and universal end to slavery in France's colonies in 1848. Though Tocqueville explicitly critiques slavery as a violation of blacks' human rights, by the time of his 1839 report to the French government on abolition, he calls for a temporary prohibition on the possession of land by freed slaves, excluding them from full citizenship. Nesbitt derives two lines of French abolitionist thought. On the one hand, he identifies a middling realistic strand stretching from Condorcet and the Société des Amis des Noirs to thinkers such as Tocqueville, who called for a gradual and partial emancipation of slaves; and on the other hand, he singles out a radical idealism that can be found in the case of Toussaint Louverture and Schoelcher, who remained faithful to the Enlightenment concept of natural right, arguing that any and all human beings are capable of autonomous action. According to Nesbitt, the events of the Haitian Revolution lay at the core of this divergence. While Tocqueville based his hesitant emancipationist realism in part upon the conventional assessment of the 1804 revolution, Schoelcher's greater familiarity with the French colonies and the political philosophy of Toussaint and 1804 led him to militate for universal abolition and full, immediate citizenship. In developing these conflicting currents of French political thought in the nineteenth century, Nesbitt highlights certain dilemmas of imperial power that become endemic sources of controversy in twentieth-century American political discourse.

Part 3 explores the views of America held by leading nineteenth-century French writers and politicians who were contemporaries of Tocqueville. Aurelian Craiutu's essay, "A Precursor of Tocqueville: Victor Jacquemont's Reflections on America," analyzes the image of America in the writings of Victor Jacquemont (1810–32), a friend of Stendhal and one of the most prominent representatives of the new French generation that came of age around 1820. A gifted natural historian, Jacquemont epitomized the romantic intellectual in love with exotic landscapes and cultures and in search of unprecedented adventures (his travel diary in India brought him posthumous fame in France). He arrived in the New World in December 1826 and spent almost six months there, visiting Philadelphia, New Jersey, New York, Haiti, and parts of Canada. Although Jacquemont's observations on America have been neglected to this day, they deserve to be retrieved from oblivion because, in many respects, he was a forerunner of Tocqueville and introduced a series of themes that were later developed further in *Democracy in America*. Craiutu's essay focuses on Jacquemont's comments on the themes of equality and equalization of conditions, self-government and the spirit of association, and Protestantism; the relationships between society and government and between religion and morality; and domestic life, journals, and political debates in America. Craiutu argues that although narrower in scope than Tocqueville's ideas, Jacquemont's reflections anticipate the latter's more subtle and nuanced analysis of democratic mores and religion in America. Jacquemont followed American journals and debates closely and noted the signs that announced a possible civil war between the North and the South. Also worth noting are his remarks on the power of public opinion and the homogenization of society. Jacquemont had serious reservations about American pragmatism and was far from being enthusiastic about its effects on American mores. Toward the end of his journey, Jacquemont did not conceal his dissatisfaction with the American way of life and the ensemble of American mores, which he found cold and vulgar. He concluded that, for all its virtues, the American way of life did not provide a civilized type of liberty.

Christine Dunn Henderson's essay, "Tyranny and Tragedy in Beaumont's *Marie*," explores Gustave de Beaumont's portrait of slavery and of racism in America from his famous novel *Marie: A Tableau of American Moeurs*. Beaumont visited America with Tocqueville in 1831–32. Their travels took them to New England, Michigan and the Ohio River area, Memphis and New Orleans, and Washington. Praised for the promise of liberty and equality held out in its founding, nineteenth-century America was justly criticized by foreigners and natives alike for betraying that promise by allowing racial slavery to continue within its borders. Beaumont's novel—which received great critical and popular acclaim upon its publication in 1835—relates a tragic tale of interracial love between a young Frenchman and a mulatto American woman, which explains its subtitle, "A Tableau of American Moeurs." A serious dimension accompanies the novel's entertaining melodrama—as Beaumont states in *Marie*'s preface, his intention is to probe "the violence of the prejudice which separates the race of slaves from that of free men." Henderson's essay examines Beaumont's portrait of "the black race" as well as the long- and short-term effects of slavery upon both blacks and whites. It also explores Beaumont's assessment of America's prospects for

overcoming racism and the legacy of slavery and draws some parallels with Tocqueville's account of the future of the three races in America.

Jeremy Jennings's contribution, "French Visions of America: From Tocqueville to the Civil War," comments on Michel Chevalier's, Guillaume-Tell Poussin's, Jean-Jacques Ampère's, Duvergier de Hauranne's, and Édouard Laboulaye's
reflections on America, which he then compares briefly to Tocqueville's *Democracy in America*. Jennings argues that Chevalier's *Lettres sur l'Amérique du Nord* is
worthy of being placed immediately beside *De la démocratie en Amérique* because
Chevalier offered an empirical economic study of America that is as valuable
and prophetic in its way as is Tocqueville's more institutional and philosophical
description. Chevalier's two-volume work, first published in 1836, remains virtually unknown (in both France and America) and has singularly failed to attain
the canonical status long since accorded to Tocqueville's own two-volume study,
published in 1835 and 1840. The comparison between the two authors can be
extended further, as both Chevalier and Tocqueville invoked the example of
America in the heated atmosphere of the Revolution of 1848 and the birth of
the Second Republic. Chevalier explored aspects of American life and society
that were completely unnoticed by his more illustrious compatriot. That Tocqueville's earlier description of America remained a point of reference for French
visitors is then amply illustrated by Jennings's brief accounts of the reflections on
America by Poussin, Ampère, Laboulaye, and Duvergier de Hauranne. As Jennings points out, each of these French travelers saw something to admire about
America, from its vigor and vitality as a young nation to the economic power of
America seen as a symbol of a future that one day, in some form or other, that
was bound to reach European shores.

Part 4 is devoted to examining three different British views of America. In his
essay "From Aristocratic *Politesse* to Democratic Civility, or, What Mrs. Frances
Trollope *Didn't* See in America," Richard Boyd comments upon Frances Trollope's visit to America in 1827 to establish a dry goods emporium in Cincinnati.
Although the trip, as Boyd points out, was an unmitigated disappointment, personally and financially, it culminated in a successful book analyzing American
society and manners, *Domestic Manners of the Americans,* that was a best seller in
England and the United States upon its appearance in 1832. Trollope's book
offered a sophisticated picture of the manners of the Americans and invites its
readers to reflect on how daily manners can serve as a foundation for democratic
political institutions. Despite the salience of this topic Trollope's book has generated little scholarly attention among political theorists when it has not been flatly
dismissed as nothing more than an embittered and condescending expression of
an aristocratic critique of American society and its system of government.
Through an analysis of Trollope's spirited account of American life, Boyd's essay

underscores important differences between her vision of American manners and that of Tocqueville. Where the latter appreciated the redeeming features of democratic manners and morals, especially the kind of easy spontaneity and democratic equality with which Americans treated one another, Trollope saw mostly "vulgarity," "grossness," "familiarity," "presumptuousness," and "universal deficiency in good manners and graceful demeanour." Yet, as Boyd argues, her musings paradoxically capture better than Tocqueville's the sense in which America's democratic norms of civility serve to communicate a sense of the equality and intrinsic dignity of all persons. Trollope's *Domestic Manners* is an especially fruitful text for exploring the suggestion that the everyday habits of democratic life are expressive of its moral virtues and vices. Trollope's stark critique of American democracy allows us to distinguish these two commonly conflated synonyms for "manners"—namely, civility and politeness—and to determine why the latter assumed such noxious and exclusionary formulations only in the wake of modern democracy.

Russell L. Hanson's essay, "Tyranny of the Majority or Fatalism of the Multitude? Bryce on Democracy in America," offers a comparative analysis of Tocqueville's and Bryce's interpretations of America. In *The American Commonwealth* (1888), James Bryce chided Tocqueville for exaggerating the danger of tyrannical majorities in the United States. The real danger, Bryce said, is a deepening "fatalism of the multitude," which induces people to accept and even endorse majority opinions. That is different from submitting to the will of a powerful entity, and it has different consequences for liberty, as Bryce suggested. Hanson clarifies the distinction between tyranny of the majority and fatalism of the multitude, and he shows how it accounts for Tocqueville's and Bryce's different assessments of political tendencies in the United States. Hanson concludes by arguing that Bryce has the more accurate analysis of American politics, but that Bryce's critique of Tocqueville's understanding of democracy in general is limited by the "exceptionalist" nature of Bryce's argument.

Patrick J. Deneen's essay, "What G. K. Chesterton Saw in America: The Cosmopolitan Threat from a Patriotic Nation," focuses on Chesterton's reflections on America, with special emphasis on Chesterton's travel essay, *What I Saw in America,* in which he at once recognized the globalizing tendency of America's philosophical underpinnings—expressed through the universalisms of the Declaration of Independence—and its propensity toward economic expansion and standardization. As Deneen points out, *What I Saw in America* contains one of the most-oft quoted and almost invariably misunderstood lines that attempts to describe the essence of America. In his first chapter, entitled "What Is America?" Chesterton famously described America as "the nation with the soul of a Church." Chesterton did, in fact, conclude that America is a religious nation, but this is not the core meaning of the famous line, according to Deneen. Rather, Chesterton was speaking of "America's creed," and argued that Americans base their identity more or less wholly on a shared set of *beliefs* in contrast to the Europeans' various identities in the form of traditions and practices. Chesterton claimed that the creedal identity resulted in a strenuously nationalistic and patriotic people. He believed that America was a country that fundamentally rested on commitments to nationality, patriotism, and its own form of particularity, however apparently universalistic in theory. Chesterton claimed that America demonstrated the limit to which the nation-state could be stretched, beyond which it would cease to be a nation—and hence, a self-governing entity—in any real sense. In contrast to his frequent intellectual nemeses, H. G. Wells and G. B. Shaw, Chesterton viewed America not as an inspiration for an eventual world government, but rather as a distinct and definitive expression of human particularity, one that accorded more closely with a traditionalist view of human nature than with any form of cosmopolitan citizenship.

As our volume makes clear, while this particular cast of distinguished writers differed regarding the accomplishments and failings of the United States as well as regarding the broader significance of American society, they agreed that American society was particularly and distinctively significant, by virtue of its relentless modernism and its effective and in some ways implacable organization of political power. Indeed, as Jeffrey Isaac makes clear in his concluding essay, this symbolic and material importance of the United States is more manifest than ever today, precisely because of the terms according to which the cold war was resolved, leaving the United States as the world's lone "superpower." At the same time, the world that American power has inherited is a world of proliferating antagonism and conflict, announcing significant shifts in power and attitudes in the process of transition from anti-Americanism to "post-Americanism."[13] While the Americans will have to accept that in the twenty-first century some roads will no longer lead to Washington, they will also have to be prepared to deal with new challenges and new rivals such as China, India, or Brazil. The working out of these antagonisms and conflicts will no doubt be determined largely by the mobilization of material forces. Nonetheless, often the strongest material force is the force of political ideas and symbols, myths and countermyths. To the extent that this is true, the debates about the "meanings" of America are likely to persist and to have important consequences well into the future. That is why the "symbolic geography" of "America" must remain a focal topic of sober historiographical inquiry and critical investigation.

13. For a recent analysis of this transition, see Fareed Zakaria, *The Post-American World* (New York: Norton, 2008).

PART ONE

AMERICA'S MANY FACES

I

THE IDEA OF AMERICA IN THE HISTORY
OF EUROPEAN POLITICAL THOUGHT

1492 to 9/11

Alan Levine

This chapter introduces the reader to how America was perceived by and what it meant to the political thinkers of Europe from Columbus until the twenty-first century. The chapter is not about American political thought but about America as a symbol; and as the recent debates over globalization, terrorism, and Iraq reveal, to this day the idea of America remains one of the most powerful symbols in the world. Beginning with the "discovery" of America, and spanning the more than five hundred years until today, this paper gives an overview of what theorists from the Old World thought about America and how they reacted to events in America at each stage of its unique development.

My project is both broader and narrower than any of the existing literature on European conceptions of America.[1] While my time frame is ambitious, my

I gratefully thank the following organizations for their generous support of my research: the National Endowment for the Humanities, the Hoover Institution, and the James Madison Program in American Ideals and Institutions.

1. The most interesting existing accounts of Europe's first encounters with the Indians include Fredi Chiapelli et al., eds., *First Images of America: The Impact of the New World on the Old,* 2 vols. (Berkeley and Los Angeles: University of California Press, 1976); Gilbert Chinard, *L'exotisme américain dans la littérature française au XVI siècle* (Geneva: Slatkine Reprints, 1978); Antonello Gerbi, *The Dispute of the New World: The History of a Polemic, 1750–1900,* trans. Jeremy Moyle (Pittsburgh: University of Pittsburgh Press, 1973); Lewis Hanke, *The Spanish Struggle for Justice in the Conquest of America* (Boston: Little, Brown, 1965); Anthony Pagden, *The Fall of Natural Man: The American Indian and the Origins of Comparative Ethnology* (Cambridge: Cambridge University Press, 1982); Edmundo O'Gorman, *The*

scope is narrow. I focus on how European *philosophers and political theorists* view America, not on the views of every European writer, traveler, or scientist, nor on the opinions of the European public as a whole, nor on the ramblings of random commentators, many of whom have written on America. (The views of some of these other writers, travelers, and commentators are discussed in other chapters of this volume.) I discuss the general cultural critiques to highlight what is unique to the philosophical debates and what is shared with the larger European critiques, and I put the philosophers' views in the context of the overall European views. I focus on philosophers because of their insight as presumably the most thoughtful commentators.

Space here permits but a brief sketch of both my findings and my analytical framework. While fuller documentation as well as nuanced qualifications will be found in my forthcoming book on this topic,[2] my overall findings are relatively straightforward. I find that throughout its history, America has stood for two different, almost opposite, things. First, it initially stands for Indians,[3] who are

---

Invention of America: An Inquiry into the Historical Nature of the New World and the Meaning of Its History (Bloomington: Indiana University Press, 1961); and Tzvetan Todorov, *The Conquest of America: The Question of the Other,* trans. Richard Howard (New York: Harper and Row, 1984). The best accounts of European reactions to the United States are James Ceaser, *Reconstructing America: The Symbol of America in Modern Thought* (New Haven: Yale University Press, 1997); Durand Echeverria, *Mirage in the West: A History of the French Image of American Society to 1815* (Princeton: Princeton University Press, 1957); Philippe Roger, *The American Enemy: The History of French Anti-Americanism,* trans. Sharon Bowman (Chicago: University of Chicago Press, 2005); and C. Vann Woodward, *The Old World's New World* (New York: Oxford University Press, 1991). On anti-Americanism, one might also profitably consult Arnold Beichman, *Anti-American Myths: Their Causes and Consequences* (New Brunswick, N.J.: Transaction, 1993); Paul Hollander, *Anti-Americanism: Critiques at Home and Abroad, 1965–1990* (New York: Oxford University Press, 1992); Paul Hollander, ed., *Understanding Anti-Americanism: Its Origins and Impact at Home and Abroad* (Chicago: Ivan Dee, 2004); Peter J. Katzenstein and Robert O. Keohane, eds., *Anti-Americanisms in World Politics* (Ithaca: Cornell University Press, 2006); Andrei S. Markovits, *Uncouth Nation: Why Europe Dislikes America* (Princeton: Princeton University Press, 2007); Jean-François Revel, *L'Obsession Anti-Américaine: Son fonctionnement, ses causes, ses inconsequence* (Paris: Plon, 2002); and Barry Rubin and Judith Culp Rubin, *Hating America: A History* (Oxford: Oxford University Press, 2004).

2. This chapter is a précis of that forthcoming book.

3. The term *Indians* is problematic for several reasons. It is inaccurate and sometimes deemed offensive. As I explain later in this section, its derivation is from the mistaken belief that those using the term had landed in India and not in a continent hitherto unknown to them. Preferred terminology today includes *Native Americans* in the United States and *First Peoples* in Canada. Of these two, *First Peoples* makes more sense, since most scholars believe that the so-called Indians were descendents of the first people who came to America via the frozen land bridge from Asia to Alaska over the Bering Strait. It should be emphasized, however, that it is also believed that these "first" arrivers came in several different waves of migration over a period of more than ten thousand years. They are lumped together as "first" relative only to later arriving Europeans. Similarly, if the Bering land bridge theory is correct, the people the Europeans found in America are "native" only from the perspective of later arriving Europeans. Hence, the terms *First Peoples* and *Native Americans* do not, in my opinion, overcome Eurocentrism as advocates of these terms intend to signify. In my experience, the descendents of the first people of America prefer to be called by the name of their people—i.e., Navajo, Iroquois, Inuit—and not by an abstract catch-all label. Nonetheless, despite its inaccuracy, since the historical texts I analyze use the term *Indian,* I have chosen to employ it, too.

heralded as "natural man" and said to represent the world's beginning. Second, it currently stands for the United States, the great political experiment based on natural rights, which has evoked responses ranging from inspiration to fear to envy. The United States inspires such strong feelings not simply because it is the most powerful nation in the world, but because it is often perceived as the world's future. America thus represents both the world's origins and its endpoint.

European views of America can be broken into four periods, two corresponding to the Indians and two corresponding to the United States. Examination of European views of America also reveals an interesting pattern of America condemned, praised, and condemned again but for different reasons. Underneath this pattern, however, a deeper struggle is taking place. While European views shed some light on America, they reveal a surprisingly consistent substantive continuity of perceptions that reveals more about Europe's own hopes, fears, and anxieties for itself. The European thinkers' battle over America is largely a proxy war over European civilization, the Enlightenment, liberalism, and modernity itself.

THE INDIANS

From 1492 until the American Revolution, and in some sense still today, in the European consciousness America evoked the image of Indians. What the Indians represent in the global imagination today is a fairly static image informed by media portrayals that starkly depict the Indians either as barbaric savages or as noble stewards of the land living in harmony with nature. These images have a long genealogy.

The First Period: First Attempts to Explain America

Although the Americas were undoubtedly visited by the Vikings around the year 1000, the European "discovery" of America is attributed to Christopher Columbus, whose voyage to America in 1492 captured the European imagination. Ironically, to Columbus's dying day, he insisted that what he had found was part of Asia. Thus, European perceptions of America have been mistaken from the very beginning. Sixteenth-century mapmakers, recognizing Columbus's mistake, named the New World not after him, but after Amerigo Vespucci—hence the name "America"—who they credited as the first to realize that the New World was its own continent.

The Indians of America were misrepresented by Europeans from the very beginning. Not only did Columbus believe America was someplace else—hence the name Indians—but his description of its inhabitants was fanciful, too. He claimed to discover cannibals, Cyclops, Amazons, Sirens, dog-faced peoples, people with no hair, and people with tails.[4] These bizarre claims were suggested to him by centuries of fanciful tales passed on through medieval times by supposedly reliable authorities.[5] Essentially, Columbus already knew what he would find, and he found what he thought he would. This self-fulfilling discovery began a pattern of preformed opinions dictating what is supposedly found in America. He saw the land as potential wealth and its people as possible converts or slaves. He takes "possession of them" and says they would make either good Christians or good slaves.[6] For him, the Indians had no independent status, no integrity of their own. They were just to be used like any other resource.

Columbus's instrumental view was shared by most of the early conquistadors and missionaries, who did not consider the Indians' beliefs and cultures as worthy human creations entitled to respect. To the extent that these Spaniards deigned to understand the Indians' beliefs at all, it was to use those beliefs against the Indians for their own purposes, as Cortes famously did.[7] Conquistadors, such as Cortes and Bernal Díaz, express revulsion at the Aztecs' human sacrifices and brutality, but they seem not to notice the barbarism and cruelty that they themselves inflict almost everywhere they go. They kill and maim not only as means of conquest but also for sport, sharpening their swords by running people through. They plunder villages and murder the inhabitants without remorse or guilt but (ironically) with piety. For example, Bernal Díaz explains how the Spanish "were going to get rid of [an Indian village] in order to save them from their false beliefs."[8] The juxtapositions of their clean-conscience, guiltless mur-

4. See the famous "Letter of Columbus" in *The Journal of Christopher Columbus,* ed. and trans. Cecil Jane (New York: Bonanza Books, 1989), 198–200. See also Columbus's journal entries for November 4, 23, and 26, 1492, and January 9, 1493.

5. Originating with a skeptical Herodotus and passed to Christendom largely through a more credulous Pliny the Elder, these stories were grossly elaborated by Pomponius Mela, Solinus, Isidore of Seville, Vincent of Beauvais, Bartholomew, Sir John Mandeville, and others. Accounts of wild men varied; but tales of cannibalism, nakedness, and the monstrously deformed, including giants, the completely hairy, and the dog-headed, had so much credence during the Middle Ages that mapmakers often put them on islands at the edge of the known world. These myths are nicely documented and traced in Richard Bernheimer, *Wild Men in the Middle Ages* (Cambridge: Harvard University Press, 1952), and Margaret Hodgen, *Early Anthropology in the Sixteenth and Seventeenth Centuries* (Philadelphia: University of Pennsylvania Press, 1964), 17–77.

6. Columbus speaks of converting the Indians on October 16, 1492, 33; November 6, 1492, 57; November 12,1492, 58; November 27, 1494, 76 and 78; December 15, 1492, 100; and December 21, 1492, 112. He speaks of enslaving them on October 14, 1492, 28; November 12, 1492, 60; and January 14, 1493, 151 (Jane, ed., *Journal of Christopher Columbus*). See also Columbus's famous letter written immediately upon his return to Europe (op. cit.), especially 192, 194, 196, and 201.

7. See Todorov's analysis of Cortes's manipulations of words and symbols, *The Conquest of America,* 53–123, 175, & 245–54.

8. Bernal Díaz Del Castillo, *The Conquest of New Spain,* ed. and trans. J. M. Cohen (London:

ders with their Christian beliefs and their professions of piety indicate a radical "othering" in their thinking about the Indians' natures. The Indians can be accepted only on Spanish terms; thus, after one gruesome battle and the Indians' capitulation, Bernal Díaz approvingly cites Cortes, stating "that now we would treat them as brothers."[9] A similar inability to "see" the Indians is evident when the conquistadors rape women and then mock their unwilling victims as whores.[10] In short, the Spanish in the New World gave the Indians so little regard as fellow human beings that they could systematically massacre them in a manner consistent with their Christian consciences.[11] They had little or no interest in an open-minded encounter with the Indians, and the writings of the conquistadors and missionaries created the popular European impression of both the New World and its inhabitants.[12]

The Spanish renaissance philosophers who first reflected on the discovery of the Indians did little better in appreciating them. Three positions dominated the Spanish debates. The first position, arguing that the Indians did not possess the faculty of reason, articulated originally by John Mair, a Scot living in Paris, and vigorously advanced by Juan de Sepúlveda in the courts of Spain, went so far as to argue that the Indians were the concrete embodiment of Aristotle's natural slave. According to this view, the Indians could be incorporated into Europe's traditional Christian-Aristotelian worldview but only in its lowest place. God created the Indians as natural inferiors, the argument went, so it was just and right that the Spanish subjugate them.[13]

The second view, most famously advanced by Francisco de Vitoria, saw the Indians as rational but underdeveloped and needing Spanish tutelage.[14] In this view the Indians possess reason and have "some order in their affairs," as evi-

---

Penguin, 1983), 122. See also Todorov, *Conquest of America*, 53–167, for a deep meditation on the Spaniards' mixture of religious piety and physical cruelty.

9. Bernal Díaz, *Conquest of New Spain*, 125.

10. Todorov, *Conquest of America*, 48–49, 139, and the book's dedication.

11. For a short and gruesome account by an eyewitness to Spanish behavior, see Bartolomé de Las Casas, *The Devastation of the Indies: A Brief Account*, trans. Herma Briffault (Baltimore: Johns Hopkins University Press, 1974).

12. For a list of the publication dates of New World travel books in Spain, see Pagden, *The Fall of Natural Man*, 57–59. For complete lists of what was published in French and English and when, see Gilbert Chinard, *L'exotisme américain dans la littérature française au XVI siècle*, chap. 1; and Myron P. Gilmore, "The New World in French and English Historians of the Sixteenth Century," in Chiapelli et al., eds., *First Images of America*, 519–21.

13. See Lewis Hanke, *All Mankind Is One: A Study of the Disputation between Bartolomé de Las Casas and Juan Ginés de Sepúlveda on the Religious and Intellectual Capacity of the American Indians* (DeKalb: Northern Illinois University Press, 1994); and Pagden, *The Fall of Natural Man*, 27–56 and 109–18.

14. Francisco de Vitoria, *On the American Indians [De Indis]*, question 1, article 6; question 2, article 5, in Vitoria, *Political Writings*, ed. and trans. Anthony Pagden and Jeremy Lawrance (Cambridge: Cambridge University Press, 1991), 250, 273.

denced by their languages, economics, and politics.[15] But according to Vitoria, the Indians have not developed their reason fully; they possess it in "potential which is incapable of being realized" due to "their evil and barbarous education."[16] Because they are human, the Indians had to be governed by consent. But because they are underdeveloped, they need not give their formal, explicit consent. They are to be governed by what they would consent to after they came to understand the natural law, which of course the Spanish thought they possessed. Unlike Sepúlveda, Vitoria concludes that the Indians are not slaves and thus must be allowed to "carry on in peaceful and undisturbed enjoyment of their property," but he also argues that where they do not follow natural law, they could justly be forced to do so.[17] They can be coerced "even against their will" as long as "everything is done for the benefit and good of the barbarians, and not merely for the profit of the Spaniards."[18] Vitoria repeatedly expresses doubts about the actual actions of the Spaniards in the New World, fearing that they have overstepped the bounds of the "permissible."[19] But he also asserts that if the Indians resist legitimate authority, then the Indians need "no longer be treated as innocent enemies, but as treacherous foes against whom all rights of war can be exercised, including plunder, enslavement, deposition of their former masters, and the institution of new ones."[20] But, Vitoria immediately adds, "All this must be done in moderation, in proportion to the actual offence."[21] According to Vitoria the Indians' interests, however, could only be truly determined by the Spanish, because they, and not the Indians, properly understood the requirements of natural and divine law.

The third view is represented by Bartolomé de Las Casas, the era's most tireless and dedicated defender of the Indians, but even he thought that the Indians were underdeveloped and needing Christianity.[22] Las Casas, famous for his view that "all the races of the world are men," was an extraordinary champion of the

15. Vitoria's account of the Indians' accomplishments is significant, because it parallels Aristotle's account of human development in *The Politics*, bk. 1, chap. 2, 1252b27–1253a40. There, Aristotle says that the uniquely human characteristic is *logos* (reason/speech). Human beings who possess *logos* come together first to make a household for the sake of securing the necessities of life (economics), and then several households form a city for the sake of securing the good life. Only in politics and its attendant debates over the good and the just does human potential reach its fruition. Languages, economics, and politics thus according to Vitoria mark the Indians as human.

16. Vitoria, *On the American Indians*, question 1, article 6 (*Political Writings*, 250).

17. Vitoria, *On the American Indians*, question 3, article 1 (*Political Writings*, 283).

18. Vitoria, *On the American Indians*, question 3, articles 2 and 8 (*Political Writings*, 285 and 291). See question 3, articles 1–8 in general (*Political Writings*, 278–91). An excellent account of Vitoria's arguments on the Indians is in Pagden, *The Fall of Natural Man*, 57–108.

19. Vitoria, *On the American Indians*, *Political Writings*, 238, 286, 291.

20. Vitoria, *On the American Indians*, question 3, article 1 (*Political Writings*, 283).

21. Vitoria, *On the American Indians*, question 3, article 1 (*Political Writings*, 283).

22. *Bartolomé de Las Casas: A Selection of His Writings*, ed. George Sanderlin (New York: Knopf, 1971), 200.

Indians, but he too favored their conversion and wanted to bring them into the "universal Church." He writes, for example, that "the goal for which divine Providence meant the discovery of those peoples and those lands . . . is none other, since we are mortal, than the conversion and salvation of those souls."[23] Las Casas differs from his Spanish contemporaries, however, because he insisted that the Indians be evangelized only through gentle means requiring their formal consent: "we can only treat them with love, peace and Christian charity which we owe them, attract them, as we would be attracted ourselves, to the holy Faith through sweet and humble evangelical preaching."[24] Las Casas praises many of the Indians' characteristics and deems them full and mature human beings, but he still finds them in need of what the Spanish possess.

In short, the Spanish thinkers were so confident in their worldview that it never occurred to them that they might be incorrect or possess only a partial truth. They all agreed the Indians needed the Christianity and civilization that the Spanish enjoyed. They disagreed primarily only on the means that could be justly used to remedy the Indians' lacks. Their cultural confidence led them to reject the Americans as underdeveloped, barbaric, or both.

The Second Period: America as the Home of Natural Man

In 1580 the French philosopher Michel de Montaigne began a pathbreaking, new way of thinking about the Indians. A skeptic and keen observer of human diversity, Montaigne argued that "each man calls barbarism whatever is not his practice; for indeed it seems we have no other test of truth and reason than the example and pattern of the opinions and customs of the country we live in."[25] Living through Europe's cruel and horrific religious wars, Montaigne, unlike the Spanish theorists before him, doubts the standards of his own place and time. In his famous essay "Of Cannibals," he describes Indian society as the best society that ever was, real or imagined, because they are "still very close to their original naturalness" and thus live in a "state of purity" according to "*les loix naturelles.*"[26]

---

23. Las Casas, *History of the Indies,* ed. and trans. Andrée Collard (New York: Harper & Row, 1971), 5.

24. Las Casas, *History of the Indies,* 8.

25. Michel de Montaigne, "Of Cannibals," in *The Complete Essays,* ed. and trans. Donald Frame (Stanford: Stanford University Press, 1957), 152. The first publication date of Montaigne's *Essays* was 1580, although he probably wrote "Of Cannibals" in 1572. On Montaigne's views of the Indians, see also Alan Levine, *Sensual Philosophy: Toleration, Skepticism, and Montaigne's Politics of the Self* (Lanham, Md.: Lexington Books, 2001), chap. 2; David Schaefer, *The Political Philosophy of Montaigne* (Ithaca: Cornell University Press, 1991); Frank Lestringant, *Le Huguenot et le Sauvage: L'Amérique et la controverse coloniale en France, au temps des guerres de religion (1555–1589)* (Paris: Diffusion, 1990); and Lestringant, *Cannibals: The Discovery and Representation of the Cannibal from Columbus to Jules Verne* (Berkeley and Los Angeles: University of California Press, 1997).

26. Montaigne, "Of Cannibals," 153.

He claims their society, held together with "little artifice and human solder," is as pure and natural as a society can be.[27] His account claims that while these Indians do fight and eat their captives, they do so not for economic gain but as a kind of aristocratic struggle for mastery. He describes their warfare as "wholly noble" and "as excusable and beautiful as this human disease can be."[28] This is the origin of the image of the noble savage.[29]

Montaigne knows that his account of the Indians' tranquility and bliss is fictitious.[30] He concedes the viciousness of some of their actions, writing, "I am not sorry that we notice the barbarous horror of [their] acts, but I am heartily sorry that, judging their faults rightly, we should be so blind to our own."[31] Here Montaigne reveals his true intentions in describing the Indians: he uses them as an emblem with which to expose the horrors and cruelty of his own world. This usage of the Indians as a countercultural marker was to become the norm. While Montaigne's account of the Indians is in the end neither anthropologically accurate nor fully desirable, he is the first to misrepresent the Indians in a positive fashion.

After Montaigne no major philosopher in Europe doubted the Indians' naturalness. To the contrary, the Indians came to represent natural man par excellence. From Montaigne until the end of the Enlightenment, every major philosopher agreed with John Locke's famous statement that "in the beginning all the World was America."[32] America represented Europe's past. In ending one debate, however, Montaigne began a new one. While every major thinker agreed that the Indians represented humanity's natural state, debate arose over the interpretation of the natural state: was it a brutishness to overcome or an innocence to recapture?

Among Enlightenment philosophers this new debate evolves in a single direction. Hobbes first argues that humanity's natural state is a horrible state of war to be avoided at all costs. Locke and Montesquieu counter that the state of nature is pacific but undesirable. Rousseau, Voltaire, and Diderot later praise the state

27. Montaigne, "Of Cannibals," 153.

28. Montaigne, "Of Cannibals," 156.

29. Two writers before Montaigne, Peter Martyr and Jean de Léry, described the Indians as living in a kind of golden age, but both severely qualified their praise by denouncing the Indians for lacking civilization as manifested in such things as clothing and, most important, for not possessing the true religion, Christianity. Their concomitant praise and criticism uneasily coexist, but ultimately and on balance, they condemn the Indians. These two and Las Casas are the only thinkers before Montaigne to substantially praise the Indians. But animated by strong faith in the legitimacy of their own worldview, none question their own core beliefs in making their judgments.

30. On the fictitious character of Montaigne's account, see Levine, *Sensual Philosophy*, 111–19, 266n2.

31. Montaigne, "Of Cannibals," 155.

32. Locke, *Second Treatise of Government*, § 49.

of natural man as happy and good. Locke's vision of the state of nature is not identical to Montesquieu's, nor is Rousseau's the same as Voltaire's and Diderot's. These philosophers' accounts are not equally systematic, and philosophical differences exist among them. For example, Rousseau's natural man is good because he lives not by reason but by the instinct of compassion or pity alone, whereas Voltaire's Hurons and Diderot's Tahitians (embodying their visions of natural man) possess highly developed senses of both compassion and reason.[33] But in contrast to what all three of the later French thinkers deem Europe's artificiality, corruption, and unhappiness, they each describe natural man as healthy, happy, and psychologically whole. Despite the differences between the accounts as they evolve, the increasing praise of the Indians over time is unmistakable. But how should one explain this trend among Enlightenment political thinkers? Is the increasing praise of the Indians an astute reflection of changes in America itself, or does it reflect a European dynamic?

European Enlightenment philosophers' views of the Indians inversely reflect their own satisfaction with the existing institutions in Europe. The philosophers are responding neither to events in America nor to the general views within Europe. They are responding to their own concerns with Europe's present and for its future. This is evident when noting three sets of facts. First, the linear development of the philosophers' views is in sharp contrast to the overall European debate where both good and bad representations of the Indians are present throughout. These positive and negative representations of the Indians are used in numerous intra-European struggles: Protestants versus Catholics, Spain versus her enemies, nobles versus kings, and in dynastic struggles. Thus, the pattern of increasing praise of the Indians is unique to the debate among political theorists. Second, it should also be noted that these changing representations do not correspond to any changes in Indian societies. There is no evidence that the Indians are in fact becoming increasingly happier from the seventeenth to the eighteenth centuries. If anything, they are becoming increasingly conquered or destroyed. Third, the linear pattern among political theorists is not in response to new information about the Indians. In truth, the available evidence was barely consulted at all by any of the great thinkers. For example, most of these Enlightenment thinkers described the Indians as atomistic individuals despite the fact that Europeans had from early on been aware of the social nature of Indian living, not to

33. On Rousseau, see his *First and Second Discourses*, in Jean-Jacques Rousseau, *The Basic Political Writings*, ed. and trans. Donald Cress (Indianapolis: Hackett, 1987), 1–109. See also Voltaire, "The Huron; or, Pupil of Nature," and his amusing "Dialogue between a Savage and a Bachelor of Arts," in *The Writings of Voltaire*, ed. and trans. E. R. Dumont (New York: Wise, 1931), 3:64–163, 4:108–17. On Diderot, see his fictitious "Supplement to the Voyage of Bougainville," in *Political Writings*, ed. and trans. John Hope Mason and Robert Wokler (Cambridge: Cambridge University Press, 1992), 31–75.

mention the Aztec and Inca civilizations. In short, the linear evolution among philosophers of the representations of American Indians as representing natural man cannot be explained by changes in the Indians or new information. Rather, these philosophers clearly used their descriptions of the Indians as support for their own ends. As dissatisfaction with the existing institutions in Europe increased, so did praise of the Indians grow as an alternative, more desirable and more natural, way of living. Neither Rousseau nor Voltaire nor Diderot wanted to go back to the state of nature or even thought such a thing possible. They use their representations of the Indians as a pawn in their anti-establishment polemics.

In sum, representations of the American Indians really reflect Europe's own debates, not the reality of America. They have left the legacies of brutishness and of the noble savage that remain with us today. But there is another legacy of these debates. In using the Indians of America to promote their own visions of freedom and legitimate institutions, the philosophers set in motion a train of thought and actions that would lead to revolution. The first of these revolutions took place in America and led to the founding of the United States.

THE UNITED STATES

The Third Period: Eighteenth- and Nineteenth-Century Reactions to the American Political Experiment

The relationship between the Old and New Worlds (and the two images of America) is intertwined and reciprocal. The American Revolution marked the first major step in the collapse of the European empires founded after Columbus encountered the New World. This revolution was inspired in part by the European philosophical doctrines based on natural rights, which had themselves been partly inspired by the original inhabitants of America. Ironically, the political experiment in the name of natural rights then helped destroy the natural people who had inspired the United States' philosophical forefathers. The American Revolution then served as inspiration for the French Revolutionaries and lovers of liberty throughout the world. The complex nature of this relationship is seen in the following quotation from the French philosopher Condorcet:

"The human race had lost its rights. Montesquieu found them and restored them to us" (Voltaire). It is not enough, however, that these rights be written in the philosophers' works and engraved in the heart of virtuous men. It is necessary that the ignorant or feeble man be able to read them in the example of a great people. America has given us this example. Its Declaration of Independence is a simple exposition of these rights, so sacred and so long forgotten. Among no nation have they been so well known, or preserved in such perfect integrity.[34]

The reciprocal relationship is evident: it moves from Montesquieu and Voltaire, who had been partially inspired by America's original inhabitants, to the Declaration of Independence then back to Condorcet, who authored France's Constitution of 1793.

Condorcet's praise of America was typical of the initial wave of *philosophes'* reactions to the United States. Immediate reaction to the American Revolution by French and British Enlightenment thinkers was largely one of enthusiastic praise. In his popular pamphlet entitled "Observations on the Importance of the American Revolution and the Means of Making It a Benefit to the World," the Welshman Richard Price writes, "I see the revolution in favor of universal liberty which has taken place in America; a revolution which opens a new prospect in human affairs, and begins a new era in the history of mankind."[35] Given the unprecedented liberties guaranteed in America, Price is hopeful, even certain, that liberty will soon spread throughout the world if unchecked by tyrannical governments. He says the revolution will "raise the species higher" and compares its effect to "opening a new sense."[36] Indeed, he goes so far as to suggest that "next to the introduction of Christianity among mankind, the American revolution may prove the most important step in the progressive course of [human] improvement."[37] So many hopes has he pinned on America that "perhaps there never existed a people on whose wisdom and virtue more depended; or to a station of more importance in the plan of Providence has been assigned."[38] Diderot similarly imagines that people in the future will say of the American revolutionaries, "These are the men who have freed half the world, and who, working for our happiness before we were even conceived, prevented our being born to the sound of chains banging on our cradles."[39] Turgot, whose brief stint as

34. Marie Jean Antoine Nicolas Caritat de Condorcet, "On the Influence of the American Revolution on Europe," in *Condorcet: Selected Writings,* ed. and trans. Keith Baker (Indianapolis: Bobbs-Merrill, 1976), 76.

35. Richard Price, "Observations on the Importance of the American Revolution and the Means of Making It a Benefit to the World," in *Political Writings,* ed. D. O. Thomas (Cambridge: Cambridge University Press, 1991), 117.

36. Price, "Observations on the Importance of the American Revolution," 118.

37. Price, "Observations on the Importance of the American Revolution," 119.

38. Price, "Observations on the Importance of the American Revolution," 120.

39. Diderot, *Political Writings,* 203. This quotation appears in a book by the Abbé Raynal, *Histoire philosophique et politique des établissements et du commerce des européens dans les deux Indes,* of which Diderot wrote approximately a third. For more on this book and the nature of the Raynal-Diderot collaboration, see Michèle Duchet, *Diderot et l'Histoire des dex Indes ou l'écriture fragmentaire* (Paris: A.-G. Nizet, 1978); Gilles Bancarel and Gianluigi Goggi, eds., *Raynal: De la Polémique à l'histoire,* Studies on Voltaire and the Eighteenth Century 12 (Oxford: Voltaire Foundation, 2000); and the essay in this volume,

finance minister in France marked the last serious attempt at reform before the French Revolution, agrees that the newly formed United States is "the *hope* of the world" and should "become a *model* to it."[40]

The Enlightenment thinkers though did not think America was perfect. Slavery was America's greatest flaw. They understood the difficulties in eradicating this execrable institution and argued that America would be judged by the manner of eliminating it as circumstances allowed.[41]

The great strengths of America, however, according to the Enlightenment philosophers, more than outweighed its imperfections. They praised the numerous liberties in the United States, including freedom of the press, speech, conscience, and religion. Moreover, America is seen as an inspiration for the world. As Condorcet writes, it is an example "so useful to all the nations who can contemplate it"; "it teaches that these rights are everywhere the same."[42] European philosophers developed these Enlightenment ideas, but due to the powerfully entrenched institutions of the Old World, they could not enact them. Enlightenment *philosophes,* however, thought that the example of America would inspire the deeds that their own words could not. As Condorcet wrote, "the example of a free people submitting peacefully to military, as to civil, laws will doubtless have the power to cure us."[43] Whether Europe has been "cured" or not as the *philosophes* might understand it, the American Revolution did in fact inspire the French Revolutionaries in 1789, many of the European revolutionaries in 1848, and various Latin American revolutionaries in the nineteenth and twentieth centuries, and it continues to inspire reformers and revolutionaries throughout the world.[44]

This assessment of America as a model for the world and the optimistic belief that permanent worldwide change would result from the American Revolution was the dominant view of Enlightenment *philosophes* immediately after 1776, but it was not a universal one. It did not take root among those who did not share the Enlightenment's sense of the inevitability of historical progress. For example,

---

"From Voltaire to Raynal and Diderot's *Histoire des deux Indes:* The French *Philosophes* and Colonial America," by Guillaume Ansart.

40. Turgot, "Letter to Price," in Price, *Observations on the Importance of the American Revolution, and the means of making it a benefit to the world* (London, 1784), 127, 123.

41. For example, Price lambastes the "Negro Trade and Slavery," decrying that "the negro trade cannot be censured in language too severe" and condemning it as "shocking to humanity, cruel, wicked, and diabolical." He insists that "nothing can excuse the United States if [abolition] is not done with as much speed, and at the same time with as much effect, as their particular circumstances and situation will allow" (Price, *Observations on the Importance of the American Revolution,* 150).

42. Condorcet, "On the Influence of the American Revolution on Europe," 77.

43. Condorcet, "On the Influence of the American Revolution on Europe," 81. Diderot and Raynal argued the same thing.

44. See, for example, Marc Lahmer, *La Constitution américaine dans le débat français, 1795–1848* (Paris: L'Harmattan, 2003).

Edmund Burke in the end supported the American Revolution as justified, but he and some figures in the Scottish Enlightenment did not see it as a world-changing event. To them, it was just an ordinary political occurrence with no major implications beyond itself. The leading philosophers of the German Enlightenment, such as Kant, also did not register the American Revolution as a world-changing event. Indeed, they barely noticed it at all.[45]

After the French Revolution went awry, European philosophers' views of America changed. Once the French Revolution devolved into terror, anarchy, and despotism, no major European thinker ever again unqualifiedly praised the American Revolution. This is a peculiar conflation of the two events. The relative success of the two revolutions might have led to more, not less, praise for America. Noting how the French got their revolution wrong, whereas the Americans got theirs right, thinkers might have concluded that the American Revolution was a great accomplishment of politically and philosophically brilliant men and worthy of intense study. Instead, European philosophers allowed the horrors of the French Revolution to color and tarnish their understanding of that in America. Their detestation of the abominations of the French Revolution led them to dismiss the American. This shows once again how the perceptions of America are based more on European dynamics than on the reality of America itself.

Despite (or because of) the failure of the French Revolution and the halting success of liberalism in Europe, nineteenth-century European thinkers projected America as Europe's future. Tocqueville and Hegel, for example, both claim that the United States represents Europe's, and perhaps the world's, future.[46] They

45. Kant, to the best of my knowledge, does not discuss the United States. The omission of the United States from his writing is perplexing. While the United States does not meet the "pure principles" of Kant's political ideal, it does have several similarities. For example, Kant describes his ideal: "This requires above all, an internal political constitution, arranged according to pure principles of right, and further, the union of it with other neighboring or distant States, so as to attain a legal settlement of their disputes by a constitution that would be analogous to a universal State" ("Perpetual Peace" in *Kant's Principles of Politics, including his essay on Perpetual Peace*, trans. W. Hastie [Edinburgh: Clark, 1891], 134). Might not a reference be warranted to the United States as one of the few, if not only, existing constitutional confederations that approximate his vision? Might one not expect the founding of such a state during Kant's lifetime to interest him? Whereas Kant is silent on the United States, he writes about the Indians in the 1770s, 1780s, and 1790s. Like many philosophers of the German Enlightenment, Kant continues to identify America with Indians. For an overview of Kant's discussions of the Indians, see Gerbi, *The Dispute of the New World*, 329–33.

46. While Tocqueville and Hegel are among the most famous thinkers associated with the idea of America as Europe's future, they are not the first. In the eighteenth century, Price saw America as a messianic forebearer of the future, and Crèvecoeur and Raynal envisioned the same thing on secular grounds. See, for example, Raynal, *A Philosophical and Political History of the Settlements and Trade of the Europeans in the East and West Indies*, trans. J. O. Justamond, 6 vols. (New York: Negro Universities Press, 1969), 6:97, 161–68; and J. Hector St. John de Crèvecoeur, *Letters from an American Farmer* (New York: Penguin, 1986), 37, 189. Earlier in the eighteenth century Bishop Berkeley also famously predicted the movement of the future to America: "Westward the course of empire takes its way." On

mean different things by this, and Tocqueville therefore goes to study America, whereas Hegel thinks its future characteristics are far off and not yet knowable. According to Tocqueville, because America did not have a feudal and aristocratic past, because the frontier exacerbated the equality that was typical of the coming world, as well as for a host of other reasons, the United States was the purest expression of what was coming for the world as a whole and Europe in particular. In short, America is seen as the purest embodiment of the future because, lacking the entrenched past that impedes the coming of modernity in Europe, America is deemed to be modernity incarnate.

Consequently, the mere existence of the United States adds a dimension to the unsettled nature of nineteenth-century European politics, aptly described by the mid-nineteenth-century romantic poet and playwright Alfred de Musset as "everything that was is no more; everything that will be is not yet. Look no further for the secret of our troubles."[47] Nineteenth-century theorists often felt their age to be unsettled, indeterminate, and transitory rather than a final destination. Tocqueville described it this way: "Aristocracy was already dead when I started life and democracy did not yet exist."[48] Feeling "in between" is in some sense true of people in every historical epoch, but the feeling was particularly acute in nineteenth-century Europe. The ancien régime had been destroyed or discredited and a stable and legitimate new order had yet to be born. Longing for the past or yearning for the future, theorists found primarily disenchantment with the present.

Different kinds of political thinkers dealt with this unsettledness and discontent in different ways. In its desire to return to the glorious prerevolution and premodern past of church, king, and aristocratic hierarchy, the radical right of Maistre, Bonald, and Carlyle, lambaste all that America represents. In contrast the radical left (socialists, communists, anarchists), thinking that liberalism, capitalism, and science represented major improvements over the ancien régime, to this extent supported what the United States represented. But since they considered the American liberal present inadequate in comparison to their respective hoped-for futures, they ultimately were critical of the United States. The liberal center, including thinkers such as Tocqueville, Mill, Guizot, Comte, Jacquemont, Chevalier, and Bryce (the latter three of whom are analyzed in detail in other chapters of this volume), accepted the liberal modern present even while

---

Berkeley's views of America, see Costica Bradatan's "Notes on Bishop Berkeley's New World," in this volume.

47. Musset quoted in Harry Levin, *The Gates of Horn: A Study of Five French Realists* (New York: Oxford University Press, 1953), 79–80.

48. Tocqueville, *Selected Letters on Politics and Society,* ed. Roger Boesche, trans. James Toupin and Roger Boesche (Berkeley and Los Angeles: University of California Press, 1985), 115.

acknowledging its drawbacks, because they thought, human nature being what it is, a modern liberal democracy as embodied in the United States was basically as good a system of government as could be hoped for. Looking for remedies to combat the problems of liberalism from within liberalism itself, this liberal center is the only group that is really supportive of what America represents. Indeed, it is the only group interested in the reality of America in both its positive and negative senses. In all cases during this time period, the American political experiment on the fringe of the world stage gets heightened attention in European debate not because of its power (relative to Europe, it had little), but because it is viewed as a living embodiment of modernity and thus, for better or worse, as Europe's future incarnate.

While nineteenth-century European thinkers on the left, right, and center had different proposed solutions to the partially realized modernity of Europe, they all agreed on the general character of this new world that the United States represented. What America had become and what they thought Europe was on the path to becoming—modern and liberal—was regarded as a mixed blessing. The greatest representative of this ambivalence is Alexis de Tocqueville, the great French thinker and statesman. According to Tocqueville, democratic government is inefficient, meandering, and petty. But it has its advantages. It gets more done by energizing the people to do things themselves: "it does that which the most skillful government often cannot do: it spreads throughout the body social a restless activity, superabundant force, and energy never found elsewhere, which, however little favored by circumstance, can do wonders. Those are its real advantages."[49] Democracy is not conducive, however, to refinement, elevated manners, poetry, glory, or heroic virtues. Theorists of the liberal center largely agreed with Tocqueville that America had these advantages, and the main political theorists of the nineteenth century from across the political spectrum largely agreed with his assessment of America's—and the budding liberal modernity of Europe's—shortcomings.

Nineteenth-century European thinkers typically saw America as the epitome of the self-interested individualism of the new commercial society and as representing the centralization of power by the new middle-class democratic regime. As such, four criticisms were repeatedly leveled at it. First, America was said to embody the disorder caused by collapsing institutions. The authority of all previous standards—experience, age, birth, genius, talent, and virtue—was undercut in America. Second, America represented a growing obsession with money. It was because of this that all other standards of human value were ignored. Third,

49. Tocqueville, *Democracy in America,* ed. J. P. Mayer, trans. George Lawrence (New York: Harper, 1966), vol. 1, pt. 2, chap. 6, p. 245.

America represented unchecked equality. The new type of man preferred equality to liberty, as Tocqueville and Mill warned. Finally, the new form of government represented the power of the majority, or the tyranny of the majority,
to use Tocqueville's famous phrase. Rule of the majority stifled creativity and
individuality. It guaranteed that society would be geared to the mediocre middle
at the expense of individual refinement, the cultivation of culture, and the emergence of spiritual sublimity and greatness.[50] These are essentially the same charges
that are leveled against the United States today by traditional authorities in Africa,
Asia, and the Middle East, by the educated elites in Europe and elsewhere, and
by the antimodern radicals, such as the Ayatollah Khomeini, Hezbollah, and al-
Qaeda.

The Fourth Period: America as Technology

The idea of America as technology has roots deep in the nineteenth-century—
that is, well before the United States became a global power. The rise of this
representation of America parallels a movement in European thought toward
America symbolizing not only the place where the future resides but also a phenomenon, "Americanization." The labels of "Americanism" and "Americanization" began with Creuzer in Germany in 1830 and Baudelaire in France in 1855,
respectively, but the idea of America coming to infect Europe is an even older
thread of German Romanticism.[51] These ideas are later most assiduously and
systematically cultivated by the German Right. The spiritual crisis that the Right
sees for the "coming future" that America represents is in Nietzsche, who writes,
"the breathless haste with which they [Americans] work—the distinctive vice of
the new World—is already beginning to infect old Europe with its ferocity and
is spreading a lack of spirituality" over the continent.[52] Arthur Moeller van den
Bruck (who reintroduces the phrase "Third Reich") systematically explores this
idea. According to him, America must be "not locally but spiritually under-

50. Aspects of this argument are also made by various literary writers, including Mrs. Trollope and
G. K. Chesterton, analyzed in Chapters 8 (Richard Boyd's "From Aristocratic *Politesse* to Democratic
Civility, or, What Mrs. Frances Trollope *Didn't* See in America") and 10 (Patrick J. Deneen's "What
G. K. Chesterton Saw in America: The Cosmopolitan Threat from a Patriotic Nation") of this volume,
respectively.

51. My thanks to Michael Ermath for this information from his forthcoming book, *Germany's
Inner America: Americanization, Counter-Americanism, and Transmodernity in the 20th Century*. According to
Ermath, Friedrich Creuzer discusses "Americanism" in his "Letter to Nebenius," and the Romantic
poet Ludwig Tieck spoke of America as infecting Germany as early as 1811. On Baudelaire, see Roger,
The American Enemy, 59–63.

52. Friedrich Nietzsche, *The Gay Science*, trans. Walter Kaufman (New York: Random House,
1974), bk. 4, aphorism 329, pp. 258–59.

stood."[53] This view of Americanization as the epitome of the culture of technology, and the mediocrity and conformity it entails, starts to be popularized during the Weimar period by people such as Stephen Zweig and Rudolf Kayser and finds a home across the ideological spectrum.[54] Thus, America, once described as the home of nature, now becomes the place where nature is most obscured, the polar opposite point of view.

Indeed, twentieth-century political theorists' main critiques of America, such as those by Heidegger and Spengler on the right and the Frankfurt School on the left, equate the essence of America with technology and materialism. Twentieth-century thinkers do not agree on the origins of America's technological morass. For example, the Frankfurt School sees technology as the result of capitalism, whereas Heidegger attributes it to a particular metaphysical way of being.[55] The characteristics that they lament in America's technological society and soul, however, are similar. They lament the mechanization of society and the way it alienates human beings from their deeper essences. They deplore the monotonization and leveling of the world and the resulting loss of individuality. They decry the way technology kills the spirit and prevents the attainment of the highest human developments. In short, their substantive list of complaints is very similar to those made during the nineteenth century. Whereas the nineteenth-century representation of America by political theorists attributed the cause of the problems to an array of social, political, and economic factors, twentieth-century political theorists tend to center the blame on technology.

Beyond the technological blame, there is another important divergence between nineteenth- and twentieth-century European thinkers' assessments of America. Whereas nineteenth-century thinkers like Tocqueville saw Russia, as well as the United States, as an emerging power, they almost all greatly prefer the American model to the Russian.[56] This is not true in the twentieth century. The creation of the Soviet Union led many revolutionary and progressive thinkers to not only turn their admiration away from the United States but to deplore it as a regressive force is world affairs. This new hostility is another example of how Europe's internal hopes and convulsions color its philosophers' views of America. Consequently, numerous twentieth-century figures on the left, such as Jean-Paul

53. Arthur Moeller van den Bruck, *Die Zeitgenossen,* 13, quoted in Ceaser, *Reconstructing America,* 174. Ceaser gives a nice genealogy of this movement (162–86).
54. See, for example, the writings collected in *The Weimar Republic Sourcebook,* eds. Anton Kaes, Martin Jay, and Edward Dimendberg (Berkeley and Los Angeles: University of California Press, 1994), 393–411.
55. The best account of Heidegger's anti-Americanism is Ceaser, *Reconstructing America,* 187–213.
56. The major exception is Friedrich Schlegel, who first saw America as the future but then refocuses his attention on the "Slavic supremacy of Russia" (Gerbi, *The Dispute of the New World,* 447 and 445–49 passim).

Sartre and Simone de Beauvoir, ideologically committed to communism, lauded Soviet approaches and condemned American ones. For example, Sartre exclaims Russia's special status in writing, "Russia is not comparable to other countries. It is only permissible to judge it when one has accepted its undertaking, and then only in the name of that undertaking."[57] Similarly, Beauvoir approvingly quotes Merleau-Ponty's account of the contemporaneous whitewashing of Stalin's terror: "In 1936, in a Soviet Russia isolated, threatened and unable to preserve the Revolution except at the price of monolithic severity, all opposition assumed the objective aspect of treason."[58] As these leftist thinkers were at least for a time unquestioningly supportive of the Soviet "undertaking," so were they "objectively" critical of its American enemy. After Soviet horrors came to light, many nonetheless maintained their anti-Americanism, some even more so, as if it was all they had left on which to hold.[59] Even on the anticommunist right, however, many considered the United States and Soviet Union to be equally bad. Heidegger, for example, says that "Russia and America . . . are metaphysically the same, namely in regard to their world character and their relation to the spirit."[60] An abstraction from politics that allows such comparisons is regrettable, but in Heidegger's case the comparison is even worse. While formally arguing that the United States and Russia are the same, when he needs a shorthand label for the phenomenon that he describes as a *"katastrophe,"* he calls it "Americanization," not Russianization, implying that the former is closer to the core of the problem.

A POSTMODERN VIEW OF AMERICA

Jean Baudrillard is the most prominent postmodern thinker who has written on America, both before and after 9/11, so as a historical epilogue it is worth concluding with a few words on his America. Baudrillard's writings bring together the whole history of European images of America and perpetuate the pattern of European indifference to the reality of America. As a postmodern thinker, Baudrillard rejects the idea that there is any humanly knowable truth, and this leads him to write contradictorily that "For me there is no truth of America" and that

57. Sartre, *Situations* [*Situations IV*], trans. Benita Eisler (New York: George Braziller, 1965), 266.

58. Beauvoir, *Prime of Life* [*La Force de l'Age*], trans. Peter Green (Cleveland: World Publishing, 1962), cited in Beichman, *Anti-American Myths,* 177.

59. Sidney Hook observes the same phenomenon among American thinkers: "the disillusioned fellow-traveling American intellectuals have bequeathed anti-Americanism rather than pro-communism to the contemporary generation of disaffected intellectuals." Sidney Hook, "Communism and the American Intellectuals: From the Thirties to the Eighties," *Free Inquiry* (Fall 1981): 15, quoted in Beichman, *Anti-American Myths,* xi.

60. Martin Heidegger, "The Fundamental Question of Metaphysics," in *An Introduction to Metaphysics,* trans. Ralph Manheim (New Haven: Yale University Press, 1959), 45.

"I knew all about this nuclear form, this future catastrophe [America] when I was still in Paris, of course."[61] There is no truth, yet he "knows" the truth of America. In addition to this contradiction, Baudrillard, as we saw with Columbus, largely knows what he will find before ever going to America. Baudrillard is learned and aware of the opposite images of America, playfully describing the United States as both "the original version of Modernity" and "the only remaining primitive society."[62] Furthermore, he cleverly combines the five hundred years of opposite European imagery of America, calling America the "Primitive society of the future."[63]

In his book entitled *America,* Baudrillard raises important questions even if he does not treat them with moral seriousness. Baudrillard fancies himself a modern-day Tocqueville who comes to the United States, rents a car, and drives around. It is only a bit of an exaggeration to say that parts of the book are written as stream of consciousness discovery: . . . the desert . . . emptiness . . . a void . . . the abyss. This is what America is![64] Yet, Baudrillard's hyperbole and exaggeration is sometimes used to pose serious questions. For example, he describes America as "the tragedy of the utopian dream made reality. In the very heartland of wealth and liberation [California], you always hear the same question: 'What are you doing after the orgy?' "[65] The after-the-orgy hyperbole leads him to pose the following question: "What do you do when everything is available? . . . This is America's problem and, through America, it has become the world's problem."[66] It is ridiculous to think of "everything" being available to everyone, as if there are currently no economic, social, or political problems and will not be so in the future. Nonetheless, as anyone who mulls Nietzsche's account of the last man will attest, the consequences for human life of excessive abundance pose serious questions. Baudrillard's self-indulgent style suits the posing of these questions even as it prevents him from wrestling with answers in a morally serious manner.

Baudrillard's views of 9/11 are equally self-absorbed and lacking in moral seriousness. Baudrillard describes 9/11 as a "gift" because it frees us from globalization, the world's dominant discourse.[67] Terrorism frees the West from its hege-

61. Baudrillard, *America,* trans. Chris Turner (London: Verso: 1988), 27, 5. Note his deployment of Heidegger's phrase of America as "katastrophe."
62. Baudrillard, *America,* 76, 7.
63. Baudrillard, *America,* 7.
64. Baudrillard writes, "for us the whole of America is a desert" (*America,* 99).
65. Baudrillard, *America,* 30.
66. Baudrillard, *America,* 30.
67. Baudrillard, *The Spirit of Terrorism,* trans. Chris Turner (London: Verso: 2002), 17. The gift is the "irruption" (16, 17) of our discourse that makes 9/11 an "event" (4, 17). Our discourse is globalization: "What is at stake is globalization itself" (11), "the capitalist system itself" (42), "a whole [Western] value-system and a world order" (41). The view that 9/11 was an attack on the dominant discourse of globalization, and not on the United States per se, is also suggested by other postmodern thinkers, including Slavoj Žižek and Jacques Derrida (see note 70, below).

monic discourse: "Terrorism is the act that restores an irreducible singularity to the heart of a system of generalized exchange."[68] But this act comes from within. Globalization is a self-undermining, that is, a suicidal, system, just as every discourse is. According to this view, the West is committing suicide, "it was party to its own destruction."[69] "The West," Baudrillard writes, "has become suicidal, and declared war on itself."[70] It is *"triumphant globalization battling against itself."*[71] And since we all suffer under this system, we all wish to destroy it. Thus, Baudrillard writes, all of us have a "deep-seated complicity" in the events of 9/11.[72] The terrorist "antagonism," he writes, "is everywhere, and in every one of us": "we can say they *did* it, but we *wished for* it."[73]

And rightly so, according to Baudrillard, for "the horror for the 4,000 [*sic*] victims of dying in those towers was inseparable from the horror of living in them."[74] Why? They were "subject to artificial conditioning," not only "air conditioning, but mental conditioning too."[75] To fail to be able to distinguish between the horror of burning alive and the horrors of a life with air condition-

---

68. Baudrillard, *Spirit of Terrorism*, 9.
69. Baudrillard, *Spirit of Terrorism*, 49.
70. Baudrillard, *Spirit of Terrorism*, 7, repeated on 50. Derrida and Žižek agree with Baudrillard that 9/11 is about the suicide of globalization and the West. Derrida's piece on 9/11 is entitled "Autoimmunity: Real and Symbolic Suicides," in *Philosophy in a Time of Terror: Dialogues with Jürgen Habermas and Jacques Derrida*, ed. Giovanna Borradori (Chicago: University of Chicago Press, 2003), 85–136. See also Žižek, *Welcome to the Desert of the Real* (London: Verso, 2002). Unlike Baudrillard, however, Žižek and Derrida do not go so far as to call 9/11 a "gift." For them, it is too early to tell what the attack's ramifications and possible benefits are.
71. Baudrillard, *Spirit of Terrorism*, 11 (italics in original).
72. Baudrillard, *Spirit of Terrorism*, 6.
73. Baudrillard, *Spirit of Terrorism*, 15, 5 (italics in original). Baudrillard's assertions of suicidal complicity in 9/11 include not only the West itself, but the actual buildings of the Twin Towers (47–49). Baudrillard personifies the towers, giving them will and intentionality, arguing that they collapsed not because of the physical damage inflicted on them but out of a kind of loss of will. It is not the physical but the symbolic that is causal, according to Baudrillard. For example, speaking of the World Trade Center Towers, Baudrillard asserts:

It was, in fact, their symbolic collapse that brought about their physical collapse, not the other way around. / As if the power bearing these towers suddenly lost all energy, all resilience; as though that arrogant power suddenly gave way under the pressure of too intense an effort: the effort always to be the unique world model. / So the towers, tired of being a symbol which was too heavy a burden to bear, collapsed, this time physically, in their totality. Their nerves of steel cracked. They collapsed vertically, drained of their strength, with the whole world looking on in astonishment. / The symbolic collapse came about, then, by a kind of unpredictable complicity—as though the entire system, by its internal fragility, joined in the game of its own liquidation, and hence joined in the game of terrorism. (48–49)

Not only are "all" of "us" and the "West" complicit in 9/11—the buildings were too.
74. Baudrillard, *Spirit of Terrorism*, 45.
75. Baudrillard, *Spirit of Terrorism*, 43. According to him, smashing the system rescues us from the "deepest despair" of our "radical comfort" (15).

ing is a level of abstraction rivaled only by Heidegger's inability to distinguish between the processing of agriculture and the processing of human beings.[76]

Yet, Baudrillard's account of 9/11 is probably more of a self-confession than an account of the actual happenings of that day. His description of the terrorists' motives, for example, portrays them not as Islamicist extremists but as postmodern philosophers. He describes them as wanting "solely" to "disrupt" the rules of the game, as "not seek[ing] the impersonal elimination of the other," and as aiming to "radicalize the relation of the image to reality" as was achieved by "the events of 1968," the magical year of upheaval for French radicals.[77] As would-be smashers of discourses, postmodern thinkers fancy themselves as a kind of intellectual terrorist. Indeed, at the end of one of his other books, Baudrillard confesses: "it would be nice to be a terrorist," if death still had some meaning; "I am a terrorist and nihilist in theory as the others are with their weapons."[78] Even Europe's postmodern thinkers, those who claim to celebrate the "other" above all else, use America to advance their own aims. Baudrillard's early work cleverly mixes five hundred years of European views of America, but he continues the five-hundred-year pattern of European thinkers using America to promote their own agendas.

CONCLUSION

America has moved from representing Europe's past to representing Europe's future and from representing the epitome of nature to the epitome of technology, polar opposite views. Four points might be noted, however, that raise questions about the validity of these representations. First, descriptions of America have been fantastical from the beginning. They are inaccurate and often intentionally so. Second, although twentieth-century thinkers blame the United States for technologizing the world, it is apparent that the technological attitude long predates the founding of the United States. Columbus and the conquistadors neither see the New World for what it is nor have any desire to do so. Rather, they seek to exploit resources and people, and this is the essence of the technological atti-

76. Heidegger stated, "as for its essence, modern mechanized agriculture is the same thing as the production of dead bodies in gas chambers and extermination camps, the same thing as the blockade and reduction to starvation of a country, the same thing as the construction of hydrogen bombs" (see Ceaser, *Reconstructing America*, 208). See also Richard Wolin, ed., *The Heidegger Controversy* (New York: Columbia University Press, 1991), 300–301.

77. Baudrillard, *Spirit of Terrorism*, 19, 25, 27.

78. Baudrillard, *Simulacra and Simulation*, trans. Sheila Faria Glaser (Ann Arbor: University Michigan Press, 1994), 163.

tude, the attitude that some claim begins only with the United States. A fair-minded observer must admit that even if the United States was later to export technology to Europe, the technological attitude began in Europe and was originally transplanted from there to America.

Third, there is a fundamental but dubious continuity in the substance of European thinkers' views about America. The Indians are described as, on the one hand, naïve, innocent, childlike, and simple, and on the other as brutish, vulgar, shallow, stupid, and lacking spirituality. These are essentially the same charges that Europe and the world level at the United States today. The United States might be all of these things, although probably no more than most countries and possibly less so than many. But the fact that ways of life as opposite as those of the Indians and the United States are described in fundamentally the same terms indicates a problem in the substantive nature of the representations. This highlights the way in which America has since its discovery served as an imagined alternative, for good and for ill, to the existing reality in Europe.

Fourth, European thinkers miss the mark in blaming America for problems that have to do with modernity itself. One must be careful about conflating the United States and modernity as if they were identical and coequal sets. On the one hand, the United States can be seen as less modern than Europe insofar as according to opinion polls the American public is more religious. On the other hand, there are plenty of modern institutions and desires outside of the United States, too. There are multinational corporations in Europe and other countries around the world, and most people wherever they live in the world desire the standard of living and freedom that the United States—and many modern countries—has. So while there is a certain justification for seeing the United States as embodying modernity, it is not modernity's sole embodiment.

EPILOGUE

I came to this project through a scholarly and not a political connection. At the beginning of my research I admired (and still do) the authenticity that European philosophers celebrate, and I to some extent lamented what I then deemed the lack of authentic culture in the United States. In the course of this research project, however, I came to question these views of both Europe and America and have come to understand them primarily as stereotypes. The very repetitiousness of European thinkers' views of America disproves many of their claims to originality and authenticity. Many leftists after World War II would be embarrassed to know the rightist roots of their views in prewar thought. And there is no European equivalent of the political wisdom and pragmatic good sense found in the American *Federalist Papers*. Indeed, the general contempt that has characterized many European philosophers' views of "practice" and things practical is a snobbish and foolish prejudice left over from aristocratic times. Intellectual rapprochement across the Atlantic, where thinkers on both sides jointly confront the problems of modernity, would be an excellent thing, but a sound transatlantic intellectual rapprochement requires both recognition of the virtues and vices found on each side of the Atlantic and also the separation of modernization from Americanization.

Many philosophers clearly understand that the fundamental phenomenon with which they wrestle is modernity and that America is just their shorthand way of referencing the more omnipresent and deeper problem. In discussing America, many of them are not interested in America itself but use America as a way to get a handle on their own hopes, fears, and anxieties about Europe's future with respect to fundamental questions of modernity. But all too often, especially in general public discussion, the shorthand is mistaken for the phenomenon itself, and America and modernity are equated. This leads people to blame problems not on modernization itself but on Americanization and the United States. It may be easy and perhaps satisfying for Europeans to foist off the problems of modernity onto an "other," to present problems as externally imposed as opposed to being issues with which their own society is implicated. To do so, however, is both wrong and potentially dangerous. It is wrong because it misses the mark. Europe is modern not primarily because of anything the United States has done but because of decisions made by its own past philosophers and leaders. It is dangerous because it creates a caricature of America that exacerbates real problems and gets in the way of potential solutions.

One part of my argument is prosaic: it turns out that those who favor modernity, especially modernity in its liberal form, favor America, whereas the Far Left and the Far Right dislike the United States. The antimodern Right is of two types, traditionalist and revolutionary. The traditionalist antimodern Right, including both Europe's defenders of the ancien régime and the defenders of traditional authority throughout the world today, are anti-American because America promotes the creative destruction of capitalism, the social-order shaking of individualism and meritocracy, and a hierarchy-destroying egalitarianism. These often threaten or undermine inherited traditions, orders, and authorities. The revolutionary Right that calls for creating a new hierarchy in the future dislikes America for what it sees as its excessive egalitarianism, race mixing, and the mediocrity considered inherent in democracy. Those on the Far Left who condemn the liberal version of modernity in favor of what they think are more advanced versions of modernity such as communism and socialism are also ultimately anti-American because they are antiliberal. Whereas many progressive thinkers celebrated America in the nineteenth century as the best that had been achieved until then, progressives and revolutionaries abandoned the United States after the rise of the Soviet Union and authored some of the most vituperative anti-American writings of the twentieth century.

It is perhaps less appreciated, however, that the Far Left and Far Right, unlike the liberal center, are but little interested in factual data and evidence about the real America. Their ideologies seem to supply almost all they need to know. The dominance of ideology among the theorists examined in this study is the most personally disappointing aspect of my findings. I initially expected to find more people who actually philosophized and thought. I was disappointed by the number and the extent of famous names that turned out to be ideological, dogmatic, and relatively shallow.

The unfortunate problem for America concerning European perceptions of it is that so few European philosophers are moderate or liberal. In the twentieth century, most European countries have but few liberal thinkers of note— Raymond Aron and his followers in France; Popper, Oakeshott, and Berlin in England; Habermas and Sternberger in Germany; Croce in Italy. They are few and far between. This should not perhaps be surprising given the historical lack of liberal political systems in Europe. Liberalism came to France for good (excluding the Vichy lapse) only in 1870. Germany had only the brief Weimar experiment before liberalism was imposed by the United States in its western half after World War II. In Italy and Greece liberalism had minimal political roots until after World War II, and it was not realized in Spain and Portugal until the 1970s. Eastern Europe had few moments of democratic rule until the collapse of the Iron Curtain in 1989. And today, at a time when Europe's peaceful coming together is lauded by Europeans everywhere, where, other than Habermas, are the European philosophers of federalism? At a time of European constitution building, why is there so little interest in the theory and practice of American constitutionalism?[79]

One final word on the limits of my study. I have examined the views of philosophers. In modern parlance, I have examined elite, as opposed to mass, views of America. These two views are not the same. European public opinion

79. Valéry Giscard d'Estaing, former president of France and the head of the European Convention that was charged with drafting a constitution for Europe, said that he wanted to be for the European Constitution what Jefferson was for the American one: "I tried to play a little bit the role that Jefferson played, which was to instill leading ideas into the system. Jefferson was a man who wrote and produced elements that consolidated the Constitution." He might have got his wish: both he and Jefferson spent the time of the respective constitutional draftings largely in France. The fact that someone in Giscard d'Estaing's position seemed not to know that Jefferson had little to do with the drafting of the American Constitution is an example of the regrettable European ignorance of American constitutionalism. See Elaine Sciolino, "United Europe's Jefferson? Giscard d'Estaing Smiles," New York Times, June 15, 2003, A6.

as a whole responds to the actions of the United States in a more or less common-sense manner. As shown by the longevity of the images I have discussed, this is not true of the elites. Opinion polls serve as another measurement of this phenomenon. For example, French elite opinion of the United States does not vary with what the United States does. Whereas after World War II and the Marshall Plan, French mass opinion was overwhelmingly in favor of the United States, French elite opinion of the United States was overwhelmingly negative.[80] The inflexible, ideological nature of elite opinion is regrettable. It is dangerous, because in this case it has created a discourse of anti-American stereotypes that can readily be tapped into and exploited by demagogues when the European masses have an unfavorable view of America. The masses respond to media portrayals of what the United States *actually does*. The elites condemn the United States for what they *think it is*.

What does this mean for today? As long as both the United States and Europe are liberal and more like each other than like any other region of the world, transatlantic relations will be relatively good. As long as there are disparities in power between the United States and Europe, there will also be fear, envy, and mutual resentment. Rivalry must inevitably emerge as the cold war fades from memory and as long as shared perceptions of a new common foe do not exist. Since the 1776 revolution in America and the 1789 one in France, European thinkers have been struggling to articulate and/or create uniquely European ways of living and to erect political institutions to promote and protect them. Their aim has been to deal with the conflict between what they deem European values and aspirations on the one hand and the modern forces they associate with America on the other. There is no reason to think European philosophers' perceptions of conflict between their deepest aspirations and what they deem America to be will end in the foreseeable future. Indeed, in 2003, in the wake of the launching of the most recent Iraq war, Habermas and Derrida called for a new Europe that can serve as an alternative to the American model and be a counterweight to it.[81] Policy makers and acute observers should thus expect continued tension in the transatlantic relationship. There is no reason why both sides of the Atlantic cannot understand and learn from each other. But whatever hap-

80. Tony Judt, *Past Imperfect: French Intellectuals, 1944–1956* (Berkeley and Los Angeles: University of California Press, 1992), 201–4.

81. Habermas and Derrida, "After the War: Plea for a European Rebirth," originally published as "Nach dem Krieg: Die Wiedergeburt Europas" in *Frankfurter-Allgemeine Zeitung*, May 31, 2003. These thinkers call for a new constitutional order for Europe to enshrine European values and "to counterbalance the hegemonic unilateralism of the United States." The European values they identify include secularization, a preference for the security guarantees of the welfare state, confidence in the state in general, distrust of markets, and a desire for a multilateral and legally regulated international order.

pens on the level of philosophical discourse, policy makers and interested observers should be prepared to deal with excessively negative reactions to the United States, when in times of disharmony, cynics and demagogues tap into the five-hundred-year-old legacy of imagery of America.

PART TWO

AMERICA AND THE ENLIGHTENMENT

2

NOTES ON BISHOP BERKELEY'S NEW WORLD

Costica Bradatan

THE UNORTHODOXIES OF AN EIGHTEENTH-CENTURY "EMPIRICIST"

George Berkeley (1685–1753) is not only the author of foundational empiricist manifestos, such as *A Treatise Concerning the Principles of Human Knowledge* or *Three Dialogues between Hylas and Philonous,* but also the writer, quasi-ignored today, of a series of texts on topics that would rather embarrass his commentators of today: utopian projects, messianism, the quest for the earthly paradise, tar-water as panacea, alchemical visions, and so forth.[1] In 1725, for example, Berkeley published a paper titled *A Proposal for the better Supplying of Churches in our Foreign Plantations, and for Converting the Savage Americans, to Christianity, By a College to be erected in the Summer Islands, otherwise called The Isles of Bermuda.*[2] The title is self-explana-

This text clarifies, develops, and re-elaborates some ideas and arguments that I first advanced in the chapter "George Berkeley's 'Bermuda Project,'" in Costica Bradatan, *The Other Bishop Berkeley: An Exercise in Reenchantment* (New York: Fordham University Press, 2006), 146–72, and in my article "Waiting for the *Eschaton:* Berkeley's 'Bermuda Project' between Earthly Paradise and Educational Utopia," *Journal of Utopian Studies* 14, no. 1 (2003): 36–50. I am grateful to Fordham University Press and *The Journal of Utopian Studies* for their kind permission to use a part of these materials.

1. In this paper, I only discuss Berkeley's "American project" and the topics associated with it (utopianism, quest for the earthly paradise, messianism). For an ampler introduction to this more obscure Berkeley, see my book *The Other Bishop Berkeley.*

2. All references to Berkeley's text will be made to *The Works of George Berkeley Bishop of Cloyne,* ed. Arthur Aston Luce and Thomas Edmund Jessop, 9 vols. (London: Thomas Nelson and Sons, 1948–57). In this edition, *A Proposal* is published in 7:343–60.

tory. Prior to that, the philosopher, since about March 1722, had written several private letters to friends and acquaintances on the same topic, each of them offering enthusiastic descriptions of the Bermuda islands and of his educational project. The letter to Lord Percival, dated March 4, 1722,[3] is of special interest, as in it Berkeley announces for the first time his intention to establish a theology and fine arts college in the New World and to spend all the rest of his life there: "It is now about ten months since I have determined with myself to spend the residue of my days in the Island of Bermuda, where I trust in Providence I may be the mean instrument of doing good to mankind."[4] Then, finally, there are those famous stanzas by Berkeley dedicated to the project, confessing his lack of satisfaction, if not disappointment, with the Old World, and famously announcing that "Westward the Course of Empire takes its Way."[5]

In this essay I discuss Berkeley's project to build a theology and fine arts college in the Islands of Bermuda as a paradigmatic case of utopian idealization and symbolic reconstruction of the New World with the means offered by the philosophical, theological, and political conceptual repertoire of the Old World. More specifically, Berkeley's American project will be analyzed through the prism of a set of traditional Western topoi, notions and conceptions such as the utopian tradition, the fascination with the "happy islands," the quest for the earthly paradise, as well as the notion of *eschaton*.[6] I will show that in designing his educational project Berkeley was, whether consciously or unconsciously, under the strong influence of these ancient notions and patterns of thought. In other words, on his (epistemic) encounter with the New World, Berkeley did not so much seek to know it on its own terms, as he mapped it out mentally using the repertoire of ancient phantasms, hopes of universal renewal, and dreams of spiritual salvation offered to him by the intellectual traditions of the Old World. I will first seek to determine the place of Berkeley's project in the utopian tradition; I will also try to place Berkeley's idealized representation of the islands

3. *The Works of George Berkeley Bishop of Cloyne,* 8:127–29.

4. *The Works of George Berkeley Bishop of Cloyne,* 8:127. As David Berman has put is, "[f]or whatever reasons, Berkeley seems to have lost confidence in the Old World and was looking hopefully to America. For it was probably in the early months of 1722 that he conceived his plan for a missionary and art college in Bermuda, which was to engage him for the next decade" (Berman, *George Berkeley: Idealism and the Man* [Oxford: Clarendon Press, 1994], 100).

5. *Verses on America,* 7:373.

6. This is, obviously, one angle, out of many possible, from which to look at how European philosophers have represented and reconstructed America over the last few centuries. Other approaches are equally possible. For example, in an interesting book, Durand Echeverria traces the image of America in eighteenth-century French philosophy and letters. See Echeverria, *Mirage in the West: A History of the French Image of American Society to 1815* (Princeton: Princeton University Press, 1957). For the way in which America has been represented in English literature in the late nineteenth and early twentieth centuries, see Peter Conrad, *Imagining America* (New York: Oxford University Press, 1980).

of Bermuda in the tradition of the search for the earthly paradise and the "happy islands," as traditionally described in ancient and medieval literature. Second, I will show that Berkeley's "Bermuda project" is hardly understandable without taking into account its messianism, which Berkeley shared with many of the early American colonists. Finally, by way of conclusion, I will point to some ways in which Berkeley's project would be relevant today in light of the general theme of this volume, America through European eyes.

BERKELEY THE UTOPIST

George Berkeley's project to build a theology college in the islands of Bermuda, far from being an isolated attempt, a personal and incomprehensible caprice, might well be placed in the long tradition of the "educational utopias." Berkeley did not gratuitously dream about the New World and the islands of Bermuda; he needed this place precisely as a spatial framework, as a setting, for his educational project. Since his main objective was to establish a college there, dedicated to learning and the cultivation of sciences, an investigation of Berkeley's Bermuda project in relation to the utopian tradition would put us in a better place to make some sense of it. Let me also add at this stage that the term *utopia* in relation to Berkeley's Bermuda project was first used more than one hundred years ago by A. C. Fraser, one of George Berkeley's prominent editors and biographers. Thus, Frazer talks about Bermuda as "a region whose idyllic bliss poets had sung, and from which Christian civilization might radiate over the Utopia of a New World, with its magnificent possibilities in the future history of the human race."[7] Notwithstanding this remark by Fraser, however, there has not been to this day any systematic investigation of Berkeley's Bermuda project in terms of utopianism.

As Northrop Frye once put it, any utopia is ultimately a discourse about education. Even if it is not conceived as an educational project per se, any utopia aims in fact at changing people's lives by means of a radically new vision of education, learning, and *Bildung*. If not in their explicit purposes and statements, at least implicitly the utopian authors very often employ a vision of education as a decisive factor in improving the minds, souls, and mores and of their fellow humans. For, of course, it is much easier to educate people differently, to inculcate new ideas in people's minds when they are still at an early age, than to change their minds suddenly and forcedly at a time when they are already mature

7. Alexander C. Fraser, *The Works of George Berkeley, D. D.; Formerly Bishop of Cloyne. Including his Posthumous Works, With Prefaces, Annotations, Appendices, and Account of his Life, by Alexander Campbell Fraser,* 4 vols. (Oxford: Clarendon Press, 1901), 4:343.

and deeply rooted into certain ways of life and accustomed to certain ways of thinking. Indeed, in Frye's view, from this perspective, any utopia seems to have a certain platonic component, whether or not the utopian writers are platonists themselves:

> And though not all utopia-writers are Platonists, nearly all of them make their utopias depend on education for their permanent establishment. It seems that the literary convention of an ideal state is really a by-product of a systematic view of education. That is, education, considered as a unified view of reality, grasps society by its intelligible rather than its actual form, and the utopia is a projection of the ability to see society, not as an aggregate of buildings and bodies, but as a structure of arts and sciences.[8]

In Thomas More's *Utopia,* to take a classic example, even if his is not primarily an educational utopia, the cultivation of learning and sciences play a central role in people's lives: "a great multitude of every sort of people, both men and women, go to hear lectures, some one and some another, as every man's nature is inclined."[9] In utopia, knowledge and instruction are democratically accessible to all its inhabitants, to the point that, in a way, learning has become a form of entertainment here. Because of the generous cultivation of arts and sciences, expertise in one or more fields is so widespread among utopians that utopia is more advanced, scientifically, than any other place on earth: "But they be in the course of the stars and the movings of the heavenly spheres very expert and cunning. They have also wittily excogitated and devised instruments of divers fashions, wherein is exactly comprehended and contained the movings and situations of the sun, the moon, and of all the other stars which appear in their horizon."[10]

To return to Berkeley's project, one might say that, in a rigorous sense, when compared to, say, Plato's *Republic,* Berkeley's is only an incomplete, partial utopia. It is not a hard but a soft utopia, so to speak. It does not aim to occupy all spheres of life but only the educational sphere. More than the ambitious ideal state envisaged by Plato, Berkeley's Bermuda resembles to some extent the *Bildungsprovinz* we come across in Hermann Hesse's *Das Glasperlenspiel (The Glass Bead Game):* an ideal scholarly society dedicated to cultivating superior arts and science, located in some privileged space, clearly separated from the corrupted and corrupting outside world, and designed to embody, preserve, and convey

---

8. Northrop Frye, "Varieties of Literary Utopias," in *Utopias and Utopian Thought,* ed. Frank Edward Manuel (Boston: Beacon Press, 1965), 37–38.

9. Thomas More, *Utopia* (London: Dent, 1974), 65.

10. More, *Utopia,* 83.

the noblest values and virtues of humankind. It is an island, not necessarily in a physical sense but in a symbolical one. The island thus becomes a spatial symbol of salvation and regeneration through learning, science, and fine arts. Bermuda is "the world of Mind—artificial, more orderly, more secure, but still in need of constant supervision and study."[11] Just like Hesse's Castalia, Berkeley's utopian island is projected as "the training ground and refuge for that small band of men whose lives were to be consecrated to Mind and to truth."[12]

The notion of utopian separation from the outside (profane) world[13] of self-protection and inaccessibility is emphasized several times by Berkeley: "The Group of Isles . . . walled round with Rocks, which render them inaccessible to Pirates or Enemies; there being but two narrow Entrances, both well guarded by Forts. It would therefore be impossible to find anywhere, a more secure Retreat for Students."[14] As a matter of fact, in doing so, Berkeley followed a pattern of thought that had been brilliantly illustrated by Thomas More. More set his utopia on a remote, well-protected, inaccessible island. One has to be already a utopian, an insider, to know how to enter utopia safely; otherwise, any attempt at forcing the entrance proves fatal. Utopia is specifically designed to keep away any unwelcome visitors. The place has its secret traps, gates, and paths; it is not for everybody to enter it unharmed:

Other rocks there be lying hid under the water, which therefore be dangerous. The channels be known only to themselves [Utopians], and therefore it seldom chanceth that any stranger, unless be he guided by an Utopian, can come into this haven, insomuch that they themselves could scarcely enter without jeopardy, but that their way is directed and ruled by certain landmarks standing on the shore. By turning, translating, and removing these marks into other places they may destroy their enemies' navies, be they never so many.[15]

Berkeley's strong emphasis on this aspect of his project is thus perfectly justified when considered in light of the utopian tradition and of the canons of utopian thinking, where remoteness, difficulty of access, and isolation play an

---

11. Hermann Hesse, *The Glass Bead Game: Magister Ludi,* trans. Richard and Clara Winston (New York: Picador, 1990), 100.

12. Hesse, *The Glass Bead Game,* 100.

13. According to some authors, this remoteness of the island from the American mainland was in fact one of the main causes of the failure of the entire project. A. Luce, for example, considers that "the tragedy of the Bermuda project was just Bermuda. Six hundred miles of ocean separate it from the nearest point of the mainland. Students might have come sixty miles, but not six hundred. The romance of Bermuda won support for the scheme, the facts of Bermuda killed it" (Arthur A. Luce, *The Life of George Berkeley Bishop of Cloyne* [Edinburgh: Thomas Nelson and Sons, 1949], 99).

14. *A Proposal,* 7:352.

15. More, *Utopia,* 55–56.

important role. But, interestingly enough, they play a double role: they are necessary not only for keeping the innocent students safe from the corrupting profane world, or for preventing it from interfering with the normal course of the
academic/utopian affairs, but also for conferring high prestige and esteem on this
scholarly community. Remoteness causes fascination; inaccessibility is what gives
birth to, and increases, desire. Therefore, the strength of such an ideal scholarly
community does only come from, say, the volume of its learning or from its
various scientific accomplishments, but also—maybe more important—from its
prestige, from its publicly and socially recognized image, and the wide fascination
that it holds.

Once all the requirements are met, Berkeley's utopia is ready to make its
debut. In *A Proposal* he describes in detail the specific conditions under which
the project takes place:

> Among a People [the inhabitants of Bermuda] of this Character, and in a
> Situation thus circumstantiated, it would seem that a *Seminary of Religion* and
> Learning might very fitly be placed. The Correspondence with other Parts of
> *America,* the Goodness of the Air, the Plenty and Security of the Place, the
> Frugality and Innocence of the Inhabitants, all conspiring to favour such a
> Design. Thus much at least is evident, that young Students would be there
> less liable to be corrupted in their Morals; and the governing Part would be
> easier, and better contented with a small Stipend, and a retired academical
> Life, in a Corner from whence Avarice and Luxury are excluded.[16]

As expected, life in such an "ideal community" is dominated by an increased
degree of artificiality: in such a place human life is not allowed to take its natural
course, but it is carefully and in detail "regulated," ordered, surveyed, controlled,
kept far away from any possible vices and temptations. In brief, life is thoroughly
rationalized and engineered here. As Giuseppe Mazzotta observed, utopians "are
necessary for many reasons." One of these reasons is that "there is always a need
to accommodate the excess of private desires to the public good, politics to ethics, moderation to freedom."[17] Private desires are systematically censored, cas-
trated even, according the compelling logic of the public good. Whatever does
not a play a role in the construction and reproduction of the public good has to
be repressed. In fact, what happens in a utopia is a drastic redefinition of the
distinction between private and public: everything should be public, even the

---

16. *A Proposal*, 7:353.

17. Giuseppe Mazzotta, *Cosmopoiesis: The Renaissance Experiment* (Toronto: University of Toronto
Press, 2001), 60.

most private things. Any utopia is designed as a sophisticated social machinery whose input is raw, uneducated humans still in a "natural state" and driven by primary instincts, and whose output is nothing other than a wonderfully redesigned, perfectly civilized, and smoothly working human community.

This process of "rationalization" is an essential characteristic of any utopian organization, starting with its very outset: recruitment of its members. As has been remarked about the recruitment of new members in Hesse's *Das Glasperlenspiel,* "an exchange between Castalian institutions and their surroundings persists: since all Castalians are celibate men and since they do not have any alternative form of perpetuating their ascetic community (immortality, regeneration, cloning, and so forth), lay children are recruited on the basis of their intellectual and artistic performance by thoroughly combing the schools of the real world."[18] In a similar fashion, Berkeley's ideal scholarly society regularly needs new members. Since its main objective is to produce worthy priests and missionaries who are to be involved in the propagation of the Gospel and the conversion of Indians, it is necessary to have an established way of replacing them and permanently renewing the utopian community. It is at this point that Berkeley's system differs significantly from that envisaged by Hesse. For, while the new members of Castalia were "elected," being invited to join the utopian community only as the final result of an extremely difficult process of selection, in Berkeley's Bermuda among the toughest procedures are those related to the recruitment of future members of the scholarly community. Basically, if peaceful methods fail, Berkeley openly recommends the kidnapping of young Indians and forcing them into his utopian machine: "The young *Americans* necessary for this Purpose, may in the beginning be procured, either by peaceable Methods from those savage Nations, which border on our Colonies, and are in Friendship with us, or by taking captive the Children of our Enemies."[19] This controversial aspect of Berkeley's Bermuda project has long been discussed among Berkeley scholars. David Berman, for example, regards this violent solution as "chilling" and, despite his constantly sympathetic reading of George Berkeley, he cannot help being rather sarcastic when it comes to Berkeley's American project: "The Indian children are to be kidnapped. Why? No doubt, for their spiritual advantage."[20] On the other hand, when he comes to discuss this issue, Harry Bracken advances an interesting millennialist hypothesis, which I will examine later in this chapter.

Apart from the provision about recruitment, there are in Berkeley's *Proposal*

---

18. Sorin Antohi, "Commuting to Castalia: Noica's 'School.' Culture and Power in Communist Romania," preface to Gabriel Liiceanu, *The Păltiniș Diary* (Budapest: Central European University Press, 2000), xi.

19. *A Proposal,* 7:347.

20. Berman, *George Berkeley,* 132–33.

clear and detailed regulations with regard to the schooling itself. Just as in other utopias, for example in Plato's *Republic,* so in Berkeley's theology and fine arts college there are similarly rationalized and detailed procedures regarding access to the utopian community, starting age, precise subject matters to be taught, and so forth:

> It is proposed to admit into the aforesaid College only such Savages as are under ten Years of Age, before evil Habits have taken a deep root; and yet not so early as to prevent retaining their Mother Language, which should be preserved by Intercourse among themselves.
>
> It is further proposed, to ground these young *Americans* thoroughly in Religion and Morality, and to give them a good Tincture of other Learning; particularly of Eloquence, History and practical Mathematics; to which it may not be improper to add some skill in Physics.[21]

This is one of the few references Berkeley makes to the specifics of the curriculum to be used in his college. Had he got the necessary funds from the British authorities, he would have had to offer a much more detailed curriculum and an ampler description of the academic program to be pursued in the college. Sketchy as it is, the *Proposal* does not allow us to know more about Berkeley's educational doctrines. It is worth noting at this point that Berkeley does not see the study of his own immaterialist philosophy as playing any role in shaping his utopian project; he did not build his utopian project on principles derived from his own philosophical system, nor did he mention that students should study it. He, rather, relied here on the traditional utopian way of thinking. The details he provides are derived not from his immaterialist theses, but from the inner logic of utopianism itself.

Several of Berkeley's commentators and admirers have been rather embarrassed when coming across the description of such cruel procedures as those recommended for the recruitment of young Indians in his *Proposal.* The conventional image of the "good Bishop" would rather exclude all these cruel procedures. Yet, it seems to me that, if we adopt the hypothesis of utopianism, such procedures, however cruel or even "totalitarian" they might appear to some, become to some extent understandable: they do not pursue severity for its own sake, but are derived from the logic of the utopian thought, from a particular way of considering the relationship between private life and public life, between what we are and what we should be. They are based on a certain understanding of what it means to be human and what "the Good" means. In such a context,

21. *A Proposal,* 7:347–48.

the tough procedures somehow lose their seeming "cruelty" and "totalitarian-ism" if considered as mere means for obtaining a greater good: an obvious improvement, or transfiguration, of the fellow humans' way of life. According to such a line of thought—which can be easily followed from Plato to, say, Lenin—the overwhelming "pluses" that such a transfiguration would bring about are more important than any of the "minuses," the possible local inconve-niences it might cause to those who happen to be involved. In More's *Utopia,* too, there are specific rules and codes of conduct regulating all aspects of private and social life. For More, these regulations are not at all about the production and reproduction of power, but are simply intended to help utopians live a happy and simple life: "After supper they bestow one hour in play, in summer in their gardens, in winter in their common halls where they dine and sup. There they exercise themselves in music, or else in honest and wholesome communication"; "to the intent the prescript number of the citizens should neither decrease nor above measure increase, it is ordained that no family . . . shall at once have fewer children of the age of fourteen or thereabout than ten or more than sixteen"; "if any be desirous to visit either their friends dwelling in another city or to see the place itself, they easily obtain licence of their Syphogrants and Tranibores."[22] It is, ultimately, the benevolence, noble motivations, and generosity of the utopian projects that result in these unpleasant side effects.

Obviously, this is not the place for me to agree or disagree with Berkeley's violent procedures in his utopia; I am simply trying to place them in a wider context of the tradition of utopian thought and see what the logic behind them is. For insofar as it is possible to talk about a "perennial utopian theme," as Frank Manuel has put it,[23] Berkeley's Bermuda project could be probably better understood if considered as belonging to the long tradition of those similar proj-ects through which this utopian theme has been approached and developed. Seen in this way, all these detailed and unpleasant provisions, regulations, and tough measures that Berkeley envisaged are born out of a genuine desire to see his neighbors happier, less distressed, and more virtuous, just as in any other utopian project. "Compassion" certainly has a different meaning in this tradition: one helps one's neighbors not by just feeding them or attending to them, and then leaving them as they are, but by involving them in an active process of (self-) transformation. Then, unlike us in the twenty-first century, Berkeley lived in a rather "innocent" age, one that had not witnessed any serious attempts at putting utopian projects into practice.

---

22. More, *Utopia,* 65, 69, 75.

23. Frank Edward Manuel, "Toward a Psychological History of Utopia," in *Utopias and Utopian Thought,* ed. Manuel, 70.

Apart from the need for physical isolation and difficulty of access, a utopian project would not in principle require any particular geographical setting for its implementation. A highly rational (and, therefore, universal) project, the utopia is, as it were, possible anywhere, disregarding the local traditions, the specific geography, and topography of the place. In Berkeley's case, however, and this is probably one of the original aspects of his project, the specificity of the place plays an important role: he needed for his utopia a place of a particular nature and with specific characteristics.

Despite the fact that he had never traveled to Bermuda (and, ironically, he never would do so),[24] Berkeley offered in both his letter to Percival mentioned above and his *Proposal* a very detailed description of the islands—of their natural landscapes, beauties, resources, richness, and prosperity; he gave plenty of details about the happy inhabitants of these islands and their way of life, praising the purity of their morals and innocence of their manners.[25] Berkeley's talent as a writer helps him portray the islands and the islanders magnificently, compensating for the absence of any direct familiarity with them. Since the description itself is an excellent piece of writing and plays a significant role in my argument, I will reproduce below some excerpts:

> The climate is by far the healthiest and most serene, and . . . the most fit for study. . . . There is the greatest abundance of all the necessary provisions for life, which is much to be considered in a place for education. . . . It is the securest spot in the universe, being environed round with rocks all but one narrow entrance, guarded by seven forts, which render it inaccessible. . . . The inhabitants have the greatest simplicity of manners, more innocence, honesty, and good nature, than any of our other planters.[26]

Read between the lines, Berkeley's text conveys something of a premonition that a place like this is predestined to become the location for some great deeds;

---

24. Berkeley would travel to, and live in, America from 1728 to 1731, for the most part in Newport, Rhode Island. This paper deals only with how he *fantasized* about the New World, before setting foot there. For his actual stay in America, see, for example, Edwin S. Gaustad, *George Berkeley in America* (New Haven: Yale University Press, 1979).

25. Interestingly enough, Berkeley's Bermudans have many things in common with the inhabitants of Thomas More's *Utopia*. Just as in Berkeley's Bermudas, the utopians "embrace chiefly the pleasures of the mind, for them they count the chiefest and most principal of all. The chief part of them they think doth come of the exercise of virtue and conscience of good life" (Thomas More, *Utopia* [London: Dent, 1974], 92). The parallel between Berkeley's *Bermuda* and More's *Utopia* will be followed in more detail later on in this paper.

26. *Letter to Percival*, 8:128.

it simply invites them. On the other hand, although *A Proposal* is written some years after this letter, it still retains the same enthusiasm and idealization. Berkeley used generously winged words to express this sense of perfection and astonishment. Everything about those islands was as perfect as something could possibly be in this world: "No Part of the World enjoys a purer Air, or a more temperate Climate, the great Ocean which environs them, at once moderating the Heat of the South Winds, and the Severity of the North-West. . . . the Air of Bermuda is perpetually fanned and kept cool by Sea-breezes, which render the Weather the most healthy and delightful that could be wished, being . . . of one equal Tenour almost throughout the whole Year, like the latter End of a fine May."[27]

A crucial part of the description is that in which the numberless natural "beauties of Bermuda" of all kinds are listed. The islands seem full of wonders and blessings, abundantly supplied with natural resources as useful as they are beautiful. On the islands of Bermuda there is no need for hard work to produce the goods necessary for living: these goods are already there, ripe, fresh, and ready for consumption. In Bermuda, as it were, the whole of nature conspired to produce one of the most beautiful and happiest places in the universe; it becomes obvious that the island has been "chosen" as a place for unusual spiritual accomplishments. The Bermudan landscape thus becomes an important part of the utopian project: Berkeley's college does not just happen to be located in Bermuda, but it is *necessary* for it to be there:

The summers refreshed with constant cool breezes, the winters as mild as our May, the sky as light and blue as a sapphire, the ever green pastures, the earth eternally crowned with fruits and flowers. The woods of cedars, palmettos, myrtles, oranges &c., always fresh and blooming. The beautiful situations and prospects of hills, vales, promontories, rocks, lakes and sinuses of the sea. The great variety, plenty, and perfection of fish, fowl, vegetables of all kinds, and . . . the must excellent butter, beef, veal, pork, and mutton. But above all, that uninterrupted health and alacrity of spirit, which is the result of the finest weather and gentlest climate in the world.[28]

The first idea that crosses one's mind when reading such a description is that the way in which Berkeley describes the islands of Bermuda is similar to the way the earthly paradise has traditionally been described and represented within the medieval *mirabilia;* in medieval, Renaissance, and early modern travel literature; and in various other "amazing" accounts of "happy islands." Exactly in the same

---

27. *A Proposal,* 7:351.
28. *Letter to Percival,* 8:128.

fashion in which Berkeley depicted the Bermuda islands, generations of ancient and medieval authors before him had seen the earthy paradise: marked by a sense of virginal perfection, overwhelmed by the enchanting beauty of nature, abundant in goods of all kind, well-protected from the outside world, a place closer to God than anywhere else on earth. What is striking about Berkeley's portrait of the islands is that behind his detailed description of them does not actually lie any actual documentation, but only the primordial fantasy, so to speak, of a wonderful, innocent, and uncorrupted world. In a way, it could be said that Berkeley did not even need to go see the islands in order to be able to describe them: he apparently found them, with all their wonderful paradisiacal appearance, right there, in the rich conceptual repertoire of his own inner intellectual world. Upon conceiving of these texts, Berkeley engaged himself in a process of "idealization," or "sacralization," of something otherwise quite profane: he ends up attributing to a neutral group of Atlantic islands almost all the ennobling characteristics of the earthly paradise as it had traditionally been imagined since Greco-Roman antiquity.[29]

First of all, it is the very notion of *island* that confers on the whole story a special character.[30] An island is not a place "like any other"; it is a privileged space, a space that—thanks to its isolation, remoteness, and difficult accessibility, to its mysteriousness and autonomy—has acquired a particular symbolic dignity from the very beginning of human culture.[31] The sophisticated interplay between water and land, their complex dialectics, gave birth eventually to a new, intermediary entity: *the island*. The island is more than land and water, as it acquires something that neither land nor water as such has: the capacity to provoke in us a greater fascination, curiosity, and awe. Islands always attract us because, among other things, they cause in us a distinct feeling of the sublime: a sense of greatness and of danger at the same time. There is something at once powerful and fragile about an island: it offers protection, noble isolation, autonomy, but it also insinuates a sense of directionless floating and of lack of roots. Not that islands are closer to heaven, but they are certainly not so close to earth. They are detached from earth, left on their own, which makes them ready for extraordinary adventures

29. Of course, Berkeley claims several times that he had been informed about the islands by very trustworthy persons ("the best Information I could get"), but, as we will see below, his description did not fit the real situation of the islands at all.

30. It is true that, later on, when the project had already started to fail, Berkeley showed himself ready to build the college somewhere on the American mainland. However, what I am particularly interested in here is his first, genuine impulse and intention, as recorded in the letters mentioned above and in *A Proposal*.

31. "Distance lends enchantment, and isolation preserves things in existence. Later on, many 'utopias,' among them that of Thomas More, would be located on islands" (Jean Delumeau, *History of Paradise: The Garden of Eden in Myth and Tradition,* trans. Matthew O'Connell [New York: Continuum Publishing, 1995], 98).

and events. As Claude Kappler put it, if there are "any places that have a special appeal for imagination it is islands. . . . An island is by its nature a place where marvels exist for their own sake outside the laws that generally prevail. . . . Ever since Greek antiquity, islands have been favorite places for the most astounding human and divine adventures."[32] This gives islands an impressive metaphorical and symbolical value. Like mountains, for example, islands are always present in the intellectual discourse, be it literary, poetic, theological, mythological, utopian, or political. An island can thus signify, from case to case, hope, survival, salvation, separation, freedom, heresy, regeneration, *una vita nuova,* certitude, danger, rootlessness, and proud independence. No wonder, then, that the earthly paradise itself has often come to be located somewhere on an island: "Dante . . . gave the earthly paradise the characteristics of an island, and in many medieval travel stories, especially Mandeville's, the kingdom of Prester John is located on an island. According to Mandeville, mysterious India is 'divided into isles on account of the great rivers which flow out of Paradise.'"[33]

The usual name under which the earthly paradise islands have been traditionally known is that of "happy island(s)." Why this particular name? Medieval scholars had their own way of explaining it. Pierre d'Ailly, for example, says that the "name 'Happy Isles' means that these islands contain all good things. It is the fruitfulness of the soil that makes people believe that paradise was located in these islands."[34] In fact, as Jean Delumeau has shown, this explanation was borrowed from Isidore of Seville, and it widely spread throughout the Middle Ages. In the *Etymologiae,* Isidore says: "The name 'Happy Isles' means that they produce all sorts of good things; that they enjoy a quasi-blessedness and have the advantage of happy abundance. By their very nature they give birth to precious trees and fruits. The slopes of the hills are naturally covered with vines. Instead of grass the soil for the most part yields crops and vegetables."[35] Therefore, the topic of the happy islands was not an isolated and marginal topos at all, but a deeply rooted and long lasting one. It was a topic onto which people projected their expectations, nostalgias, and fantasies, a topic that caused them to daydream, desire, and hope. If the heavenly paradise was still remote and inaccessible, the earthly one was perceived as being somewhere closer, at least close enough to allow them to turn it into a major topic of their narratives.

This fascination that surrounded the happy islands in the Middle Ages played an essential part in the formation and dissemination of a complex symbolic geog-

---

32. Quoted in Delumeau, *History of Paradise,* 98. Kappler's book, cited by Delumeau, is *Monstres, demons, et merveilles à la fin du Moyen Âge* (Paris: Payot, 1980).

33. Delumeau, *History of Paradise,* 98.

34. Quoted in Delumeau, *History of Paradise,* 99.

35. Quoted in Delumeau, *History of Paradise,* 99.

raphy, one that, as we will see below, would to an important degree shape the geographical conceptions and representations of the Western discoverers and travelers at the dawn of modern era:

> The Happy Islands stand in a Greco-Roman poetic tradition that is based on passages in Homer, Hesiod, and Plutarch. According to this tradition, beyond the towering Atlas there lie islands with enchanted gardens, a constant temperate climate, and fragrant breezes, where human beings have no need to work. In the Christian era Isidore of Seville gave this belief a new popularity by assigning it a place in his geography, which then exerted a lasting influence on Western culture.[36]

Based on the imaginary account that Berkeley gives of the islands of Bermuda, and on the various similar accounts by ancient, medieval, or early modern authors, to which some were referred above, it can be safely argued that Berkeley's representation of the New World (in particular, the islands of Bermuda) was deeply marked by a certain nostalgia for an earthly paradise. When conceiving of his educational project Berkeley, knowingly or unknowingly, placed himself in a long tradition of representations of the earthly paradise that in Europe (and not only in Europe) went back many centuries, gave birth to a sophisticated symbolic geography (in terms of people's cultural projections upon place, space, and distance), and eventually shaped to a significant extent their understanding of the real geography. As a result, in formulating his Bermuda project Berkeley makes use of the conceptual and imagistic repertoire provided by this symbolic geography. Then, it was probably the religious dimension of this nostalgia for the earthly paradise that gave him an extraordinary strength and determination to pursue his project for so many years and overcome all the criticisms it encountered from the side of the more practical politicians of the day or simply from those too deeply attached to the values, habits, and patterns of living of the Old World. It may also have been this nostalgia for the earthly paradise that made him so enthusiastic and, as we shall see below, particularly unrealistic about the situation of and problems with those islands.[37]

It would therefore be fair to say that the right place of Berkeley's Bermuda

---

36. Delumeau, *History of Paradise*, 99.

37. Sometimes his enthusiasm infected others. For example, one of his contemporaries said, "Young and old, learned and rich, all desirous of retiring to enjoy peace of mind and health of body, and of restoring the golden age in that corner of the world" (Dan Dering, a contemporary, quoted in Arthur A. Luce, *The Life of George Berkeley*, 97).

islands—with all their countless wonders and amazing resources and ideal landscapes, with their perfect situation, the "gentlest climate in the world," "the
securest spot in the universe"—is to be found not in the real world, but on one
of those "detailed maps from the end of the Middle Ages [that] still teaches" us
that "there exist in the West paradisiacal islands 'that abound in all good things.'
These islands combine most of the elements that make for an earthly paradise:
pleasant warmth, perpetual spring, delicious and fragrant fruits."[38] Somewhere
on the same (imaginary) map, Thomas More's island is to be found, too. There,
just as in Berkeley's Bermuda, the visitor is instantly welcomed by the same
enchanting landscape, so rich in promises of unusual encounters: "all things begin
by little and little to wax pleasant; the air soft, temperate, and gentle; the ground
covered with green grass; less wilderness in the beasts."[39] However, in Berkeley
the synthesis between the utopian tradition and the quest for the earthly paradise
is almost complete. While in More the paradisiacal appearance of the island does
not play an essential (but only a decorative) role in the economy of the utopian
project, in Berkeley it is crucial that his educational project takes place *there,* in
Bermuda, and not somewhere else. As a matter of fact, for theological reasons I
will discuss later, Berkeley *needed* this synthesis: he had to root his utopia into the
soil of a strong theological tradition. His was an educational utopia, true, but
with a specific theological mission.

Quite expectedly, the project eventually failed, Berkeley being much laughed
at, and even considered mad, by some London wits of his time.[40] However, as I
will show below, despite its failure, this project is significant not only for what it
shows about Berkeley's personality, but also about the deeper theological perspectives that nourished his intellectual life and philosophy, as well as about his
rapport with the past. Just as the platonic tradition, the alchemical way of thinking, or the tradition of the *liber mundi* deeply permeated Berkeley's metaphysics
and, to different degrees, left their mark on it,[41] so it could be followed in some
detail how various cultural and mythical representations of place and space (of
the New World in particular), how various notions of symbolic geography had a
distinct impact on his philosophy of history.

38. Delumeau, *History of Paradise,* 100–102.
39. More, *Utopia,* 17.
40. For the most part, criticisms were about the impracticability of Berkeley's project. Many people "found the entire enterprise absurd. . . . those with first-hand experience of the American Church
or educational scenes were profoundly distressed with Berkeley's ignorance. It is clear that for many
years, Berkeley was seen as something of a nut" (Harry Bracken, "Bishop Berkeley's Messianism," in
Millenarianism and Messianism in English Literature and Thought 1650–1800, ed. Richard Popkin [Leiden:
E.J. Brill, 1988], 68).
41. For these aspects of Berkeley's work, as well as other similar topics, see my book *The Other
Bishop Berkeley.*

A (VERY) REAL WORLD

If a "state of mind is utopian when it is incongruous with the state of reality within which it occurs,"[42] then Berkeley's state of mind when conceiving and proposing his Bermuda project was certainly utopian. The huge and unbridge-able gap (or "incongruity," in Mannheim's terminology) between the real (geo-graphical, natural, and social) situation of the islands of Bermuda and their ideal situation in Berkeley's mind (the way he misrepresented them) is revealed by both some of the contemporary opponents of his plan and—maybe more impor-tant—by several accounts of the real Bermuda from the first colonists there, dated some decades before Berkeley's project was conceived. Some of these accounts are still extant.

Arthur Aston Luce, who studied the whole affair thoroughly, found that—when the issue of giving the project financial support came to be discussed in the British Parliament—the opposition to Berkeley's Bermuda project was not always malevolent or unjustified. There were realistic people ("enlightened opposition") who criticized Berkeley's project on the basis of their own knowl-edge of the real situation of the islands. Among them William Byrd of Virginia, "who with local knowledge opposed the project, not as undesirable, but as impracticable," brought pertinent arguments against the project. He regarded George Berkeley as "a Don Quixote in zeal" and his project as a "visionary scheme." A. A. Luce summarizes Byrd's argument:

There is no bread in Bermuda; there is nothing fit for the sustenance of man but onions and cabbages; its inhabitants are healthy, because, forsooth, they have so little to eat; the air is pure because swept by storms and hurricanes. . . . There are no Indians in Bermuda, "nor within two hundred leagues of it upon the continent, and it will need the gift of miracles to persuade them to leave their country and venture themselves upon the great ocean, on the temptation of being converted."

Dean Berkeley must take "the French way" and force them into Christianity. He must take half a dozen regiments, and "make a descent upon the coast of Florida, and take as many prisoners as he can." Behind the sarcasm is the assur-ance of the man with local knowledge.[43]

On the other hand, there are those accounts from the first colonists in Ber-muda, mainly private letters published some time ago under the title *The Rich*

42. Karl Mannheim, *Ideology and Utopia. An Introduction to the Sociology of Knowledge,* trans. Louis Wirth and Edward Shils (New York: Harcourt, Brace and C., 1936), 192.
43. Luce, *The Life of George Berkeley,* 137.

Papers: Letters from Bermuda 1615–1646: Eyewitness Accounts Sent by the Early Colonists to Sir Nathaniel Rich, describing both the exact conditions in which the islands were then planted and administrated, but also the numerous other problems encountered, such as the serious troubles caused by the drunkenness, immorality, and general unreliability of the inhabitants. The sharp contrast between the poor "state of reality" in Bermuda and Berkeley's too enthusiastic "state of mind" is marked at times by such chilling fragments as the following one: "If the Adventurers [the company then administrating the islands] send noe clothes to this poore people before this time 12 months, many of them will be naked if not dead."[44] No doubt some of the problems might have been solved by Berkeley's time, but it is unreasonable to believe that the unfriendly climate, for example, had changed very much in the meantime.

These accounts depict a small world, with its fortunes and misfortunes, its happy and unhappy events, bearing apparently no resemblance to any earthly paradise. Life in Bermuda was taking its course in a more or less bearable manner, but sometimes there were events so frightful that they seriously jeopardized the very minimal conditions of living there. For example, as it is recorded, one such event was a tremendous invasion of rats: "Rattes have been and are a great judgement of God upon us. All the Ilands have been in a manner like so many Cunny [coney, rabbit] warrens, which did put the people much out of heart. It is incredible how they did swimme from Iland to Iland, and suddainly like an armie of men did invade the Ilands from one end to an other, devouring the fruites of the earth in strange manner."[45]

As for the morals of the inhabitants, highly praised by Berkeley, they were not, at the time of writing of these accounts, as exemplary as one could wish. For example, some of the Bermudans seem to have often resorted to the virtues of wine. To the extent that, far from being overwhelmed by innocence, moderation, and other noble virtues, some of them had come to be seriously fond of drinking. A Bermuda priest wrote once to Sir Nathaniel Rich: "Good sir, for God sake do what you can to send hither godly preachers, before sinne hath got the upper hand. It is lamentable to see how sinne aboundeth every day more and more as the people do increase. I am not able to expresse the abhominable

44. Vernon Arthur Ives, ed., *The Rich Papers: Letters from Bermuda 1615–1646: Eyewitness Accounts Sent by the Early Colonists to Sir Nathaniel Rich* (Toronto: University of Toronto Press, 1984), 14.

45. *The Rich Papers,* 14. In addition, far from being "the best air in the world," as Berkeley thought, Bermuda's air was often violently agitated by "terrible winds," causing much trouble and many falls to the Bermudans: "Mr Lewis [a settler] . . . hath taken a greate hurt by a fall, which hath bruised him much, and his [he is] att this instant very weake, the force of the wind beeing soe terrible. Att the same tyme the like was never seen. Mr Lewis, goeing to the governors, the wind beeing so stronge that it bente hime to the ground. And the same day there were many of our howses blowne downe. We have hadd a very unseasonable summer and winter that it hath hinred [hindered] much labour, which otherwise might hadd been performed" (*The Rich Papers,* 85).

drunkeness, loathsome spuing [spewing, vomiting], swearing, swaggering and quarrelling, while the ship is in harbour with any wine or strong waters in her."[46]

THE ESCHATOLOGICAL CONTEXT

Let us recall that Berkeley's college was not designed as an end in itself, as a purely educational institution, but simply as a means: its supreme mission was to produce worthy priests and theologians, "missionaries" to persuade the "savage Indians" of the New World to accept Christianity. Yet, such a mission had at that time special connotations. What I argue in this essay is that, in close connection to the topics of the earthly paradise and utopianism discussed above, a consideration of Berkeley's *Proposal* within the context of the religious (apocalyptic, millennialist, and eschatological) ideas and attitudes that lay behind the early transoceanic voyages of discovery (and colonization) of the New World would be of great importance for a better understanding of this project. As Mircea Eliade and especially Harry Bracken and David Berman have shown, Berkeley's American project is hardly understandable without taking into account its messianism. In his essay "Bishop Berkeley's Messianism" Bracken argues that in his *Proposal* Berkeley embraced the then-popular analogy between the American Indians and the "Lost Tribes of the Israel," whose conversion would have had a special value according to Saint Paul.[47] As such, Berkeley's eagerness to convert the Indians might well be regarded as an attempt to prepare for the Second Coming.

It is this messianic feature of Berkeley's project that is indebted to the religious and theological background against which the first transatlantic voyages, and then the early colonization of America, took place. There is agreement among many historians and religious scientists that a crucial factor in realizing the new geographic discoveries was, as Mircea Eliade has put it, "the nostalgia for the earthly paradise that the ancestors of the American nations had crossed the Atlantic to find."[48] According to this line of thought, the deeper causes and motivations of the transatlantic voyages undertaken by the early discoverers and colonists were not only of an economic or political nature, but they also had something to do with a certain religious atmosphere that characterized the European world

46. *The Rich Papers,* 161–62.

47. And, as Bracken openly recognizes, messianism was not unique to Berkeley. Even if for different reasons, "there is hardly a single great mind of the period which is not involved in millennial thinking. Henry More, Sir Isaac Newton, and Sir Robert Boyle may be the names best known to academic philosophers" (Bracken, "Bishop Berkeley's Messianism," 78).

48. Mircea Eliade, "Paradise and Utopia: Mythical Geography and Eschatology," in *Utopias and Utopian Thought,* ed. Manuel, 261.

toward the end of the Middle Ages: an atmosphere marked by eschatological expectations, millennialist dreams, hopes for universal renewal, and, most important, a need for radical "moral transformation" and spiritual "regeneration." And it was within "this messianic and apocalyptic atmosphere that the transoceanic expeditions and the geographic discoveries that radically shook and transformed Western Europe took place. Throughout Europe people believed in an imminent regeneration of the world."[49]

Mircea Eliade and Jean Delumeau are proponents of this line of thought.[50] They employ an impressive knowledge and deep understanding of the cultural, religious, and intellectual context of this confused and multifaceted age:

[T]he search for paradisiacal islands was an important stimulus to voyages of discovery from the fourteenth to the seventeenth centuries. Nostalgia for the garden of Eden; the conviction of Christopher Columbus and missionaries that the end time was at hand; the will to bring religion to new lands; and the desire to find gold, precious stones, and other rare commodities: all these combined to spur travelers, religious, sailors, and conquerors on to new horizons. Their culture and the dreams it brought with it led them, at least in the beginning, to see in the strange lands opening up before them the characteristics of those blessed countries that had haunted the Western imagination since antiquity.[51]

Eliade's and Delumeau's interpretations rely on what the discoverers and first colonists themselves thought about what they were then doing, seeing, and experiencing. There is significant textual evidence pointing to a close relationship between the tradition of the search for the earthly paradise in Europe and the way in which the first travelers and colonists experienced their encounter with the New World. For example, in a letter Amerigo Vespucci sent to Lorenzo de Medici sometime between 1499 and 1502 the famous navigator talks about "the friendly land, covered with countless very tall trees that do not lose their leaves and emit sweet and fragrant odors and are loaded with tasty fruits that promote the body's health; the fields of thick grass that are filled with flowers which have a wonderfully delightful perfume; the great throng of birds of various species,

---

49. Eliade, "Paradise and Utopia," 262.

50. Of course, Eliade and Delumeau are not the only scholars to endorse and follow this idea. I have chosen to discuss them only because they offer a rather synthetic view of the phenomenon. There are numerous other authors who have, in recent decades, discussed the discovery of the New World in relation to the tradition of the search for the earthly paradise. See, for example, Joseph Duncan, *Milton's Earthly Paradise: A Historical Study of Eden* (Minneapolis: University of Minnesota Press, 1972), and George Williams, *Wilderness and Paradise in Christian Thought* (New York: Harper, 1962).

51. Delumeau, *History of Paradise*, 109–10.

whose feathers, colors, and songs defy description. . . . For myself, I thought I was near the earthly paradise."[52] If in the case of Vespucci these things were veiled in a rather poetic and somewhat vague form, Christopher Columbus openly considered his transoceanic enterprise in terms of sacred history, and conceived of his mission as part of a divine plan. He "did not doubt that he had come near the Earthly Paradise" and consequently—however strange this might appear today—he considered his adventurous navigation in theological and mystical (rather than secular) terms. Columbus was convinced, for example, that the freshwater currents that he came across in the Gulf of Paria originated nowhere else than in the Garden of Eden. The discovery of the New World had for him a clear "eschatological implication." He was "persuaded that the prophecy concerning the diffusion of the Gospel throughout the whole world had to be realized before the end of the world—which was not far off. In his *Book of Prophecies,* Columbus affirmed that this event, namely, the end of the world, would be preceded by the conquest of the new continent, the conversion of the heathen, and the destruction of the Antichrist."[53]

Thus, what is equally important is that such a state of mind not only persisted even after the establishment of the first colonies, but that it also increased in intensity, developed, and spread widely throughout America.[54] The first colonists' dreams of renewal and fantasies of spiritual salvation proved to be so intense that it was as if what they found out after crossing the ocean confirmed literally all their eschatological expectations and millenarian ideas: "the most popular religious doctrine in the Colonies was that America had been chosen among all the nations of the earth as the place of the Second Coming of Christ, and the millennium, though essentially of a spiritual nature, would be accompanied by a paradisiacal transformation of the earth, as an outer sign of an inner perfection."[55] The awareness of their being "chosen," the sense of their blessing, election, and mission made them feel in some way "associates" or "partners" of God, trustful implementers of his plans. As it were, theirs were not simply human enterprises,

52. Quoted in Delumeau, *History of Paradise,* 110.

53. Eliade, "Paradise and Utopia," 262.

54. Some pioneers already saw Paradise in the various regions of America. Traveling along the coast of New England in 1614, John Smith compared it to Eden: "heaven and earth never agreed better to frame a place for man's habitation. . . . we chanced in a lande, even as God made it." George Alsop presents Maryland as the only place seeming to be the "Earthly Paradise." Its trees, its plants, its fruits, its flowers, he wrote, speak in "Hieroglyphicks of our Adamitical or Primitive situation." Another writer discovered the "future Eden" in Georgia—a region located on the same latitude as Palestine: "That promis'd Canaan, which was pointed out by God's own choice, to bless the Labours of a favorite People." For Edward Johnson, Massachusetts was the place "where the Lord will create a new Heaven and a new Earth." Likewise, the Boston Puritan John Cotton informed those preparing to set sail from England for Massachusetts that they were granted a privilege of Heaven, thanks to "the grand charter given to Adam and his posterity in Paradise" (Eliade, "Paradise and Utopia," 264–65).

55. Eliade, "Paradise and Utopia," 264.

their doings were not just facts of social history; they perceived themselves as being deeply involved in the unfolding of an apocalyptic process, in affairs of a divine nature:

> The first English colonists in America considered themselves chosen by Providence to establish a "City on a Mountain" that would serve as an example of the true Reformation for all Europe. They had followed the path of the sun toward the Far West, continuing and prolonging in a prodigious fashion the traditional passing of religion and culture from East to West. . . . The first pioneers did not doubt that the final drama of moral regeneration and universal salvation would begin with them, since they were the first to follow the sun in its course toward the paradisiacal gardens of the West.[56]

Very broadly speaking, this was the religious context against which Berkeley's *Proposal* emerged, and we should keep this fact in mind when considering the "boldness," "savagery," as well as the "unrealistic" character of his project.

WAITING FOR THE MESSIAH?

Since one of the main aims of his projected college was to supply the colonies with virtuous, well-prepared priests and missionaries,[57] some Berkeley scholars— based also on the last stanza of the famous poem that Berkeley dedicated to America—concluded that his motivation in initiating and pursuing the project was ultimately one of an eschatological and millennialist nature. The poem is called "America; or, the Muse's Refuge: A Prophecy" and is an excellent piece of verse in its own right. In the first place, Berkeley wrote and disseminated it in order to get more support for his project. Originally it was circulated anonymously, but eventually he published it in the *Miscellany* (1752) under his own name. In his book on Berkeley, David Berman discusses in some detail "the eschatological aspect of Berkeley's poem and project," and one of his conclusions is that it is "evident that his poem is apocalyptic and eschatological."[58] (Berman follows Bracken's interpretation.)[59] I reproduce here only the last stanza of the poem, namely, the portion that has received special interest from commentators:

56. Eliade, "Paradise and Utopia," 264.

57. To "provide, in the first Place, a constant Supply of worthy Clergymen for the English Churches in those Parts; and in the second Place, a like constant Supply of zealous Missionaries, well fitted for propagating Christianity among the Savages" (*A Proposal*, 7:345).

58. Berman, *George Berkeley*, 116, 118.

59. It is worth pointing out that Mircea Eliade has a rather similar interpretation of this poem. See Eliade, "Paradise and Utopia."

Westward the Course of Empire takes its Way,
The four first Acts already past.
A fifth shall close the Drama with the Day,
The world's great Effort is the last.[60]

Seeking to interpret the symbolism of the five acts Harry Bracken resorts to the Old Testament, namely, to the Book of Daniel: "I take the symbolism of the final stanza, the four plus one Acts, to be from *Daniel,* chapter 2, where the four kingdoms, usually taken to be Babylon, Persia, Greece and Rome, shall be succeeded by a fifth: 'And in the days of these kings shall the God of heaven set up a kingdom, which shall never be destroyed' (2:44)."[61] Given the complex millennialist and apocalyptic context briefly presented above, with all its great expectations and intensely religious feelings, an interpretation like Bracken's seems reasonable.

Bracken epitomizes his demonstration with a decisive scriptural argument. According to him, "the key to this extraordinary proposal is that Berkeley accepts the [then] popular view that the American Indians are the Lost Tribes of Israel. As Jews, their conversion is especially dear to God and each conversion promises, as Paul tells us in *Romans XI,* to bring closer the Second Coming."[62] Then, he undertakes a detailed research of some of the beliefs then current in America, beliefs according to which the American Indians were—in some way or other—of Jewish origin.

If we follow Bracken's hypothesis, the theology graduates from Berkeley's college, by converting the native Indians would have converted the Lost Tribes of Israel, which—according to Saint Paul—was a clear sign of the much-expected, triumphal end of history and of our sufferings and misery in this world. In Berkeley's mind the propagation of gospel in America and the conversion of the Indians living there would have had a highly spiritual value as these activities would have been at the same time preparation for, and a sign of, the approaching Second Coming. Hence the urgent need for building a missionary college in Bermuda: "Given what we know about Berkeley, we must find a reason not only for his committing himself so completely to his American dream, but especially for the savagery he was prepared to inflict on Indian children."[63] This messianic interpretation gives us such a reason, allowing us to see Berkeley's project in a different light.

Harry Bracken's documented interpretation, even if one does not accept it

---

60. *Verses on America,* 7:370.
61. Bracken, "Bishop Berkeley's Messianism," 71.
62. Bracken, "Bishop Berkeley's Messianism," 73.
63. Bracken, "Bishop Berkeley's Messianism," 80.

entirely,[64] has the merit of underlining the theological complexity of the Bermuda project and suggesting ways of explaining several of the confused aspects of Berkeley's enterprise. Moreover, it is perfectly consistent with the complex religious context sketched above. Then, needless to say, Bracken's interpretation fits pretty well into—and, to a great extent, is supported by—my own attempt, earlier in this essay, to place Berkeley both in the tradition of educational utopias and in the tradition of the search for an earthly paradise. On the other hand, Bracken's reconstruction of Berkeley's way of thinking, as far as this particular issue is concerned, might also be applied to the way in which many of his contemporaries were then thinking. For, as it has been argued, in "the eyes of the English . . . the colonization of America merely prolonged and perfected a Sacred History begun at the outset of the Reformation. Indeed, the push of the pioneers toward the West continued the triumphal march of Wisdom and the True Religion from East to West. For some time already, Protestant theologians had been inclined to identify the West with spiritual and moral progress."[65]

At least two fundamental Christian ideas were inextricably interwoven in Berkeley's Bermuda educational project: a nostalgia for an earthly paradise and "the expectation of a kingdom of happiness that is to be established on our earth and to last for a millennium."[66] The "happy islands" of Bermuda, despite their imaginary, utopian nature—if not precisely because of that—have been the chosen space for such an enterprise, its privileged environment. They have played a central role in this story: their isolation from the outside world, purity, difficult accessibility, exoticism, paradisiacal appearance, beauties, innocence of the inhabitants, and so on—all these are attributes that enable us to consider those islands as some unearthly or unnatural place, a place where marvels or such supernatural events as the Second Coming are at any time possible.

Then, the millennialist interpretation of Berkeley's Bermuda project presented above adds to his utopia a character somehow different from that of a simply political/social project. Berkeley's utopia has a certain theological flavor, which we do not find in many utopias. It still is a utopia in the tradition of Plato, Campanella, and Thomas More, but—in addition to that—Berkeley's utopia is also characterized by certain chiliastic elements. His is a religiously modeled utopia, an educational utopia with a certain soteriological mission. Even if the main emphasis is not placed, in his project, on messianism, the chiliastic features are

---

64. Bracken is very careful and scrupulous in his analysis. He admits that his is only a partial and possible interpretation, with the possibility of other points of view: "if it is granted that Berkeley hoped to use the traditional symbolism of Daniel so that he might characterize America in messianic terms then we have a partial answer to the point of the American Project" (Bracken, "Bishop Berkeley's Messianism," 73).

65. Eliade, "Paradise and Utopia," 263.

66. Delumeau, *History of Paradise*, 1.

present and explain the ultimate specificity of the Bermuda project. This messianism belongs not so much to the project itself (explicitly), as to its unspoken presuppositions, to the intellectual and religious background against which it was conceived. As it were, the millennium is rapidly approaching; under such circumstances, getting ready is the crucial and most urgent thing to do. Hence the imperative of preparing a body of worthy, well-trained, and dedicated people, ready to prepare, in turn, their neighbors for the great event. Instructing such special people is an extremely difficult and demanding job. In fact, it is a job that is made possible only within the firm boundaries of a highly disciplined educational utopia. And this is where Berkeley's project comes in.

CONCLUSION

There is a sense in which Berkeley's Bermuda project, although it failed long time ago, is still curiously relevant today. In several respects, this seed, which died somewhere in the offices of the British government sometime at the beginning of the eighteenth century, has brought forth unexpected fruit in several places, but especially in the United States. Ever since Berkeley launched his American project many North American campuses have been designed as "islands" of peace and serenity in the middle of a relentless world, cities of learning and science, relatively separated from the "worldly" sphere, and kept safe, insofar as it is possible, from the corrupting influence of the profane world. There is something puritanical and rigid about living and working on many of these campuses: life here is not left on its own, as it were, but it is strictly regulated and channeled toward higher and loftier aims; to the point that, sometimes, it is precisely this Castalia-like appearance of the university life that gives the greatest charm to such places. Safely away from the many distractions and vanities of the world, what appeals to us here is precisely the monasticism of scholarship. (Sometimes, even visually, many North American campuses look like monasteries.) While Berkeley's utopian project has never been tried in practice, it would therefore be wrong to say that his bold proposal has left the world unchanged either. It has changed it, even if long after its failure, and in ways not foreseen by Berkeley himself. In a way, then, Berkeley's utopia has had the same ironic fate that all utopias have had: it died, but—in doing so—it changed the world around it. The main role of utopias is, as it were, to never be put into practice, but to be dismantled and joyfully burnt down; sometimes, ironically, their ashes are exactly what the world needs to be a better place. At least this is what the various utopias of the twentieth century seem to teach us: they are not to be taken seriously, but just read between the lines.

On the other hand, the way in which Berkeley imagined (or, better, fantasized about) the New World, as a mythical place where dreams can come true and the grandest projects, no matter how utopian, can be put into practice, is traceable in the way in which America has been, and still is, represented today, not only by Americans, but also (or, rather, *especially*) by the outside world. A place where the past is not a burden, a place where one can always start everything from scratch, where one can renew and reinvent oneself. America is the place where one can become what one virtually is. America is par excellence the world of the self-made. The same "promised land" that Bishop Berkeley, disenchanted with the Old World, looked upon as the ideal venue for the realization of his projects, has ever since continued to nourish hopes and fascinate generations of immigrants and self-made people from all over the world, who have been attracted to America (not only North America, but sometimes South America as well) precisely by the same promise of rebirth, renewal, and self-fulfillment. Read between the lines, Berkeley's American project is an invitation to self-experimentation and self-realization.

It would be hardly an exaggeration to say that the self-representation of many Americans today is still markedly Berkeleyan: America is nothing other than an enormous island (sometimes, moreover, a "besieged" island), far away from the rest of the world, and *different* from the rest of the world. Its geography keeps it graciously safe from the corrupting influence of the Old World (and from whatever else, for that matter), from its many vices and its continuing decadence, even though it makes it, at the same time, even more desirable. On our island, salvation comes not from interaction with the outside world, but from the cultivation and preservation of what is our own. This logic of the island still dominates much of the public discourse in the United States, as well as the way in which many Americans see themselves.

Last but not least, George Berkeley's poem on America (significantly subtitled "A Prophecy") strikes us today as disturbingly "prophetic"—almost everything that has happened since Berkeley wrote that piece has done nothing but confirm his insight: "Westward the Course of Empire takes its Way." Certainly, it remains to be seen if "the world's great Effort is the last," just as being a prophet remains a risky, and not always pleasant, business. The fact is, however, that the shape of the world is, for better or for worse, similar to that drawn by Berkeley in his poem.

3

FROM VOLTAIRE TO RAYNAL AND DIDEROT'S
HISTOIRE DES DEUX INDES

The French *Philosophes* and Colonial America

Guillaume Ansart

The last third of the eighteenth century witnessed the development in France of an increasing interest in American political and social life. Before the late 1760s, the colonies had attracted only modest attention. After the beginning of the rebellion, however, widespread enthusiasm for the American cause, the cultlike admiration inspired by Franklin during his visits (1767 and 1769) and stay in France (1776–85), as well as French military involvement on the American side, prompted the publication of a rich body of texts. Some of the most significant among these early French works on America issued from the most progressive ideological milieu of the end of the Old Regime, that of the *philosophes,* the rationalist, liberal, reform-minded intellectuals (writers, philosophers, scientists, members of the academies, enlightened administrators, and so forth) who most actively championed the values of the Enlightenment and whose spirit found its fullest expression in the *Encyclopédie* of Diderot and D'Alembert (1751–80). By temperament, these men were predisposed to be "Americanists,"[1] to see in America a sort of philosophical promised land. As a rule, they had no direct knowledge of the colonies, relying instead on written or secondary sources for their information.

---

1. Not all *philosophes,* of course, turned out to be pro-American, but it was certainly a dominant trend among them. See Durand Echeverria, *Mirage in the West: A History of the French Image of American Society to 1815* (Princeton: Princeton University Press, 1957), 3–174.

Yet, the *philosophes* were not entirely divorced from American reality. They were social and political critics eager to collect factual information for study. In addition to books and newspapers from England or America, they had access to a substantial and growing amount of knowledge on the colonies: during their stays in France, Franklin and later Jefferson, who arrived in Paris in 1784, did their best to educate their French friends on America and to dispel misconceptions; and many *philosophes,* among them Raynal and Condorcet, became members of the American Philosophical Society or the American Academy of Arts and Sciences and corresponded with their American counterparts.

The image of America that emerged within these most influential reformist intellectual circles of the end of the Old Regime—in other words, the blend of historical analysis and liberal political aspirations that constituted the America of the *philosophes,* up to the start of the rebellion—will be the focus of the present study. However, this chapter cannot cover all the literature on colonial America generated by the *philosophes.* Instead, it will examine a small number of outstanding texts that were particularly influential and/or highly representative of a wider corpus: Guillaume-Thomas Raynal's *Histoire philosophique et politique des établissements et du commerce des Européens dans les deux Indes* (1770–80) and several earlier works by Voltaire.

Raynal's *Histoire des deux Indes,* an encyclopedic philosophical history of European colonization, was one of the most important and successful works of the French Enlightenment. In fact, the chapters devoted to the thirteen colonies and the United States in the *Histoire* constitute what was probably the single most influential account of America written in eighteenth-century France.[2] First published in 1770, Raynal's *Histoire* was then revised and substantially expanded in 1774 and 1780.[3] The total number of its editions between 1770 and 1820 ranges from thirty to fifty, depending on whether one considers only official editions or pirated ones as well.[4] It was rapidly translated into the main European languages, another sign of its success.[5] The importance of the *Histoire des deux Indes* for modern criticism is also enhanced by the fact that it was not the work of Raynal alone but of several contributors, chief among them Diderot.[6] And the very

2. Chapters 1–5 and 18–30 of book 17 and the whole of book 18, or approximately five hundred pages. Chapters 38–52 of book 18 cover the Revolution and will not be considered here.

3. This essay follows the 1780 edition (see below, note 8).

4. See Cecil P. Courtney, "Les métamorphoses d'un best-seller: L'*Histoire des deux Indes* de 1770 à 1820," in *Raynal, de la polémique à l'histoire,* ed. Gilles Bancarel and Gianluigi Goggi (Oxford: Voltaire Foundation, 2000), 109–20.

5. On the reception and impact of the *Histoire des deux Indes* throughout Europe and America, see, in addition to the volume just cited, Hans-Jürgen Lüsebrink and Manfred Tietz, eds., *Lectures de Raynal: L'*Histoire des deux Indes *en Europe et en Amérique au XVIIIe siècle, Studies on Voltaire and the Eighteenth Century* (Oxford: Voltaire Foundation, 1991).

6. Diderot's contribution to the *Histoire des deux Indes* was significant, to say the least. In sheer volume, up to a third of the entire work could be attributed to him, according to some contemporaries.

mode of its composition (the plurality of collaborators, the successive revisions and additions, Raynal's practice of borrowing freely from various sources), while it led to inconsistencies and a certain lack of cohesion in structure and content, made the *Histoire* a remarkably representative work. By incorporating so much of the ideological material current in philosophical circles of the period, it became a reflection of that intellectual milieu and a sort of encyclopedia of liberal ideas that had been widely adopted among the *philosophes*.

As for Voltaire, his observations on the colonies are brief and scattered among several works. They tend to deal chiefly with the question of religious tolerance. Yet his praise for William Penn, the Quakers, and the government of Pennsylvania, found most notably in the *Lettres philosophiques* (1734), had such lasting influence that several articles of the *Encyclopédie* as well as Raynal's *Histoire* still bear its mark some thirty or forty years later.

Voltaire, Raynal, and Diderot contributed greatly to the propagation in France and Europe of a powerfully seductive early image of America. So seductive, indeed, that it has survived to this day, in still more or less recognizable form, on both sides of the Atlantic. We shall see that its power resides perhaps mostly in its tendency to conceptualize the promises of the "New World," the new social and political possibilities that America symbolized for Europe, in terms of a return to an idealized past. And this idealizing impulse could prove as irresistible to the American imagination as to the European. It can be argued, therefore, that the *philosophes,* and Raynal in particular, played a part in the formation of American national identity. One of the founding fathers of American literature, St. John de Crèvecoeur, apostle of the "melting pot" and one of the first writers to articulate a distinctly American sense of national consciousness, was so enthusiastic an admirer of the *Histoire des deux Indes* that he dedicated his *Letters from an American Farmer* (1782) to Raynal and proclaimed:

A few years since, I met accidentally with your *Political and Philosophical History* and perused it with infinite pleasure. For the first time in my life I reflected

---

In terms of the nature of his collaboration, Diderot authored most of the general developments in political and moral philosophy. Michèle Duchet, in her study *Diderot et l'Histoire des deux Indes ou l'écriture fragmentaire* (Paris: Nizet, 1978), has identified with great precision all the segments of the *Histoire* that can be credited to him with a reasonable degree of certainty. As far as the chapters on the United States or future United States are concerned, Diderot contributed chapters 4 and 21 of book 17 and chapters 1, 42, 43, 44, and 45 of book 18 as well as many shorter fragments that I will identify when appropriate (on Diderot and the *History of the East and West Indies*, see also Yves Benot, *Diderot, de l'athéisme à l'anticolonialisme* [Paris: Maspero, 1970], 162–259; Michèle Duchet, *Anthropologie et Histoire au siècle des lumières* [Paris: Maspero, 1971], 170–77, 407–75; Anthony Pagden, *European Encounters with the New World: From Renaissance to Romanticism* [New Haven: Yale University Press, 1993], 141–88; Sankar Muthu, *Enlightenment against Empire* [Princeton: Princeton University Press, 2003], 72–121; J. G. A. Pocock, *Barbarism and Religion,* vol. 4, *Barbarians, Savages and Empires* [Cambridge: Cambridge University Press, 2005], 229–328).

on the relative state of nations. . . . You viewed these provinces of North
America in their true light: as the asylum of freedom, as the cradle of future
nations and the refuge of distressed Europeans. . . . I conceived your genius to
be present at the head of my study; under its invisible but powerful guidance, I
prosecuted my small labours; and now, permit me to sanctify them under the
auspices of your name.[7]

Lastly, the *philosophes'* vision of America as a land of virtuous republicanism has
crucial historical significance: from the American and French Revolutions on
through the nineteenth century and beyond, it informed fundamental debates
regarding the nature of republican government, the question of American exceptionalism, and what form of liberty is appropriate or possible in modern nations.

The *Histoire des deux Indes* contains a detailed treatment of the colonies and
their history from their origins to the eve of the rebellion. Chapters dealing with
the colonies as a whole survey a broad range of issues such as religion, government, principles of moral and political philosophy, population, manners, agriculture, industry, commerce and currencies, geography, flora and fauna. The same
wide array of topics is taken up again in additional chapters retracing the social
and political history of each individual colony from New England to Florida.
The following remarks will concentrate on the major colonies: New England
and Pennsylvania in the North, Virginia and the Carolinas in the South. Within
these chapters, revealing sets of implicit or explicit oppositions emerge.

RELIGION: TOLERANCE VS. FANATICISM

The role of religion in society and the question of tolerance in religious matters
were topics of prime importance for the *philosophes,* so it is not surprising that
the influence of religion on the development of the colonies receives extensive
attention in the *Histoire.* From the beginning, Raynal points to religious discord
in England as the original factor in the establishment of the colonies: "Nothing
less than some extraordinary commotion could . . . have sent inhabitants even
into an excellent country. This emigration was at length occasioned by superstition, which had given rise to commotions from the collision of religious opin-

---

7. J. Hector St. John de Crèvecoeur, "To the Abbé Raynal, F. R. S.," in *Letters from an American
Farmer* (Harmondsworth: Penguin, 1981), 37–38. On Raynal and Crèvecoeur, see David Eisermann,
"La 'Raynalisation' de l'*American farmer:* La réception de l'*Histoire des deux Indes* par Crèvecoeur," in
Lectures de Raynal, ed. Lüsebrink and Tietz, 329–39.

ions."[8] But the imputation of superstition, it will turn out, is meant to apply mostly to early Puritan New England. The authors of the *Histoire* were well aware of the differences that existed among the colonies in terms of religion as in many other respects.

One colony in particular, Pennsylvania, provided Raynal and Diderot with the antithesis to the example of New England. In chapter 1 of book 18, penned by Diderot, Pennsylvania is mentioned as a fitting illustration of a good government, a government approaching the ideal of being founded on virtue.[9] Thanks chiefly to Voltaire, when the *Histoire des deux Indes* first appeared the educated French public had for some time been familiar with a certain image of Pennsylvania. In fact, no other colony had received the same level of attention in France up to this point. With his *Lettres philosophiques,* Voltaire had spread the idea of the virtuous and tolerant Quaker: "He [William Penn] began by making a treaty with his neighbors the [native] Americans. It is the only treaty between these people and the Christians that has never been confirmed by oath and never broken." Penn "made wise laws," the first of which was "to prohibit maltreatment of anyone because of his religion, and to consider as brothers all those who believe in God."[10]

Three decades later, the Quakers are again cited as models in the *Traité sur la tolérance* (1763). Although their customs might seem ridiculous, their virtuous and peaceful behavior deserves admiration: "Discord and controversy are unknown in the happy homeland they have made for themselves. And the very name of their city of Philadelphia, which reminds them constantly of the brotherhood of

---

8. Guillaume-Thomas Raynal, *A Philosophical and Political History of the Settlements and Trade of the Europeans in the East and West Indies,* 6 vols. (New York: Negro Universities Press, 1969), bk. 17: 282. All references to the English text will be to this edition, reprint of the 1798 translation published by J. Mundell & Co., London, which itself reproduced the translation by John Justamond based on the 1780 French text and first published in 1783. The chapters on colonial America are in vol. 5, 278–303, 355–88, and vol. 6, 1–122. Selections from these chapters can be found in a new English translation: Raynal, *A History of the Two Indies,* trans. and ed. Peter Jimack (Aldershot: Ashgate, 2006), 242–61. Because Justamond's translation is sometimes inaccurate and even omits certain passages, I will also provide references to the original French text used, the "definitive" 1780 edition (chapters are not numbered in the translation, and the division in volumes is different from the original; on the other hand, the division in books remains identical): *Histoire philosophique et politique des établissements et du commerce des Européens dans les deux Indes,* 10 vols. (Geneva: Jean-Léonard Pellet, 1780), bk. 17:314. The chapters on colonial America are in vol. 8, 309–54, 444–512, and vol. 9, 1–218.

9. Raynal, *History of the East and West Indies,* bk. 18:3; *Histoire des deux Indes,* bk. 18:4.

10. Voltaire, *Philosophical Letters. Or, Letters Regarding the English Nation* (Indianapolis and Cambridge: Hackett, 2007), letter 4, 12. Cf. these passages from the *Essai sur les moeurs* (1756–85): "This is not a usurpation similar to all those invasions we have seen in the old world and in the new. Penn bought the land from the natives, and became the most legitimate of owners" (Voltaire, *Essai sur les moeurs et l'esprit des nations* [*Essay on the Manners and Spirit of Nations*] [Paris: Garnier, 1963], 2:383 [my translation]); "Half [of these new citizens] are Germans, Swedes, or other populations which form seventeen religions. The Quakers who govern regard all those foreigners as brothers" (Voltaire, *Essai sur les moeurs,* 2:384; my translation).

man, is both an example and a reproach to those nations who have yet to learn tolerance."[11] In addition to a spirit of tolerance, Voltaire saw in the Quakers a return to the original spirit of Christianity and to the qualities embodied by the apostles: virtue, simplicity, and equality. The *Dictionnaire philosophique* (1764) declares: "If there is any sect that recalls the times of the first Christians, it is undoubtedly that of the Quakers. Nothing more resembles the apostles."[12] The same idea is developed in the *Essai sur les moeurs:*

> The type of Christianity that he [Penn] brought with him no more resembles that of the rest of Europe than his colony resembles the others. His fellow colonists professed the simplicity and equality of the first disciples of Christ. No other dogmas than those that issued from his mouth; thus almost everything was limited to loving God and humanity: no baptism, because Jesus never baptized anybody; no priests, because the first disciples were all led by Christ himself.[13]

Clearly, Voltaire's descriptions of Pennsylvania have strong utopian, or at least pastoral, overtones and are intended to evoke images of the Golden Age: equality and harmony among citizens, "a government without priests, a people without weapons." So, "William Penn might well have boasted that he brought back the golden age of which so much is spoken and which in fact never really existed save in Pennsylvania."[14]

By the time the *Histoire des deux Indes* was published, French liberals were already accustomed to associating Pennsylvania with a few very positive ideas: freedom of conscience, virtue, simplicity, and equality. Raynal and Diderot continue in the same vein. As with Voltaire, a strong symbolic significance is attached to the way Penn treated native populations: "His [Penn's] arrival in the New World was signalized by an act of equity, which made his person and principles equally beloved. Not thoroughly satisfied with the right given him to his extensive territory, by the grant he had received of it from the British ministry, he determined to make it his own property by purchasing it of the natives."[15] Penn's purchase of his land from Native Americans is called "an example of moderation and justice in America, which was never thought of before by the

11. Voltaire, *Treatise on Tolerance* (Cambridge: Cambridge University Press, 2000), 22.
12. Voltaire, *Philosophical Dictionary* (Harmondsworth: Penguin, 1971), 392 (article "Toleration").
13. Voltaire, *Essai sur les moeurs,* 2:383 (my translation).
14. Voltaire, *Philosophical Letters,* letter 4:13. The simplicity of what Voltaire considered "natural religion" will also be, of course, one of the main features of the utopian kingdom of Eldorado in *Candide* (1759).
15. Raynal, *History of the East and West Indies,* bk. 18:9; *Histoire des deux Indes,* bk. 18:15.

Europeans,"[16] and is the subject of the engraving by Moreau le jeune placed on the frontispiece of volume 9 (book 18) in the 1780 Pellet edition (see illustration).[17] By contrast, the history of the other colonies seems to offer only cases of mistreatment of native populations. In New England, natives were simply deprived of their land,[18] and a reward was granted to any settler for the death of an American Indian.[19] English greed and dishonesty led to countless atrocities in Virginia.[20] Random massacres of entire nations took place in Carolina.[21]

The unparalleled act of justice marking the foundation of Pennsylvania is emblematic of the entire history of the colony.[22] Freedom of conscience is the first principle of its legislation: "The virtuous legislator made toleration the basis of his society. . . . he left every one at liberty to invoke the Supreme Being as he thought proper, and neither established a reigning church in Pennsylvania, nor exacted contributions for building places of public worship, nor compelled any persons to attend them."[23] Raynal and Diderot further emphasize the fact that Quakers do not engage in theological dogmatism but instead prefer to encourage the practice of a morality inspired by the simplicity of early Christians. George Fox, the founder of the sect, is described as a Christlike figure: "He often wandered alone in the woods, without any other amusement but his Bible. In time he even learned to go without that, when he thought he had acquired from it a degree of inspiration similar to that of the apostles and the prophets."[24] In Pennsylvania, religion, with its particularisms receding into the background, acquires the validity of a near-universal moral system: "Without being dogmatic, without arguing about ceremonies, in a country where every sect has its own, people honor the supreme Being with their virtues rather than with their prayers. Innocence and simplicity protect public morality more surely than precepts and controversies."[25] This tendency toward universalism greatly appealed to the *philosophes,* and the *Histoire des deux Indes* underscores the positive social effects of religion in Pennsylvania:

16. Raynal, *History of the East and West Indies,* bk. 18:9; *Histoire des deux Indes,* bk. 18:15.

17. Each volume of the 1780 Pellet edition in ten volumes (there is also a version in four volumes) contains only one illustration, placed on the frontispiece.

18. Raynal, *History of the East and West Indies,* bk. 17:357; *Histoire des deux Indes,* bk. 17:449.

19. Raynal, *History of the East and West Indies,* bk. 17:364–65; *Histoire des deux Indes,* bk. 17:465–66.

20. Raynal, *History of the East and West Indies,* bk. 18:39; *Histoire des deux Indes,* bk. 18:68–69.

21. Raynal, *History of the East and West Indies,* bk. 18:52; *Histoire des deux Indes,* bk. 18:91–92.

22. By freeing their slaves the Quakers later set another "example which ought to make an epocha in the history of religion and humanity" (Raynal, *History of the East and West Indies,* bk. 18:104; *Histoire des deux Indes,* bk. 18:186).

23. Raynal, *History of the East and West Indies,* bk. 18:10–11; *Histoire des deux Indes,* bk. 18:17.

24. Raynal, *History of the East and West Indies,* bk. 18:6; *Histoire des deux Indes,* bk. 18:9. See also Voltaire, *Philosophical Letters,* letter 3:7–9.

25. Raynal, *Histoire des deux Indes,* bk. 18:33 (my translation). These two sentences are omitted from the 1798 translation.

Penn achette des Sauvages le pays qu'il veut occuper

Guillaume-Thomas Raynal, *Histoire philosophique et politique des établissements et du commerce des Européens dans les deux Indes* (Genève: Jean-Léonard Pellet, 1780), vol. 9, frontispiece. "Penn purchases from the natives the land he wants to settle." Courtesy Lilly Library, Indiana University, Bloomington, Indiana.

The most edifying, and at the same time the most extraordinary circumstance, is the harmony that subsists between all the sects established in Pennsylvania, notwithstanding the difference of their religious opinions. Though not all of the same church, they all love and cherish one another as children of the same father. They have always continued to live like brethren, because they had the liberty of thinking as men. To this delightful harmony must be attributed more particularly the rapid progress of the colony.[26]

Tolerance, freedom, and equality lead to a climate of peace and social harmony, which in turn leads to prosperity. Pennsylvania thus provided the *philosophes* with a rare example illustrating the practical applicability in a contemporary society of a central tenet of their political credo. In their eyes it demonstrated the falsity of an objection all too often presented to them by their opponents: that religious and civil liberties would be destructive of social order and harmony and lead to chaos. Quite the opposite, the *philosophes* could argue, just consider the peace and prosperity of Pennsylvania!

As indicated above, New England figures in the *Histoire* as the antithesis of Pennsylvania from the point of view of religion. To the sober universalism of Quaker morality is opposed the strict severity of Puritanism with its rigorous theocratic application of Old Testament norms: "[The criminal laws] of the Jews were adopted. Witchcraft, blasphemy, adultery, and false testimony, were punished with death."[27] "The government forbade, under penalty of death, the Puritans to worship images, just as in the past Moses had prohibited the cult of foreign gods among the Hebrews."[28] Raynal condemns such practices in the strongest terms: "This conduct reveals a people given to the vilest superstition."[29] Diderot agrees: "All of Europe was shocked by so revolting an intolerance."[30] Religion and its peculiarities tend to penetrate all aspects of life: it is regarded as ungodly for men to wear long hair;[31] inoculation against smallpox is prohibited by law as contrary to the decrees of divine Providence.[32]

Thus, in the case of New England, the *Histoire des deux Indes* insists on the negative social effects of religion. Superstition and fanaticism promote intolerance and weaken social bonds. Man becomes "insociable" and distrustful of his

26. Raynal, *History of the East and West Indies*, bk. 18:16; *Histoire des deux Indes*, bk. 18:28.
27. Raynal, *History of the East and West Indies*, bk. 17:357; *Histoire des deux Indes*, bk. 17:450.
28. Raynal, *Histoire des deux Indes*, bk. 17:450–51 (my translation). The comparison with Moses is omitted from the 1798 translation.
29. Raynal, *Histoire des deux Indes*, bk. 17:450 (my translation). This sentence begins a paragraph on superstition omitted from the 1798 translation.
30. Raynal, *Histoire des deux Indes*, bk. 17:451 (my translation). This sentence begins a long discursion by Diderot on intolerance and superstition (17:451–54) omitted from the 1798 translation.
31. Raynal, *History of the East and West Indies*, bk. 17:358–59; *Histoire des deux Indes*, bk. 17:455–56.
32. Raynal, *History of the East and West Indies*, bk. 17:363–64; *Histoire des deux Indes*, bk. 17:464–65.

fellow man,[33] which can lead to deep social disturbances, as the episode of the Salem witch trials vividly illustrates.[34] But even in less extraordinary circumstances, Puritanism remains adverse to Nature and to the general welfare of society in a colony in need of population. Hence Diderot's inclusion of the story of Polly Baker, a young woman who had five children out of wedlock and each time was brought before the judges and prosecuted for the crime.[35]

LIBERTY AND PROSPERITY: NORTH VS. SOUTH

The other significant opposition running through the North American chapters of the *Histoire des deux Indes* is the difference in cultural and political traditions between the northern and southern colonies. Pennsylvania, of course, but also New England, exemplify the more democratic and economically progressive North. From this perspective, New England appears in a much more favorable light. Now, the positive consequences of Puritanism are emphasized. One remarkable feature is the orderly, rational organization of the colony:

> The clearing of the lands is not directed by chance, as in the other provinces. This matter, from the first, was subjected to laws which are still religiously observed. No citizen whatever has the liberty of settling even upon unoccupied land. The government, desirous of preserving all its members from the inroads of the savages, and of placing them in a condition to share in the protection of a well-regulated society, hath ordered that whole villages should be farmed at once. . . . The district assigned [new families] always borders upon the land already cleared, and generally contains six thousand square acres. These new people choose the situation most convenient for their habitation, which is usually of a square figure. The church is placed in the center. . . . It is thus that New England is constantly enlarging its territory, though it still continues to make one complete and well-constituted province.[36]

Puritan mistrust of all worldly, temporal forms of authority fosters a republican spirit[37] reflected in a government "where the people . . . have the legislative

33. Raynal, *History of the East and West Indies*, bk. 17:359; *Histoire des deux Indes*, bk. 17:456.

34. Raynal, *History of the East and West Indies*, bk. 17:361–63; *Histoire des deux Indes*, bk. 17:460–63. Voltaire's treatment of the same events is very similar. He underlines the social division caused by this "epidemic disease," a term also used by Raynal (*Essai sur les moeurs*, 2:384–85).

35. Raynal, *Histoire des deux Indes*, bk. 17:466–73. Also included in another work by Diderot, *Supplément au voyage de Bougainville* (1772); omitted from the 1798 translation. The source of this anecdote is thought to be Franklin.

36. Raynal, *History of the East and West Indies*, bk. 17:366; *Histoire des deux Indes*, bk. 17:474–75.

37. Raynal, *History of the East and West Indies*, bk. 17:367; *Histoire des deux Indes*, bk. 17:477.

power in their own hands."[38] Furthermore, trade and industry have made more progress in New England than anywhere else in the colonies.[39] So much so that life in Boston offers as much comfort and sophistication as in London itself: "The houses, furniture, dress, food, conversation, customs and manners, were so exactly similar to the mode of living in London, that it was scarce possible to find any other difference, but that which arises from the greater numbers of people there are in large capitals."[40]

As can be expected, though, the true model of enlightened government is Pennsylvania. Reflecting upon the entire history of European colonization in the New World, Raynal expresses in lyrical terms what could be called a theory of Pennsylvanian exceptionalism:

> The mind of the writer and of his reader dwells with pleasure on this part of modern history, and feels some kind of compensation for the disgust, horror, or melancholy, which the whole of it, but particularly the account of the European settlements in America, inspires. Hitherto we have only seen these barbarians depopulating the country before they took possession of it, and laying every thing waste before they cultivated it. It is time to observe the dawnings of reason, happiness, and humanity, rising from among the ruins of a hemisphere, which still reeks with the blood of all its people, civilized as well as savage.[41]

Penn's legislation is based on "those two first principles of public splendour and private felicity, liberty and property."[42] Equality should also be mentioned, for in Pennsylvania every child is obliged to learn a profession, a regulation that preserves "the natural equality of mankind" by encouraging all men to work.[43] In addition, poverty is unknown: "There are no poor in all Pennsylvania. All those whose birth or fortune have left them without resources, are suitably provided for out of the public treasury."[44]

---

38. Raynal, *History of the East and West Indies*, bk. 17:365; *Histoire des deux Indes*, bk. 17:474.

39. Raynal, *History of the East and West Indies*, bk. 17:369; *Histoire des deux Indes*, bk. 17:480.

40. Raynal, *History of the East and West Indies*, bk. 17:373; *Histoire des deux Indes*, bk. 17:487–88.

41. Raynal, *History of the East and West Indies*, bk. 18:10; *Histoire des deux Indes*, bk. 18:16–17.

42. Raynal, *History of the East and West Indies*, bk. 18:10; *Histoire des deux Indes*, bk. 18:16–17.

43. Raynal, *History of the East and West Indies*, bk. 18:12; *Histoire des deux Indes*, bk. 18:20.

44. Raynal, *History of the East and West Indies*, bk. 18:17–18; *Histoire des deux Indes*, bk. 18:30. It is quite possibly the appeal of this image of Pennsylvania relayed by the *Histoire des deux Indes* that prompted Crèvecoeur to make his fictional American farmer a citizen of Penn's colony instead of New York, where his own estate, Pine Hill, was located. Much in the style of Raynal, Crèvecoeur's American farmer writes, for instance: "O Penn, thou best of legislators, who by the wisdom of thy laws hast endowed human nature, within the bounds of thy province, with every dignity it can possibly enjoy in a civilized state and showed by this singular establishment what all men might be if they would follow thy example!" (*Letters from an American Farmer*, 92). See Eisermann, "La 'Raynalisation' de l'*American farmer*," 334.

In spite of its original form of government, known as "proprietary govern-ment," Pennsylvania enjoys all the advantages of a popular, representative gov-ernment. Although ownership of the colony shall remain in Penn's family, "he deprived them of any decisive influence in the public resolutions, and ordained, that they should not exercise any act of authority without the concurrence of the deputies of the people. All the citizens who had an interest in the law, by having one in the object of it, were to be electors, and might be chosen."[45]

In the end, civil and religious freedoms, well-established property rights, equality, and a representative government all contribute to the general prosperity. Civil and religious liberties have attracted "the Swedes, Dutch, French, and par-ticularly some laborious Germans" into Pennsylvania, and the prosperity of the colony "has been the joint work of Quakers, Anabaptists, members of the Church of England, Methodists, Presbyterians, Moravians, Lutherans, and Cath-olics."[46]

By comparison, freedom and religious tolerance are not as deeply rooted in the South as in the North, and the spirit of commerce and industry is not as developed. In Virginia, property rights were slow to be established: "Till this time the colonists had known no true enjoyment of property. Every individual wan-dered where chance directed him, or fixed himself in the place he liked best, without consulting any titles or agreements. At length boundaries were ascer-tained; and those who had been so long wanderers, now become citizens, had determined limits to their plantations. The establishment of this first law of society changed the appearance of every thing."[47] Later, however, Charles II "granted to rapacious courtiers immense territories, which absorbed the possessions of a great number of obscure citizens,"[48] a clear obstacle to the colony's progress, in Ray-nal's opinion. The same uncertainty that weakened property rights also under-mined civil and religious liberties. In 1679 the new governor of Virginia, Lord Colepepper, proposed a law "which should condemn to one year's imprison-ment, or to a fine of 11, 250 livres (468l. 15s.), all those citizens who should speak or write any thing against their governor; and to three months imprisonment, or

45. Raynal, *History of the East and West Indies,* bk. 18:11; *Histoire des deux Indes,* bk. 18:17–18. See also "In Pennsylvania, the governor named by the proprietary family, and confirmed by the crown, is not supported by a council, which gives a kind of superiority, and he is obliged to agree with the commons, in whom is naturally vested all authority" (18:112; 18:201).

46. Raynal, *History of the East and West Indies,* bk. 18:14; *Histoire des deux Indes,* bk. 18:24. Cf. Crèvecoeur and his idea of melting pot: "The next wish of [the enlightened English] traveller will be to know whence came all these people. They are a mixture of English, Scotch, Irish, French, Dutch, Germans, and Swedes. From this promiscuous breed, that race now called Americans have arisen" (*Letters from an American Farmer,* 68).

47. Raynal, *History of the East and West Indies,* bk. 18:37–38; *Histoire des deux Indes,* bk. 18:65–66. Compare with the description of New England quoted above.

48. Raynal, *History of the East and West Indies,* bk. 18:38; *Histoire des deux Indes,* bk. 18:67.

to a fine of 2250 livres (93l. 15s.), those who should speak or write against the members of the council, or against any other magistrate."[49] Nor was freedom of conscience protected any better. Nonconformists were not welcome in the colony, and "in 1624 a law was made, which expelled from the province all those inhabitants who did not belong to the church of England." And although "this fatal decree" was soon revoked, "a small number only of Presbyterians, Quakers, and French refugees, ventured to put any trust in this repentance. The religion of Henry VIII continued to be the prevailing one, and was almost exclusive."[50]

The legislation of Carolina (originally one colony), despite having been drawn up by Locke himself, is not judged much more favorably by Raynal and Diderot.[51] Locke was guilty of setting limits to the principle of religious tolerance: he ordered that every citizen should be registered in some Christian communion, a provision to which the authors of the *Histoire des deux Indes* strongly object since "the liberty of conscience admits of no kind of modification. This is an account which man owes to God alone. In whatever manner the magistrate may be made to interfere in it, it is an act of injustice. A Deist could not possibly subscribe to such terms."[52] Civil liberty was even less well treated in Locke's system: "The code of Carolina, by a singularity not to be accounted for in an Englishman and in a philosopher, gave to the eight proprietors who founded the settlement, and to their heirs, not only all the rights of sovereignty, but all the powers of legislation." The proprietors used their authority to establish a new aristocracy by creating three orders of nobility. The house of commons of the province was granted considerably more limited powers than its English model.[53] As in Virginia, this lack of democracy impeded the development of the colony: "A form of constitution ill-arranged, was the principal cause of an almost general indolence. The lords who were proprietors, imbued with despotic principles, used their utmost efforts to establish an arbitrary government. The colonists, on the other hand, who were not ignorant of the rights of mankind, exerted themselves with equal warmth to avoid servitude."[54]

49. Raynal, *History of the East and West Indies*, bk. 18:41; *Histoire des deux Indes*, bk. 18:72.

50. Raynal, *History of the East and West Indies*, bk. 18:44–45; *Histoire des deux Indes*, bk. 18:78–79. The original French text correctly gives 1642 as the date of the expulsion.

51. Here Raynal and Diderot differ sharply from Voltaire, whose admiration for Locke's legislative plan for Carolina was without reservation. See *Essai sur les moeurs*, 2:381–82, and *Treatise on Tolerance*, 22.

52. Raynal, *History of the East and West Indies*, bk. 18:50; *Histoire des deux Indes*, bk. 18:88–89.

53. Raynal, *History of the East and West Indies*, bk. 18:51; *Histoire des deux Indes*, bk. 18:90.

54. Raynal, *History of the East and West Indies*, bk. 18:52; *Histoire des deux Indes*, bk. 18:92. In Georgia the absence of civil liberty was even more egregious. There, the proprietors made themselves "entirely masters, not only of the police, justice, and finances of the country, but even of the lives and estates of its inhabitants. Every species of right was withdrawn from the people" (18:65–66; 18:115). See also, regarding fiscal matters: "From its infant state, Georgia had been subjected to the fines of a feudal government, with which it had been, as it were, fettered" (18:66–67; 18:117).

It is a recurring theme in the *Histoire des deux Indes* that the southern colonies exhibit features characteristic of an aristocratic, in some respects even feudal, culture.[55] The initial form of government in most of the South (proprietary government) meant that the lord proprietors naturally favored the constitution of an aristocracy of large landowners whose interests were often in conflict with those of the general population. We saw that in Carolina the proprietors even established three orders of nobility based on land ownership. But more than purely political tradition is involved here. Proprietary governments eventually disappeared. A certain aristocratic culture and way of life, however, remained:

> Men, who prefer the tranquillity of a rural life to the tumultuous abode of cities, ought naturally to be economical and laborious; but this was never the case in Virginia. Its inhabitants were always very expensive in the furniture of their houses; they were always fond of entertaining their neighbours with ostentation. They always liked to display the greatest luxury before the English navigators, whom business brought to their plantations. They always gave themselves up to that effeminacy, and to that negligence, so common in countries where slavery is established.[56]

"Luxe," or luxury, was of course the subject of many moral and economic debates in eighteenth-century France.[57] Conflating the two perspectives, Raynal condemns luxury as the distinctive mark of a particular morally tainted class—the aristocracy of wealthy landowners—and of a particular economic system based on slavery. Luxury goes hand in hand with corruption and exploitation. Indeed, the negative attitude toward luxury in the *Histoire des deux Indes* reflects a deep aversion to all forms of exploitative commerce. But it certainly does not express any blanket condemnation of trade in general. Raynal's indictment is specifically directed here at the economy of the South. As the counterexample of New England shows, enlightened free commerce based on free labor is a different story altogether.

55. This theme, of course, would become a major one in Tocqueville's *Democracy in America* (1835–40).

56. Raynal, *History of the East and West Indies,* bk. 18:47; *Histoire des deux Indes,* bk. 18:83. See also, on South Carolina: "the taste for the conveniencies of life is generally prevalent, and the expences are carried as far as luxury" (18:60; 18:106). Cf. Crèvecoeur, *Letters from an American Farmer,* 166–67.

57. In *The Spirit of the Laws* (1748), for example, Montesquieu had argued that luxury is incompatible with the spirit of democracy, which he characterized as a love of equality and frugality (bk. 7, chap. 2), but is appropriate in monarchies where it constitutes the main foundation of commerce (bk. 7, chap. 4; bk. 20, chap. 4). Voltaire, for his part, consistently extolled the social benefits of luxury and commerce in general. Rousseau, on the other hand, unambiguously condemned luxury as destructive of good morals. For an excellent recent survey of the question, see Jeremy Jennings, "The Debate about Luxury in Eighteenth- and Nineteenth-Century French Political Thought," *Journal of the History of Ideas* 68 (2007): 79–105.

However, for a work whose general stance is resolutely anticolonial and anti-slavery, the *Histoire des deux Indes* devotes surprisingly little attention (about half a dozen pages out of five hundred) to the problem of slavery in North America. Two reasons can be invoked to account for this apparent negligence. The first and most obvious is that slavery had already been dealt with in preceding sections, particularly those on the Antilles (bk. 11). There is perhaps also a tendency to downplay the evil of slavery in the North American context in observations like this one, for example: "It will not be disowned, that they [the slaves] may be better fed, better clothed, less ill treated, and less overburdened with toil, than in the islands. The laws protect them more effectually, and they seldom become the victims of the barbarity or caprice of an odious tyrant."[58] Nevertheless, Diderot and Raynal's fundamental position, that slavery can never be justified, is made abundantly clear in the chapters on the American Revolution; in a sense, the existence of slavery in a free country like the United States is all the more shocking: "I shall never comprehend by what fatality that legislation, which is the most happily planned of any that hath ever existed, hath been capable of preferring the interest of a few of its merchants to the dictates of nature, of reason, and of virtue."[59]

It seems manifest to Raynal that the aristocratic way of life of the South inhibits the development of commerce and industry. In Virginia, for example, the tobacco trade is hampered by the absence of large cities and ports; British ships are forced to sail from plantation to plantation to get their cargo.[60] More generally, southern colonists are not only less industrious than their northern counterparts, they are also less civic minded. Raynal writes in the chapter on North Carolina: "These colonists are seldom assembled together, and they are therefore the least informed of the Americans, and the most indifferent to the public interest. Most of them live dispersed upon their plantations, without ambition or foresight. They are but little inclined to labour, and they are seldom good planters. Though they have the English form of government, the laws have very little force among them."[61]

Broadly speaking, the depiction of the southern colonies in the *Histoire des deux Indes* evokes more traditional societies. Less freedom and tolerance, an agricultural economy, aristocratic customs, barriers to trade and industry—all these features imply that the South is politically and economically less progressive than the North.

58. Raynal, *History of the East and West Indies*, bk. 18:103; *Histoire des deux Indes*, bk. 18:184–85.

59. Raynal, *History of the East and West Indies*, bk. 18:105–6; *Histoire des deux Indes*, bk. 18:189.

60. Raynal, *History of the East and West Indies*, bk. 18:46–47; *Histoire des deux Indes*, bk. 18:82–83.

61. Raynal, *History of the East and West Indies*, bk. 18:56; *Histoire des deux Indes*, bk. 18:99–100. Cf. Crèvecoeur, *Letters from an American Farmer*, 79.

PROGRESS OR VIRTUOUS SIMPLICITY?

In his classic study of the image of America in France up to the fall of Napoleon, Durand Echeverria distinguishes two interpretive paradigms of American society prevalent among Americanist *philosophes*.[62] Both paradigms emphasize the ideas of liberty and enlightenment, but in one, virtue and simplicity provide the other dominant themes, whereas in the second, it is rather the notion of progress that completes the picture. The "virtue and simplicity" paradigm is more backward-looking, it sees in America a recreation of an ideal past. The "progress" paradigm is naturally more forward looking and views America as inaugurating a new and better type of society. In its general assessment of the colonies, the *Histoire des deux Indes* shows signs of both trends, though with a definite predominance of the "virtue and simplicity" thesis.

Franklin, of course, appears as the perfect embodiment of the enlightened American. He is living proof that the emerging country can produce great men of science and eloquent philosophers. Philadelphia, the subject of a whole chapter in the *Histoire,* is described as a modern city with wide streets and sidewalks.[63] Particularly noted are its cultural institutions, two libraries, and a college, so that "if ever despotism, superstition, or war, should plunge Europe again into that state of barbarism out of which philosophy and the arts have extricated it, the sacred fire will be kept alive in Philadelphia, and come from thence to enlighten the world."[64] And Diderot is convinced that soon not only the sciences but the arts too will flourish in America: "Works of imagination, and of taste, will soon follow those of reasoning and observation." New England will soon have "its Homer, its Theocritus, and its Sophocles" because it offers better and more accessible education to the mass of the population than is the case in Europe.[65]

Yet Diderot hesitates between the image of a return to ancient Greece and the idea of progress in comparison with the contemporary state of Europe. In the end, and in contrast to modern European societies, with their luxury and inequalities, simplicity and equality form the main characteristics of life in the colonies according to the *Histoire des deux Indes:*

> Throughout the families in general, there reigns economy, neatness, and regularity. Gallantry and gaming, the passions of indolent opulence, seldom inter-

---

62. Echeverria, *Mirage in the West,* 144–61.

63. Raynal, *History of the East and West Indies,* bk. 18:22; *Histoire des deux Indes,* bk. 18:39.

64. Raynal, *History of the East and West Indies,* bk. 18:24; *Histoire des deux Indes,* bk. 18:42.

65. Raynal, *History of the East and West Indies,* bk. 18:97; *Histoire des deux Indes,* bk. 18:175. See also, on a small settlement in Florida: "Why should not Athens and Lacedemon be one day revived in North America? . . . The new colony is less distant from this flourishing state than were the barbarous Pelasgians from the fellow-citizens of Pericles" (18:77; 18:136–37). And on Pennsylvania: "All [nations] were delighted to see those heroic days of antiquity realized, which European manners and laws had long taught every one to consider as entirely fabulous" (18:12; 18:21).

rupt that happy tranquillity. . . . One general sentiment of benevolence unites every family. Nothing contributes to this union so much as a certain equality of station, a security that arises from property, hope, and a general facility of increasing it . . . Instead of luxury, which brings misery in its train, instead of this afflicting and shocking contrast, an universal ease, wisely dealt out in the original distribution of the lands, has, by the influence of industry, given rise in every breast to the mutual desire of pleasing; a desire, without doubt, more satisfactory than the secret disposition to injure our brethren, which is inseparable from an extreme inequality of fortune and condition.[66]

In America humankind can return to earlier and better times, to its legendary origins, and the vision of a renewal of the "heroic days of antiquity," the heroic days of Athens and Sparta, turns into a sentimental tableau of pastoral Golden Age:

It is in the colonies that men lead such a rural life as was the original destination of mankind, best suited to the health and increase of the species: probably they enjoy all the happiness consistent with the frailty of human nature. We do not, indeed, find there those graces, those talents, those refined enjoyments, the means and expence of which wear out and fatigue the springs of the soul, and bring on the vapours of melancholy, which so naturally follow the disgust arising from sensual enjoyment; but there are the pleasures of domestic life, the mutual attachments of parents and children, and conjugal love, that passion so pure and so delicious to the soul that can taste it, and despise all other gratifications. This is the inchanting prospect exhibited throughout North America.[67]

On the other hand, it would be misleading to assert that, in its understanding of North America, the *Histoire* relies exclusively on a strict and simple opposition between history (the Old World) and nature (the New World). In his recent reading of the *Histoire des deux Indes,* J. G. A. Pocock alleges that Raynal and Diderot's work "cannot get beyond the vision of a Pennsylvanian utopia to an assessment of the now independent English colonies as a force acting in history and making a history of their own."[68] According to Pocock, the two *philosophes* "could not see how settler peoples could re-create themselves as Europeans beyond Europe, beyond such picturesque exceptions as the republic of the fili-

66. Raynal, *History of the East and West Indies,* bk. 18:108; *Histoire des deux Indes,* bk. 18:193–94.
67. Raynal, *History of the East and West Indies,* bk. 18:108–9; *Histoire des deux Indes,* bk. 18:194–95.
68. Pocock, *Barbarism and Religion,* 4:323.

busters or the utopia of the Quakers."[69] As a result, the *Histoire* "fails as philosophic enquiry at the point where it fails to provide an account of the development of economies of free land and free labour in the New World."[70] The *Histoire,* it would seem, is no history at all: it is guilty of having relegated the New World in general and North America in particular to a sphere outside history (nature, utopia, or conversely barbarism in the case of the Spanish and Portuguese colonies).

This does not do justice to the complexity of the inner tensions running through the North American sections of the *Histoire des deux Indes.* Even without considering the nearly two hundred pages devoted to the American Revolution, the depiction of New England alone is sufficient to reveal how Raynal and Diderot could get beyond the confrontation between nature and history. As we have noted, despite a history tainted by religious fanaticism, New England is praised for its orderly development, its laws regarding property, its prosperous trade and industry, its education system, its popular government, and so forth. The authors of the *Histoire* used at least three different models in their political treatment of the North American colonies: the utopian model represented by the Quakers, but also, and most significantly, the ancient Greek model, which reappears on several occasions, and a modern model based on open trade and free government as illustrated by New England.[71] No doubt, the *Histoire* often yields to the temptation of conceiving the "new" simply in terms of the "old," of theorizing the colonies as a return to some form of idealized communal past: virtuous ancient republicanism, pastoral Golden Age, early Christianity (in Quaker Pennsylvania). It thus contributed to the spread of a seductive mythical image of America, an image destined to endure across the centuries and, most important, to feed into various versions of the theory of American exceptionalism. But then, if the *Histoire* can be said, judging from our modern perspective, to suffer from any particular failure in its philosophical enquiry on the English colonies, it is less because of a reliance on utopia or on the opposition between history and nature than because of its hesitation between two visions of America and of liberty: one "ancient," inspired by the communal, virtuous republicanism of Antiquity, the other "modern," based on individual freedom, industry, and enlightened open commerce. In failing to opt between "ancient" and "modern" liberty, the *Histoire des deux Indes* failed to take a clear position in what would become, during

---

69. Pocock, *Barbarism and Religion,* 4:324.

70. Pocock, *Barbarism and Religion,* 4:327.

71. Even in the case of Pennsylvania the utopian-pastoral paradigm is only partially relevant. The examples of Franklin as scientific genius and Philadelphia as a great modern center of enlightenment point in a different direction.

the following decades and until at least the end of the nineteenth century, a fundamental debate about the nature of liberty in the modern age.[72]

To claim that Raynal and Diderot's *Histoire* and Voltaire's brief remarks on the colonies cover the whole range of opinions on colonial America in pre-revolutionary France would, of course, be an exaggeration.[73] On the other hand, these texts stand out as particularly significant, influential, and representative of the types of Americanism widespread among the intelligentsia of late eighteenth-century France, the *philosophes*. With regard to Americanism, the preceding pages have also shown that there is a clear, continuous line of influence extending from Voltaire to Raynal and Diderot, and from Raynal and Diderot to Crèvecoeur. Not only did the *History of the East and West Indies* contain the most widely read discussion of America produced in late Enlightenment France, but its influence was further magnified by the extraordinary success of the *Letters from an American Farmer* in Europe. Not only did the *Histoire* help define the image of early America throughout Europe, it also played a role in shaping America's own self-image. Through Crèvecoeur, the French aristocrat avid reader of the *Histoire des deux Indes* who became one of the first great American writers, Raynal and the *philosophes'* ideas on the colonies participated in the formation of American national identity. Then as now, America's self-image was not a purely homemade construct, it was and remains inseparable from its image in Europe and the rest of the world. Better than other authors of the same period, Voltaire, Raynal, and Diderot thus illustrate the reciprocal impact of American colonial history on French liberal thought and of French philosophical idealism on American national consciousness on the eve of both the American and French Revolutions. They provide an excellent window into a defining, seminal early chapter in the ongoing Franco-American dialogue about the politics of democracy.

72. See, notably, Condorcet's political writings, Benjamin Constant's "De la liberté des anciens comparée à celle des modernes" ("On the Liberty of the Ancients Compared with that of the Moderns," 1819), and Fustel de Coulanges's *La Cité Antique* (*The Ancient City,* 1864). All three authors insisted on the radical difference between ancient and modern conceptions of liberty and on the inapplicability of ancient models of freedom to the modern world.

73. For such a survey, we again refer the reader to the still indispensable study by Echeverria, *Mirage in the West.*

4

ON THE POLITICAL EFFICACY OF IDEALISM
Tocqueville, Schoelcher, and the Abolition of Slavery

Nick Nesbitt

The problem of slavery and its abolition was of enormous import for thinkers across the spectrum of what we would now call left-wing thought in nineteenth century France. In the period of the July Monarchy of Louis-Philippe (1830–48), two public intellectuals in particular forcefully and repeatedly placed the problem of slavery in France's American colonies before the French public and paved the way for its eventual abolition on April 27, 1848: Alexis de Tocqueville and Victor Schoelcher.[1] Each traveled extensively throughout the Americas, and each brought the experience of their New World encounters to bear upon their attempts to eradicate French participation in what they viewed as an enormous crime of inhumanity. While Schoelcher's thought is relatively little known outside the field of abolition studies, the same cannot be said of his contemporary Tocqueville. Despite the centrality of Tocqueville to the fields of political theory, history, and American studies, however, relatively little attention has been given to his writings on the problem of slavery in the New World.[2] In what follows, I

1. See Robin Blackburn, *The Overthrow of Colonial Slavery, 1776–1848* (London: Verso, 1988), on the history of abolitionism in the July Monarchy.
2. Jennifer Pitts's introduction to her translation of Tocqueville's *Writings on Empire and Slavery,* (Baltimore: Johns Hopkins University Press, 2001) offers readers a balanced and convincing account of Tocqueville's complex, often contradictory views on what were, for him, inextricably connected issues.

would like to consider Schoelcher's and Tocqueville's respective positions on abolition, before widening the focus of my discussion to consider the historical and philosophical context within which they made their respective interventions.

Alexis de Tocqueville unambiguously condemned slavery as a "violation of blacks' human rights" and called for its abolition on multiple occasions, in both *Democracy in America* and in his later writings and letters.[3] From 1835 on, he was a member of the abolitionist Société française pour l'abolition de l'esclavage. Like many other liberal abolitionists of the period, however, he argued that enfranchisement should occur gradually, as the slaves were "prepared" for liberty; that is, they were to receive a sort of civic education in the rights and responsibilities of democratic society until such a time as the French state and the colonial plantocracy had successfully weathered the transition from a slaveholding system to one based upon wage labor.

Tocqueville's position in favor of the French imperial project, while common to French liberal thought of the period, stood in stark contrast to the condemnation of imperialism that had developed in eighteenth-century Enlightenment thought.[4] The inherent contradiction between the defense of individual rights and the defense of the democratic nation-state that assured and implemented those rights forced liberal July Monarchy politicians to make difficult choices; for Tocqueville after 1839, that choice repeatedly tended to favor the interests of the democratic state. When context favored the defense of the Rights of Man, as in the question of slavery, so much the better. When it did not, as in the case of the colonization of Algeria, the rights of the colonized were to be sacrificed to greater French glory.[5]

Previous to Pitts's edition, Sally Gershman's "Alexis de Tocqueville and Slavery" (*French Historical Studies* 9, no. 3 [1976]: 467–83) presented the most balanced treatment of this element of Tocqueville's thought, though the article tends to underplay the inherent conflict between Tocqueville's simultaneous dedication to both democracy and the economic liberalism of the July Monarchy. Also of interest are Melvin Richter's polemical "Tocqueville on Algeria" (*Review of Politics* 25, no. 3 [1963]: 362–98), which concludes that in his support for French colonization of Algeria, the historian was "deceived" and "inconsistent" with his own convictions; and Seymour Drescher's *Dilemmas of Democracy* (Pittsburgh: University of Pittsburgh Press, 1968), 151–95, which discusses Tocqueville's views on abolition.

3. Alexis de Tocqueville, *Democracy in America,* trans. G. Bevin (London: Penguin Books, 2003), 402.

4. As Jennifer Pitts argues, "Postrevolutionary France offers a particularly stark example of antiimperialism's retreat to the margins of political debate. The nation's unstable and unsettling domestic regime for much of the nineteenth century led liberals, including Tocqueville, to embrace imperialism as a kind of national salvation. . . . The dominant strand of liberalism that was forged during this period was to be exclusionary and nationalist; and it would sit uneasily with the Revolution's apparent legacy of universal human equality and liberty" (introduction to Toqueville, *Writings on Empire and Slavery,* xxxiv). On the Enlightenment critique of European imperialism, see Sankar Muthu, *Enlightenment against Empire* (Princeton: Princeton University Press, 2003).

5. "How were European societies to make the transition from the old autocratic regimes to republics without succumbing to anarchy or state terror? Tocqueville's writings on Algeria imply that this transition required the exploitation of non-European societies, that nation-building legitimated the

In contrast to the liberals' subordination of human rights to the interests of the nation-state, Victor Schoelcher argued that the ideals of 1789 demanded nothing less than the full and immediate granting of the Rights of Man and Citizen to the slaves France had held in bondage. The distinction I wish to draw in this chapter, then, is not the one between colonialists who defended slavery in the interests of French imperialism and abolitionists dedicated to its eradication, but rather the inherent one between abolitionists such as Tocqueville who were willing to subordinate human rights to those of property, and those such as Schoelcher who, while attentive to property rights and the needs of the state, maintained that defense of the rights of all citizens must come before democratic state-building, even if this priority should cost France her American colonies.

Among French abolitionists of the period extending from 1789 to 1848 one might thus distinguish between a pragmatic and an idealist approach to the elimination of slavery. The former might be best characterized by Condorcet's 1781 "Réflexions sur l'esclavage des nègres," where the philosopher-mathematician's radical universalist call for human rights was tempered by the historical expediency of a graduated and rational "preparation" of slaves for freedom. Condorcet offered a series of "objective" mathematical formulas to deduce the need for a *gradual* elimination of slavery over the course of one or two generations, rather than its immediate abolition.[6] Never was there any discussion on his part whether those directly involved, the objects of such cold calculation, might prefer or merit a more rapid emancipation. For all Condorcet's concern for what we would now call human rights, these were to be sacrificed in the present for hundreds of thousands of subjects in the interest of the state's smooth transition to a regime based on wages rather than slave labor.[7]

The arch-realist in matters of French slavery was no doubt Napoleon himself, who stands as the logical fulfillment of this utilitarian approach to the question of slavery in the period, insofar as he followed through the logic of placing the property rights of slave owners before the human rights of 1789. His 1802 reimposition of slavery in all of France's American colonies was an attempt to recover the economic productivity of the world's most profitable colonial enterprise (Saint Domingue's sugar alone accounted for over a third of the country's foreign trade in 1789), a project predicated in turn upon the renewed attempt to reduce humans to mere machinic quotas of productive capacity.

---

suspension of principles of human equality and self-determination, and that French glory justified any aggression the nation could muster" (Pitts, introduction to *Writings on Empire and Slavery*, xxxv).

6. Jean-Antoine-Nicolas, Marquis de Condorcet, *Réflexions sur l'esclavage des Nègres* (Paris: Mille et une nuits, 2000), 38, 44.

7. In France's New World colony of Saint Domingue alone, by 1789 some five hundred thousand African slaves were kept in servitude.

TOCQUEVILLE'S POSITION ON SLAVERY

Tocqueville echoed Condorcet's hesitation before the outrage of slavery. In *Democracy in America,* he explicitly criticized slavery as the "violation of blacks' human rights."[8] He articulated a principled and consistent critique of the institution in his most famous work, a stance grounded on both his Christian faith and a fidelity to the human rights tradition of the French Revolution.[9] *Democracy in America* only addressed the problem of American slavery in passing, however, since, as he put the matter, slavery was "American but not democratic and it was the portrait of democracy I wanted to paint."[10] Instead, Tocqueville referred his readers in search of a more detailed exploration of American slavery to his friend Gustave de Beaumont's novel *Marie.*[11] Nonetheless, his condemnation of the institution was total, calling it an "evil which has crept secretly into the world. . . . [It] is cast like an accursed seed somewhere on the soil; it then feeds itself, grows without effort, and spreads naturally inside the society which has accepted it."[12]

When it came to the French state's institution of slavery in the Americas, Tocqueville repeatedly and unambiguously called for its elimination in his public and private writings in the years leading up to 1848. His critique of slavery and the attendant plantocracy that sustained it was detailed and insightful. These writings fully reveal Tocqueville's subtly evolving views on the proper course for French abolition in light of the experience of France's imperial rival, England, which had abolished its own slavery regime in 1833. Tocqueville joined the French Chamber of Representatives as a liberal representative in 1839. During these final years of the July Monarchy, from 1839–48, Tocqueville wrote repeatedly on what were for him the inextricably intertwined problems of French imperialism and slavery. The bulk of his analysis of the former focused on the contemporary French initiative to colonize Algeria,[13] and attention to his argu-

---

8. Tocqueville, *Democracy in America,* 170.

9. Tocqueville, *Democracy in America,* 399. See also Gershman, "Alexis de Tocqueville and Slavery," 467.

10. Cited in Gershman, "Alexis de Tocqueville and Slavery," 469.

11. "Those who want to understand to what excesses of tyranny men are steadily driven, once they begin to abandon nature and humanity, should read M. de Beaumont's work" (Tocqueville, *Democracy in America,* 399). As Christine Dunn Henderson points out in her contribution to this volume ("Tyranny and Tragedy in Beaumont's *Marie*"), Beaumont's novel is more accurately described as a reflection upon racial prejudice in the United States, rather than the institution of slavery itself.

12. Tocqueville, *Democracy in America,* 399.

13. These include his first and second "Letter[s] on Algeria" (1837), "Notes" on "the Koran" (1838) and on his 1841 voyage to Algeria, the "Essay on Algeria" (1841), an "Intervention on the Debate over the Appropriation of Special Funding" (1846), and his first and second "Report[s] on Algeria" (1847), all reproduced in Tocqueville, *Writings on Empire and Slavery.* For more on these texts, see Richter, "Tocqueville on Algeria," 362–98.

ment there reveals the degree to which the problem of slavery for Tocqueville must be understood as a problem less of human rights than of the greater good of French imperialism.

Tocqueville's writings on Algeria consistently subordinated the Rights of Man to those of the French citizen. These texts reveal that in the context of his political functions, Tocqueville placed the rights of French citizens and the need to shore up an infirm French democratic tradition before the human rights of its colonial subjects. Tocqueville could simultaneously defend the use of violence against Algerian subjects while condemning French slavery because his predominant criterion in all of these writings was not the problem of human rights, but the glory and solidity of the democratic French state.[14] That such recourse to violence (if only against noncitizens) in defense of the ideals of 1789 might actually undermine those same ideals was not a line of argument he chose to pursue. The imperial project, and the conquest of Algeria in particular, were essential, Tocqueville argued, to enhancing France's international standing; if the rights of Algerians were to suffer under French hegemony, this was an unfortunate but necessary evil. His writings on Algeria, albeit by 1847 coming to condemn the violence of Marshal Bugeaud's military conquest as counterproductively excessive, unanimously defended a certain degree of imperialist violence as necessary to the greater good of successful colonization.[15]

His writings on imperialism and slavery reveal a fundamental tension in Tocqueville's liberalism, one inhering between the defense of individual liberties and the need to shore up and defend the democratic state that assured the implementation of those liberties for its citizens. If Tocqueville had condemned the American extermination of native peoples in *Democracy in America,* in matters of democratic nation-building, he nonetheless understood the colonized (like slaves) to be less-developed, "barbarous" peoples who, standing outside the democratic polis, failed to qualify for the full civil rights of French citizenship.[16] In the "Essay on Algeria," Tocqueville explicitly defended the practice of the *razzia,* the need to "burn harvests, empty silos, and capture unarmed men, women,

14. "France, in Tocqueville's view, required new occasions for virtuous or glorious action. The conquest of Algeria, and in the 1840s the debate over the abolition of slavery in the French Antilles, provided precisely such occasions. The abolition of slavery would be a noble, moral act and would regain for France some of the luster of her humanitarian reputation, which had passed over to Britain when that country abolished slavery in its colonies in 1833. Conquering and settling Algeria would constitute a national project: it would capture the public's attention, unify the fractured political scene, and gain Europe's respect" (Pitts, introduction to Toqueville, *Writings on Empire and Slavery,* xvii).

15. The problem with French colonial violence in Algeria, Tocqueville's 1847 texts argue, is not that it is inherently wrong, but rather that its *excessive* application under Bugeaud had left "Muslim society much more miserable, more disordered, more ignorant, and more barbarous than it had been before knowing us" (cited in Pitts, introduction to Tocqueville, *Writings on Empire and Slavery,* xxvii).

16. Pitts, introduction to Tocqueville, *Writings on Empire and Slavery,* xv.

and children," and the destruction of Arab towns to secure French colonial hegemony.[17] Tocqueville understood French colonialism as a conflict between lesser- and more-developed human races, and it was this inequality that justified the use of violence on the part of the French colonizers: "In order for us to colonize to any extent," he wrote, "we must necessarily use not only violent measures, but visibly iniquitous ones. The quarrel is no longer between governments, but between races."[18]

In addition to the comments on North American slavery in *Democracy in America,* Tocqueville wrote two principal texts on the problem of French abolition. The first is the report of the government commission Tocqueville headed in 1839, and the second his 1843 essay "The Emancipation of Slaves," written for the journal *Le Siècle.*[19] In all these texts his condemnation of slavery is unambiguous: "Man has never had the right to possess another man," he wrote in the 1839 report, "and the fact of possession has always been—and is still— illegitimate."[20] "Emancipation," he stated in the language of universal natural rights, is the realization of the "principles of justice, humanity, and reason."[21] The commission's report, which Tocqueville authored, began with the assertion that their task was neither to disprove the justifications put forward in the past to defend slavery, nor even to argue for the necessity of abolition. These, it asserted, could by 1839 be taken as given; that slavery "can and must one day be ended," Tocqueville wrote, "is today a universally recognized truth, one that slave owners themselves do not deny."[22] The commission instead had addressed a question of "practical politics": not to investigate the philosophical question of whether slavery is wrong and must end, but "when and how it must end."

Tocqueville's position on abolition was complex. Both his 1839 report and the articles of 1843 make similar arguments, though his intended audiences differed: one that of his fellow representatives, the other a French public opinion that he wished to influence in favor of abolition. In consonance with Victor Schoelcher, he refuted in his 1839 text the idea that slaves should be "prepared" for freedom before emancipation can occur. Tocqueville argued that none of the processes such gradualists call for (civic and religious training, strengthening the institution of marriage) could be accomplished within the slaveholding system. The system itself fatally undermined their development. Given this fact, "to

---

17. Cited in Pitts, introduction to Tocqueville, *Writings on Empire and Slavery,* xxi.

18. Cited in Pitts, introduction to Tocqueville, *Writings on Empire and Slavery,* xxiii.

19. While the first text is not reproduced in Pitts's volume, the report is available as Tocqueville, Alexis, *Rapport fait au nom de la commission chargée d'examiner la proposition de M. de Tracy, relative aux Esclaves des colonies, 23 July, 1839,* http://gallica.bnf.fr/ark:/12148/bpt6k845061.

20. Tocqueville, *Writings on Empire and Slavery,* 19.

21. Tocqueville, *Writings on Empire and Slavery,* 22.

22. Tocqueville, *Writings on Empire and Slavery,* 2.

demand that they be accomplished before slavery is ended [is] to declare that it should never end."[23] Tocqueville placed the blame for the slave's moral underdevelopment (he accepted this underdevelopment unquestioningly) not with the slave, but with the slaveholders who had systematically impeded that development. "How could one," he asks, "enlighten and fortify the reason of a man as long as he is kept in a state where it is useless to him and where it could be harmful for him to reason?"[24] Instead, Tocqueville argued that "only the experience of freedom . . . can suggest and give to men the opinions, the virtues, and the habits appropriate for the citizen of a free country."[25] The process of emancipation would inevitably be uncertain, Tocqueville asserted. One must accept this fact or else "eternalize slavery."[26] Given this, Tocqueville's commission recommended that the French government not delay abolition, arguing moreover that it could be "perilous" to do so.

Despite this firm support for universal, immediate abolition, Tocqueville remained more hesitant as to the precise modality of the emancipation process itself. Emancipation should be universal, he argued, rather than gradual. Anything less—as was attempted in the English colonies—would lead to chaos.[27] The only question then was whether emancipation would be unprepared and disorderly or (relatively) systematic. Tocqueville's most problematic recommendation was his repeated suggestion that the colonists be partially indemnified for the loss of their slaves (who would nonetheless presumably continue to work for them).[28] This despite his own recognition, in *Democracy in America*, that "the Negroes may remain slaves without complaining but once they join the ranks of free men they will soon be indignant at . . . not being able to become the equals of the whites. . . . There is no intervening state that can last between the excessive inequality created by slavery and the complete equality naturally promoted by independence."[29] Such an indemnity would smooth the period of transition from the slave system to remunerated labor. The cost of indemnification, he argued, was a burden the state should shoulder for its past misdeeds. That this money should go to the slaveholders themselves rather than to benefit the slaves in some way, however, makes this a decidedly unconvincing argument.[30]

23. Tocqueville, *Writings on Empire and Slavery*, 3.
24. Tocqueville, *Writings on Empire and Slavery*, 4.
25. Tocqueville, *Writings on Empire and Slavery*, 6.
26. Tocqueville, *Writings on Empire and Slavery*, 6.
27. Tocqueville, *Writings on Empire and Slavery*, 11, 14.
28. Tocqueville, *Writings on Empire and Slavery*, 22.
29. Tocqueville, *Democracy in America*, 423, 425.

30. Gershman is at pains to square Tocqueville's support of indemnification, both in his 1839 report and the 1843 articles, with his belief that "man never had the right to possess man, and the fact of possession has always been and still is unlawful" (cited in Gershman, "Alexis de Tocqueville and Slavery," 476).

Tocqueville understood and professed to sympathize with the desire of former slaves both to possess and farm their own personal plots of land. Speaking of the English Caribbean colonies, where former slaves retained such plots and devoted much attention to their cultivation, he observed that, quite reasonably, "blacks prefer, in cultivating [these gardens], to work for themselves, rather than serving another."[31] Tocqueville flatly rejected this form of autonomy, however, in the context of abolition: "If it is judged necessary for the exploitation of colonial crops and for the permanence of the white race in the Antilles that the freed black sell his services permanently to the plantation owners, it is evident that no domain should have been created [in these English colonies] where he could live in comfort by working for himself alone."[32]

Though Tocqueville rhetorically distanced himself in his official document from this qualification of the former slaves' freedom by the use of the third person conditional, it is precisely this conclusion that the report would go on to recommend. Though perhaps a reflection of Tocqueville's lifelong desire to "moderate" the forces of democracy,[33] in other words, to find a balance in this case between the rights of slaves and colonial property owners, such a limitation of rights could only be called a deliberate form of discrimination. When it came to the economic success of the French plantation system, suddenly Tocqueville's penchant for human autonomy was notable by its absence, and property rights came before the natural rights of man. "Your Commission," he writes, "thinks that a trial period, in which the Blacks, already given *certain* rights of the free man, would still be forced to work, is indispensable . . . to prepare the education of the black population, and to bring it to *a state able to bear liberty [la mettre en état de supporter la liberté"]*."[34]

Tocqueville saw his approach to abolition as a pragmatic, rhetorical gambit oriented toward attaining the final goal of abolition. He wrote to Pierre-Paul Royer-Collard that in the report "you will see that I have avoided, to the point of *coldness,* all that smacks of harangue. Both my own natural penchant and the desire to avoid unnecessarily exciting the passions of the colonies led me to it. I wanted to be scrupulously just and moderate in an affair in which until now I think others have been violent even when they have been right. . . . [In] working on the report, I always thought of the success of the measure and never of the success of the report."[35] For all his willingness to compromise, Tocqueville never

31. Tocqueville, *Writings on Empire and Slavery,* 45.
32. Tocqueville, *Writings on Empire and Slavery,* 46.
33. On Tocqueville's complex political moderation, see Aurelian Craiutu, "Tocqueville's Para-doxical Moderation," *Review of Politics,* 67, no. 4 (2005): 599–629.
34. Tocqueville, *Writings on Empire and Slavery,* 48 (my emphasis).
35. Cited in Gershman, "Alexis de Tocqueville and Slavery," 477

managed to bring the government in which he participated to implement abolition. Instead, the government issued a series of reports in the 1840s, each of whose recommendations were either ignored or postponed by the decision to form a new committee on the subject.

When confronted with the need to ensure the regular flow of profit from the colonies, Tocqueville adopted a decidedly paternalistic tone that stood in marked contrast to the condemnations of slavery one finds elsewhere in his oeuvre. He asserted to his readers that plantation owners could profit from the former slaves' (putative) inclination to subservience, the result of their long experience of forced labor: "During the period in which already promised freedom is not yet completely given; in which habits of respect that slavery had engendered are still maintained by forced labor, but in which the slave's spirit already looks forward to the approach of independence; in this intermediary period the application [*action*] of power [to ensure their continuous labor] is easy and effective."[36] Not human rights, autonomy, or democracy, but merely the effective domination of the former slave's spirit by sovereign power stood at this point as Tocqueville's moral criterion. Why should the former slave not be free, as a human being, to formulate his or her own conception of autonomy? The answer for Tocqueville and his colleagues was so obvious that he had no need to state it explicitly: because, in matters of colonial policy, the economic viability of the large-scale plantation system overrode the natural right of slaves to articulate the conditions of their own freedom. Though Tocqueville called for "destroying in a single blow all the former relations that existed between the master and his slave,"[37] these relations would immediately be replaced by a system of forced plantation labor that only differed from slavery in that it would be remunerated. In other words, Tocqueville recommended replacing outright slavery with remunerated serfdom.

In this 1839 text Tocqueville understood the former slaves not as fully autonomous human beings, but as moral and juridical minors who required the guardianship of the state after their long period of servitude: "The state thus becoming [upon emancipation] the tutor of the former slaves, it finds itself free to use all means that can best and most quickly prepare the latter for the use of independence."[38] Tocqueville's language is revealing: it was not the former slaves who would be free upon emancipation, but the state that should be "free" to model these beings—not into slaves, as it had attempted for two centuries—but, now, into a docile, infantilized, and subaltern agricultural proletariat. The state "can impose upon them the conditions it judges indispensable, and force them to

36. Tocqueville, *Writings on Empire and Slavery*, 49.
37. Tocqueville, *Writings on Empire and Slavery*, 49.
38. Tocqueville, *Writings on Empire and Slavery*, 52.

undergo the necessary ordeals before giving them over to themselves."[39] Tocqueville then concluded his recommendations by calling for a limited period of servitude and indoctrination after emancipation, a status without juridical limitation
upon the state's actions. During this period, the state would enjoy "full freedom"
to create a submissive labor force. That this social engineering would be limited
in time and applied only to Africans would have been strictly irrelevant from the
point of view of natural rights. That, however, was neither Tocqueville's nor the
commission's point of view.

TOCQUEVILLE'S EUROCENTRIC PERSPECTIVE

While Tocqueville's 1839 and 1843 texts both offered similar arguments in favor
of abolition, the latter was in fact the more progressive document, given its
immediate historical context. The French chamber had rejected Tocqueville's
1839 report and convened a new commission, this time headed by the Duc de
Broglie. The commission then called in its 1843 report for a ten-year delay in
implementing emancipation in order to "prepare" slaves for republican citizenship. Though he does not say so in his article, Tocqueville had again argued, but
this time unsuccessfully, that abolition should be immediate, though still qualified
by state supervision of former slaves and counterbalanced by the indemnification
of former slaveholders. The articles were an attempt to influence public opinion
in the hope that this report would not be ignored and shelved, as had his earlier
initiative. Tocqueville's rhetoric in the 1843 articles ranges from the condemnation of the "detestable institution"[40] of slavery to pragmatic considerations of
the proper timing and implementation of abolition in light of France's imperial
economic and political interests.

Tocqueville's series of articles "On the Emancipation of the Slaves" began by
celebrating the "bold and remarkable" event that was Britain's 1833 abolition of
slavery. This occurred, he commented, "not by the desperate effort of the slave,
but by the enlightened will of the master; not gradually," but "in an instant."[41]
The colonists, Tocqueville implied, are an aristocracy like any other; like that of
1789, their unjust "privileges" must be stripped from this race-based "nobility"
in the interest of the democratic state.[42] While Tocqueville qualified both the
slave trade and slavery itself as "infamous," this moral condemnation remained

39. Tocqueville, *Writings on Empire and Slavery*, 52,
40. Tocqueville, *Writings on Empire and Slavery*, 222.
41. In Tocqueville, *Writings on Empire and Slavery*, 199. All further references to this text refer to
this edition. The "desperate effort of the slave" is no doubt an oblique, dismissive reference to the
Haitian Revolution, as well as to New World slave revolts in general.
42. Tocqueville, *Writings on Empire and Slavery*, 200.

secondary in his argument to the question of the good of the imperial nation-state that he went on to explore in depth: "[H]ow can the colonists who belong to the freest and most democratic nation of the European continent," he asked, "flatter themselves that they can preserve [slavery]?"[43]

The interest France holds in its New World colonies, Tocqueville argued, is predominantly not an economic but a geostrategic one. The islands of Guadeloupe and Martinique were "colonies where 200,000 inhabitants speak our language, share our mores, obey our laws."[44] Given the growing ascendancy of U.S. global hegemony that Tocqueville so presciently foresaw, he argued to his readers that the citizens of these colonies must become free members of the French nation as a geostrategic counterweight. "These two islands form two citadels from which France can observe at a distance what happens in these waters, which are to have such a great destiny, and where France can be ready to play the role that her interest or greatness indicates."[45] These positions, Tocqueville argued, would be fatally weakened if France should attempt to maintain slavery on islands surrounded by free territories, sites whose status would inevitably infect the enslaved population with a will to revolt in the name of their freedom.[46] Slavery must be abolished in order to "resist an external attack that would take as its point of departure the evident interests and passions [i.e., for freedom], so often excited, of the immense majority of its inhabitants." The "foremost truth" of emancipation, for Tocqueville, is not one of social justice or human rights, but rather "that keeping the colonies is necessary for the strength and greatness of France."[47]

Tocqueville took an unambiguously Eurocentric perspective when discussing the origins of the idea of emancipation. The question he repeatedly asked was a paternalist one: "Should we, like the English, seek to abolish slavery?"[48] The movement for abolition emanated unilaterally, he argued, from an enlightened Europe to its colonies. That the slaves of Saint Domingue whom this eminent historian never mentions might have actually seen beyond the French bourgeois consensus of 1791 that actively silenced and sidelined the issue of slavery, that these former slaves may have actually radicalized the process of democratization in the French Revolution and compelled the first French abolition of 1794, fully

43. Tocqueville, *Writings on Empire and Slavery*, 201.
44. Tocqueville, *Writings on Empire and Slavery*, 206.
45. Tocqueville, *Writings on Empire and Slavery*, 206.
46. Here again, the memory of the Haitian Revolution, ever-present yet perpetually disavowed, is undoubtedly the spectral, unnamed other lurking beneath Tocqueville's text. On this widespread tendency of nineteenth-century thinkers to repress the political implications of the Haitian Revolution, see Sibylle Fischer, *Modernity Disavowed: Haiti and the Cultures of Slavery in the Age of Revolution* (Durham: Duke University Press, 2004).
47. Tocqueville, *Writings on Empire and Slavery*, 203.
48. Tocqueville, *Writings on Empire and Slavery*, 200.

four decades before the British abolition, is a possibility Tocqueville never admitted.[49] Instead, we are told that "this great event [British abolition of 1833] was
produced by the movement of the century. . . . The ideas, the passions, the ways
of all European societies have pressed in this direction for fifty years. . . . The idea
of slavery in a sense grew from all our other ideas."[50] Tocqueville's suppression of
the events of the Haitian Revolution, events that led directly to the first immediate and total abolition of 1794, is total. Attention to its progression, to say nothing
of the accomplishments of its leader Toussaint Louverture, might have led him
to pause before concluding that "if [the slave] gains his freedom, he often feels
independence as a shackle heavier than slavery itself. . . . When reason becomes
his only guide, he cannot recognize its voice."[51] Instead, Tocqueville flattered his
readers in asserting that the desire to end slavery arose purely from the French
Revolution. The events of 1789, he claimed, gave to the world "this sentiment,
disinterested yet impassioned with the love of men, which all at once made
Europe hear the cries of the slaves—who propagated it, directed it, illuminated
it? We were the ones."[52]

Tocqueville's 1843 text, like that of his earlier report, reduced the problem of
emancipation to a question of costs and benefits: given the unambiguous need to
abolish slavery, how, Tocqueville inquired, could this be achieved with the least
cost and greatest benefit for the French imperial nation-state? In seeking an
answer, one must, he argued, take "the necessary precautions to ensure the benefits and to restrict the costs and perils" in order to guarantee the "most economical means of succeeding" in this endeavor.[53] Since the political and economic
benefit of the French nation remained Tocqueville's point of reference in these
later reflections, the problem of work stoppage by freed slaves came to stand as
the single most important impediment he perceived to a successful emancipation.
Nowhere did Tocqueville stop to wonder whether there might exist a model of
human autonomy that would give priority to the reappropriation of labor-free
time as a valid measure of freedom for someone who had been a slave laborer.[54]

49. The classic discussion of this process remains (C. L. R. James's *The Black Jacobins: Toussaint
Louverture and the San Domingo Revolution* [New York: Vintage, 1989]). I explore this question, along
with other dimensions of the Haitian Revolution to be discussed below in Nick Nesbitt, *Universal
Emancipation: The Haitian Revolution and the Radical Enlightenment* (Charlottesville: University of Virginia
Press, 2008).

50. Tocqueville, *Writings on Empire and Slavery*, 201.

51. Tocqueville, *Democracy in America*, 372.

52. Tocqueville, *Writings on Empire and Slavery*, 207.

53. Tocqueville, *Writings on Empire and Slavery*, 207–8.

54. Carolyn Fick has shown in detail how the conflict in late 1790s Saint Domingue between the
peasant class and Toussaint Louverture centered around precisely this dispute over the nature of the
freedom they had won from France. See Carolyn Fick, *The Making of Haiti: The Saint Domingue
Revolution from Below* (Knoxville: University of Tennessee Press, 1990).

Tocqueville recognized that the British decision to implement an "apprenticeship" after the nominal abolition of slavery in essence amounted to slavery under another name. Upon the completion of this delay, however, Tocqueville faulted the British for immediately granting full citizenship rights to the former slaves: "The workers of the colonies had precisely the same rights those of the metropole enjoyed; like them, they could, at their pleasure, decide with sovereign power how to use their time, set their rates, and determine what to do with their wages. This complete transformation of colonial society into free society," Tocqueville concluded, "was premature."[55] Many of those who formerly worked the sugar plantations as slaves, Tocqueville observed, quite naturally preferred to work elsewhere. "That a certain number of workers would leave the sugar refineries, preferring other industries, was the necessary consequence of freedom." The result of this labor scarcity was a rise in wages and decline in sugar production. The solution Tocqueville proposed was, here as in 1839, "to prohibit them for a certain time from becoming landowners."[56]

This remedy Tocqueville favored subordinated the bourgeois defense of a free and open labor market to the need of colonial capitalism to maintain a sufficient supply of wage laborers. The choice of former slaves to invest whatever capital they possessed in small, private landholdings rather than in their own wage labor on the sugar plantations threatened, Tocqueville maintained, the survival of the plantation system itself. The English experience had shown that the possession of privately held land sufficient to meet one's basic needs meant that free laborers could demand higher wages than a landless proletariat. Tocqueville never stopped to ask whether this incipient turn toward self-sufficiency would be to the benefit of the former slaves. Instead, he argued that self-sufficiency would "deliver a fatal blow to the sugar industry," which in turn would necessarily lead to "a general crisis that, after first striking the whites, will necessarily extend to all the other classes."[57]

In his concluding comments on the Broglie report, Tocqueville observed that the committee decided, in light of the British experience of emancipation, to institute a ten-year delay on abolition. He remarked that upon abolition, the former slaves would not immediately enjoy the full rights of French citizens, but instead the commission recommended "to qualify the freedom of the emancipated Negroes in the following three ways: The former slaves will be required to reside in the colony; although free to choose their profession and the master under whose direction they want to work, they will be neither permitted to remain idle nor to work only for themselves; the maximum and minimum wages

55. Tocqueville, *Writings on Empire and Slavery*, 214.
56. Tocqueville, *Writings on Empire and Slavery*, 215.
57. Tocqueville, *Writings on Empire and Slavery*, 216.

will be fixed by the governor."[58] Tocqueville commented that "these arrangements are transitional" in order to ensure the smooth change from a slaveholding regime to one based upon the free labor of the landless Negroes, or what his contemporary Karl Marx would call a proletariat, that is, a class forced to undertake capitalist wage labor due to their nonpossession of the means of production. If "the emancipated Negroes were neither allowed to live as vagabonds nor to procure a little domain for themselves, and were reduced to hiring out their services for a living," Tocqueville concluded approvingly, "it is very likely that most of them would remain in the sugar refineries, and that the cost of running these establishments would not increase immeasurably."[59] This period of transition, the committee advised, "could end after five years."[60] This five-year maintenance of servitude was, Tocqueville maintained, something the state "owed the colonists."[61] What France might have "owed" to the Africans it had enslaved is a question Tocqueville never bothered to ponder in these writings. Of apparently greater interest to him was the calculation of the proper indemnity due to the colonists for their loss of "property": "As the capital owed for the colonies' 250,000 slaves, at 1,200 francs a head, comes to 300 million, half that, or 150 million, represented by interest at 4 percent of 6 million, would be granted the colonists."[62] The black slaves would then be called upon to pay through their own labor for the remaining half of this indemnity, a cost to be added to the apparently insufficient price in suffering and forced labor they had already paid to that point.

VICTOR SCHOELCHER AND THE INVIOLABILITY OF THE RIGHTS OF MAN

Among Tocqueville's contemporary abolitionists there existed others who defended both immediate abolition (like Tocqueville) as well as immediate enfranchisement. Victor Schoelcher stands as the protypical example of this strain of radical abolitionism in the period. Schoelcher, the architect of France's second universal and immediate abolition of slavery (the first had occurred in 1794 but was reversed by Napoleon in 1802), was the son of a successful porcelain maker. Schoelcher's inheritance allowed him to live as a bourgeois *rentier,* and he used his inheritance in large part to travel around the world. Schoelcher made his first trip to the Americas (Mexico, Cuba, the southern United States) in 1829–30,

58. Tocqueville, *Writings on Empire and Slavery,* 219–20.
59. Tocqueville, *Writings on Empire and Slavery,* 221.
60. Tocqueville, *Writings on Empire and Slavery,* 220.
61. Tocqueville, *Writings on Empire and Slavery,* 222.
62. Tocqueville, *Writings on Empire and Slavery,* 224.

where he first encountered the reality of slavery, a discovery that would reshape his life. In 1833 he published his first major condemnation of slavery, *On the Enslavement of Blacks and Colonial Legislation*. He traveled again to the Americas in 1840–41, this time visiting for an extended period the Caribbean islands of Jamaica, Antigua, Dominica, Martinique, Guadeloupe, and Haiti. There, Schoelcher gathered extensive data on actually existing slavery, as well as on the results of its recent abolition (1834) in the English colonies.[63] The result of this second trip was Schoelcher's most famous book: *Des Colonies françaises: Abolition immédiate de l'esclavage* (On the French Colonies: Immediate Abolition of Slavery).[64] As its title indicates, by the time of this second trip, Schoelcher had abandoned his early defense of gradual abolition and called instead for universal and immediate abolition with no intermediary period of "acculturation" to liberty or wage labor for the slaves.[65]

Following the revolution of 1848, François Arago, the Minister of the Marine and Colonies in the revolutionary government, appointed Schoelcher vice-secretary of state to the colonies and president of the government's Commission on the Abolition of Slavery. Schoelcher subsequently served as representative of Martinique and Guadeloupe in the French National Assembly, before going into a long period of political exile (1850–70) following Louis Napoleon's coup d'état. He once again served as representative for Martinique under the Third Republic, publishing regularly on subjects such as colonialism, slavery, and musicology until his death in 1893. Long familiar with the events of the Haitian Revolution, Schoelcher published in 1889 his monumental study *Vie de Toussaint Louverture* (The Life of Toussaint Louverture), which still ranks as one of the finest studies of the Haitian Revolution to date.[66]

The key moment in Schoelcher's life undoubtedly occurred on March 4, 1848, when, upon his return from a trip to Senegal, he met with Minister of the Colonies François Arago. Arago had already held meetings with colonial delegates, who assured him of the need to proceed slowly with any eventual emancipation decree, which, they maintained, would inevitably lead to the economic ruin of the colonies.[67] On March 4 Schoelcher met with Arago and convinced him to call on the government to adopt the principle of universal, immediate emancipation with full rights of citizenship. Arago proceeded to put Schoelcher himself in charge of the process, charging him to lead a commission that would

63. Schoelcher was in fact the founder of comparative historical study of the Americas in France.
64. Victor Schoelcher, *Des Colonies françaises: Abolition immédiate de l'esclavage. Préface de Lucien Abenon* (1842; Paris: Editions du CTHS, 1998).
65. See Nelly Schmidt, *Victor Schoelcher et l'abolition de l'esclavage* (Paris: Fayard, 1994), 30.
66. Victor Schoelcher, *Vie de Toussaint Louverture* (1889; Paris: Ed. Karthala, 1982).
67. Schmidt, *Victor Schoelcher et l'abolition de l'esclavage,* 103.

"prepare without delay the act of the emancipation of the blacks and the measures necessary for its success."[68] Tocqueville actually served on this commission
alongside Schoelcher, frequently taking the side of the colonists in their debates,
arguing against Schoelcher's call to indemnify the slaves as well as the colonists.[69]
Though Schoelcher only retained this position until July 21, in that short period,
he was able to oversee the transformation of his ideas into political reality upon
the abolition of French slavery on April 27, 1848. "I accomplished a great thing,"
he wrote in 1849, "I had this extraordinary happiness, rarely granted to a man,
to witness the triumph of a cause by my efforts that was the object of my life."[70]
In addition to this success, his proposals and speeches in the French Assembly
would define in large part the development of the French Caribbean Overseas
Colonies, to the point that in 1946 these would be declared "French Overseas
Departments" as Schoelcher had explicitly called for over a century before.

While both Tocqueville and Schoelcher were socially progressive in the context of the politics of the July Monarchy, the distinction between the two can be
readily discerned if one compares Tocqueville's call for an immediate but limited
emancipation with Schoelcher's defense of immediate emancipation with full
civil rights in his 1842 text. *Des Colonies françaises: Abolition immediate de l'esclavage*
explored in some four hundred pages the contemporary situation of slavery in
the French colonies of the period. The book accumulated a wealth of detailed
description, the result of Schoelcher's onsite investigations, to convince the
reader of the soundness of its judgment. Successive chapters survey topics such as
"The Condition of Slaves," marriage, punishment, "the color prejudice," labor,
indemnification, religion, and the process of emancipation itself.

Though Schoelcher spent the majority of the volume analyzing in detail the
actual conditions of French slavery, he made clear at a number of points that he
based his call for abolition on the absolute inviolability of human rights. "One
can no longer simply examine the [empirical] vices and abuses of servitude . . . :
we argue our case in the name of the imprescriptible rights of man; we pursue
slavery, beyond any practical consideration, because it offends humanity. . . . It is
not a question of beneficent or cruel treatment. It is a question of principle."[71]
The crime of slavery was precisely that it imposed limits on the autonomous
development of a portion of humanity: "Does man have in his brain but mere
instincts? Is man made to remain at the instinctual level, is it not a crime of
lèse-humanité to impose limits upon his development?"[72] Schoelcher understood

68. Cited in Schmidt, *Victor Schoelcher et l'abolition de l'esclavage*, 103. All translations are mine unless
otherwise noted.
69. Schmidt, *Victor Schoelcher et l'abolition de l'esclavage*, 120.
70. Cited in Schmidt, *Victor Schoelcher et l'abolition de l'esclavage*, 144.
71. Schoelcher, *Des Colonies françaises*, 27.
72. Schoelcher, *Des Colonies françaises*, 49.

slavery as the bestialization of humanity and its exclusion from society: "Servitude is the annihilation of all rights and faculties, an eternal civil and moral mutilation. . . . A slave has hardly anything in common with a man, save his animal form. He is an isolated being who has no legal relation with the other members of society, he is a cultivation machine; he is a mere thing."[73] And yet a slave is undeniably a human being: "he thinks, he feels the emotions of happiness and the anguish of pain; the desire for approbation leads him to heroic deeds, and egoism to reprehensible acts."[74] The apparent differences between the races may "make of him another type of human, but they will never prevent him from being human; and that being so, nothing can excuse his enslavement."[75]

Like Tocqueville, Schoelcher argued that abolition was an inevitable process. "Whether the colonists agree or not, they must resign themselves to it. There is no longer any force in the world that can prevent its triumph; it is carried by the current of progressive ideas [idées de réforme] at such a height of demonstrated truth that to deny it today would be to lose oneself in mere opinion."[76] The cause of abolition is absolute: the colonists should recognize that "it is in the name of the progress of human morality that torture is abolished and that France demands the abolition of servitude; [it is] in the name of charity that the nation has resolved to purify a social state that offends reason, justice, and all humanity."[77] As Kant had argued in the Conflict of the Faculties, the idea of the French Revolution had become a world historical fate: "Liberty, Equality, Fraternity; in these three words, lie the inevitable destiny of humankind. Whoever wishes to stand against it will be broken, in the Antilles as in Europe."[78] Unlike Tocqueville, who invoked these same ideals of the French Revolution in reference to nationalistic grandeur, Schoelcher sustained the Jacobin view that they must apply to all humans.

In contrast to Tocqueville's recommendations to the French government, Schoelcher maintained a strict fidelity to an uncompromised abolition. For Schoelcher, any intermediary period between abolition and full accession of former slaves to their civic and human rights would amount quite simply to a continuation of slavery under another name: "If to give the blacks the freedom due to them one thinks it necessary to pass through an intermediary regime; and if to obtain the desired and desirable assent of the colonists one left it up to them to indicate the nature of this regime, I submit that [the result would be] the prolon-

73. Schoelcher, Des Colonies françaises, 54.
74. Schoelcher, Des Colonies françaises, 149.
75. Schoelcher, Des Colonies françaises, 152.
76. Schoelcher, Des Colonies françaises, 255.
77. Schoelcher, Des Colonies françaises, 256.
78. Schoelcher, Des Colonies françaises, 257.

gation of slavery under another name."[79] Unlike Tocqueville, who repeatedly based his analysis on the needs of French capital or of the imperial nation-state when discussing the possible modalities of emancipation, Schoelcher analyzed the question of emancipation and its modality from the subject position of the slave. "This half-liberty [in a postemancipation transitional period], after the heightened expectations that the proclamation of principle leads the blacks to conceive, [would be] a cause for discontent."[80] Schoelcher argued that the future of French Caribbean society depended on an uncompromising equality of citizenship. "Any compromise could only embitter and poison the atmosphere. . . . Either leave servitude as it is or grant total liberty. . . . No intermediary class, no newly freed wards of the state, no half citizens, these would destroy the homogeneity that a society must have to move forward."[81] While Tocqueville recommended forbidding freed slaves from owning plots of land for a limited period, Schoelcher recommended (though his commission refused to endorse) proactive land reform, the distribution of small plots of land, along with the much more radical proposal for remuneration not only to the slave owners, but also to the former slaves themselves.[82] Schoelcher had no illusions that the process of emancipation could be engineered to eliminate any possible social upheaval. "One must simply resign oneself to the turmoil that follows any great disruption of a political order, just as is true in the natural world."[83]

Schoelcher argued against those defenders of slavery and more pragmatic abolitionists such as Tocqueville who claimed that freedom could only be learned by delaying its implementation. "I will always believe that mass emancipation alone can permit the slaves to learn the duties of citizenship. . . . To think one could teach freedom to a being remaining outside freedom! One might just as well try to teach an infant to swim without putting them into the water. . . . The blacks will become accustomed to their rights by practicing them, to their duties in fulfilling them, just as French bourgeois become good jurors by exercising the eminent function of juror."[84]

Schoelcher explicitly placed human rights and a radical vision of remunerative justice above the economic good of both the state and slave owners. Like Robespierre before him, he went so far as to call explicitly for the abandonment of the colonies if they should prove to be workable only by slave labor. "I proclaim 'no

79. Schoelcher, *Des Colonies françaises*, 366.
80. Schoelcher, *Des Colonies françaises*, 367.
81. Schoelcher, *Des Colonies françaises*, 367. Schoelcher is likely explicitly addressing many of his comments to Tocqueville's report, which he refers to at one point as "the famous Tocqueville report" (*Des Colonies françaises*, 373).
82. Schmidt, *Victor Schoelcher et l'abolition de l'esclavage*, 109.
83. Schoelcher, *Des Colonies françaises*, 368.
84. Schoelcher, *Des Colonies françaises*, 370, 371.

colonies if they cannot exist without slavery.' Slavery violates the principle of liberty, a principle that is not only a convention made among men, but also a natural truth that has become fully evident; . . . it is the supreme destiny of man."[85] Schoelcher, alone in his era, then concluded his most famous book in visionary and truly prophetic terms with precisely the point that Tocqueville never deigned to consider: *why*, in fact, should the former slaves, if they are to be considered full citizens subject to all human and civic rights, be forced at all to work on the plantations where they had spent their lives as tortured captives? "All the sophisms in the world cannot go against right. The blacks must be free, because it is just. If, when they are free, they do not wish to cultivate the land beyond their own needs, as we are told, either they should be replaced by immigrants who will work, or we should give back the islands to nature, which did not make them fit for man, since it is impossible to exploit them without violence toward our fellow man."[86]

While arguing for the universal abolition of slavery, Tocqueville, as we have seen, viewed slaves as morally unformed beings; humans, certainly, but beings not yet able to function autonomously in democratic society. The roots of Tocqueville's paternalistic and condescending views of blacks are perhaps to be found in a laconic passage in *Democracy in America,* in which the author observed with authority: "Up to the present, everywhere where the whites have been the strongest, they held the Negroes in debasement or in slavery. Everywhere where the Negroes have been the strongest, they destroyed the whites; this is the only account that has ever been opened among the races."[87] Here, Tocqueville's tone of scientific objectivity does no more than repeat his epoch's racist condemnation of the only successful struggle in human history to have overthrown a slaveholding system: the Haitian Revolution. In 1832 Tocqueville could be referring to no other event, one that had so outraged a world grounded and dependent upon the enslavement of a portion of the human population that enormous efforts had been made to silence it, to falsify it, and to demonize it as an eruption of pure, barbaric violence—in short, to reduce Haiti as both idea and reality to no more than the "poorest country in the Western Hemisphere."[88] Tocqueville in turn repeated the predominant nineteenth-century clichés that saw Haitians as bloodthirsty barbarians. In his 1839 report he in fact referred more explicitly to the

---

85. Schoelcher, *Des Colonies françaises,* 385.

86. Schoelcher, *Des Colonies françaises,* 387. The former option is exactly what would happen in the decades following the 1848 emancipation, when Martinique and Guadeloupe would bring significant numbers of East Indian and Chinese workers to the sugar plantations.

87. Tocqueville, *Democracy in America,* 160.

88. See Michel-Rolph Trouillot, *Silencing the Past: Power and the Production of History* (Boston: Beacon, 1995); and David Geggus, ed., *The Impact of the Haitian Revolution in the Atlantic World* (Columbia: University of South Carolina Press, 2001).

Haitian Revolution: the memory of Saint Domingue (Tocqueville used the name not of the world's first black republic, but referred nostalgically to the former French colony) signified for him only "bloody confrontations, where expulsion, and the massacre of whites must follow."[89] That the Haitian Revolution may have signified more than this, that it may indeed have surpassed in some respects the French Revolution that inspired it and that Tocqueville knew so well, he either did not know or could not admit. Schoelcher, who had traveled to Haiti and studied its revolution in detail, knew better, and perhaps one may locate his faith in the maturity and enlightenment of the slaves in this familiarity.

DE LA DÉMOCRATIE EN HAÏTI

In fact, had Tocqueville spent the time to inform himself *de la démocratie en Haïti* as he had seen fit to do in the United States, he would have found that, in contrast to the European vision of bloodthirsty barbarians, the Haitian abolition of slavery in its constitutions of 1801 and 1804 instituted the world's first de jure postracial society. All those who set foot upon Haitian soil, where slavery had been universally and without reserve abolished, were declared to be "black" citizens.[90] In light of the conflict between property rights and human rights that I have argued distinguish Tocqueville's and Schoelcher's respective views on abolition, it is worth recalling the tradition of political thought from which the latter's claim stemmed. Louverture's 1801 constitution was the first in western modernity to have resolved the conflict between universal human rights based on natural law and the defense of private property. As Florence Gauthier has shown, the French Declarations of the Rights of Man and Citizen (1789, 1793) had left this contradiction unresolved.[91] On the one hand, the natural right of all human beings to their freedom is inalienable and universal; on this point the American, French, and Haitian revolutions all agreed. If this is so, however, the right to property must be a subsidiary, secondary right that can only be sustained insofar as it supports the primary human right to "life, liberty, and the pursuit of happiness." The right to property cannot be absolute. When it infringes on natural human rights (as in the case of slavery, where one human would constitute the "property" of another), it must be limited.

From 1789 to the definitive abandonment of natural right in the convention's liberal constitution of *l'An III* (1795), this contradiction remained unresolved.

89. Tocqueville, *Rapport fait au nom de la commission,* 25.
90. See Fischer, *Modernity Disavowed,* on this unique aspect of the Haitian Revolution.
91. Florence Gauthier, *Triomphe et mort du droit naturel en Révolution: 1789–1795–1802* (Paris: PUF, 1992).

Both universal natural rights and the social right to property were posited as absolutes.[92] Before 1801 the only attempt to resolve this contradiction had been Robespierre's project for a Declaration of the Rights of Man and Citizen submitted to the convention on April 24, 1793.[93] This document explicitly subordinated the right to material property to natural human rights (the right to existence, liberty, and the fullest possible development of one's human faculties). "The goal of all political association," Robespierre maintained in his proposed declaration, "is the maintenance of the natural and imprescriptible rights of man, and the development of all his faculties."[94] The right to property, Robespierre maintained, "can prejudice neither security, nor liberty, nor existence, nor the property of one's fellow men. All possessions, all traffic that violates this principle is illicit and immoral."[95]

For Robespierre, society had only one goal, a raison d'être that grounded and determined all other secondary considerations regarding its structure: this was not the fulfillment of the imperial destiny of the nation-state, nor to assure the material prosperity of its citizens, but to realize the right of all humans to self-preservation, freedom, and self-realization. Though the Jacobins adopted his proposal on April 21, 1793, this radical subordination of property rights to natural rights was eliminated in the final, compromise declaration adopted by the convention on May 29. The foundation of a society based on an unequivocal, uncompromised fidelity to human rights would be delayed until Toussaint's constitution of 1801.

That Toussaint Louverture forced the masses of freed slaves to return to the plantation when he came to power in Saint Domingue in the late 1790s is both unfortunate and well known. His increasing recourse to forced labor after 1796 unarguably betrayed to an important extent the revolution he had helped to focus on the single criterion of undivided, universal freedom. Historians will no doubt continue to debate whether this political choice was warranted, given the need to rebuild the colony's economic base to ensure the continuation of the abolition of slavery, or a mere regression on the part of Toussaint into relative tyranny and personal alienation from the mass of former slaves. The publishing of the 1801 Saint Domingue constitution, however, was nonetheless the culmination of Toussaint Louverture's decadelong attempt to reorient the society of Saint Domingue away from the arbitrary violence of slavery and to ground social

92. This is the case even in the otherwise highly progressive constitution of 1793, which only defended "les droits de l'homme *en société*" (Gauthier, *Triomphe et mort*, 99). Here, in the most radical constitution of the period, natural rights were already reduced to mere goods, an object given to citizens by governments, rather than to all humans by their nature.

93. See Gauthier, *Triomphe et mort*, 74–92.

94. Robespierre, *Discours et rapports à la Convention* (Paris: Union Générale d'Éditions, 1965), 123.

95. Robespierre, *Discours et rapports à la Convention*, 120.

relations on the universal human right to autonomy. Its publication marked the moment in which a colonized society first became an autonomous society, in the sense not only of a society that gives itself its own laws[96]—the same could be said of the slaveholding societies of America in 1776 or France in 1789—but autonomous in the more limited, Kantian sense of a society in which such auto-constitution is specifically directed by a criterion of universality. In the long and complex history of the struggle for such a self-constituted society, the date of 1801 can rightfully take pride of place as the *first* moment in human history in which a society not only composed itself, but did so, for all its secondary contra-dictions and shortcomings, upon the constitutional basis of universal rights.

In contrast to both the delaying tactics of the abolitionist pragmatists such as Condorcet and Tocqueville, as well as to their paternalist assurances that slaves were not "ready" for freedom and had to be prepared for its coming over many years, Schoelcher's human rights–based approach to continental abolitionism managed to implement a full and uncompromised transformation of slaveholding society in 1848. The architect of France's 1848 abolition was the most radical, uncompromising champion of an idealist conception of emancipation from slav-ery since Toussaint Louverture himself. "The right of man to freedom, to the possession of one's self," Schoelcher wrote, "contains at once for him both the moral and material good. This is not a convention of the age, of place and cir-cumstances, it is a universally recognized truth, and it takes by this title the name of principle, in the same way that fidelity to a sworn faith is a principle that no one in the world can contradict."[97] Like Tocqueville, Schoelcher traveled to the Americas, in his case to New Orleans and the Caribbean, but he took from this empirical observation of slavery a principled determination that the claims of human rights trumped those of capital. He expressed this conviction to the world in the violent idealist equation encapsulated in the subtitle of his most famous book: *Immediate Abolition of Slavery*. When the moment came in 1848 to abolish slavery, it was Schoelcher alone who argued for an uncompromised, total, and immediate abolition, against the tergiversations of his colleagues. Schoelcher's was an unyielding and effective fidelity to a radical conception of universal human rights, one he inherited from the architects of the Haitian abolition of slavery. Schoelcher's most famous interjection into the debate on abolition thus stands in stark contrast to Tocqueville's celebration of French colonial violence (in Algeria) and the defense of the rights of property holders over the indivisible

96. Cornelius Castoriadis defines an autonomous society in such a fashion, as one that gives itself its "own laws, and [that] can change them when the need presents itself" (*Une société à la dérive: Entretiens et débats 1974–1997* [Paris: Seuil, 2005], 123).

97. Cited in Aimé Césaire, *Victor Schoelcher et l'abolition de l'esclavage, suivi de trois discours* (Paris: Le Capucin, 2004), 13.

human rights of the enslaved: "One can no more abolish slavery humanely than one can redeem a murder."[98]

CONCLUSION

If both Tocqueville and Schoelcher brought their travels in the Americas to bear upon the legacy of human rights inherited from 1789 and its relation to French imperialism and slavery, their reflections might well serve as a spur to readers to carry forward this reflection into the contemporary context of global imperialism. This is a period when slavery, as commonly defined, far from having disappeared, currently exists in greater numbers—at least twenty-seven million—than at any other point in human history.[99] To undertake such reflection might also involve interrogating the systematic attempts of both the United States and France over the past two centuries to isolate a nascent black republic that dared in 1804 to call for—and actually to implement within its own territory—the universal destruction of slavery amid a world system that would continue to depend on it for many decades. This was a republic from which France would extort a ninety-million-franc payment—for loss of "property"—to obtain recognition of its independence in 1826, and that the United States would not formally recognize until 1862. This was a republic the United States would occupy from 1914 to 1934, and again (in cooperation with the United Nations) in 1994 and 2004. This was a republic whose first democratically elected president, Jean-Bertrand Aristide, was overthrown by a CIA-supported coup in 1991, and again—following a 2001 reelection unanimously vetted by international observers—in 2004. Though each of us must draw our own conclusions from the available evidence, the United States' multifaceted attempts systematically to weaken, if not destroy, Haitian sovereignty since 1804 are by now well documented.[100]

More generally, it seems clear that since at least the end of the Second World War, "democracy in America" has meant, in part, imperialist intervention in other democratic states whose leaders—including democratically elected presidents such as Allende and Aristide—were seen as a threat to various dimensions

98. Cited in Césaire, *Victor Schoelcher et l'abolition de l'esclavage,* 24.

99. See *Hidden Slaves: Forced Labor in the United States,* available online at: http://freetheslaves.net/home.php. See also http://www.antislavery.org/index.htm.

100. See Paul Farmer's now classic study *The Uses of Haiti* (Monroe, Maine: Common Courage Press, 1994) for an extensive description and referencing of this sad history. More extensive documentation of the most recent phase of U.S. interventionism appears in Robert Fatton, *Haiti's Predatory Republic: The Unending Transition to Democracy* (Boulder, Colo.: Lynn Rienner Publishers, 2002); Alex Dupuy, *The Prophet and Power: Jean-Bertrand Aristide, the International Community, and Haiti* (Lanham, Md.: Rowman and Littlefield, 2007); and Peter Hallward, *Damming the Flood: Haiti, Aristide, and the Politics of Containment* (London: Verso, 2007).

of U.S. regional or international hegemony. In short, the conflict between hegemonic needs of the imperial nation-state and the ever-elusive implementation of universal human rights remains as much a problem for us today as in the time of Tocqueville and Schoelcher. Tocqueville's repeated and ultimately failed attempts to push the July Monarchy toward the immediate abolition of slavery, and Victor Schoelcher's successful conclusion of that process in the brief window of opportunity that was France's revolutionary Second Republic, should compel us to interrogate further the problematic imbrication of human rights deployment within the global network of imperial nation-states. These are states that were once responsible for the systematic institution of slave labor within the modern world system of agrarian capitalism, and that, long after the nominal abolition of slavery, continue to undermine the process of democratization abroad in the name of "life, liberty, and the pursuit of happiness" within their own borders. As citizens of such democracies, it is our responsibility to offer systematic, critical dissent to such policies undertaken in our name, whenever we find that they conflict with the norms of human rights that we, like Tocqueville and Schoelcher before us, have inherited from the American, French, and Haitian Revolutions.

PART THREE

FRENCH VIEWS OF AMERICA

5

A PRECURSOR OF TOCQUEVILLE
Victor Jacquemont's Reflections on America

Aurelian Craiutu

> Nulle part il n'ya plus d'esprit d'association et moins
> de société.
> —*Victor Jacquemont*

THE FRENCH DIALOGUE WITH AMERICA

In the past few years, the political and cultural dialogue between France and the United States has been marked by controversies and tensions that have given to the most vocal French critics of America an unexpected opportunity to recruit new converts and gain renewed popularity.[1] Many French intellectuals have voiced their dissatisfaction with various aspects of American society, culture, and politics, which they have taken as a symbol of the irreversible decline of the Western civilization.[2] Nonetheless, as Jacques Portes has recently reminded us,

A previous version of this chapter was presented at the conference "America Seen through Foreign Eyes," Indiana University, Bloomington (March 2005), co-sponsored by Indiana University's College of Arts and Humanities Institute, the WEST Institute, the Department of Political Science, and the Office of International Scholars. Some of the arguments of this chapter draw upon the ideas that I originally developed in Aurelian Craiutu, "In Search for Happiness: Victor Jacquemont's Travel to America," *The European Legacy* 13, no. 1 (2008): 13–33. I would like to thank Doina Harshanyi, Jeremy Jennings, Nick Nesbitt, Vladimir Protopopescu, and K. Steven Vincent for their valuable comments and suggestions on previous drafts of this essay. Also, special thanks are due to the Earhart Foundation and the Social Philosophy and Policy Center at Bowling Green State University for a generous research fellowship that allowed me to revise and complete this chapter for publication in due course.

1. See, for example, John J. Miller and Mark Molesky, *Our Oldest Enemy: A History of America's Disastrous Relationship with France* (New York: Doubleday, 2004).

2. Such a recent critique can be found, for example, in Emmanuel Todd, *Après Empire* (Paris:

the prominence of these French critics of America should not make us ignore the complexity of Franco-American relations over the past two centuries.[3] America has had many friends in France, some of whom (like Tocqueville) are well known today, while others have remained in relative obscurity until now.

As René Rémond pointed out in his magisterial study of the image of the United States in France, during most of the Bourbon Restoration, French public opinion looked favorably at America and was optimistic with regard to the stability and future of its political institutions.[4] To give just a few examples, the French Ideologues admired the American constitution and institutions, and their appreciation of America resonated with Thomas Jefferson, who translated into English Destutt de Tracy's commentary on Montesquieu's *Spirit of the Laws* (the book first appeared in English in 1811 and only eight years later in French).[5] In part 6 of her *Considerations on the Principal Events of the French Revolution,* the bible of all French Restoration liberals, Madame de Staël unambiguously expressed her appreciation for the American political experiment and equated the government of the United States with the government of reason: "There is a nation which will one day be very great, the Americans. . . . What is there more honorable for mankind than this new world which has established itself without the prejudices of the old? This new world where religion exists in all its fervor without needing the support of the state to maintain it, where the law commands by the respect it inspires although no military power backs it up."[6] Shortly before her untimely death in 1817, she confessed to an American friend, George Bancroft, who paid her a visit in Paris: "You are the vanguard of the human race, you are the future of the world."[7]

Madame de Staël was not alone among her compatriots in expressing her confidence in America's radiant future. Her views were echoed a few years later by Charles-Arnold Scheffer (1796–1853), the former secretary of La Fayette who

---

Gallimard, 2003). Todd's book was reviewed by Henri Astier in the *Times Literary Supplement,* January 10, 2003, 3–4.

3. Jacques Portes, *Fascination and Misgivings: The United States in French Opinion, 1870–1914* (Cambridge: Cambridge University Press, 2000). Also see Jeremy Jennings's contribution ("French Visions of America: From Tocqueville to the Civil War") in this volume.

4. René Rémond, *Les États-Unis devant l'opinion française, 1815–1852,* 2 vols. (Paris: Armand Colin, 1962). Also worth consulting are Durand Echeverria, *Mirage in the West: A History of the French Image of American Society to 1815* (Princeton: Princeton University Press, 1958); and Philippe Roger, *L'Ennemi américain* (Paris: Seuil, 2002). An English translation of Roger's book, *The American Enemy,* was published by the University of Chicago Press in 2005.

5. See Rémond, *Les États-Unis devant l'opinion française,* 2:631–34. The political ideas of the French Ideologues are discussed in Cheryl Welch, *Liberty and Utility: The French Ideologues and the Transformation of Liberalism* (New York: Columbia University Press, 1984).

6. See Madame de Staël, *Considerations on the Principal Events of the French Revolution,* ed. Aurelian Craiutu (Indianapolis: Liberty Fund, 2008), 707.

7. *Life, Letters, and Journals of George Ticknor* (Boston and New York, 1909), 1:132–33.

in his influential history of the United States published in 1825 claimed that "the American federation showed the entire world the "true popular government and liberty."[8] For Scheffer and his colleagues who contributed to the *Revue américaine* (edited by Armand Carrel from July 1826 to June 1827), the republican political experiment that succeeded in America had a *universal* importance and was expected to pave the way for similar political developments in Europe. The French admired the wisdom of American laws, principles, and institutions,[9] and regarded the American constitution as a model document that successfully combined the highest degree of individual liberty with social order.[10] Finally, many French observers of the American scene emphasized the connection between liberty and religion in the United States and pointed to the important role played by religious toleration, liberty of conscience, and freedom of the press in securing individual liberty and general prosperity.

A ROMANTIC MIND IN AN AGE OF TRANSITION

The wide range of French attitudes toward America can be best explored in the writings of Victor Jacquemont, one of the most prominent representatives of the new generation that came of age around 1820.[11] Born in Paris on August 8, 1801, to a family that was close to the French Ideologues, Jacquemont was fortunate to live in a period of unprecedented social and political change, in which the old battle between the Revolution and the Old Regime was waged once again by new actors pursuing widely different political agendas. The first years of the Bourbon Restoration were a remarkable golden age of political thought; social, political, and economic changes were accompanied by new currents in music, literature, painting, and philosophy.[12] The enthusiasm and energy of the postrevolutionary generation seemed boundless as many young minds were engaged in a fervent quest for a new "secular ministry," to use Paul Bénichou's words.[13]

In one of the most important intellectual manifestos published during this

---

8. As quoted in Rémond, *Les États-Unis devant l'opinion française*, 2:532. Unless otherwise noted, all translations are mine.

9. On this topic, see Rémond, *Les États-Unis devant l'opinion française*, 2:540–43.

10. *Le National*, May 29, 1832.

11. For a comprehensive analysis of this generation, see Alan B. Spitzer, *The French Generation of 1820* (Princeton: Princeton University Press, 1987).

12. For more information, see Aurelian Craiutu, *Liberalism under Siege: The Political Thought of the French Doctrinaires* (Lanham, Md.: Lexington Books, 2003), chaps. 2–3; Paul Thureau-Dangin, *Le Parti libéral sous la Restauration* (Paris, 1888), 191–264; and Guillaume de Bertier de Sauvigny, *The Bourbon Restoration* (Philadelphia: University of Pennsylvania Press, 1966), 328–62.

13. Paul Bénichou, *The Consecration of the Writer, 1750–1830*, trans. Mark K. Jensen (Lincoln: University of Nebraska Press, 1999), 11.

period, "How Dogmas Come to an End" (1823), Théodore Jouffroy, who belonged to the same generation as Jacquemont, offered a powerful account of the mission of his generation. Born in the bosom of a society prone to apathy, fatigue, and skepticism, its young members grew up immunized against the seduction of old political and philosophical dogmas. Restless and impatient, these young Turks sought to break free from the mold of the past and launched themselves into new adventures with a renewed confidence in their unique mission. Unlike their parents, who had focused only on the destruction of the Old Regime, the young minds concentrated on the other half of their task, the building of a new political system for postrevolutionary France.[14] They knew that the future was dependent on their choices and believed that they were called to discover a new doctrine suitable to their rapidly changing world.

In many respects, Victor Jacquemont epitomized the restless intellectual in love with exotic landscapes and cultures and in search of romantic adventures. He achieved posthumous fame primarily because of his letters and diaries that made him one of the greatest *écrivains voyageurs* of the nineteenth century, whose life abounded in unusual adventures and experiences. Jacquemont traveled to America and India and left behind original accounts of his voyages. Although close to the young members of the staff of *Le Globe* (born between 1795 and 1805), his heart remained immune to the temptations of the political and spiritual eclecticism preached by Cousin, Jouffroy, and their followers. Victor's father, Vinceslas, was a philosopher and close friend of Destutt de Tracy, the famous Ideologue whose commentary on Montesquieu had been translated into English by Jefferson in 1811. Vinceslas was arrested and imprisoned by Napoleon in 1808. The Jacquemonts were regular guests of the Tracys at Paray-le-Frésil and La Grange, where Victor came into contact with the legendary figure La Fayette, who played a key role in his intellectual formation. Due to La Fayette's generous hospitality, the young Victor eventually made the acquaintance of many other distinguished individuals, such as the painter Ary Scheffer, the Duke and Duchess de Broglie, and Sir and Lady Morgan. It was in this circle centered around La Fayette that the young Victor familiarized himself for the first time with the principles and institutions of the American democracy.

Politics proved, however, to be little else than a *violon d'Ingres* for Victor Jacquemont, who initially pursued classical studies and chemistry. An unfortunate laboratory accident eventually prompted him to switch to botany, geology, and mineralogy. A founding member of the Société d'Histoire Naturelle in Paris,

---

14. Théodore Jouffroy, "How Dogmas Come to an End," in *Philosophical Miscellanies,* trans. and ed. George Ripley (Boston: Hilliard, Gray & Co., 1838), 2:137. For a good overview of eclecticism, see Bénichou, *The Consecration of the Writer,* 170–82. On *Le Globe,* see Jean-Jacques Goblot *La jeune France libérale. Le Globe et son groupe littéraire* (Paris: Plon, 1995).

Jacquemont was destined to become one of the most famous travelers and explorers of the nineteenth century, one who embraced his new career with unbound enthusiasm. It was during one of his early trips in southern France that he made the acquaintance of Achille Chaper and Jean de Charpentier, who became two of his closest friends and confidants.

In Paris, Victor Jacquemont attended some of the most prestigious social circles and spent long hours at the Jardin des Plantes. He was welcomed (along with J. J. Ampère, Vitet, and Dubois) into the highly selective salons of Baron Gérard, Baron de Mareste, and Baron Cuvier, and he regularly attended the reunions organized by Tracy and La Fayette. It was there that he made the acquaintance of Delècluze, Mérimée and Stendhal (Stendhal's *Rome, Naples, and Florence,* was one of the favorite books of Madame de Tracy).[15] Although eighteen years older than Jacquemont, Stendhal developed a particular appreciation for Victor's talents and enthusiasm and admired his courage to speak his mind freely.[16] What brought Stendhal and Jacquemont together, despite their age difference, was their common passion for music and opera. Both were devotees of Italian music and rarely missed the best concerts in Paris, staged by Rossini and featuring stars like the soprano Giuditta Pasta, who would soon become a close acquaintance of Victor. It was not long after that that he succumbed to the charms of Eros, again in the guise of another Italian singer, Adélaïde Schiasetti, whose beauty and graceful spontaneity exercised a strong spell on Victor, who was in search of romantic adventures.[17] What followed, however, was an unhappy love story that ended with Schiasetti's sudden departure for Dresden that threw Jacquemont into a deep emotional crisis, tormented by uncertainty, hope, and disappointment. It was at the recommendation of his brother Porphyre that Victor decided to travel to America in order to find solace in the company of an old friend, Dr.

15. For more information, see Yannick Resch, *Le rêve foudroyé de Victor Jacquemont* (Marseilles: Editions Eurisco, 1998), 19–41; and Pierre Maës, *Un ami de Stendhal: Victor Jacquemont* (Paris: Desclée de Brouwer, 1934), 95–180. The surviving correspondence of Victor Jacquemont and his friend Pierre Achille Marie Chaper (1795–1874) consists of 106 letters and was published as *Letters to Achille Chaper: Intimate Sketches of Life among Stendhal's Coterie,* ed. J. F. Marshall (Philadelphia: American Philosophical Society, 1960). These letters provide insight into the salon culture of Paris in the early 1820s, and specifically the circle around Stendhal and Mérimée. Several letters describe Jacquemont's sojourn in the United States.

16. For example, Jacquemont and Stendhal disagreed on Napoléon. In a letter from 1824 Jacquemont went so far as to take Stendhal to task for espousing a vulgar admiration for Napoléon (see Resch, *Le rêve foudroyé de Victor Jacquemont,* 28). In a letter of December 31, 1825, Jacquemont wrote to Stendhal: "J'ai pour le grand homme . . . une haine parfaite et de plus du mépris. Je l'exècre pour les infâmies qu'il a faites. Je le méprise pour ses petitesses. Je le méprise pour avoir été, à bien des égards, aussi bête, aussi plat, aussi pitoyable qu'un roi légitime. Et ici, le jugeur est supérieur à celui qui juge, c'est-à-dire moi à Bonaparte, sous le rapport de la chose jugée, qui est la *vertu*" (quoted in Resch, *Le rêve foudroyé de Victor Jacquemont,* 28).

17. See Resch, *Le rêve foudroyé de Victor Jacquemont,* 35–41.

John B. Stevenson (Victor's brother, Frédéric, had also lived in New York for two years before moving to Haiti).

Having received letters of introduction from La Fayette, Jacquemont boarded *Cadmus,* the ship that had also been used by the general during his previous voyages to the New World. Upon leaving for America on November 3, 1826, Jacquemont expressed his doubts that he would ever be able to attain true and lasting happiness. But as the journey across the Atlantic went on, he began to regain confidence and took delight in learning and speaking English. His medical training also proved to be useful, as he was able to help an injured black man who was neglected by his superiors.

Jacquemont arrived on the soil of the New World on December 9, 1826, after a monthlong voyage, determined not only to retrieve his inner peace but also to use his voyage in order to make botanical expeditions in the western parts of the country. Alas, Jacquemont's arrival in New York did not put an end to his misfortunes. While departing after a pleasant dinner at the home of François Réal, a former supporter of Napoleon living in exile in America, Jacquemont was offended by some remarks made by another guest of Réal, General Lallemand (1774–1839). Jacquemont wanted to avenge his wounded honor but was prevented by New York law from dueling there. As a result, he decided to travel to Haiti, where his brother Frédéric lived and where dueling was allowed. Jacquemont went there waiting for Lallemand, who ultimately declined Jacquemont's invitation after sending an apology to his younger countryman.[18]

In January 1827 Jacquemont received an invitation from Pierre Louis Cordier of the Muséum d'Histoire Naturelle in Paris to undertake a scientific survey in India, with full pay and full discretion over the course of the expedition. He decided to return from Haiti to France via the United States, where he spent almost half a year. This time, Jacquemont had a more pleasant and fruitful sojourn. Anticipating Tocqueville's itinerary a few years later, Jacquemont visited a good part of the country, including Philadelphia, New Jersey, upstate New York, Niagara, and parts of Canada. On returning to Paris he immediately began preparing for his travel to India (he also had to go to England to obtain a permit from the East India Company in order to visit India).

Jacquemont departed for India on August 26, 1828. His trip was not devoid of unforeseen events and accidents. He ran out of money but was able to continue his voyage due to the generous help of India's governor general, Lord William Bentink. Jacquemont traveled from Punjab to Kashmir, and from Bombay to Bengal, admiring the majestic landscapes of the Himalayas and Tibet. He

18. Jacquemont's own account of the Lallemand affair is reprinted in Maës, *Un ami de Stendhal,* 259–74.

carried out geological research in the mountains and explored the Indian flora that dazzled him. At the same time, Jacquemont maintained a rich correspondence with his friends at home while also following from the distance the political developments in Paris, where a new king and a new constitution emerged from the days of the July 1830 revolution.[19] The major (posthumous) publication resulting from Jacquemont's travel to India was his monumental *Voyage dans l'Inde* containing his perceptive reflections and notes on the botany, zoology, ethnography, colonial administration, and the jurisprudence of India.[20]

In the end, the extremely high temperatures and tough travel conditions took a high toll on Jacquemont's fragile health. Avoiding eating any meat and drinking only water and tea, he was determined, however, to continue his explorations, ignoring at his own peril the specter of cholera and other deadly diseases looming large around him. Alas, Jacquemont's decision to continue his journey to Bombay proved to be an imprudent one. He fell ill on the way and died on December 7, 1832.[21]

THE LAND OF EQUALITY WITH AN UNCERTAIN FUTURE

If Jacquemont's Indian travel diary was hailed as a masterpiece of the genre in France, his reflections on America have largely passed unnoticed until now.[22] Although in America his name is arguably unknown not only among political scientists but also among historians of France, Jacquemont's thoughts on American society deserve to be retrieved from oblivion because he was a first-rate observer of the American scene who made perceptive remarks on the future of Native Americans, the different forms of religion, and the domestic manners of

19. Jacquemont's political pessimism was clearly conveyed in a letter to M. de Melay from December 31, 1831: "Je vois comme vous en sombre l'avenir de notre pays: anarchie, guerre civile, coalitions étrangères, toutes ces cruelles épreuves nous menacent" (quoted by Resch, *Le rêve foudroyé de Victor Jacquemont,* 166).

20. François Guizot was instrumental in the publication of Jacquemont's *Voyage dans l'Inde,* 6 vols. (Paris: 1836–44). An enlarged edition of Jacquemont's *Correspondence* with his family and friends was published a few decades later, in 1867, with an introduction by Prosper Mérimée. Jacquemont's Indian journal was partly published as *État politique et social de l'Inde du Nord en 1830* (Paris: Leroux, 1933) and *État politique et social de l'Inde du Sud en 1832* (Paris: Société de l'histoire des colonies françaises, 1934). There are a few interesting comparisons with America in Jacquemont's Indian journals.

21. For an introduction to Jacquemont's life, see *Letters to Achille Chaper,* 3–17. Also, Maës, *Un Ami de Stendhal,* 45–247; and Resch, *Le rêve foudroyé de Victor Jacquemont,* 17–61.

22. A few exceptions worth noting: Lionel J. Friedman, "One of the 'Happy Few': The American Voyage of Victor Jacquemont" (Ph.D. diss., Harvard University, 1950); Michel Crouzet, *Stendhal et L'Amérique: L'Amérique et la modernité* (Paris: Editions de Fallois, 2008), 165–76. On Jacquemont's travel to India, see Lloyd Kramer, "Victor Jacquemont in India: Travel, Identity, and the French Generation of 1820," in *The Human Tradition in Modern France,* ed. K. Steven Vincent and Alison Klairmont-Lingo (Wilmington, Del.: Scholarly Resources Books, 2000), 49–68.

the Americans. By raising a number of interesting questions about the aesthetic and emotional education of young Americans, Jacquemont can be regarded as a forerunner of Tocqueville even if he paid considerably less attention to political institutions in general. If toward the end of his journey Jacquemont concluded that "America is made more for stirring the curiosity of those who do not know it than for satisfying those who have seen it,"[23] he perceptively grasped key aspects of American life and society such as the impact of equality on individual lives and mores, a theme that also loomed large in Tocqueville's work.

As already mentioned, Victor Jacquemont arrived in America on December 8, 1826, in a peculiar state of mind, undoubtedly influenced by his unfortunate love affair with Schiasetti. As Jacquemont wrote in his travel notes, he left Europe, where he was "dead to all sorts of pleasures and interests," and went to the other side of the Atlantic to soak his ailing soul in a new world and to rejuvenate his emotional and intellectual faculties.[24] Like Chateaubriand, Jacquemont dreamt of encountering exciting new landscapes, majestic mountains, mysterious deserts and forests. But his romantic longings and imagination clashed with the reality he encountered upon arriving in the New World. Indeed, his very first impressions upon reaching the New Jersey shore proved to be rather disappointing. All he could see were desolate shores and river banks, made even uglier by man's intervention and punctuated by uninspiring and colorless houses.[25] His first impressions of the New York harbor were hardly more reassuring. To the young Frenchman the city seemed distant and cold, hiding beyond a "fantastic forest of masts"[26] that gave the traveler the uneasy feeling of having arrived in a hyperactive world that never rests. This sight only increased Jacquemont's uneasiness and sense of solitude.

His initial plans included a short visit to Philadelphia, a longer sojourn in Washington (where he wanted to attend some of the sessions of Congress), and an expedition to the western parts of the country that interested him as a botanist. He also seemed interested in examining American intellectual life and the organization of judicial power, and he was intent on taking copious notes, with plenty

23. *Correspondance inédite de Victor Jacquemont avec sa famille et ses amis 1824–1832*, ed. Prosper Mérimée (Paris: Calmann-Lévy, 1885), 1:153. Henceforth abbreviated as *Correspondance*.

24. "Je quittais l'Europe où j'étais mort à toutes espèces de plaisirs et d'intérêts, et j'allais au-delà de l'Atlantique essayer de retremper dans un monde nouveau mon âme affaissée, et mes facultés trop longtemps courbées sous le poids du malheur" (from Jacquemont's notes published in Maës, *Un Ami de Stendhal*, 253).

25. "Tout ce que le paysage eût pu avoir de charme agreste se trouvait ainsi détruit," writes a disappointed Jacquemont (in Maës, *Un Ami de Stendhal*, 254). The whole passage from Jacquemont's journal that Maës quotes is worth reading (*Un Ami de Stendhal*, 253–55). For a comparison between Chateaubriand's and Jacquemont's romantic imagination, see Friedman, "One of the 'Happy Few,' " 117–21.

26. Maës, *Un Ami de Stendhal*, 255.

of details about various aspects of American society.[27] He planned to return to New York in early summer, when he was hoping to continue his trip north. All these plans were foiled by the unfortunate incident with Lallemand.

Jacquemont's travel experience gave him the opportunity to reflect not only on the culture and mores of the world he was visiting, but also on his own French background in comparative perspective. His most perceptive observations on the American mores can be found in a seminal forty-page letter that Jacquemont sent to his friend, Victor de Tracy (the son of Destutt de Tracy), in September 1827.[28] In a speech on the commemoration of the centenary of Jacquemont's death, André Chevrillon, member of the French Academy, did not hesitate to claim that Jacquemont's letter to Victor de Tracy represented *in nuce* the substance of a great book that, had it ever been written, would have preceded Tocqueville's masterpiece. At the same time, one can find interesting observations on America in other writings by Jacquemont, including his correspondence and journals. In particular, he acquired a more positive view of the United States while visiting India (his Indian travel journal contains a few interesting notes about America). As Lionel Friedman argued, "if one follows him from his first voyage to America through his voyage to India, one can see the transformation and refinement that his thought has undergone. Banalities and external differences begin to give way before more penetrating insights into the nature of social systems and social problems."[29]

What makes this document so interesting and precious is Jacquemont's ability to draw a remarkable portrait of American society, religion, and mores. While not devoid of certain ambiguities that might lead Jacquemont's readers to believe that he was entirely hostile to American society, his observations bear a number of striking resemblances to Tocqueville's reflections on America, although they occasionally lack the latter's fine nuances. At the end of his voyage in America, Jacquemont thought that the soundness of political institutions depends on many unquantifiable variables (habit, custom, etc.) and that individual happiness is, to a large degree, independent from particular forms of government. If the young Frenchman returned home being critical of American mores, which he found "severe, cold, flat, and vulgar,"[30] he was far from becoming yet another represen-

27. Writes Jacquemont: "J'écrirai beaucoup: tout ce que j'aurai vu de choses nouvelles dans le jour, et ce que ces choses m'auront fait pensé. Peut-être, plus tard, pourrais-je faire quelque chose de cela" (quoted in Resch, *Le rêve foudroyé de Victor Jacquemont*, 46).

28. Victor de Tracy (1781–1864) served for a long time as a member of the Chamber of Deputies. In this capacity he endorsed many humanitarian causes and was deeply involved in debates on the emancipation of slaves in the French colonies. Also worth consulting is another letter to Fouchard from July 17, 1827, in *Correspondance*, 1:33–43.

29. Friedman, "One of the 'Happy Few,'" 445. Also see André Chevrillon, "Victor Jacquemont," *Revue de France*, July 1, 1933, 178–79.

30. Letter to Tracy, September 1827, in *Correspondance*, 1:153.

tative of that branch of anti-Americanism that saw in American society nothing but disquieting signs of cultural, political, and spiritual decline.[31]

In his long letter to Victor de Tracy, Jacquemont commented on important issues as diverse as equality, self-government, the spirit of association, the relationship between society and government, religion and morality, Protestantism, domestic life, journals, and political debates (similar observations can be found in his journals). Jacquemont closely followed American journals and debates and observed those signs predicting a possible civil war between the North and the South. He noted the rising power of public opinion and paid special consideration to the growing homogenization of American society. While traveling in India a few years later, Jacquemont took the opportunity to reflect on his prior journey to America. This time, he unambiguously praised the *"moeurs toutes constitutionnelles"* of the American nation and claimed that the American government was appropriate "only to enlightened and laborious populations,"[32] being an outcome of the admirable social virtues of American citizens. Jacquemont clearly understood—and accepted—the democratic direction in which the American society as a whole was advancing at that time. His notes are important because they contain perceptive reflections on the causes that fostered the process of equalization of conditions of America, which he regarded—much like Tocqueville—as an irresistible and irreversible phenomenon.

While Jacquemont admired the novelty of the American experiment of self-government, he contemplated it with a mixture of respect and uneasiness that was not uncommon among other nineteenth-century European visitors of the New World. It is worth noting that a few years before Tocqueville, Jacquemont highlighted the social and cultural foundations of democracy and was impressed by the degree to which Americans governed themselves and managed to successfully reconcile equality with liberty. Jacquemont perceived a fundamental revolution in the fabric of American society at work and attributed it to the powerful influence of equality in all spheres of life. The predominant passion for equality in America, he noted, played a key role in promoting a new form of education, blurring the distinctions between classes and ultimately lowering the barriers between individuals in society. "America," Jacquemont wrote, "is entirely democratic in its mores" (note the reference to mores), and its laws express the general interests and wishes of the country. The American government does not look down at society and is neither better nor worse than the latter. The situation, he

31. On this issue, see Rémond, *Les États-Unis devant l'opinion française,* 2 vols., and Roger, *L'Ennemi américain.* On the image of America in the works of European writers, see Peter Conrad, *Imagining America* (New York: Oxford University Press, 1980).

32. This note was written in India, a few years after his sojourn in America. It is quoted by Friedman, "One of the 'Happy Few,'" 435–36.

added, was entirely different in France, where society was more creative than the government, and where the agents of the government tended to act in a paternalistic manner and distrusted all initiatives that they were unable to control or supervise.[33]

Moreover, like many other foreign travelers, Jacquemont was surprised by the equality with which education was disseminated among the diverse classes of society. He remarked: "There is not between individuals this enormous distance that separate them in our country."[34] In America, the gradual breakup of the barriers between people furthered the ever-growing equality of conditions and contributed to social leveling, two phenomena that also made a lasting impression on Tocqueville upon his arrival in the New World four years later. While Jacquemont realized that inequalities of wealth might create significant distinctions between individuals, he did not believe that a new aristocracy could ever arise in America.

Although America was entirely democratic in its mores, Jacquemont feared that this process of democratization was bound to clash eventually with slavery, triggering significant changes in the institutions, laws, ideas, and customs of the country. Like many other European travelers, Jacquemont regarded slavery as an anomaly in a democratic and civilized country such as the United States. He attributed the existence of racial prejudices and slavery to custom and habit,[35] which enforced docility, obedience, and passivity. Jacquemont took extensive notes for two articles on this topic that he intended to publish in 1827. In the long letter to Tracy he unambiguously expressed his opposition to slavery, which he found utterly offensive and wrong: "In a democratic country in which the principle of government is equality, this terrible inequality established by society almost in defiance of the law revolts me."[36] Jacquemont predicted the gradual abolition of slavery as well as the persistence of deeply seated racial prejudices that it would take decades to eradicate fully:

In the southern United States, in Jamaica, and in general, everywhere in America where the population of African origin, free and slave, is mixed, but in great majority, with a white population of English origin, no fusion can be hoped for between these two peoples; the contempt, on the one hand, and the hatred on the other will survive after the extinction of slavery, if slavery is

33. *Correspondance*, 1:155.
34. *Correspondance*, 1:168–69.
35. *Correspondance*, 1:119–20. Also see 1:135–36.
36. *Correspondance*, 1:180. The two articles he wanted to publish were "Aperçu de l'état social et politique de la République de Haiti" and "Saint-Domingue." See Jacquemont, *Correspondance*, 1:213–20.

ever going to be abolished; and the greatest number, one day or another, will destroy the smallest.[37]

In this regard, Jacquemont espoused much the same views as Tocqueville a few years later. Both foresaw the impending clash between the white and the black populations and believed that a peaceful solution would be quite difficult, if not impossible, to find. After coming into contact with some Indian tribes from the New York state (the Buffalo reservation occupied by the Senecas, Cayugas, and Onondagas), Jacquemont feared that the proximity with the white race would eventually deprive the Indians of their lands and traditions and would slowly pervert their mores: "From North to the South, on the whole western frontier, they will disappear in front of the new settlements. The neighborhood of the European civilization pushes them further and more often destroys them."[38] When Indian tribes were successful in resisting the advance of the whites' settlements, the whiskey, Jacquemont wryly added, was going to destroy forever their "independent sovereignties."

But what was the deeper cause of this evolution that was destined to alter the spirit of American republican institutions? Was it possible to distinguish between temporary and permanent causes of this inevitable process? To these questions, Jacquemont gave a clear answer. In his view, at the root of this phenomenon lay the trend toward greater equality and uniformity that, in turn, changed the ways in which people related to and cooperated with one another. In America, he argued, equality was irresistible and all individual lives and careers followed similar patterns and were cast in the same mold, much the same as houses were build according to the same plan and people were pursuing more or less similar occupations.[39] It was this growing uniformity that gave Jacquemont the impression that America was not a country where profound and original characters could flourish, but one in which the majority pursue the same daily occupations and have more or less identical material interests. As equality advances and penetrates more deeply into the fabric of society, a growing number of people live under similar conditions and perform similar tasks that end up limiting their intellectual horizon. The wild and exotic America that had once caught the imagination of previous visitors was no longer as exotic and picturesque as Chateaubriand or Crèvecoeur had described it. What Jacquemont experienced firsthand was an increasingly bourgeois America, a country that was gradually losing its originality and was becoming less picturesque and original in the eyes of European travelers.[40] In emphasizing that the progress of equality came at a certain

37. *Correspondance*, 1:182. Also see 1:334–35.
38. *Correspondance*, 1:191.
39. *Correspondance*, 1:176.
40. "Nul pais n'est aussi dépourvu de toute originalité nationale; nulle population n'est aussi anti-pittoresque" (*Correspondance*, 1:175).

price, Jacquemont proved to be a perceptive forerunner of Tocqueville, who in volume 2 of *Democracy in America* analyzed how equality changes the way in which people live, write, feel, and relate to one another in modern democratic societies.

HAPPINESS AND DOMESTIC MANNERS IN AMERICA

In his private correspondence, Jacquemont made a number of interesting comments on domestic life and mores in America. In this regard, his reflections were close to the observations made by Stendhal, who never visited the United States. In *On Love* (1821), Stendhal drew an unflattering portrait of daily life in America, being impressed at the same time by the strenuous efforts made by all Americans to improve their material condition. Unlike Jacquemont, Stendhal did not see American mores as rude. On the contrary, it was their politeness and rationality that he found problematic and ultimately unsatisfying. "All their attention," Stendhal wrote, "seems to be concentrated on a sensible arrangement of the business of living, and on foreseeing all mishaps."[41] But these efforts ended up taking a high toll on people's inner life: "When at last they reach the point of harvesting the fruit of so much care and orderly planning, they find no life left with which to enjoy."[42] Although America had a free government that "does its citizens no harm, but rather gives them security and tranquility,"[43] this was not enough (in Stendhal's view) to create true happiness, which is different from political happiness. For all its virtues, the spirit of American liberty was "a coarse spirit" that gave individuals the illusion of being happy simply because they enjoyed security and tranquility.[44]

True happiness, Stendhal believed, means much more than being free from the interference of a bad, harmful, and incompetent government. Although the American government "fulfils its functions as it should, and harms no one . . . we see that the Americans, without the misfortunes created by governments, feel themselves to be lacking in something."[45] What Americans were lacking, in Stendhal's view, were genuine feelings and great passions: "It is as though the springs of sensitiveness had dried up in these people; they are just, they are ratio-

---

41. Stendhal, *On Love*, trans. Gilbert and Suzanne Sale (London: Penguin, 1975), 164. On Stendhal's political thought, see Richard Boyd, "*Politesse* and Public Opinion in Stendhal's *Red and Black*," *European Journal of Political Theory* 4 (2005): 367–92. For a comparison between Stendhal and Tocqueville, see Francesco Spandri, "La vision de l'histoire chez Stendhal and Tocqueville," *Revue d'Histoire littéraire de la France* 106:1 (2006): 240–67. Also see André Daspre, "Stendhal et la démocratié américaine," *Europe* 519–21 (July–September 1972): 79–88; and Crouzet, *Stendhal et L'Amerique*.

42. Stendhal, *On Love*, 164.

43. Stendhal, *On Love*, 163.

44. Stendhal, *On Love*, 163.

45. Stendhal, *On Love*, 164.

nal, but they are not at all happy."[46] His examples described a society in which people were polite and civil but incapable of deep and profound sentiments. In turn, it was this lack of warmth that prompted Stendhal to refer to the Americans' political happiness as the happiness "of beings of a different and inferior species."[47] America, he concluded, was a country incapable of providing the finest pleasures of civilization.

It is no coincidence that the alleged absence of genuine passions in America also loomed large in Jacquemont's account, as he had carefully read Stendhal's *On Love* (as well as Madame de Staël's *Corinne*) prior to his arrival in the New World.[48] A few years later, another reference book for Jacquemont would be Frances Trollope's *Domestic Manners of the Americans,* which he mentioned in his letters from India. Writing about the relations between husbands and wives, Jacquemont noted with disappointment that they were characterized by coldness, reserve, emptiness, and superficiality, which he found both unsatisfying and inappropriate. In America, he wrote to Tracy,[49] young men are forced into early marriage and procreation by deeply seated social conventions that push them to fulfill early on their spousal duties, without much attention being paid to marital harmony and happiness. The communication between spouses, Jacquemont continued, is often limited to a few words, being focused on finding the best means for improving living arrangements. Furthermore, Jacquemont pointed out that in America, men often took upon themselves a number of tasks that in Europe traditionally belonged to women and were performed by them.[50] As for the lot of the unmarried young men in America, he added, it is somewhat worse than in other places. In this regard, Jacquemont differed from Stendhal, who argued that in the New World the youth of both sexes enjoy a true freedom, unhindered by old and ultimately stifling class-based conventions.

It is worth pointing out that Jacquemont painted a less flattering picture of American women than Tocqueville, who attributed many of the virtues of American democracy to the great qualities of American women. In his peregrinations, Jacquemont came into contact largely with upper-class women from the New York area and was led to believe that most American women lacked charm and grace in social relations. By entering too early into society and being forced

46. Stendhal, *On Love,* 164.

47. Stendhal, *On Love,* 165.

48. Referring to Staël's *Corinne,* Jacquemont wrote: "Oh! Que je me suis souvent rappelé, pendant mon séjour aux États-Unis, cette peinture de la vie d'une petite ville d'Ecosse, faite par Madame de Staël dans sa *Corinne!* C'était cette même teinte plate, sombre, et glacée!" (quoted in Friedman, "One of the 'Happy Few,'" 359–60).

49. *Correspondance,* 1:160–61.

50. "L'homme dans le ménage passe sa vie à gagner de l'argent: il remplit dans la maison des soins qui sont chez nous, et partout, je crois, en Europe, le partage de la femme; il ne voit celle-ci pendant le jour qu'aux heures de repas et lui parle très peu (*Correspondance,* 1:162).

to mature early, he argued, American women are less likely to pay enough attention to the cultivation of their minds and are more prone to acquire a certain unpleasant austerity and coldness. Their main virtue, Jacquemont argued, is resignation. If there are fewer detestable marriages in America than in France, he added, there are certainly fewer happier or glamorous ones.[51] Comparing the role and life of an English woman to the one played by women in America, Jacquemont was surprised by the intellectual and social separation between men and women in America (Frances Trollope made the same point in her famous book on American manners a few years later).[52] For Jacquemont, a happy family life was predicated upon tenderness on the part of the husband and a rich emotional life, and as such it was incompatible with the isolation in which American women lived. He concluded: "Such is their existence, such are the external relations with men, that they seem to be in no way half of the conjugal community."[53]

The deeper cause of all this was the materialism and pragmatism reigning in America. The Americans' obsessive concern for the utilitarian aspects of their lives was one such consequence; the narrow, unidimensional education of their offspring was another. Anticipating Tocqueville's analysis of the American democratic mind, Jacquemont was surprised to discover how many Americans strain their faculties to the utmost to make a name for themselves in honorable but ultimately uninspiring occupations, most often in commerce or industry. As such, their lives displayed a surprising uniformity in the eyes of the European traveler. "They all resemble each other to a great extent, regardless of their status,"[54] and all of them end up pursuing similar occupations and living almost identical lives.

Among other things, what all Americans share, according to Jacquemont, is a certain pragmatic belief in indefinite progress, grounded in the idea that life is an endless competition that sorts out the worthy ones and rewards only the virtuous individuals. In order to be successful in the world, wrote Jacquemont, the Americans tend to cut short their intellectual evolution and have an acute consciousness

---

51. *Correspondance*, 1:162. Also: "Il y a en Amérique moins de detestable ménages que chez nous, il y en a peut-être autant de mauvais, et certainement beaucoup moins de très bons. La réserve, sinon la froideur des deux sexes ne leur permet peut-être jamais de connaître ce nous apellons intime" (162). Compare with Beaumont's account: "American women generally have well-informed minds but little imagination, and more reason than sensibility" (Gustave de Beaumont, *Marie: Or Slavery in the United States: A Novel of Jacksonian America*, trans. Barbara Chapman [Stanford: Stanford University Press, 1958], 16).

52. *Correspondance de V. Jacquemont avec sa famille et plusieurs de ses amis pendant son voyage dans l'Inde (1828–1832)*, 4th ed. (Paris: Garnier Frères, 1846), 1:302. Friedman also comments on the similarities between Jacquemont and Trollope ("One of the 'Happy Few,'" 349–55). For more information, see Frances Trollope, *Domestic Manners of the Americans*, ed. Donald Smalley (Gloucester, Mass.: Peter Smith, 1974).

53. *Correspondance*, 1:162.

54. *Correspondance*, 1:162.

of time that permeates all their actions and thoughts. They encourage their children to become adults early on by giving them a predominantly utilitarian education that prevents them from experiencing adolescence in the full sense of the
word. The young, Jacquemont pointed out, are taught early on that they must
behave seriously and responsibly if they are to succeed in the world. At an age
when in Europe young people still live in a blissful ignorance of the worries of
adult life, the young Americans already know how to be rational and calculating.
The way in which the young Americans spend their time is dictated by the need
to learn quickly those skills that are meant only (or mostly) to further their careers
and wealth. In so doing, Jacquemont claimed, they miss the transition from
childhood to adulthood, a period supposed to be a rite of passage that allows one
to become a harmoniously developed person. Instead, young Americans skip
moral adolescence and are taught how to cope responsibly with the tough
demands of the real world.[55] As a result, most young Americans begin their voca-
tional education early on and voluntarily relinquish any dreams of pursuing a
truly liberal education. They seek to learn only what is strictly necessary for
advancement in their professions and lack curiosity and interest in exploring
other fields. If everyone is very diligent, the drawback is that "the pleasure of
study is very little known in America."[56]

Furthermore, Jacquemont also remarked that the relations between children
and parents were characterized by respect rather than tender feelings and noted
that their family life was not devoid of a certain coldness and reserve that he
found surprising. He went as far as to argue that the family as a traditional political
unit did not (and could not) exist in such a restless country as America. The
justification of this rather surprising claim is that the traditional family cannot
survive in a country in which the permanent social mobility constantly uproots
individuals from their birthplace and forces them to adjust to new territories and
communities in search of new opportunities for profit. Paradoxically, Jacquemont argues the high social mobility and restlessness called into question the
originality of America: "No country is as deprived of national originality [as
America]; no population is as anti-picturesque [as the Americans]," Jacquemont
wrote to Tracy. "They often repeat a few old sentences from Europe on the
fatherland; it is obvious that they do not feel them. They are not the sons of this
land they inhabit, and, from various points of view, they seem to be nothing else
than strangers who inhabit it while passing through it. M. de Bonald would
have had hard time finding in the entire United States what he calls a family."[57]

55. "Ils passent des jeux de l'enfance au travail aride et positif, à la dure préoccupation du monde
réel, sans connaître cet âge de timidité honteuse, d'ingénuité, d'espérances vagues qui sépare chez nous
l'enfance de la jeunesse. Ils n'ont point d'adolescence morale" (*Correspondance*, 1:163).

56. *Correspondance*, 1:164.

57. *Correspondance*, 1:175.

Surprisingly, in Jacquemont's view, it was the very propriety and austerity of mores that denied Americans the possibility of a rich and emotionally fulfilling family life.

RELIGION, THE FREE PRESS, AND THE ART OF ASSOCIATION IN AMERICA

Jacquemont's remarks on religion further revealed his disagreement with one of the core aspects of American social and political life. Anticipating another insight of Tocqueville, Jacquemont noted that most Americans tended to treat not only their affairs in a clear and dry language deprived of any ornament, but applied the same attitude to religion. Arguably, his musings about religion in America had to do a lot with his distrust of Protestantism and his rejection of the supremacy of individual judgment in matters pertaining to religion. Furthermore, as a note from his Indian travel diary shows, Jacquemont was skeptical about the immortality of the soul and did not believe that the existence of a religious instinct in human beings requires the corresponding existence of many denominations and cults.[58] For him, "the pleasures of faith must be independent from the form of the cult."[59] Coming from a liberal background, Jacquemont was deeply suspicious of all forms of religious zealotry and was convinced that the basic religious needs of human beings can be fulfilled by a sort of vague, nondenominational deism compatible with liberal political principles.

It will be recalled that in the early decades of the nineteenth century (after 1810), America witnessed a remarkable religious revival that manifested itself in an unprecedented growth of religious sects, revival meetings, and theological controversies. The strength of the religious life and sentiment in America caught Jacquemont's attention, and this might account for some of his bold claims about religion in the New World. There he found many Protestant sects that seemed to promote a peculiar type of fanaticism that he unambiguously rejected. After two months spent in the United States, Jacquemont confessed to Charpentier that he had been exposed there to more theological issues and controversies than in this entire previous life in France, and he deplored the paradoxical social intolerance with regard to religious matters in America:

58. For more information on Jacquemont's own religious beliefs, see Friedman, "One of the 'Happy Few,'" 310–43. As Jacquemont put it in a letter to Charpentier, "janséniste, molinistes, quiétistes, jésuites, ce m'est tout un. . . . Moi, je suis rieniste" (quoted in Friedman, "One of the 'Happy Few,'" 314).

59. Quoted in Friedman, "One of the 'Happy Few,'" 333 (Friedman's translation). Also see the following passage from the letter to Tracy: "Appeler au jugement de l'esprit, au libre examen de la raison, de la vérité d'une croyance religieuse, cela ma paraît le comble de l'absurdité. Toute religion qui se dit éclairée, qui se prétend raisonnable, est la plus mesquine et la plus fausse conception" (Correspondance, 1:160).

There are thirty-three religious sects in New York that co-exist without fighting one another; yet this country is marked by religious intolerance. In Europe, or on the Continent, at least, we only know the intolerance of governments. But that is nothing compared to the intolerance of society. In Ferrara, Bologna, the Pope's representative and his spies observe all the time if you go to the liturgy on Sunday. But in New York it is the entire city, your neighbors, your friends who, out of religious zeal, constantly look at you and spy on you; and if they find in you a fault with the good God, they would report it to the whole world. Since everyone passionately sides with the good God, you will be poorly regarded and isolated in society.[60]

While the multiplicity of religious sects could temper religious zealotry, Jacquemont argued that in reality their diversity tended to increase each group's dogmatic fervor and enforced conformism, without always promoting sound moral principles. Even if the constitution officially promoted and consecrated the principle of toleration, the powerful social clout of sects diminished the influence of this principle in society.[61] Jacquemont's position on this issue amounted to questioning the existence of true religious tolerance in America, where the mere failure to observe the Sabbath could expose everyone to serious communal persecutions: "One of the statutes of the thousands of the religious associations of this country includes the obligation of each member not to hire any worker known for his negligence in his religious duties, or not to buy anything from merchants suspected of the same infamy."[62] Too often religious practices hid deeper forms of prejudice, hypocrisy, or dogmatism. Jacquemont criticized the use of religion for public purposes and suspected furthermore that many public officials were professing only a superficial form of religion that did not take seriously the dogmas of Christianity. In Jacquemont's opinion, most American politicians only attempted to appear religious without really being so. Viewed from his perspective, the need to seem religious was another facet of American conformism that Jacquemont found problematic. Equally interesting, he found the Protestant service to be excessively rational and lacking mystery, true nobility, and simplicity (with the notable exception of the Quakers). A true reli-

---

60. *Lettres de Victor Jacquemont à Jean de Charpentier,* 2nd ed. (Paris: Masson, 1934), 188–89. The letter is also quoted by Friedman, "One of the 'Happy Few,' " 319–20 (Friedman's translation).

61. "Depuis, les prêtres de toute secte ont acquis une extrême influence; ils ont modifié les opinions de la société, ils l'ont rendue intolérante. . . . A cet égard, la loi est donc aujourd'hui plus libérale que la société; elle vaut mieux" (*Correspondance,* vol. I, 155–56). Comparing Jacquemont's categorical views on the observance of the Sabbath with those held by other visitors of America, Friedman quoted Grund, who argued that 'no universal practice exists, in this respect, in the United States" ("One of the 'Happy Few,' " 328).

62. *Correspondance,* 1:138.

gious sentiment, he believed, is an instinct implanted deeply into the heart of a person, which explains why religion must speak directly to the heart rather than the mind.

Jacquemont's skepticism explains the strong claim he made in his letter to Victor de Tracy: "The Bible seems to me to be the scourge of America."[63] In this regard Jacquemont's opinion stands in stark contrast to what Tocqueville had to say about the ways in which Americans applied the doctrine of self-interest to religion and used the latter to promote and moderate democracy. More important, it was his American experience that led Jacquemont to question the relation between religion and morality, or to put it differently, the extent to which religion can serve in practice as an instrument of morality and education essential to modern society: "What I had seen in the United States made me give up one of my opinions, namely that religious ideas can be an instrument of morality useful to human societies."[64] By the end of his American sojourn, he was convinced that it would be difficult—if not utterly impossible—to distinguish proper religious claims from mere superstitions and worried that religious dogmas were deeply entrenched in local laws and regulations.[65] Furthermore, he believed that although the U.S. Constitution provided for the separation of state and church, there was, however, a state religion *sui generis* in America, the religion of the majority—the greatest number—which could always oppress the minorities.[66]

Jacquemont's thoughts on the art of association and newspapers in the United States are equally interesting because they add a critical dimension to Tocqueville's well-known description of the practice of self-government in America. "American of all ages, all conditions, all minds constantly unite," Tocqueville famously wrote. "Not only do they have commercial and industrial associations in which all take part, but they also have a thousand other kinds: religious, moral, grave, futile, very general and very particular, immense and very small."[67] Like Tocqueville, Jacquemont was impressed by the multifarious ways in which American citizens made continuous and systematic use of the right of association to found schools, build churches and roads, and promote temperance. He attrib-

---

63. *Correspondance,* 1:158.

64. *Correspondance,* 1:159.

65. "L'intolérance religieuse a reçu successivement la sanction inconstitutionnnelle de presque toutes les législations particulières. . . . À mesure que la loi est plus locale, à mesure qu'elle est faite par et pour un plus petit nombre d'individus, comme par exemple les réglements de police municipale, elle est plus fanatique et plus intolérante" (*Correspondance,* 1:156).

66. "Il y a donc, de fait, une religion d'état aux États-Unis. Au lieu d'être la communion catholique, comme en France, or la communion épiscopale comme en Angleterre, c'est la religion chrétienne dans la plus vaste extension de ce mot; mais peu importe. Là, comme ailleurs, la religion du plus grand nombre fait la loi à celle du plus petit, et l'opprime" (*Correspondance,* 1:157).

67. Alexis de Tocqueville, *Democracy in America,* trans. Harvey C. Mansfield and Delba Winthrop (Chicago: University of Chicago Press, 2000), 489.

uted Americans' propensity to form civil and political associations to the principle of equality reigning supreme in a democratic society. Jacquemont noticed that Americans of all ages and professions displayed an unusual ability to choose common goals and to advance them skillfully with the aid of various associations. They shied away from carrying out these activities in isolation and viewed civil associations as powerful means of action that created new social bonds.

Yet at the same time Jacquemont feared that the spirit of association might turn into a caricature when everyone acquires the habit of association and carries it to the extreme. He ironically noted that "ten Americans do not know how to dine, play, or meet for any reason without electing a president and a secretary."[68] But, he added, all these organizations resemble small armies in which there is no soldier and in which everyone is a general. This, he opined, was the effect of equality and republican education on mores. While applauding the habit of forming associations for pursuing common projects, Jacquemont doubted that civil associations could ever serve as a substitute for what European called *society* in the proper sense of the word.

On a larger note, Jacquemont expressed concerns about the gradual standardization of life that might bring forth an extreme simplicity in manners and a stultifying uniformity in ideas and feelings: "All individual existences seem to have been cast in a similar mold; as all houses are built exactly according to the same plan, everyone's life is enclosed in the same framework. In this country people are born with many unequal faculties, and all the mores tend to bring them closer to each other."[69] Observing the daily conversations among Americans, Jacquemont was struck by their plainness and banality. Proud of their democratic mores, the Americans "carry even into their most frivolous conversations the slow forms and the heavy tone of a public deliberation."[70] That is why Jacquemont doubted that a true art of conversation could ever exist in the New World. Most of the time, he claimed, the exchanges between Americans are nothing more than an endless series of banalities, an odd mixture of sentimentality and superficiality in stark contrast to the sophisticated exchanges of Europeans, who were less prone to succumb to the temptation of overwork and pragmatism.

As Jacquemont pointed out in a letter to Fouchard,[71] it is the lack of leisure that explains why respectable people in America never manage to read classic authors such as Lord Byron and Walter Scott. Where everyone seems eager to make as much money as possible, the time spent on reading books becomes

68. *Correspondance*, 1:166.
69. *Correspondance*, 1:176.
70. *Correspondance*, 1:166.
71. *Correspondance*, 1:140–41; also quoted in Friedman, "One of the 'Happy Few,'" 377.

extremely costly. What the French call society, Jacquemont concluded, could hardly exist in America. Although Americans had developed the art of association to perfection, they still lacked the graces of gentle social interaction. Hence, for Jacquemont, the paradox of America lay in its unusual combination of a strong spirit of association and a weak spirit of gentle society:

> The intellectual habits, the tastes of a doctor are the same as those of a court-
> ier; take people from all the so-called liberal professions, bring them together
> in a salon for an evening, and listen to the general conversation that is estab-
> lished sometimes among them . . . ; I would challenge you to find among
> them the smallest excitement for your mind. It seems to me that the Ameri-
> cans lack the humor of the English; and certainly they completely lack this
> graciousness of spirit that is not rare among us, in such a way that they have
> nothing with which to hide their excessive ignorance. They lack both the
> content and the form. The conversation never rises above a subject of local
> interest or, if someone who considers himself capable wants to rise even
> higher and on a general tone, he only manages to provoke a deluge of the
> most banal and pretentious truisms. . . . What we call society, nothing of this
> kind exists in America. . . . There is nowhere else more spirit of association
> and less spirit of society.[72]

In his long letter to Victor de Tracy, Jacquemont also commented on Ameri-can newspapers that played a key role in the daily life of American democracy. He was baffled by the unprecedented proliferation of journals in America, where every single town had its own newspaper and press through which ordinary citizens shared their ideas and made use of their knowledge to improve the con-dition of their communities.[73] This was an undeniable sign of civic vitality that demonstrated that America was not only the country of the middle class par excellence, but also the country with the greatest number of newspapers and grassroots associations. Jacquemont understood that in a democratic society newspapers play a seminal role in connecting individuals who are dispersed over a great space and might otherwise have the inclination to retreat from the public sphere in order to pursue their private interests. By disseminating information and giving voice to sentiments common to many individuals, journals bring peo-ple in contact with one another and facilitate their communication, while also

---

72. *Correspondance*, 1:165–66. Interestingly, the lack of true society was also a major criticism in Frances Trollope's account of America. For more details, see Conrad, *Imagining America*, 33–34, 47–48; and Trollope, *Domestic Manners of the Americans*.

73. Referring to local newspapers, Jacquemont wrote: "Le nombre en est immense; chaque grande ville du litoral en publie vingt ou trente, et chaque village un peu populeux de l'intérieur a le sien" (*Correspondance*, 1:169).

furnishing them the means of undertaking in common the designs that they had previously conceived.

Yet in spite of all these virtues, Jacquemont was struck by the low quality of many American newspapers which, in his opinion, only disseminated "half-knowledge" and prevented the most enlightened part of the public from learning more.[74] The time devoted to browsing these journals, he argued, would be much better spent by reading valuable books such as Adam Smith's *Wealth of Nations* or Destutt de Tracy's *Commentary on Montesquieu*. Jacquemont noted with surprise that a good part of newspapers' space was taken up by paid advertisements: "You can easily guess what the prose of local journalists looks like: it resembles the sermons of our local priests."[75] He attributed the low quality of American newspapers to a great extent to the particular nature of public debates revolving around a small number of narrow issues. These debates mirrored—and were influenced by—the structure of the American political system, based on two major parties that often shared similar agendas and platforms. Jacquemont suggested that the low quality of American newspapers was a direct outcome of the progressive leveling of society and was related to the absence of an "aristocracy of knowledge" comparable to that existing in European countries.[76] Jacquemont also remarked that Washington's generation, which had created America, was being replaced by a new political elite whose taste and instincts were in stark contrast to those of its predecessors. "There are no longer those intellectually superior minds that rise high above the level of the masses," he confessed with a hint of sadness. "Those men of 1776 were Englishmen."[77]

Last but not least, noting the chronic restlessness of the Americans, Jacquemont expressed concerns about the consequences of being exposed to an inordinately large amount of irrelevant information in the media. Democratic individuals, he argued, tend to forget easily what they previously learned, and since they can never stand still, they are bound to pursue projects for which they have not been properly prepared. Furthermore, Jacquemont added, in the United States where there are no legal limits on what may be published, newspapers often convey a multitude of insignificant details that make it difficult to distinguish between relevant and irrelevant information. Not only is people's curiosity satisfied cheaply by the petty news disseminated by the media, but many individuals prefer to know a lot quickly rather than know anything well and are bound to remain in a peculiar state of ignorance *sui generis*.

74. *Correspondance*, 1:170.
75. *Correspondance*, 1:170.
76. *Correspondance*, 1:168.
77. *Correspondance*, 1:168. Interestingly, Jacquemont referred to the great American leaders as "republicans by principle and aristocrats in their mores."

The similarity with Tocqueville's ideas on the habitual inattention of democratic citizens is striking here. Unable to be an expert in all matters, individuals living in democratic regimes tend to become satisfied with half-baked ideas and do everything in a hurry, rarely pausing for more than one moment to consider properly what they do. That is why Jacquemont believed that given the nature and poor quality of printed news in America, little could be gained by being exposed to a huge amount of irrelevant information. As such, Jacquemont's claim reminds us of Tocqueville's point about the two types of ignorance; the first derives from *too little* information while the second is the outcome of *too much* information. In Jacquemont's opinion American citizens were prone to this second type of ignorance resulting from extreme publicity, a phenomenon that can be found in all democratic nations, regardless of their particular culture.

AMERICAN OR FRENCH EXCEPTIONALISM?

Jacquemont ended his American trip on a sour note, as he came to believe that for all its virtues the American way of life could *not* serve as a model for European nations in search of a new form of civilization. In this regard he echoed the criticism voiced by other observers of the American scene who had pointed out that America had too much equality that was likely to create, in the words of Jouffroy, "a type of mediocre civilization."[78] But it was Americans' money-centered utilitarianism that seems to have disturbed most nineteenth-century French visitors irrespective of their political affiliation. "The main question here (and it's the *alpha* and *omega* of life)," the ultraconservative Benjamin Saint-Victor wrote, "is to gain money, then to use this money to gain ever more. . . . The entire world does not seem to suffice to their cupidity."[79] On this view, the restless competition and frantic commercial life in America created a "perpetual and boundless movement of all cupid passions, the endpoint of all the worried thoughts of this multitude of people, who constantly turned to earth, exhaust themselves under the sun in order to build a treasure or to increase without measure the one that they have already amassed."[80] It is hardly surprising then that in the eyes of the more hedonistic French, life in America was marked by monotony, coarseness, and a lack of *savoir-vivre*.[81]

78. Jouffroy as quoted in Rémond, *Les États-Unis devant l'opinion française*, 2:721.
79. Benjamin Saint-Victor, *Lettres sur les États-Unis d'Amérique* (Paris: Perisse Frères, 1835), 1:26–27 (my translation). The second letter describes in detail American mores. It is worth pointing out that Saint-Victor's letters, written in 1832–33 from America, were published in France in 1835, about the same time as volume 1 of Tocqueville's *Democracy in America*.
80. Saint-Victor, *Lettres*, 1:30–31.
81. For a few interesting passages on this topic, see Rémond, *Les États-Unis devant l'opinion française*, 2:724–25.

In this regard, Jacquemont was far from being the only one to express concern that the spirit of calculation and rationalism might stifle or weaken all generous sentiments in the human heart. That is why Jacquemont's reservations about America must be placed in their proper historical context in order to be fully comprehended and evaluated. His misgivings about American society expressed in the letter to Tracy mirrored the growing doubts in France about the proper functioning of American institutions that reached a peak around 1832 or 1833, by the time Tocqueville drafted volume 1 of *Democracy in America*. As more information about American political institutions became available in the French press, the old image of a successful and accomplished American democracy eventually came to be replaced by the image of a country with a rather uncertain future, facing a complex set of problems and challenges (slavery was only one of them), and therefore unable to play the role of political model for the rest of the world.[82]

Jacquemont's letter to Tracy clearly shows his uneasiness toward the tendency of American institutions and mores to simplify the natural complexity of society and human character.[83] He illustrates the emergence of a distinctive type of aesthetic critique of America among French travelers, who (in the footsteps of Talleyrand) were surprised to discover a country with thirty-two religions and lacking a proper *esprit de société*. As such, he gave voice to a certain cultural skepticism toward America that has been shared by many European writers and philosophers over time.[84] Nevertheless, a fine line separates the cultural critics who complain that American mores efface human character from the anti-Americans who profess a deep-seated hostility toward American values and principles. This line must always be kept in mind when evaluating the anti-American rhetoric that is raging today across the world. For as both Alan Levine and Andrei Markovits have pointed out, European critics of America and anti-American attitudes have been much more concerned with the imaginary "essence" of America (sometimes constructed by Europeans for their own purposes) than with its actual social and political activities and practices. More so than anywhere else

---

82. Some of the French critics mockingly referred to the *États-désunis* instead of *États-Unis* to express their growing skepticism about the long-term viability of American institutions and way of life. For more details, see Rémond, *Les États-Unis devant l'opinion française*, 2:650–51. The phrase "*États-désunis*" belongs to Saint-Victor, *Lettres*, 1:2.

83. Also see Roger, *L'ennemi américain*, 61–65.

84. For an excellent analysis of the complex relationship between French intellectuals and America, see Jean-Philippe Mathy, *Extrême-Occident: French Intellectuals and America* (Chicago: University of Chicago Press, 1993). For an informed survey of nineteenth-century French visions of America, see Jeremy Jennings's chapter ("French Visions of America: From Tocqueville to the Civil War") in this volume. It would also be interesting to compare Jacquemont's and Tocqueville's ideas with those of Achille Murat from his book *A Moral and Political Sketch of the United States of North America* (London: Effingham Wilson, 1833).

in the world, the European representation of America has been a particularly loaded concept and complex entity and served a wide variety of purposes, some political, others cultural.[85] As Europe's "Other," America's image has been constructed in such a way as to stir imagination, provide escape, or give comfort to its friends and critics alike.

Jacquemont's misgivings about the possibility of achieving happiness in America did not lead to a more articulated and trenchant political critique of American democracy. Reflecting back at his visit of the New World, he had words of appreciation for the Americans' science of self-government and common sense. As such, Jacquemont's travel to America was an opportunity to compare critically two different cultures and types of civilization. In this regard, he was a precursor of those French republicans who made a fundamental distinction between the *moral* aspects of American democracy that they openly questioned and its *political* institutions and principles that they embraced.[86] What is particularly interesting in Jacquemont's case is that his conclusion that individual happiness is more or less independent of forms of government coexisted with a sincere appreciation of many political aspects of American democracy. Although Jacquemont's reflections on America evinced a few (mostly French) stereotypes—he "saw America with Stendhal's eyes," Crouzet argued[87]—he correctly grasped the general trends of American society that made it the laboratory of a new and unique democratic experiment in the entire world. In this respect, Tocqueville followed a few years later in Jacquemont's footsteps, even if he probably never knew it.

85. See Andrei Markovits, *European Anti-Americanism (and Anti-Semitism): Ever Present though Always Denied,* Working Series Paper 108 (Cambridge, Mass.: Minda de Gunzburg Center for European Studies, Harvard University, 2004); also Markovits, *Uncouth Nation: Why Europe Dislikes America* (Princeton: Princeton University Press, 2007). For more information, see Alan Levine's chapter, "The Idea of America in the History of European Political Thought: 1492–9/11," in this volume.

86. For more details, see Rémond, *Les États-Unis devant l'opinion française,* 2:667–72. This dichotomy appeared, for example, in an article published in *Revue républicaine* in 1834: "From the moral point of view, we do not belong to the American school. . . . From the practical point of view, . . . we belong to the American school . . . in this sense that we invoke the example of America as a practical proof that demonstrates the application of the republican doctrine of universal vote and its consequences" (quoted in Rémond, *Les États-Unis devant l'opinion française,* 2:668; my translation).

87. Crouzet, *Stendhal et L'Amerique,* 167.

6

TYRANNY AND TRAGEDY IN BEAUMONT'S *MARIE*

Christine Dunn Henderson

The storm is visibly gathering, one can hear its
distant rumblings;
but none can say whom the lightning will strike.
—*Gustave de Beaumont,* Marie (1835)

"Thus, in the beginning, all the world was *America*,"[1] wrote John Locke, articulating one of the main strands through which America has been viewed by European visitors—as a virgin nature, a bountiful point of departure from which free and equal human beings are able to write their own destinies, unencumbered by the orders and hierarchies of a European past. The image of the noble savage and Chateaubriand's romanticized portraits of Native American life exemplify this perspective.[2] Linked to the idea of an unencumbered past is the image of America as the future, a clean slate upon which political and social arrangements better suited to human nature could be created. America, then, offered a glimpse of the future. Alexis de Tocqueville's famous statement that "in America I saw more than America; I sought there an image of democracy itself, of its penchants, of its character, of its prejudices, of its passions; I wanted to understand it if only at least to know what we ought to hope or fear from it"[3] reminds us of the force

---

1. John Locke, *The Second Treatise,* ed. C. B. Macpherson (Indianapolis, Ind.: Hackett Publishing Company, Inc., 1980), §49.

2. François-René de Chateaubriand, *Travels in America,* trans. Richard Switzer (Lexington: University of Kentucky Press, 1969).

3. My translation. The original passage reads, "dans l'Amérique j'ai vu plus que l'Amérique; j'y ai cherché une image de la démocratie elle-même, de ses penchants, de son caractère, de ses préjugés, de ses passions; j'ai voulu la connaître, ne fût-ce que pour savoir du moins ce que nous devions espérer ou craindre d'elle" (Alexis de Tocqueville, *De la Démocratie en Amérique,* in *Oeuvres* [Paris: Gallimard, 1992], 2:15).

of that image of America as a future,[4] and also of the Guizotian context within which both Tocqueville and his friend Gustave de Beaumont understood their shared journey to America to be an investigation into the unfolding of a history of equality.[5]

Tocqueville's study of nineteenth-century America is the most famous and perhaps the best synthetic account ever written about this country; worth bearing in mind, however, is that Tocqueville did not initially envisage *Democracy in America* as a single-authored work. In its original conception, *Democracy in America* was to be a joint endeavor between Tocqueville and Beaumont, his intellectual partner and his companion during the 1831–32 voyage to the United States. Tocqueville and Beaumont's plan for co-authored *Democracy in America* seems to have included a division of labor, according to which Tocqueville would analyze American institutions and Beaumont would focus his energies upon Anglo-American mores. Yet somewhere along the way, they abandoned the idea of a common project and turned instead to separate endeavors.

That the two young Frenchmen envisaged a joint reflection on and analysis of America would have been surprising to none of their contemporaries, for their personal closeness and intellectual similarity was striking to friends and foes alike. The German poet Heinrich Heine described them as "these two inseparables,"[6] while Jean-Jacques Ampère put it more lyrically, referring to Beaumont as "that other you" in verse addressed to Tocqueville.[7] The fact that Beaumont and Tocqueville both applied the pronoun "our" to their political ideas and intellectual undertakings indicates the depth as well as the extent of their partnership. Yet within this similarity were some differences. Three years Tocqueville's senior, Beaumont was lively and outgoing where Tocqueville was taciturn, cheerful where Tocqueville was melancholy. These were largely temperamental differences; otherwise, the duo formed two complementary halves of a whole, "pefect[ing] each other superbly." As Heine noted, "One, the severe thinker, the other, the man of gushing feeling, go together like a bottle of vinegar and a bottle of oil."[8]

4. One counterimage to America as a land of possibility is America as the symbol of degeneracy. James Ceasar's discussion of this is excellent, particularly in the context of America and racial theory. See especially chapters 1 and 4 of James W. Ceasar, *Reconstructing America: The Symbol of America in Modern Thought* (New Haven: Yale University Press, 1997).

5. During 1829–30, Tocqueville and Beaumont attended François Guizot's lectures on French history and on the history of European civilization.

6. Heinrich Heine, *Allemands et Français,* quoted in Seymour Drescher, "Tocqueville and Beaumont: A Rationale for Collective Study," in *Tocqueville and Beaumont on Social Reform,* ed. and trans. Seymour Drescher (New York: Harper and Row, 1968), 201.

7. Jean-Jacques Ampère, *La Démocratie: À M. de Tocqueville,* quoted in Drescher, "Tocqueville and Beaumont," 201. For more information, see Jeremy Jennings's chapter, "French Visions of America: From Tocqueville to the Civil War," in this volume.

8. Heine, quoted in Drescher, "Tocqueville and Beaumont," 201.

These differences in Tocqueville's and Beaumont's temperaments are discernable in the projects each pursued once the idea of a collaborative *Democracy in America* had been abandoned; the year 1835 witnessed the publication of the fruits of both their labors, with Tocqueville issuing the more institutionally oriented first volume of *Democracy in America,* and Beaumont bringing forth a quasi-novel entitled *Marie: Or, Slavery in the United States,* and carrying the subtitle *Tableau of American Mores.*[9] That Beaumont would ultimately concentrate on America's racial situation is not surprising, for the plights of freed blacks and of Indians seem to have captured his attention quite early during the voyage to America. *Marie*'s focus on racial inequality is, moreover, consistent with the sympathy for the downtrodden and the interest in democratic social justice that seem to have motivated much of Beaumont's political activism. That these themes continued to hold Beaumont's attention throughout his public life can be seen in his writings on prison reform and the Algerian question; his speeches on child labor and on abolition, and his activism for these causes;[10] these concerns also characterize Beaumont's other major work, the two-volume *Ireland.*

While *Democracy in America* brought Tocqueville immediate and lasting renown, *Marie*'s fate was more complicated. Beaumont's novel achieved quick success with critics and readers in France, winning the prestigious Montyon Prize from the French Academy, and *Marie* has been cited as "the most influential work of its generation in French on slavery in America" as well as one of the most important factors in shaping the image of America throughout Europe.[11] Yet within a generation *Marie* had faded into relative obscurity in France. To say that the novel's success on this side of the Atlantic was even shorter lived would be a gross overstatement, for no English translation of the novel was published until 1958; not surprisingly, scholarship on *Marie*—and on Beaumont more generally—is fairly sparse.[12] *Marie*'s failure to find lasting audiences may be partly attributed to the novel's highly romanticized style, and its neglect in the United States is certainly also due to the social and political climate of the mid-nineteenth century, which was unfavorable to Beaumont's explorations of miscege-

9. The second volume of *Democracy in America,* which focuses more explicitly on *moeurs,* appeared in 1840.

10. Seymour Drescher's *Tocqueville and Beaumont on Social Reform* contains some of these shorter writings and speeches. Because of Tocqueville and Beaumont's collaborative relationship, Jennifer Pitts's edition of Tocqueville's *Writings on Empire and Slavery* (Baltimore: Johns Hopkins University Press, 2001) offers an additional window into the political and social issues which interested both men.

11. Drescher, *Tocqueville and Beaumont on Social Reform,* 204.

12. Which is not to say nonexistent. The 1999 reissue of the Chapman translation of *Marie,* together with the 2006 republication of Beaumont's *Ireland,* give some cause for optimism that interest in Beaumont's thought might undergo a revival. The three-volume *Correspondence d'Alexis de Tocqueville et de Gustave de Beaumont* (Paris: Gallimard, 1967) and the extensive Tocqueville and Beaumont materials available in Yale's Beinecke Library provide rich sources for future studies.

nation, slavery, and racial prejudice. George W. Pierson views all of these factors as contributing to *Marie*'s slip into obscurity, finding that the novel "was badly done; it was published in the wrong country; and it came twenty years too soon."[13]

Despite its flaws, *Marie* is worthy of serious study, and I propose turning attention to it here, with the suggestion that the novel, like its creator, is "inseparable" from Tocqueville's *Democracy in America*. Indeed, the relationship between the two books is akin to the relationship between the two Frenchmen, for at first glance the differences between the two works are most striking: *Democracy in America* is a treatise, whereas *Marie* is a sentimental novel; *Democracy in America* explores a range of topics, whereas *Marie* is explicitly framed by the theme of race and racial prejudice; Tocqueville chooses an analytic tone and approach, whereas Beaumont seeks actively to engage the reader's emotions in the main text and relegates the more technical analyses to the appendixes. But a closer inspection belies the depth of these differences. Most obviously, the works are connected by their creators' awareness of the magnitude of the question of "the three races" for the future of American democracy; as evidence of this shared awareness, we see Tocqueville devoting the longest chapter of *Democracy in America* to this very theme. Moreover, just as Tocqueville is not neutrally analytic in *Democracy in America, Marie* is also not simply a novel.[14] Rather, *Marie* is a half-novel in which Beaumont balances his dramatic narrative with thirteen scientific appendixes on topics as diverse as race relations, religion, family life, and Native American social organization.[15] Although the combination of romantic novel and theoretical treatise is somewhat jarring to the reader and may partially account for the novel's consignment to obscurity, Beaumont envisioned a balance between the fictional and the theoretical, hoping that the storyline would draw

13. G. W. Pierson, "Gustave de Beaumont: Liberal," *Franco-American Review/Revue franco-américaine* 1, no. 4 (1937): 315. André Jardin, who does acknowledge Beaumont's originality in focusing on racial inequality rather than slavery, is nevertheless sharply critical of the novel as "un livre sans unité, alourdi de longueurs, qu'il s'agisse de digressions morales ou de descriptions où l'influence d'*Atala* est trop sensible" (Gustave de Beaumont, *Lettres d'Amérique*, ed. André Jardin and G. W. Pierson [Vendôme: Imprimerie des Presses Universitaires de France, 1973], 18).

14. While they differ in genre, both *Democracy in America* and *Marie* are—to borrow René Rémond's classification—"works of sythesis" that begin from accurate reportage of facts but aim ultimately to investigate the underlying causes of the facts, their relations, and their effects (Réne Rémond, *Les Etats-Unis devant l'opinion française* [Paris: Librairie Armand Colin, 1962], 1:383). Beaumont and Tocqueville, "allant plus profound que la masse des écrits simplement descriptifs et des ouvrages de pure information, projetait sur les aspects principaux et les pus charactéristques de la réalité américaine un faisceau d'explication, un réseau d'interprétations que renouvelaient sensiblement la répresentation des Etats-Unis" (1:390).

15. Rémi Clignet asserts that the themes treated in the appendices directly or indirectly affect the novel's main action (Rémi Clignet, "The Contributions of Beaumont to Democracy in America: His Analysis of Race Relations and Slavery," *American Studies International* 39, no. 2 [2001]: 35). See also Rémond, *Les Etats-Unis*, 1:388.

in readers who would be further persuaded by the informative appendixes.[16] *Marie* is a "roman à thèse," whose pleasing form masks a more serious purpose.[17] As Beaumont explains in his foreword, "I have tried to clothe my work in less severe garb in order to attract that portion of the public which seeks in a book ideas for the intellect and emotions for the heart."[18]

In suggesting that despite their differences in form, tone, and style, Tocqueville's *Democracy in America* and Beaumont's *Marie* are as connected as their creators, I am saying nothing new here, for both authors attested to the books' relationship. Tocqueville acknowledges the link between the two works and the importance of his friend's novel in the introduction to the first volume of *Democracy in America* by commenting, "Another author is soon to portray the main characteristics of the American people and, casting a thin veil over the seriousness of his purpose, give to truth charms I could not rival."[19] Beaumont offers a similar cross-reference in the opening pages of *Marie:* "At the very moment when my book will be published, another will appear which will shed the most brilliant illumination upon the democratic institutions of the United States. I refer to the work of M. Alexis de Tocqueville" (*Marie,* 4).

Of course, Tocqueville's work goes beyond institutional analysis, branching out into investigations of American *moeurs* via explorations of topics as diverse as American commerce, literature, religion, and philosophy. Beaumont's novel, by contrast, focuses explicitly on *moeurs* alone, and within that focus, one theme dominates: the moral consequences of slavery, especially as manifested through racial prejudice against African Americans. Via this theme, Beaumont is able to

16. Diana Schaub observes that "*Marie*'s fate was that of so many half-breeds—it was rejected by both camps" (Diana J. Schaub, "Perspectives on Slavery: Beaumont's *Marie* and Tocqueville's *Democracy in America,*" *Legal Studies Forum* 12, no. 4 [1998]: 609).

17. Rémond, *Les Etats-Unis,* 1:407–8. Beaumont makes a similar point in the novel's introduction.

18. Gustave de Beaumont, *Marie: Or, Slavery in the United States,* trans. Barbara Chapman (Baltimore: Johns Hopkins University Press, 1999), 3. Subsequent references to the novel will be within the text, as *Marie,* followed by page numbers referring to this edition.

19. Alexis de Tocqueville, *Democracy in America,* ed. J. P. Mayer and trans. George Lawrence (New York: Perennial Library, 1988), 19. Unless otherwise noted, subsequent references to *Democracy in America* will be within the text, as *DA,* followed by page numbers referring to this edition.

Tocqueville offers an assessment of the purpose and significance of Beaumont's novel in the note following that passage. He writes, "M. de Beaumont's main object was to draw emphatic attention to the condition of the Negroes in Anglo-American society. His book threw new and vivid light on the question of slavery, a vital question for the united republics. I may be mistaken, but I think M. de Beaumont's book, after arousing the vivid interest of those who sought emotions and descriptions therein, should have a more solid and permanent success with those readers who seek, above all, true appreciations and profound truths." In *Democracy in America*'s chapter on America's three races, Tocqueville again refers to Beaumont's work, directing the interested reader to *Marie* and commenting that "Beaumont has plumbed the depths of a question which my subject has allowed me merely to touch upon. . . . His book should be read by all those who want to know into what excesses men may be driven when once they abandon nature and humanity" (*DA,* 340n30).

explore the limits of equality within a society whose political and social forms are democratic. *Marie*'s focus on racial prejudice rather than slavery accounts for the novel's Baltimore setting as well as the fact that neither slaves nor slaveholders nor plantations are depicted in what has often been described as novel about slavery. Beaumont attributes the continued separation of blacks from whites to racial prejudice, which he finds throughout the United States, in states in which slavery has been abolished as well as in the slaveholding states. "Slave or free," he writes, "the Negroes everywhere form a people apart from the whites" (*Marie,* 4). That this prejudice, born of the institution of slavery, has remained after the abolition of slavery in the North suggests the grave nature of this problem within a society founded upon the idea of equality. As Beaumont writes:

> Each day it deepens the abyss which separates the two races and pursues them in every phase of social and political life; it governs the mutual relations of the whites and the colored men, corrupting the habits of the first, whom it accustoms to domination and tyranny, and ruling the fate of the Negroes, whom it dooms to the persecution of the whites; and it generates between them hatreds so violent, resentments so lasting, clashes so dangerous, that one may rightly say it will influence the whole future of American society. (*Marie,* 5–6)[20]

The novel's focus on racial prejudice's extralegal dimension is one of its truly original and groundbreaking characteristics.[21] Beaumont's emphasis on the informal forces that shape democratic societies reveals his connection to Tocqueville, and *Marie*'s treatment of this raises several Tocquevillean motifs—especially the tyranny of the majority, the relation of *moeurs* and laws, the legacy of slavery, and the question of racial identity. These themes merit further investigation in this essay, both because they pose perennial questions for democratic societies, and because they ask us to consider the status of unequals among nominal equals. *Marie* essentially asks us to confront the question of whether a truly multicultural society is possible, and for this reason, it is of particular importance today.

20. Beaumont echoes Jefferson's understanding of slavery's harmful effects on both masters and slaves. See Jefferson, *Notes on the State of Virginia,* Query XVIII: "The whole commerce between master and slave is a perpetual exercise of the most boisterous passions, the most unremitting despotism on the one part, and degrading submissions on the other" (in Jefferson, *Writings,* ed. Merrill D. Peterson [New York: Library of America, 1984], 288).

21. Rémond finds *Marie* to be the first French novel—if not the first novel—focusing on this particular theme (Rémond, *Les Etats-Unis,* 2:736). In his introduction to his collection of Beaumont's 1831–32 correspondence from America, Jardin also notes the originality of *Marie*'s focus on racial inequality (Jardin, introduction to Beaumont, *Lettres d'Amérique,* 18).

A TRAGIC ROMANCE

Before moving forward to explore these themes more closely, however, a brief outline of the novel is in order. *Marie* depicts the tragic romance between Ludovic, a young Frenchman, and Marie, a beautiful American woman of mixed-race ancestry. Marie is the daughter of Daniel Nelson, a prosperous Baltimore gentleman, and his now-deceased wife, Theresa, a native of New Orleans. Nelson is among the Americans with whom Ludovic's family was previously acquainted, and upon his arrival in the United States, Ludovic becomes associated with the family,[22] striking up a friendship with Daniel's son, George, a social and political activist, and falling in love with his daughter, Marie, who devotes herself to charitable works and who seems to avoid him. Ludovic eventually learns the "mystery" of Nelson's children's heritage: although their mother appeared to be white, her great-grandmother had been black.[23] Nelson did not learn of Theresa's heritage until after their marriage, and the revelation about his wife's ancestry did not diminish Nelson's love for her or their children; because of the majority's prejudice against blacks, however, the spread of that knowledge cost the Nelsons most of their New Orleans friends, led to his wife's death, and seems to have been the reason for the family's subsequent flight to Baltimore and the relatively low profile they keep in that city.[24]

As a foreigner untouched by American racial prejudice, Ludovic embodies the Enlightenment-born notion of a colorblind France, which Beaumont contrasts to the prejudices lurking beneath America's rhetoric of fundamental equality of all in creation and in rights. Because the rational ideals of liberty and equality operate without obstacle in Ludovic's character, his knowledge of Marie's heritage does not alter his feelings—which are reciprocated by Marie—nor does it deter him from his desire to wed her. Cautioned about American

---

22. Beaumont's description of the Nelsons as "An American Family" is thought provoking, in terms of the racial theme and in considering Marie as a young American woman. His depiction of the family's interactions merits comparison to Tocqueville's analysis of the democratic family in volume 2, part 3 of *Democracy in America*.

23. Also called a "shame" and a "misfortune" (*Marie*, 52, 53, 57), Marie and Nelson's mixed parentage is described as "the great abyss which separates" them (*Marie*, 48); Beaumont verbally associates their racial heritage with grief, with fate, with sorrow, and with cursedness (e.g., *Marie*, 51, 52, 120, 133).

24. Ludovic's relative is singled out by Nelson as the only friend who remained faithful even after the public revelation of Theresa Nelson's racial heritage (*Marie*, 55). Not only do the colorblind attitudes of Ludovic and his family approximate Beaumont's own stance, but they also exemplify the French relative unconcern with race and racial mixing during this period. For an opposing account of the attitudes of white Frenchmen toward Africans, see William Cohen, *The French Encounter with Africans: White Responses to Blacks (1530–1880)* (Bloomington: Indiana University Press, 1980), or David Brion Davis, *The Problem of Slavery in Western Culture* (1966; repr., Oxford: Oxford University Press, 1988).

prejudice toward racial mixing and about the force of majority opinion in all aspects of American society, though, Ludovic agrees to Nelson's requirement that he journey throughout the United States before marrying Marie in order to observe American attitudes toward race. Upon Ludovic's return from his travels, the young lovers attempt to marry in New York, but the ceremony is disrupted by a race riot.[25] The couple leaves civilization, seeking happiness outside of society and beyond reach of the majority's disapproval; in Michigan's wilderness, Marie succumbs to a mysterious illness and dies. Adding to the tragic tableau, George is also killed while participating in a rebellion of Native Americans against the U.S. government. Grieving and disillusioned, Ludovic retreats to a hermit's existence, choosing to remain outside of the society he and Marie had fled.

LAW, MORES, AND THE LEGACIES OF SLAVERY

In Beaumont's view, America's problem with racial prejudice is closely linked to dangers inherent in any democratic society, and he shares Tocqueville's understanding of the scope and force of majority rule in America as well as Tocqueville's alertness to the possible dangers of majority tyranny. The travels that Nelson commands Ludovic to undertake awaken the young Frenchman to the extent of the majority's power beyond the legal forms, and his eyes are opened to the deep-seated prejudice against blacks found throughout the United States. During this voyage throughout the United States, Ludovic—who might well be a stand-in for Beaumont—comes to understand that the "slave problem" is less the legal forms that permit chattel slavery than the "prejudice, powerful, inflexible, widespread in all classes, which dominates America, with *no voice* raised against it" (*Marie*, 71, emphasis added). On one hand, the situation seems to be improving, for slavery is gradually disappearing throughout America,[26] yet the abolition of slavery as an institution solves only one part of the problem, for it does little to ameliorate racial tensions, prejudice, and discrimination. Tocqueville shares Beaumont's assessment of this difficulty, observing, "I see clearly that in one part of the country the legal barrier that separates the two races is tending to descend, but not the barrier of mores. I see slavery receding; the prejudice to which it gave birth is immovable."[27]

25. Beaumont's depiction of the riot is based on the New York City race riot of July 1834, which he attributes to the "offended pride of the whites at the pretensions to equality shown by the colored people" (*Marie*, 243). Beaumont's full account of the race riot is found in appendix L.

26. Beaumont and Tocqueville seem to agree that this is due at least as much to white economic self-interest as to the force of any moral principles (*Marie*, 60; *DA*, 348–50).

27. My translation. The original passage reads: "je vois bien que, dans certaine partie du pays, la barrière légale qui sépare les deux races tend à s'abaisser, non celle des moeurs: j'aperçois l'esclavage qui recule; le préjugé qu'il fait naître est immobile" (Tocqueville, *Oeuvres*, 2:397).

The condition of emancipated blacks in free states best illustrates the nature and magnitude of America's real problem, for although Northern laws extend legal and civil equality to free blacks, they are unable to enjoy that equality. Their freedom is hollow: while they are technically equal to their white co-citizens, they are "covered with disgrace perhaps worse than slavery; all people of color branded by public contempt, overwhelmed with abuse, more degraded by shame even than by misery" (*Marie,* 71). The majority no longer legally oppresses a minority, yet it continues to make its force felt by excluding that minority from equal membership in society. Although no juridical barriers between the races exist in the North, the social conventions maintain a more rigid separation than even in the South. Describing the isolation of the Northern emancipated black, Beaumont comments that "as a slave, he had no place in human society; now he is counted among men, but as the last" (*Marie,* 72). Tocqueville observed this as well, offering the following account of the separation white Americans strive to maintain: "In the North, the white man no longer clearly sees the barrier that separates him from the degraded race, and he keeps the Negro at a distance all the more carefully because he fears lest one day they be confounded together" (*DA,* 343). Tocqueville's manuscript notes at this point reveal the extent to which he shared Beaumont's moral outrage, for he condemns the situation as a "miserable mockery" of the principle of equality.[28]

Northern segregationist attitudes are attributable to a deep-seated belief in black inferiority, originally advanced by whites in order to justify slavery, but continuing well after the institution's abolition in that part of the country. Attempting to explain why this belief has endured after slavery's abolition, Tocqueville finds a "natural prejudice that leads men to scorn the one who has been his inferior, long after he has become his equal." The experience of legal inferiority, it seems, gives rise to a corresponding moral sense, or an "imagined inequality rooted in mores" (*DA,* 314). In *Marie,* however, Beaumont provides another account of this prejudice's genesis. During an exchange with Ludovic and George, Nelson offers a two-part description of white American attitudes, revealing that "the black race is despised in America because it is a race of slaves; it is hated because it aspires to liberty" (*Marie,* 58). The description is instructive, demonstrating the power of the ideas of liberty and of equality within democratic hearts as well as the troubling truth that those ideals are not necessarily congruent. Liberty and equality are generally understood as positive forces, leading to ever-expanding circles of free and self-governing peoples, yet Beaumont's depiction of American racial attitudes presents a darker possibility, in which the force

---

28. Alexis de Tocqueville, *De la Démocratie en Amérique,* ed. Eduardo Nolla (Paris: J. Vrin, 1990), 1:265.

of those ideals helps justify the continuation of the enslavement of large groups of humans. In America, the majority's attachment to liberty and equality does *not* inevitably lead to a more enlightened society in which people are freed from their bondage. Instead, those ideals work against their own diffusion, and we witness lovers of liberty and equality judging the slaves, apparently condemning them for their plight and concluding that an insufficient love of liberty among blacks has either caused their enslavement or keeps them from throwing off their chains. As a consequence of this distorted logic, the force of the love of equality in the American heart turns to the hatred of a supposedly inferior race and to the exclusion of that race from the basic right to live freely.[29] As Nelson notes, "No people are more attached than we to the principles of equality; but we will not allow a race inferior to ours to share in our rights" (*Marie,* 58).

Beaumont's appendix on the New York race riots of 1834 amplifies this exchange among Nelson, George, and Ludovic, for the appendix highlights still another unsavory dimension of the force with which the love of liberty can take hold of the human heart. The appendix's description of the New York race riots reveals the manner in which pride and anger can reinforce majority views and help people who hold those views avoid a critical reexamination of them. In a passage reminiscent of Tocqueville's ominous observation that the love of liberty exerts less force in the human heart than the love of equality, Beaumont describes how the claim of free blacks to the equality that is their due both extinguishes white pity for the blacks' plight and arouses fierce hostility against them. He writes, "But as soon as they announce their claims to equality, the pride of the whites is aroused, and the pity inspired by misfortune gives way to hatred and scorn" (*Marie,* 243). As long as freed blacks do not disrupt the hierarchy that places them beneath whites, the two races live together peacefully. In the lines preceding the passage just quoted, Beaumont describes this equilibrium: "As long as the freed Negroes show themselves submissive and respectful to the whites, as long as they hold themselves to a position of inferiority, they are assured of support and protection. The American sees in them only those poor unfortunates whom religion and humanity command him to aid" (*Marie,* 243).

The racial character of American slavery further complicates the issue, for color serves as "a constant reminder" (*Marie,* 63) of slavery, of its degradation, and of the beliefs in racial inequalities justifying it. As Nelson notes, "The black who is no longer a slave has been one; and, if he is born free, everyone knows that his father was not" (*Marie,* 63). Modern slavery's racial basis lends it a new character and gives a greater longevity to its legacy. In the ancient world, the

29. Ironically, the grounds for determining a race's inferiority would seem to be its members' attachment to the cause of liberty; in this manner, the circle becomes a vicious one.

distinctions between slave and master vanished once their legal equality was established. In the nineteenth-century context in which Beaumont and Tocqueville wrote, however, removing legal inequalities between blacks and whites had proven insufficient to bring out genuine equality. Tocqueville observes that "memories of slavery dishonors the race, and race perpetuates memories of slavery" (*DA*, 341). The most difficult work of the modern advocates of liberty and equality begins where the greatest task facing those ancient advocates ended. Mores and prejudices must be changed, and given Beaumont's assessment that "custom is more powerful than the law" (*Marie*, 214), this transformation is a formidable task indeed. Beaumont's personal correspondence from America puts this even more forcefully. Writing about the situation of free blacks in Pennsylvania in 1831, he observes, "According to the Constitution, they are equal to Whites and have the same political rights; but laws do not change mores: it is customary here to see a slave in a Negro and to continue to treat him as such."[30]

Through the complexity of Daniel Nelson's character, Beaumont brilliantly underscores the difficulty of changing mores and democratic beliefs. Although Nelson is a native New Englander who avows that "slavery offends the laws of morality and of God" (*Marie*, 59) and who stood by his wife once her origins were revealed, his actual position lies somewhere between enlightenment and bigotry, for he also shares at least some of the Southern prejudices and beliefs in black inferiority that justified slavery and its continuance. In Nelson's analysis, their "naturally restricted" minds cause blacks to "attach little value to liberty." He concludes that this deficiency generally makes emancipation a "fatal gift" for blacks, for they do not know how to use their independence wisely (*Marie*, 59). Nelson believes that because of their inability to support themselves, most emancipated slaves would judge freedom as a less happy condition than bondage. Nelson's belief in blacks' inherent mental inferiority is resistant to reason, and he is impervious to Ludovic's attempts to change his thinking by the rational argument that one cannot make accurate judgments about the natural capacities of blacks by considering slaves, for slavery has deprived them of the opportunity to develop. Ludovic observes that not only can we not know blacks in their natural condition, but generations in bondage may also have rendered the race *less* capable of living freely than it once had been. In a passage worth quoting in its entirety, Ludovic argues:

It is natural that the slave who suddenly becomes free does not know how to use or enjoy independence. Like a man whose legs have been bound from

30. My translation. The original reads, "D'après la Constitution, ils sont égaux aux blancs et ont les mêmes droits politiques; mais les lois ne changent pas les moeurs: on est habitué ici à voir dans un nègre un *esclave* et on continue à le traiter comme tel" (Beaumont, *Lettres d'Amérique*, 171.) The Ameri-

childhood, who is told suddenly to walk, he staggers at every step. Liberty is a deadly weapon is his hands, with which he wounds all about him; and most often, he is his own first victim. But should one conclude that slavery, once established, should be respected? Of course not. Only it is just to say that the generation which receives its freedom is not the generation to enjoy it: the benefits of liberty are reaped only by the following generations. (*Marie*, 59)[31]

Nelson's refusal to accept Ludovic's logic points to the intractability of his beliefs, and it highlights the insufficiency of reason—or even reason as embodied in the law—in the face of belief and mores. Nelson's character provides Beaumont with an ideal vehicle for conveying the depth of his pessimism about the transformation of white Americans' prejudices, for while Nelson's background and personal history ought to make him amenable to a reassessment of majority opinions held without question, he resists such reexamination throughout the novel. Casting further doubt on the hope for change is the fact that while Beaumont acknowledges Christianity's force in the United States, and he understands the opposition between Christianity's fundamental assertion of the "moral equality of man" and slavery (*Marie*, 201), he seems less optimistic about religion's potential to change racial prejudice. Daniel and Marie Nelson are both strongly tied to religion, yet if their religiosity is an accurate indicator of Beaumont's stance, Christianity appears impotent in transforming these particular mores.

If reason makes few inroads against Nelson's (or the majority's) prejudices, emotion and experience are similarly impotent. Although Nelson's experience as a husband and father causes his beliefs about racial inferiority to pain him,[32] that experience proves insufficient to change those beliefs. In George's words, "You were first an American, then a husband" (*Marie*, 59). Here, Beaumont goes beyond Tocqueville's pessimism about the condition of the three races in the United States, for while Tocqueville sees racial amalgamation as one possible (albeit unlikely) way of breaking down white prejudice and black hatred, *Marie* suggests that Beaumont is less optimistic. Tocqueville writes, "It is the mulatto who forms the bridge between black and white; everywhere where there are a great number of mulattoes, the fusion of the two races is not impossible" (*DA*,

---

can situation to which Beaumont attests contrasts with France's Enlightenment-based understanding of equality and idea of inclusive citizenship.

31. In *Democracy in America,* Tocqueville describes the distortion of Native American character because of their contact with Europeans: "In its dealings with the North American Indians, the European tyranny . . . has changed their customs and increased their desires beyond reason, making them more disorderly and less civilized than they had been before. At the same time, the moral and physical condition of these peoples has constantly deteriorated, and in becoming more wretched, they have also become more barbarous" (*DA*, 318).

32. Responding to George, Nelson cries, "Do you not believe that my heart has not bled in judging as I have the race to which your mother was related?" (*Marie*, 61).

356). This comment obviously parallels what Tocqueville writes about half-caste Indians, whose white parentage moves them further away from their *sauvage* condition.[33] Yet *Marie* reminds us that the suggestion may also have this dimension: the possibility that the prejudiced white will be forced to rethink his views of black racial inferiority when the races mix. In other words, when self-interest conflicts with prejudice—for example, when one's child, who is an extended form of the self, is a mulatto—prejudice might be defeated by self-interest. Tocqueville holds out at least faint hope that racial mixing could lead to a fundamental change in *moeurs* and to the gradual erosion of the majority's belief in black inferiority. Beaumont, however, appears more pessimistic than his friend, for despite his belief that "intermarriages are certainly the best, if not the unique, means of fusing the white and the black races" (*Marie*, 245), both the novel's general plot and its depiction of Daniel Nelson reveal grave doubts about the likelihood that intermarriages and racial mixing could make any significant inroads against the democratic majority's prejudices in the short run.[34]

AN OMNIPOTENT AND ALL-REACHING MAJORITY

The difficulties to which Beaumont's analysis of the American racial situation points are but part of more general problems inherent in all democratic societies, for they remind us that an empowered and untempered majority does not always exercise its power benignly. Whether at the ballot box or in the formation of taste, it seems true that public opinion rules absolutely in the United States, with virtually no mechanisms to diffuse or thwart the majority's desires. In Tocqueville's analogy, "The people reign over the American political world as God rules over the universe" (*DA*, 60).[35] *Marie* testifies to the darker possibilities of an omnipotent majority, and Beaumont observes that "in the United States, under the rule of popular sovereignty, there is a majority whose actions are irresistible, which crushes, breaks, annihilates, everything which opposes its power and impedes its passions" (*Marie*, 251). Rather than "refining and enlarging the public view" as James Madison envisaged in *Federalist* 10, American democratic politics merely reflects the majority's opinions and gives them the force of law. In Beau-

---

33. About the half-caste, Tocqueville writes, "Sharing his father's enlightenment without entirely giving up the savage customs of his race on his mother's side, the half-caste forms the natural link between civilization and barbarism. Everywhere that half-castes have multiplied, the savages have gradually changed their social condition and their mores" (*DA*, 329).

34. While intermarriages are a means to the erosion of racial prejudice, Beaumont also understood them as an indicator of that erosion having already transpired. See *Marie*, 245.

35. The quotation concludes, "It is the cause and the end of all things; everything rises out of it and is absorbed back into it" (*DA*, 60).

mont's analysis, American democracy lacks intermediate bodies and institutions capable of breaking the majority's force. For better or worse, the power of the majority extends into all areas of life, and it is able to exert its political and moral power to systematically exclude those it deems unworthy of full membership into society. As Tocqueville observed, "though the form of government is representative, it is clear that the opinions, prejudices, interests, and even passions of the people can find no lasting obstacles preventing them from being manifest in the daily conduct of society."[36] Admittedly, Tocqueville does suggest that quasi-aristocratic bodies such as the courts and the legal profession more generally might counter the majority's wishes; Beaumont, however, does not emphasize these potential protections.

Beaumont and Tocqueville shared concerns about the unstoppable force of democratic power, and the specter of the tyranny of the majority emerges at least as strongly in Beaumont's work as in Tocqueville's. Hence, Beaumont's judgment that all white Americans share in the oppression of blacks, for

in a land of equality, all citizens are responsible for social injustices; each is a party to them. Not a white man exists in America who is not a barbarous, iniquitous persecutor of the black race.

In Turkey, there is but one tyrant responsible for the most frightful distress; in the United States, there are, for each act of tyranny, ten million tyrants. (*Marie*, 73–74)

RACE, IDENTITY, AND SOCIETY: THE LIMITS OF SELF-MAKING

While Beaumont's awareness of the majority's tyrannical tendencies is clearly manifested in his discussions of white Americans' racial prejudices, his treatment of this theme contains an additional (and very postmodern) wrinkle, for he depicts race as a socially constructed identity, defined almost entirely by the majority's opinion.[37] *Marie* seems to have been inspired by an event Beaumont witnessed in Baltimore, which he relates in the novel's preface. He describes his puzzlement over the presence of a beautiful white woman among the mulattoes in a segregated theater audience. Upon inquiring, he learned that "local tradition has established her ancestry, and everybody knows" her racial makeup and, therefore, how society ought to treat her. Similarly, the presence of an apparently

36. *DA*, 173. See also *Democracy in America*, vol. 1, part 2, chap. 1 more generally.
37. Given the extent of the majority's extrapolitical powers, Beaumont's statement that "the fact is that in America the very race of the slaves is a more serious problem than their slavery" (*Marie*, 214) is particularly telling in this context.

mulatto woman among the whites was justified, for "local tradition" had established her Spanish heritage (*Marie*, 5). Appearances, or even facts, matter little once the majority has made up its mind, and its opinions define social relations as completely as its will defines the political sphere.

Like the woman in the Baltimore theatre, Marie Nelson also appears white, yet her society defines her as black. Marie accepts the majority's definition of her racial identity; in her own mind, she is black rather than 1/32 black, or mixed race. Her language of separation and shame—she "blushes at her African origin" (*Marie*, 61)—also suggests her acceptance of the majority's opinions concerning African American abilities and the place of African Americans in American society.[38] Despite the fact that she has lived her entire life as a free, white woman, her self-understanding more closely mirrors that of the slave described by Tocqueville: "From birth, he has been told that his race is naturally inferior to the white man and almost believing that, he holds himself in contempt. . . . If he could, he would gladly repudiate himself entirely" (*DA*, 319). Marie's shame at her origins reveals yet another dimension of Beaumont's pessimism about the possibilities for change—Marie's apparent whiteness does not lead others to rethink their opinions about race; instead, the power of majority opinion assigns an identity to her, and she seems incapable of resisting that imposition of identity or of redefining it.

Marie is not the only member of the Nelson family whose understanding of race and identity seems to have been determined by the majority rather than through individual experience. George's character also reveals the extent to which racial identity is constructed by majority opinion, for like his sister, George views himself as a member of the black race rather than a mulatto. Yet George accepts the social definition of race only to the extent that he understands his own fate as linked to the fate of the black race; unlike Marie, however, George is proud of his racial heritage and does not accept the white assertions of black inferiority. In a spirited rebuttal to Nelson's statement that the "natural restriction" of black minds makes them "unfit" for liberty, George asserts, "It is true that according to law a Negro is not a man; he is chattel, a thing. Yes, but you will see that he is a thinking thing, an acting thing, that can hold a dagger!" Laws

38. Amazingly, Marie also claims "that God himself separated the white from the black" (*Marie*, 66), and she accepts other elements of the white stereotype of blacks (*Marie*, 61). Beaumont's interest in using Marie's self-understanding as a means of reflecting the majority opinions of white Americans can also be seen by comparing Marie's self-presentation to the figure of the *métis* in Afro-Caribbean literature, for the *métis*'s mixed heritage often elevates her above the purely African slave, whereas for Marie (and nineteenth-century Americans, generally), the presence of black blood consigns her to the level of the slave. For some discussion of representations of the *métis* in Afro-Caribbean literary, see Beverley Ormerod's "The Martinican Concept of 'Creoleness': A Multiracial Redefinition of Culture," *Mots Pluriels* 7 (1998), http://motspluriels.arts.uwa.edu.au/MP798bo.html.

and public opinion might oppress blacks, but "some day he will stand up and look you in the eye, and kill you. . . . He has but one thought: vengeance" (*Marie,* 60). For George, the "festering sore of slavery" (*Marie,* 62) can only begin to heal through the cathartic bloodletting of a slave rebellion. Both Tocqueville and Beaumont thought slave uprisings were likely, for they believed that despite attempts to dehumanize African Americans, neither the hatred of enslavement nor the love of liberty could ever be extinguished from within the human heart. The struggle for freedom seems part of human existence; for the slave, this struggle eventually places him or her, just as it places George, "in a state of open rebellion against the society and the laws which have enslaved him" (*Marie,* 192).The vengeance George craves, however, is both an assertion of independence from white society as well as an illustration of the extent to which his identity remains connected to it, because he is only capable of defining himself in opposition to it.

George's rebellion is doubly unsuccessful, for at the crucial moment, the slaves who had planned to join the Indians abandon them, and George is killed in the defeated uprising. His death is but part of the tableau of sorrow with which the novel concludes: Marie has died of a mysterious illness that is probably a manifestation of sorrow or shame,[39] the broken and grieving Nelson turns to Christian missionary work among the Indians, and the disillusioned Ludovic rejects society, living instead as a hermit beyond the borders of "civilized" America. Ludovic's rejection of American society inverts the image of the American as the new Adam,[40] for his discovery that the new world is flawed rather than paradisiacal leads him to renounce it permanently. If the resolution of the novel's plot is any indication, Beaumont sees no possibility for amelioration of race relations within American borders, and the America he depicts has no place—literally or figuratively—for those who question or who stand outside the dominant narratives about race.

CONCLUSION

Both Beaumont and Tocqueville grasped the gravity of the racial situation they observed on American soil, and they concluded that it posed one of the greatest threats to the survival of American democracy. Their own liberal convictions and their belief in the moral equality of human beings led both to oppose the institution of slavery and to actively support abolitionist causes in France. In recogniz-

39. Gerard Ferguson suggests that Marie's death can also be read as a metaphor for the likely failure of interracialism as a means of breaking down racial barriers as long as slavery exists (*Marie,* xiv).
40. Davis, *The Problem of Slavery in Western Culture,* 7.

ing American slavery's evils, however, each also understood it within a broader context that took into account the related problems of a tyrannical majority, the presence of legal inequalities within a democratic society, and the difficulties of changing the mores that justify such inequalities. Both also perceived the depth and durability of mutual prejudice and hatred—legacies of slavery that continue to haunt the United States. Their analysis of American mores and of the resistance of those mores to change—even by appeals to either individual reason or reason embodied in the law—led each to grave doubts that the situation could be peacefully resolved on American soil. *Marie* testifies eloquently to Beaumont's pessimism. *Democracy in America,* in which Tocqueville also concludes that a peaceful resolution to the problem of America's "three races" is unlikely, offers an equally bleak vision of America's future.

The tableau of sorrow with which the novel concludes is Beaumont's starkest commentary on America's failure to fulfill the promise of her founding principles. Yet somehow the novel avoids depicting America simply as dystopian or degenerate, and Beaumont does not merely become another foreign observer whose disenchantment with America's reality eroded his belief in her ideals. Jean-Phillippe Mathy's account of "how French liberals such as Tocqueville, Stendhal, or Jacquemont became disenchanted with the American dream and traded, like Mrs. Trollope, their admiration of the *political* achievements of the new republic for a deep distrust in the *cultural* constraints of a democratic society" seems an overstatement of both Tocqueville and Beaumont's positions.[41] Beaumont's treatment of America is more balanced than this—certainly pessimistic, but also standing somewhere between the utopian and dystopian extremes. The gap between the image of America as the land of promise and the reality Beaumont witnessed during his travels is depicted unflinchingly in the novel, but while the novel ends unhappily, its very tragedy underscores the moral rectitude of America's founding principles. Moreover, the tragedy may be read as a particular one—the case of particular individuals, or even, perhaps, the case of a particular country—rather than a universal one. If the novel is understood this way, Beaumont does not prophesy the inevitable failure of democratic equality, of multiculturalism, or of a color-blind society. Rather, *Marie* becomes a cautionary tale, Beaumont's warning to democratic societies of the dangers and difficulties in living up to their professed philosophy of liberty and equality for all.

That America continues to struggle with race relations and with slavery's legacy gives witness to the force and durability of mores, especially among democratic peoples. As Tocqueville observed, "Of all governments, those which have

---

41. Jean-Phillippe Mathy, *Extrême-Occident: French Intellectuals and America* (Chicago: University of Chicago Press, 1993), 32. Also see Aurelian Craiutu's chapter, "A Precursor of Tocqueville: Victor Jacquemont," in this volume.

the least power over mores are free governments."[42] Yet mores can shift over time, and while the American race situation remains imperfect, it shows undeniable improvement. As we look back at *Marie* with almost 175 years of perspective, perhaps the lesson we should draw from Beaumont's novel is *not* one of the future's hopelessness and the impotence of individual effort. Instead, today's vantage point inverts Beaumont's pessimism and imparts a cautiously optimistic note to his novel. With the passing of time, we are able to look beyond the individual tragedies of Marie, Ludovic, and George, and we are able to see what they could not: mores can shift over time, and race relations are gradually improving. In this gradual amelioration, we find evidence that Tocqueville is correct in his perception of history broadly understood as the spread of equality of conditions and of democracy. Individual efforts may fail and particular histories may end in sorrow, but viewed from a long-range perspective, even failed individual effort can be understood as something other than tragic.

---

42. My translation. This comment is found in the margins of *Democracy in America,* vol. 1, part 2, chap. 10. See Nolla's comment in Tocqueville, *De la Démocratie,* 1:273na.

7

FRENCH VISIONS OF AMERICA
From Tocqueville to the Civil War

Jeremy Jennings

When Alexis de Tocqueville arrived in America in early May 1831 he quickly made up his mind about what he saw there.[1] Writing to Ernest de Chabrol from New York, scarcely a month later on June 9, 1831, he asked his friend to imagine "a society formed of all the nations of the world . . . : in a word, a society without roots, without memories, without prejudices, without routines, without common ideas." It was, Tocqueville went on, a society held together by interest alone and for which a republic was the best of governments. Its physical situation was so fortunate that private interest never acted contrary to the public interest. There was no public power and no need of one, and consequently there was no army, no taxation, and no central government. Executive authority was as nothing, possessing neither money nor power. All people could reasonably expect to attain the comforts of life, and all, if they worked hard, knew that their future was secure. Everything was valued by the money it brought in, and all Americans were ready to try their luck at making a fortune. The ancient European traditions of honor and virtue did not exist. America was well ordered and with pure mores.[2]

1. The best account of the visit to America made by Tocqueville and Gustave de Beaumont remains that of George Wilson Pierson, *Tocqueville in America* (Baltimore: Johns Hopkins University Press, 1996).
2. Olivier Zunz and Alan S. Khan, *The Tocqueville Reader: A Life in Letters and Politics* (Oxford: Blackwell, 2002), 40–42.

Some three weeks later, having traveled as far as Yonkers, twenty miles from New York, these first impressions were supplemented by further insights into the character of the American people and the nature of American society. To Louis de Kergorlay he announced that the great majority in America understood republicanism "in the most democratic sense" and that they had a faith in human wisdom and perfectibility. "They believe," he wrote, "in the excellence of the government that rules them, they believe in the wisdom of the masses, provided that they are enlightened, and they do not seem to suspect that there is some education that can never be shared by the masses and that nonetheless can be necessary for governing a state." America convinced him that civilization was moving "toward a democracy without limits" and that this was a movement pushed forward by "an irresistible force."[3]

It would be unnecessarily unkind to suggest that these first impressions were hardly modified by what Tocqueville saw during the rest of his nine-month stay in the New World; on the other hand, it can be said that they contained strong intimations of what would in due course form the content of the most famous (and, some would say, best) book ever written about the United States. Yet it was not the only book written about America by a Frenchman and Tocqueville was only one of many Frenchmen who made a similar voyage of discovery. Nor did the picture presented in *Democracy in America* go unchallenged or without comment, even if, to a large extent, it provided the frame of reference within which other accounts were written. Tocqueville's America, in short, was not the only French America in the nineteenth century.[4]

The component parts of the French vision of America were various and had been a long time in the making.[5] Certainly, by the mid- to late eighteenth century the idea of America as a land of virtue, liberty, and enlightenment had been firmly established, but this Arcadian myth was often counterbalanced by the recognition that between a civilized and refined (some would say debauched) France and the rural simplicity of American life there existed an unbridgeable chasm.[6] To this were added concerns about the damaging effects of the climate upon both people and animals, a notion supported not only by the evidence of the parlous state of Native Americans but also by Cornelius de Pauw's curious claim that in America dogs did not bark. Nevertheless, in the years that immediately preceded Tocqueville's arrival, there had emerged a relatively standardized

3. Zunz and Khan, *Tocqueville Reader*, 42–49.

4. See especially René Rémond, *Les Etats-Unis devant l'opinion française 1815–1852* (Paris: Fondation nationale des sciences politiques, 1962).

5. See Durand Echeverria, *Mirage in the West: A History of the French Image of American Society to 1815* (Princeton: Princeton University Press, 1957).

6. See Philippe Roger, *L'Ennemi Américain: Généalogie de l'antiaméricanisme français* (Paris: Seuil, 2002).

set of questions that drew the French investigator to America. Was America to provide a new order of liberty that would enable people to escape the constraints of civilization? Could America realize the dream of universal equality and fraternity? Would economic prosperity and urbanization destroy the simple virtues of the American farmer? Was the mercantile spirit, especially when combined with the absence of a fixed and established aristocracy, compatible with the flourishing of the arts and sciences? Would America escape the dominant influence of England and of English culture and religion? How would America set out to tame the vast continent that lay before it? Would America's federal system stand the test of time, and did it provide a valuable demonstration of democracy in action? Above all, nineteenth-century Frenchmen were drawn to America by their sense that it was there that important aspects and developments of a shared future were being realized for the first time.

Among these French visitors was the former Saint-Simonian Michel Chevalier, author of *Lettres sur l'Amérique du Nord,* first published in 1836.[7] According to Seymour Drescher, "Chevalier's journey to America is, after that of Tocqueville and Beaumont, the most noteworthy of their generation."[8] To the trained eye of the Saint-Simonian, Seymour notes, "the wedge of industrial feudalism was already insinuating itself beneath the democratic institutions of the American Republic."[9]

Chevalier's stay postdated that of Tocqueville (which ran from May 1831 until February 1832), although it was considerably longer in duration (October 1833 to November 1835).[10] From the headings provided to each of Chevalier's published chapters it is possible to trace his itinerary with some accuracy, and from this itinerary we learn that he and Tocqueville made two very different journeys. Tocqueville spent the greater part of his time in New York and New England. In addition, he and Beaumont made a brief sojourn in French-speaking Lower Canada and a monthlong expedition to the frontier region around the Great Lakes. Only toward the end of their time did they travel to the South. In contrast, Chevalier, having spent a month in New York, headed northeast and then

7. Michel Chevalier, *Lettres sur l'Amérique du Nord* (Paris: Gosselin, 1836). All references will be to Hauman (Brussels: Hauman Cattoir et Cie, 1838, 2 vols.). Chevalier's text has been translated into English as *Society, Manners and Politics in the United States, being a series of letters on the United States* (Boston: Weeks, Jordan & Co., 1839). It has since been reprinted only once, in 1961, by Doubleday. The English translation is not complete. References to the first English edition have been added in brackets. All translations are therefore my own.

8. Seymour Drescher, *Dilemmas of Democracy: Tocqueville and Moderation* (Pittsburgh: University of Pittsburgh Press, 1968), 53.

9. Drescher, *Dilemmas of Democracy,* 53.

10. For a fuller discussion of Chevalier that brings out the comparisons with Tocqueville, see Jeremy Jennings, "Democracy before Tocqueville: Michel Chevalier's Democracy," *Review of Politics* 68 (2006): 398–427.

south, eventually reaching Charleston. June 1834 found him in Lowell, Massachusetts, and afterward Boston, but by August he had reached Elmington, Virginia. He then set out to New Orleans, stopping off at Pittsburgh, Cincinnati, Louisville, Memphis, and Natchez. He also visited Buffalo and various small towns in Pennsylvania. There is, however, one very significant similarity between the journeys undertaken by Chevalier and Tocqueville. Both went beyond their specific assigned areas of investigation in order to take the European reader to the heart of a new civilization.

CHEVALIER'S AMERICA

As with Tocqueville, Chevalier's inquiry began from the premise that America offered lessons from which Europe, and France in particular, could profit. "The progress achieved by the populations of the New World," he wrote in his introduction, "is of the very highest significance for the general progress of the species."[11] Yet, their points of departure were markedly different. While Tocqueville commenced his analysis of America with the examination of the "exterior form" of North America and the origin of the "Anglo-Americans," quickly to arrive at what he deemed to be two of the central principles determining the character of American democracy—the laws of inheritance and the sovereignty of the people—Chevalier began with the major political issue of the day, President Andrew Jackson's campaign against the second Bank of the United States. This controversy, and the broader context in which it arose, scarcely received mention in Tocqueville's two volumes, but for Chevalier these events, when combined with the earlier nullification crisis that had pitted South Carolina against the federal government over the issue of tariffs, featured as the wider backdrop to the whole tenor of his argument. America, in this view, was entering a period of economic crisis, and this had become a matter of political concern for the simple reason that here was a country where the "industrial interest" was the most important of all.[12] At issue were not minor questions relating to the reform and management of the banking system but the very future of the country.

Nonetheless, this different point of departure took Chevalier directly to the question that was to obsess Tocqueville, for what Chevalier perceived was that the clash between Jackson and the Bank revealed a fundamental conflict between the principles of democracy and aristocracy.[13] In America democracy turned the law "against capitalists, manufacturers, and traders." At one and the same time

---

11. Chevalier, *Lettres sur l'Amérique du Nord*, 1:6 [11].
12. Chevalier, *Lettres sur l'Amérique du Nord*, 1:52 [37].
13. Chevalier, *Lettres sur l'Amérique du Nord*, 1:78–83 [52–55].

democracy possessed "physical force and political power." The bourgeoisie inspired neither fear nor respect. It was numbers alone, rather than natural superiority, enlightenment, or wealth, that counted; and the "democratic party," ready to take its revenge for past humiliations, was the best organized of all.[14] So the Bank, an institution tainted with the reputation of aristocracy, was the subject of uninformed and malign criticism that went against the long-term interests of the country.

Here Chevalier was again led to make an observation that mirrored Tocqueville's own analysis. Dynastic egoism, he remarked, has its equivalent in republics, "especially under a system of *absolute* equality that distributes political power in *absolutely* equal proportions between the expert and the ignorant, between the business elite and writers and the unruly and drunken Irish peasant who has just attained the status of citizen." A people with *absolute* power was just as likely as an *absolute* king to disregard the dictates of experience and wisdom, "a people as much as a king could have its courtesans," especially when its authority was not limited by any "counterbalances."[15]

The difficulties facing the Bank were compounded further by the federal system. In America, Chevalier wrote, "there is no government in the proper sense of the word."[16] Everyone was left to their own devices; there existed a system of "self-government in its purist sense." Both federal and local government operated in "a state of permanent eclipse." Such a system, Chevalier countered, denoted an "abnormal" extension of the principle of individuality; however, in America self-government was a source of progress and "the only political regime to which the American character could adapt itself."[17]

Beneath this concern lay the awareness that a situation of abundance and newness gave rise to a different style of politics. "The word *politics*," Chevalier explained, "cannot have the same meaning in America as it does in Europe."[18] America did not have to concern itself with past treaties and troublesome neighbors or with clashes between interests from the past and those of the present. Rather, the politics of the United States amounted to no more than "the extension of its commerce and the invasion through agriculture of the vast territory bequeathed it by nature."[19] It was these matters that enflamed political and individual passions.

In that sense the Americans were a people who sought, above all, to "econo-

14. Chevalier, *Lettres sur l'Amérique du Nord*, 1:67–69 [46–47].
15. Chevalier, *Lettres sur l'Amérique du Nord*, 1:88–89 [58].
16. Chevalier, *Lettres sur l'Amérique du Nord*, 1:75 [50].
17. Chevalier, *Lettres sur l'Amérique du Nord*, 1:76 [50–51].
18. Chevalier, *Lettres sur l'Amérique du Nord*, 1:118 [76].
19. Chevalier, *Lettres sur l'Amérique du Nord*, 1:118 [76].

mize on time," who were fervent about everything that was fast, brief, and expeditious.[20] In America, Chevalier recounted, the railroads had become "a passion and universal preoccupation" because Americans were "always in a hurry."[21] The same vigorous spirit was evident in political activity. However, this passion for politics was something of an illusion and hid an important truth. The "propagandists" of representative government, Chevalier stated, speak only of the existence of executive, legislative, and judicial power, but the time will soon arrive when they will be forced to recognize the existence of "financial power," or "at the minimum" that the banks will soon constitute a "branch of government" as powerful as any other. This was so because the Bank of the United States was more important to the prosperity of the country than was executive power in its present form. "The true or real government," Chevalier wrote, "is to be found in the banks as much as in any other body or power created by the Constitution."[22]

Chevalier thus took note of an important transition occurring in America that, with the exception of one short (but well-known) chapter in volume 2 of *Democracy in America* devoted to the question "How Aristocracy could issue from Industry," Tocqueville chose largely to leave unexplored. Power was shifting from the representatives of military and legal power toward financial interests. The former had managed to unite and temporarily turn the "multitude" against the latter, but they were bound eventually to be defeated because "the multitude had more to gain from [the latter] than from [the former]." In sum, the great increase in America's wealth derived from Wall Street rather than the activities of the military or the lawyers. In this society, therefore, it was riches, rather than the classical virtues of honor and glory, that constituted the measure of an individual.[23]

These comments upon the perceived comparative merits of wealth and honor take us to the heart of Chevalier's vision of American society. Here, he wrote, everything can be bought. From this it followed that all work, including intellectual work, could be equated with industrial work and paid accordingly. Americans displayed no emotional attachment to places or to homes and lacked a sense of beauty. Family homes were dispensed with like old clothes. Consequently, behind every act and every pronouncement made by an American there lay a financial calculation.[24]

The American, then, was consumed by a passion for wealth. The source of

20. Chevalier, *Lettres sur l'Amérique du Nord*, 1:108 [69].
21. Chevalier, *Lettres sur l'Amérique du Nord*, 1:127–35 [82–87].
22. Chevalier, *Lettres sur l'Amérique du Nord*, 1:119 [76–77].
23. Chevalier, *Lettres sur l'Amérique du Nord*, 2:133 [292].
24. Chevalier, *Lettres sur l'Amérique du Nord*, 2:133–60 [292–304].

wealth, however, was work, and Chevalier was quick to note its centrality to the American way of life. From the moment the American got up, he worked. No day was more dismal than the Sabbath. Speculation, business, and trade were the very life blood of American society, and it was to these activities that Americans devoted themselves with "an ardor bordering on relentlessness." The same went for the practices and customs of Americans. "The American," Chevalier wrote, "is brought up with the idea that he will have a position, that he will be a farmer, an artisan, a manufacturer, a trader, a speculator, a doctor, a lawyer, or a clergyman, perhaps all of these in turn, and that if he works hard and is intelligent, he will arrive at a position of opulence."[25]

The American obsession with work had other important dimensions. Chevalier was struck by the fact that American cities (unlike Paris) were so constructed as to assist the activity of work. In fact, Chevalier devoted much of his energies to the close examination of the structure and character of America's cities, especially Cincinnati.[26] Here was a new city, expanding at inordinate speed, at the center of a communications infrastructure composed of railroads, canals, and rivers, producing what was required by an ever-expanding market as America moved westward. Some six months prior to his stay in Cincinnati Chevalier had visited Lowell. This was not a trip made by Tocqueville, but it was one, according to René Rémond,[27] that was soon to attain the obligatory status later accorded visits to the Chicago slaughterhouses. The scene that Chevalier described was that of a town dominated by massive factories. The inhabitants lived as if regulated by the clock. Salaries were good and the cost of living low. The mostly young female labor force lived a life of sober propriety far removed from that of their European equivalents. Above all, the conclusion Chevalier drew from his visit was that social and economic progress could be combined and that America provided vital clues as to how this could be attained.[28]

THE CAUSES OF AMERICA'S SUCCESS

What then were the factors that explained the "general ease" and "lack of poverty" in American life and that fueled the belief of Americans in their own success? The first was the American passion for work. Such a constant commotion, Chevalier conceded, would incline the onlooker to believe that the social order might collapse, but an additional cause of American vigor was the existence of

25. Chevalier, Lettres sur l'Amérique du Nord, 2:117 [283].
26. Chevalier, Lettres sur l'Amérique du Nord, 1:282–96, 319–50 [166–75, 190–209].
27. Rémond, Les Etats-Unis, 772–74.
28. Chevalier, Lettres sur l'Amérique du Nord, 1:216–47 [125–44].

various "fixed points" in society. One of these was the domestic home and "conjugal bed."[29] Both Chevalier and Tocqueville agreed that America reinforced the position of women *within* the family. The next fixed point was "religious sentiment." Here Chevalier showed himself to be just as aware of America's Protestant heritage as Tocqueville. The people of the United States, he affirmed, were "imbued with Protestantism to their very marrow."[30] Protestantism inclined toward a recognition of the rights of the individual. Both saw the Puritanism of New England as the cradle of American democracy.[31]

The third factor behind America's commercial success and social amelioration was the education of the populace.[32] The young American, Chevalier believed, was naturally disposed to learn about trade and industry. Primary education was of a more practical bent in America than in France but, above all, the American learned a trade by watching and imitating a master at work. Next came America's banks and credit institutions. America was better provisioned with banks than France, and Americans had a greater faith in the value of paper money than the French did.[33]

Finally, Chevalier drew attention to the aspect of American life that had led him to cross the Atlantic in the first place: the ever-expanding system of communication.[34] There was, he fancied, no finer spectacle than that of a "young people building in the short space of only fifteen years a network of communications that the most powerful Empires of Europe, with populations three or four times larger, had been frightened to attempt."[35] The benefit to public prosperity was and would continue to be incalculable.

SLAVERY AND THE SOUTH

There was, of course, an important institutional exception to the rule of democracy: the existence of slavery in the South. Chevalier located its origin in the different geographies and economies of the North and South.[36] The former had been established upon the basis of small holdings distributed approximately equally, thereby producing "truly democratic republics." The latter were built around large cotton-producing estates, with slaves, and as such constituted "aris-

29. Chevalier, *Lettres sur l'Amérique du Nord*, 1:170 [310].
30. Chevalier, *Lettres sur l'Amérique du Nord*, 2:125 [289].
31. Chevalier, *Lettres sur l'Amérique du Nord*, 2:287 [367–68].
32. Chevalier, *Lettres sur l'Amérique du Nord*, 2:234–44 [347–48].
33. Chevalier, *Lettres sur l'Amérique du Nord*, 2:244–57 [347–48].
34. Chevalier, *Lettres sur l'Amérique du Nord*, 2:29–106, 258–63 [227–76, 355–57].
35. Chevalier, *Lettres sur l'Amérique du Nord*, 2:104 [274–75].
36. Chevalier, *Lettres sur l'Amérique du Nord*, 2:260–66, 274–80 [145–57, 360–64].

tocratic republics." From this had arisen what amounted to two different types of civilization and two different types of individual, the Yankee and the Virginian. What Chevalier saw was that it was the Yankee who had come to dominate, that it was he who had come to be the "arbiter in morals and customs." Chevalier also recognized that the economic and political interests of the North and South were increasingly in opposition.

If there was a solution, Chevalier suggested, it might lie in the eventual dominance of the West, thus superseding the historic political, cultural, and economic divisions between North and South. With great clarity he recognized that America was moving westward to the Ohio and beyond, and that in the near future it would be the West that would come to lead the North and the South, both politically and economically.[37] So too he saw that, in addition to the Virginian and the Yankee, there was emerging a "third kind of American," the "man of the west." If his contours, like his future, remained unclear, he nevertheless "seemed destined to dominate the other two."[38] Here was a dynamic internal to America of potentially profound consequence.

THE MEANING OF LIBERTY IN AMERICA

Writing from Richmond, Virginia, Chevalier could not disguise his profound unease at the sight of a town where half the inhabitants were treated morally, if not physically, as "bipeds foreign to human nature." This led to reflection upon the real meaning of liberty in America, and it should not come as a surprise that for Chevalier it was, above all, related to matters of internal and external trade. "American liberty," he wrote, "is not a mystical, indefinite liberty, it is a special liberty, related to the special genius of its people and its special destiny; it is a liberty of work and of movement."[39] It was the liberty to choose a profession and to change it, to go about one's business as one wished, to move from the center of the country to the periphery and back again. It was, moreover, a liberty that was exercised largely independently of the authority of the state.

Nevertheless, this did not mean that the American was free from control by authority. It simply came in different forms from those familiar to the European. Chevalier listed them as follows: religious authority (which always maintained a "watchful eye"); the authority of opinion (which was "severe to the point of harshness"); legislative authority (which tended toward "omnipotence"); and the "authority of the riot." The second and third inevitably remind us of the argu-

37. Chevalier, *Lettres sur l'Amérique du Nord*, 2:24–27 [223–25].
38. Chevalier, *Lettres sur l'Amérique du Nord*, 1:172–96 [109–24].
39. Chevalier, *Lettres sur l'Amérique du Nord*, 1:201–2 [330].

ments of Tocqueville. These are the terms in which they were described by Chevalier: "the general interest is the supreme law; thus it lifts its head and takes its revenge every time it imagines itself to be injured by private interest. The regime of this country is becoming less a regime of liberty and of laissez-faire than a regime of equality, or rather it is assuming the character of a government of the majority."[40]

These worrying developments toward the dominance of a capricious public opinion raised a whole series of pressing questions. What was the precise nature of the revolution taking place? What institutions would it give rise to? What would perish in the process and what would emerge out of the storm? Chevalier declined to attempt "to penetrate the mysteries of the destiny of the new world," but he readily acknowledged that the union could well face the danger of disintegration; such were the incompatible demands being placed upon it.[41] However, he saw that there were important countervailing forces that could keep the union together. One of these was commerce and "the community of interests" that it created. Another was improved transport links. Still another was to be found in the fact that, while the individual states themselves opposed the power of the federal government, they were setting about strengthening and centralizing their own power. Above all, Chevalier trusted the American people themselves. "Despite their unique faults," Chevalier wrote, "the American people . . . are truly great and strong."[42] For such nations the most violent of storms only served as sources of strength.

CHEVALIER'S CONCLUSIONS

To summarize, Michel Chevalier explored aspects of America that were largely unreported by his more illustrious compatriot. In general, he provided a more positive evaluation of the economic dynamism of the United States than is to be found in Tocqueville and he was certainly more aware of the impact of trade and commerce upon the evolution of American life and society. Conversely, Chevalier largely ignored the political and legal institutions that figure at the heart of Tocqueville's description. For all their differences in perspective and subject matter, however, the two accounts reveal marked similarities and parallels. Chevalier's description of economic expansion, the improvement of the condition of the workers, the importance of credit and banking, and systems of communication can be seen to complement, rather than contradict, the more explicitly and

40. Chevalier, *Lettres sur l'Amérique du Nord*, 1:214–15 [336–37].
41. Chevalier, *Lettres sur l'Amérique du Nord*, 1:346 [395].
42. Chevalier, *Lettres sur l'Amérique du Nord*, 1:347 [395].

self-consciously political depiction of American democracy provided by Tocqueville. Specifically, Chevalier, as much as Tocqueville, realized that the driving force of American society was democracy and that the dominion of public opinion was expanding. America's "great democratic experiment," Chevalier wrote, had produced "a completely new political and physiological specimen, a variety of human species unknown until that point."[43] It was, he concluded, "the first time that the multitude had fully enjoyed the fruits of its labors and that it has shown itself worthy of wearing the robe of manhood."[44] In essence, both *Lettres sur l'Amérique du Nord* and *De la Démocratie en Amérique* amounted to extended comparisons between aristocratic and democratic societies, between an old and a new world, between the past and the future.

CRITICISMS OF TOCQUEVILLE

The success of Tocqueville's *De la Démocratie en Amerique* was immediate, and in 1841, at the tender age of thirty-six, he was elected to the Académie française. However, not everyone found his account of America to be a convincing one. In particular, criticism came from the improbably named Guillaume Tell Poussin, a man who was to dog Tocqueville over the next decade. Poussin was born in France around 1795. With the fall of Napoleon he left for America and in 1817 became a topographical engineer in the U.S. Army. He subsequently became a naturalized American citizen but later returned to France, where in 1848 he played a decisive role in convincing Richard Rush, American minister to France, to recognize the new French Republic.[45] The following year, when Poussin was himself appointed French minister in Washington, D.C., his appointment was warmly welcomed by President Buchanan.

Eight years earlier, in 1841, he had published *Considérations sur le Principe démocratique qui régit l'Union Américaine et d'autres états*. In essence, this was an extremely detailed commentary on Tocqueville, written by a man who, as he immediately told his readers, had spent fifteen years in the United States. He was, he believed, therefore saved from the errors that arose out of the "brevity" of Tocqueville's visit, a brevity that meant Tocqueville had seen America from the outside, through European eyes. Poussin's text is littered with critical remarks about Tocqueville's conclusions: Americans do not regret the absence of uniform

---

43. Chevalier, *Lettres sur l'Amérique du Nord*, 1:401 [427].

44. Chevalier, *Lettres sur l'Amérique du Nord*, 1:415 [437].

45. Richard Rush, *Occasional Productions, Political, Diplomatic, and Miscellaneous, including, among others, A Glance at the Court and Government of Louis Philippe and the French revolution of 1848, while the author resided as envoy extraordinary and minister plenipotentiary from the United States at Paris* (Philadelphia: J. B. Lippincott, 1860), 299–520.

rules imposed by the state but regard it as an advantage; projects do not get abandoned because Americans act on sudden impulse; Tocqueville was wrong to believe that he could discern the remnants of an "aristocratic party" because no such party had ever existed in the United States; democracy had not reduced the vigor of intellectual life, and the American nation—"not yet fifty years in existence"—had already made a significant contribution to the arts, sciences, and literature; the sentiments and morals of Americans had not been weakened by democracy; the possible emergence of "an aristocracy of wealth" posed no dangers as it would not have a permanent composition.

However, at the heart of Poussin's commentary was a fundamental disagreement about the mechanisms of American democracy. Here he began by observing that it was incorrect to assert that democracy did not always choose the best people or that the quality of America's political leaders had declined since the days of the revolution. Accordingly, it was not true that American governments were incapable of sustained, decisive action or that they were a prey to venality and corruption. This in turn led Poussin to articulate his most serious misgiving about Tocqueville's analysis. In brief, Poussin doubted that the majority had the power to impose their views on the state and thus to oppress the minority. This conclusion, he admitted, might possibly be true of one state operating outside the federal structure, but with regard to the union as a whole it was palpably false. "Upon such a vast territory," Poussin wrote, "in the midst of so many different interests and such different parties and religious sects there could never be formed a compact majority covering the whole of society except with regard to principles touching upon justice and the national interest."[46] This was to be a criticism that others were to make of Tocqueville.

Poussin therefore did not share the profound worries about American democracy that concerned Tocqueville. Nor did he share the fears for America's future articulated in Tocqueville's final chapter of volume 1 of *Democracy in America,* devoted to the probable future of the three races. The question of the place of black Americans in a postslavery society was not beyond solution. The American continent, Poussin contended, was sufficiently vast to allow black Americans to have their own territory and to form a "separate nation of the Union," linked to the whole by shared customs and commerce.[47] Similarly he did not share Tocqueville's views on the possible disintegration of the union. No state, regardless of the superiority of its resources or its wealth, would quit the union, because the latter was "the safeguard of the liberties and of the independence of each

---

46. Guillaume Tell Poussin, *Considérations sur le Principe démocratique qui régit l'Union Américaine et d'autres états* (Paris: Gosselin, 1841), 144. Gosselin also published Tocqueville's *Democracy in America.*
47. Poussin, *Considérations sur le Principe démocratique,* 177.

individual state."[48] Poussin's overall conclusion was that "American democracy, founded upon the equal distribution of enlightenment and intelligence and upon a people deeply imbued with religious belief, presents to the world a social state as new as it is imposing, as powerful as it is durable."[49] It was remarkable, he generously conceded, that Tocqueville had been able to understand so much about America in such a short time, but where he went wrong was when he could not free himself from his aristocratic, European prejudices. Viewed thus, America was incorrectly seen as being threatened by the same perils and dangers as the monarchies of the Old World.

POUSSIN'S AMERICA

Later that decade Poussin produced his own analysis of America, and what he described was an America not remotely glimpsed by Tocqueville: the United States as an emerging world power. The title alone gave a strong indication of the argument that was to come: *De la Puissance américaine*. When translated into English the title was equally explicit: *The United States: Its Power and Progress*.[50] The immediate context of Poussin's account was the annexation of Texas in 1845 and the quarrel with Great Britain over the contested territory of Oregon. For Poussin the outcome of this struggle was beyond doubt. "The desire of this active and colonizing race," he wrote, "is one day to cover the whole of North America."[51] And this was how he described "the gigantic proportions of the American Union": it was "a colossus whose head we perceive coming out of the mists which cover the polar regions, whose feet extend as far as the isthmus of Panama, while with one arm he threatens Europe by means of the Atlantic, and grasps with the other, through the great ocean, the rich archipelagoes and continents of Asia."[52] Poussin did not seek to conceal the brutality of what he saw as the colonization of the North American continent. It had been "a violent act of usurpation," where the colonizers had arrogated to themselves, "in the name of civilization and religion . . . the right of reducing the natives to a state of slavery and of appropriating the wealth of this unknown land to themselves."[53] But the means, though "unjust," had produced "useful results." Poussin also saw that the

---

48. Poussin, *Considérations sur le Principe démocratique*, 181.

49. Poussin, *Considérations sur le Principe démocratique*, 308.

50. The French editions appeared in 1843 and 1848. The English edition of the second French edition was published by London-based publishing house, Thomas Delf, in 1851. Quotations will be cited from this edition.

51. Guillaume Tell Poussin, *The United States: Its Power and Progress* (London: Thomas Delf, 1851), 283.

52. Poussin, *The United States*, 292.

53. Poussin, *The United States*, 285.

driving force behind this brutal process had been "the Anglo-Saxon race, which alone remained mistress of the American soil" and whose capacities as colonizers far exceeded that of their French and Spanish rivals.[54] Only the Pacific Ocean would place limits upon this progress.

The second part of Poussin's account looked at the resources—natural, human, and institutional—that made possible this relentless drive to ascendancy. It was a truly extensive list, but the broad outlines and conclusions were easily discerned. Like so many visitors to America, both before and since, Poussin saw as the "distinctive feature" of the American people that they were "eminently productive." It was through the railroads—built with no undue luxury and intended to serve the interests of the people—that Americans manifested their "characteristic intelligence and their unerring instinct." He similarly commented upon the climate, but drew the unusual conclusion that the American climate was "favorable to the greatest development of the physical and intellectual faculties of man."[55] As for the "astonishing" growth of America's population, this could be attributed to its free institutions and its respect for liberty combined with "an extensive territory, where the means of existence are abundant and of easy access." In the vein of Chevalier, Poussin considered Cincinnati to be the most remarkable American city of all. The great metropolis and market of the West, it was the product of the clear-sighted and indefatigable industry of the people themselves. The Americans, Poussin believed, had perceived the harmony that existed between their Christian faith and their political principles. The source of their democratic instincts, he affirmed, thereby echoing Tocqueville, was their religion. In the United States, churches of all denominations tended to display a disdain for religious ceremony. Poussin, again recalling Tocqueville, was also aware of the social significance of religion in American life. The potency of religious conviction checked the inroads of vice and of loose morals, thereby protecting Americans from the two greatest enemies of liberty.

Religion likewise served to maintain "the true principles of liberty and equality" and led Americans to understand that equality could only be maintained "through the common enjoyment of adequate means of education." If the natural resources of America provided the bedrock of future wealth, it was the "intelligence, activity, perseverance, religious sentiment, education, and social and political freedom"[56] of the Americans that allowed this immense resource to be turned into the prosperity of all. This led Poussin again to reflect on the genius for enterprise displayed by Americans. The American, he wrote, "is undoubtedly peculiarly a man of business" who felt the constant necessity of laboring for his

---

54. Poussin, *The United States*, 286–90.
55. Poussin, *The United States*, 401.
56. Poussin, *The United States*, 451.

own advancement. It was here that was to be found the community of national interest that ensured the power and prosperity of America.

All, however, was not as it should have been. Poussin expressed concern about the "unmeasured development" of the "speculative tendencies" of Americans and warned that they should guard against their "cupidity." Since the banking crisis of the 1830s there had developed "an unbounded love of speculation, of luxury" that had sown the seeds of corruption throughout American society. His hope was that Americans would learn to "live with more simplicity." Of greater concern was the issue of slavery. However, Poussin largely absolved the Americans themselves from blame. "This leprosy," he announced, "was imposed upon them through the avarice, cupidity, and jealousy of the mother country."[57] Moreover, the condition of the slave was no more unfortunate than that of other workers. Poussin personally had always found the slaves to be "happy and contented," commenting that of late years their condition had considerably improved due to the "kind treatment and careful attention" of their masters. Liberated slaves were generally "degraded" and "of vicious habits and morals."

THE SOURCES OF AMERICAN POWER

To what causes could American power be attributed? One cause was preeminent: "the manner in which the early immigrants blended their religious opinions with the practice of political economy."[58] Each individual was assured the fruits of his labor and encouraged to look forward to the increase of his domestic prosperity. Next, Poussin listed the binding of one state to another through the federal system, so that in cases of emergency the whole nation could unite. Americans also lived in peace and harmony, and this was one of "the principal sources of public happiness." The "principles of political life," most notably universal suffrage, acted to safeguard the liberty of people. Here Poussin was adamant that "political agitation is not disorder." America, he avowed, existed in "the vigor of its early youth" and therefore the maintenance of its "admirable" institutions was "secured by the faith which yet characterizes its people."

Beneath these conclusions lay a clear political message. Poussin, like Tocqueville before him, recognized that the achievements of the young republic could largely be attributed to "the preponderance of the Anglo-Americans."[59] Yet, despite their common origins, the English and the Americans were "essentially different in the vital principles of their political organizations." The one was

57. Poussin, *The United States*, 471.
58. Poussin, *The United States*, 482.
59. Poussin, *The United States*, 295.

irredeemably aristocratic, while the other was dominated by "the great democratic mass." Thus, Poussin wrote, "an immense void will one day separate these
two commercial nations, which springing from one stock, a community of origin
and religious opinions ought to bring together."[60] Poussin returned to this theme
at the very end of his text. The spirit of enterprise, he wrote, would push
America forward, bringing it inevitably into conflict with England over its material interests. He expected America to prevail. No such clash of interests existed
between France and America, between whom there existed a "natural alliance"
and a common antipathy toward "the intolerable insolence of a power whose
cupidity is as insatiable as its ambition is cruel." "It is written on high," Poussin
announced, "that the defenders of liberty on either side of the Atlantic must one
day make common cause, and fight under the same colors in the war that shall
be waged for the rights of man."[61]

1848 AND THE SECOND FRENCH REPUBLIC

Few men were truer to their word. On February 26, 1848, Richard Rush, the
United States minister to France, received a visit from Major Poussin. "He makes
an earnest appeal to me," Rush recorded, "to recognize the new Republic . . .
and says it will be of unspeakable service."[62] Two days later, without seeking
authorization from his government in Washington, Rush unilaterally recognized
the new regime and was accompanied by Poussin when he attended the new
government at Paris's Hotel de Ville. In the heady months that followed, Rush
found himself constantly interrupted by a succession of "French gentlemen calling for information about our constitution," to the point that he became its
unofficial interpreter to the committee preparing France's new constitution.
Among those gentlemen was Alexis de Tocqueville.[63]

In 1848 Tocqueville added a new preface to *Democracy in America*, stating
boldly that the "institutions of America, which were a subject only of curiosity
to monarchical France, ought to be a subject of study for republican France."
While France should not make "a servile copy" of American institutions, it did
mean that the "principles of order, of the balance of powers, of true liberty, of
deep and sincere respect for right, are indispensable to all republics."[64] That same

60. Poussin, *The United States*, 295.

61. Poussin, *The United States*, 488.

62. Rush, *Occasional Productions*, 364.

63. In addition to Rush's own account, see J. H. Powell, *Richard Rush: Republican Diplomat 1780–
1859* (Philadelphia: University of Pennsylvania Press, 1942).

64. Tocqueville, *Démocratie en Amérique*, in *Oeuvres Complètes* (Paris: Gallimard, 1951), 1:xliii–xliv
(my translation).

year he made an impassioned speech before the citizens of Cherbourg in which he pointed out that "in America, the Republic is not a dictatorship exercised in the name of liberty; it is liberty itself, the real and true liberty of all the citizens; . . . property is secure, order firmly maintained, industry free, taxation light, the tyranny of one or of several individuals unknown."[65] It was this vision of a moderate republic that Tocqueville defended as a member of the Second Republic's constitutional committee.

Chevalier's contribution to these heated polemics came in the form of a long article in the *Revue des Deux Mondes* exploring "La Liberté aux Etats-Unis" and a set of seven articles entitled "Étude sur la Constitution des États-Unis" published in *Le Journal des Débats*.[66] Explicitly seeking to complement, rather than to contradict, what Tocqueville had written, Chevalier provided an account of how "an American citizen, having achieved adulthood, exercises his own faculties freely to his own advantage." In brief, Americans enjoyed both political *and* civil liberty. In the United States, he concluded, it was a well-established principle that "the republic has no other solid foundations than in religion, morality, and simplicity." The mistake made in France was to believe that liberty amounted to "a savage liberty whose principal objective was to destroy established government, frighten peaceful people, and threaten everything which exists."[67]

For both Chevalier and Tocqueville, writing in the wake of the 1848 Revolution, there was then much to be admired about American democracy. They were by no means alone in believing this. The federal constitution was retranslated and republished, and the press contained numerous articles examining its strengths and weaknesses.[68] Yet the traditional hostility of French republicans towards bicameralism and federalism prevailed, and once again France found itself with a constitution that prioritized unity over liberty.

Nevertheless, the opinion that France had lessons to learn from America continued to be heard. In his inaugural lecture to the Collège de France, Édouard Laboulaye was unequivocal in affirming that, within the next fifty years, the American Republic would become "the most extensive, the most powerful, and the most homogenous that had ever appeared on the globe and, for the first time, Europe will be obliged to take account of this new people which will come, if it has not done so already, to share with it the empire of the seas."[69] Specifically,

65. Tocqueville, "Banquet populaire de Cherbourg," in *Oeuvres Complètes* 3, book 3, 44–45 (my translation).

66. Michel Chevalier, "La Liberté aux États-Unis," *Revue des Deux Mondes* 19, no. 3 (1849): 91–124. The seven articles in *Le Journal des Débats* were published from May 25 through July 21, 1848.

67. Chevalier, "La Liberté aux États-Unis," 93, 119, 105 (my translation).

68. See Marc Lahmer, *La Constitution américaine dans le débat français, 1795–1848* (Paris: L'Harmattan, 2001), 291–381.

69. Édouard Laboulaye, *De la Constitution américaine et de l'utilité de son étude* (Paris: Hennuyer, 1850), 8–9 (my translation). For more on Laboulaye, see See Walter D. Gray, *Interpreting American*

the American Republic was the largest and most complete democracy of modern times. It had resolved the problem of establishing a republic over a large territory and with a sizeable population. The sovereignty of the people was no mere abstraction, while government was popular and not demagogic. American foreign policy was based upon the principles of nonintervention and neutrality. Individual liberty was not only guaranteed but it was done so energetically and efficiently. Commercial liberty and the right to work were there better protected than they were in France and, most important, in America there existed complete freedom of religion. Laboulaye informed his audience that he could quite easily draw their attention to other features of America worthy of praise, but this was not required to substantiate his overall conclusion: America was "not an imaginary but a real and living republic" with a constitution that could adapt to the development of the nation and "to the progress of commerce, industry, and civilization."[70]

Laboulaye, like Tocqueville, was a liberal and he was here using the American model as a means of criticizing his own compatriots and the republic they themselves had just brought into existence. He would later perform the same maneuver under the Second Empire, using America to encourage the French to think about the conditions under which liberty could prevail. The oddity was that this fervent admirer of the United States, who was the first to conceive the idea of the Statue of Liberty, never once set foot on the American shore. But this did not diminish the passion with which he studied America, nor did it lead him to turn a blind eye to the one institution in America that he considered to be antithetical to liberty: slavery. When the Civil War broke out, he unhesitatingly supported the North, believing that the desire to perpetuate and extend slavery was the true cause of the rebellion. This was not the position adopted by Michel Chevalier, nor was it that of the French government and of majority opinion.[71] Unfortunately, we will never know how Tocqueville would have responded. The fact was, however, that after 1850 the issue of slavery came more and more to the fore in French accounts of America. Slavery, the possibility of secession by the South, and America's ever-growing industrial power now became the principal sources of interest and preoccupation.

AMPÈRE'S AMERICA

In September 1851 Jean-Jacques Ampère, member of the Académie française, set out for the United States. He returned to France in May 1852, resuming his

---

Democracy in France: The Career of Édouard Laboulaye, 1811–1883 (Newark: University of Delaware Press: 1994).

70. Laboulaye, *De la Constitution américaine*, 10.

71. See Roger, *L'Ennemi Américain*, 100–138.

teaching at the Collège de France one day later. In his letters to Ampère, Tocqueville remarked to his close friend: "I am longing to know in which direction you are going to direct your steps. The United States are so well known to me and still so present after twenty years that you will not be able to be anywhere where I cannot follow you in my thoughts." By the same token, he was intrigued to know what had changed since his visit.[72] For his part Ampère did not hide the fact that his interest had been awoken by a reading of *Democracy in America*. Accordingly it was to Tocqueville that Ampère's *Promenade en Amérique* was dedicated.[73]

There were indeed few places where Tocqueville was not able to follow Ampère in his thoughts, as their travels were roughly similar. Ampère did, however, visit the industrial town of Lowell, being as impressed as Chevalier had been by the moral and intellectual culture of the workers, and he, unlike Tocqueville, was clearly astounded by the slaughtering of pigs made famous in Mrs. Trollope's description of Cincinnati. Nevertheless, as with his illustrious predecessor, Ampère recognized that the point of visiting America was to study institutions and people.

For our purposes, the most intriguing of Ampère's encounters was with John C. Spencer, author of a preface to the first American edition of *Democracy in America*. Ampère introduced his account of this discussion by noting that Americans almost universally agreed on one thing that Tocqueville had been mistaken: the possibility of a tyranny of the majority was unfounded. In this view, the ever-changing nature of majority opinion ensured that no "lasting tyranny" could be established. Spencer himself attributed Tocqueville's error to the peculiar political circumstances pertaining during his stay: namely, the support of the overwhelming majority for General Jackson's populist measures. Ampère, however, was not convinced by Spencer's argument. That the oppressed could themselves become the oppressors was no safeguard for liberty. Moreover, the new majority might simply continue to voice many of the opinions of the previous majority. This was especially true in the states of the South where freedom of expression on the subject of slavery did not exist. Tocqueville, he consequently affirmed, had been right to diagnose the existence of a "radical infirmity" existing at the heart of American society: "the possible tyranny of number where numbers counted for everything."[74]

Not surprisingly, therefore, there was much in Ampère's account that echoed that of Tocqueville. Like so many visitors before him, for example, he saw the importance of religion in American life and recognized the place attributed to

---

72. Alexis de Tocqueville, *Correspondance d'Alexis de Tocqueville avec P. P. Royer-Collard et avec J-J. Ampère*, in *Oeuvres Complètes* (Paris: Gallimard, 1979), 11:200–203 (my translation).

73. J-J. Ampère, *Promenade en Amérique*, 2 vols. (Paris: Michel Lévy, 1856).

74. Ampère, *Promenade en Amérique*, 1:337–41 (my translation).

hard work in individual success. He was surprised, however, by the relative sophistication and European character of American cultural life. In New York City he found not just science but the beaux arts and philosophy. But, with an eye to the future, he saw two problems looming on the near horizon. The first was that of keeping the union intact. Having witnessed the "hideous scene" of seeing slaves sold at market, he observed that nothing could justify slavery and that all the talk of "humane" masters changed none of this. Yet the differences over slavery were so deep that it was hard to discern a workable political solution. Secondly, Ampère wondered what foreign adventures would be produced by the growing sense among Americans themselves of their own superiority. Here he was clearly thinking of American designs on Mexico and Cuba. But his broader concern was that expansion would pose problems for the federal system and that it would change the character of America. The United States, Ampère wrote, was formed "under the discipline of severe virtues." They should be worried that they might perish through the weakening of these principles.

TOWARD CIVIL WAR

It was precisely this apprehension that informed Alexis de Tocqueville's increasingly pessimistic assessment of America during the 1850s.[75] For the first time he voiced concerns about a nascent American imperialism, fueled by a spirit of conquest. America, Tocqueville now contended, had most to fear from its own excesses. Its political life was ever more characterized by a violent and lawless spirit while its institutions were prey to corruption and incompetent leadership. The endless quest for prosperity had not only produced "a race . . . which combines the passions and the instincts of the savage with the tastes, needs, vigor and vices of civilized men"[76]: it had also fostered an unbridled materialism. In contrast to the accomplished and stable democracy he had described in the 1830s Tocqueville now discerned a young and immature democracy behaving like a child that could not control its emotions.

Yet these criticisms were as nothing when compared to the vehemence with which he responded to the possibility of the extension of slavery. Tocqueville's basic position was that slavery retarded America's progress, gave comfort to her detractors, and imperiled the union. To grant slavery a new lease of life by extending it westward, however, was "one of the greatest crimes that men can commit against the general cause of humanity." He viewed this prospect with

75. For a fuller assessment, see Aurelian Craiutu and Jeremy Jennings, "The Third Democracy: Tocqueville's Views of America after 1840," *American Political Science Review* 98 (2004): 391–404.

76. Quoted in Craiutu and Jennings, "The Third Democracy," 400.

horror and despair. In a letter written to Francis Lieber only three years before his death, Tocqueville wrote: "Your America itself, to which once turned the dream of all those who lacked the reality of liberty, has for some time in my view given little satisfaction to these friends."[77]

A FRENCHMAN IN LINCOLN'S AMERICA

That Tocqueville's earlier description of America remained a point of reference for French visitors is amply illustrated by the account provided by a young liberal of the next generation, Ernest Duvergier de Hauranne. By his own admission, his description was neither a condemnation nor a defense of democracy but a digest of the "naïve emotions" evoked by being "thrown without preparation into the tumult of American society." In brief, America, with all its imperfections, allowed him to see the reality of a democratic and free country thrust into civil war. To state the obvious: Duvergier de Hauranne did not dispute the justice of the federal case. Slavery and the arrogance of the South were the causes of war. The war itself was not the occasion to display "brilliant virtues" but a grim necessity to be met with courage and determination. He denied that the outcome would be military despotism, believing that there was no evidence of a new "praetorian" spirit among the citizenry. Making the comparison with France's experience of revolution, he wrote that "America, after its military 93, marches boldly towards a pacific 89."[78]

What then was the reality of democratic society that Duvergier de Hauranne glimpsed? His first impressions were of vulgarity, ugliness, and squalor. The brutality of popular mores was shocking, and one could quickly tire of the mediocre intellectual nourishment that was provided. On the face of it, religion was not a serious affair. Americans opened a church in much the same way as they published a newspaper. He was similarly dismayed by what he first saw of American political life. Fraud, lying, and violence were integral to the electoral process and low-level corruption the norm among politicians. Upon closer inspection, he saw more serious problems. "The great evil of American democracy," Duvergier de Hauranne wrote, "is not so much the arbitrariness, which occurs rarely and is, moreover, held in check by long-established habits of unlimited freedom, as it is the apathy of the general public."[79] Americans now boasted of not being involved in politics and of leaving it to "intriguers and underlings." The explana-

---

77. Quoted in Craiutu and Jennings, "The Third Democracy," 403.
78. Ernest Duvergier de Hauranne, *Huit Mois en Amérique* (Lacroix: Paris: 1866), 1:ix, 2:257 (my translation).
79. Duvergier de Hauranne, *Huit Mois en Amérique,* 1:78–79 (my translation).

tion lay in "the egotism which continually increases in the hearts of the newly-rich."

Yet, in much the same way that Duvergier de Hauranne saw beyond the "religious anarchy" so as to conclude that a "people that mixes prayer with all the acts of its public and private life is certainly a religious people,"[80] he likewise came to a fuller appreciation of the nature of America's democratic politics. First, he saw that parties now played a crucial role in the organization and success of democracy. "For Americans to be a people," he wrote, "it is necessary that all the passions, the interests, the local factions should form a common idea, and this is exactly the service that parties perform."[81] This was a lesson that Duvergier de Hauranne would seek to teach his compatriots in the early years of the Third Republic.[82] Next, he saw that the "great merit" of American democracy lay in its capacity to form "men and citizens." This arose from the daily practice of liberty. Americans therefore did not see their government as an alien power or enemy. Accordingly, they rallied to its defense in times of trouble. Just as important, American democracy did not suffer from the "fundamental vice" that had for so long been an affliction in France: the division between rich and poor, aristocrat and proletariat. "Americans," he wrote, "are united in a mutual independence instead of being divided under a common subjection."[83] Should we therefore despair and see in democracy an eternal obstacle to liberty? "If such," Duvergier de Hauranne replied in his last sentence, "has been the true lesson we can draw from the spectacle before our eyes in our own country, it would be good to turn our thoughts elsewhere and dream with hope of the great and encouraging experience provided to the modern world by the free democracy of America."[84]

CONCLUSION

The "America as degeneracy" thesis has had a long life, dating back to at least the early eighteenth century, and has remained to this day a core component of what James W. Ceaser has called "symbolic America."[85] By the mid-nineteenth century its contours were firmly established: American cities were ugly and its

---

80. Duvergier de Hauranne, *Huit Mois en Amérique*, 2:134.
81. Duvergier de Hauranne, *Huit Mois en Amérique*, 2:26.
82. See Jeremy Jennings, "Doctrinaires and Syndicalists: Representation, Parties and Democracy in France," *Journal of Political Ideologies* 11 (2006): 270.
83. Duvergier de Hauranne, *Huit Mois en Amérique*, 2:495.
84. Duvergier de Hauranne, *Huit Mois en Amérique*, 2:496.
85. James W. Ceaser, *Reconstructing America: The Symbol of America in Modern Thought* (New Haven: Yale University Press, 1997).

people uncivilized; there was no serious intellectual and artistic culture to speak of; the dollar alone was what mattered; capitalism and capitalists in America were particularly brutal; political institutions were corrupt and its politicians venal. To this, French observers could add their own prejudices: America was Anglo-Saxon and Protestant. So too there was the looming vision of the emergence of a new world power that might topple not just England but also France from its perch. And, of course, there was the abomination of slavery.

To some extent, all the writers discussed in this chapter shared some of these perspectives. All saw that America was quite definitely not France and not Europe. Yet, for all their own differences in interpretation, they each saw something to admire about America. The vigor and vitality of a young nation setting out to conquer a virgin continent could not fail to impress. The sheer power and potential of America could not be ignored. Likewise, American democracy seemed to capture the spirit of the modern age and, for all its difficulties, to demonstrate that liberty and democracy could flourish together. Above all, America revealed the future, a future that one day, in some form or other, would arrive on Europe's shores.

Herein has lain the central dilemma for France and for her politicians, writers, and people. No one has better expressed this predicament than Richard Kuisel.[86] Speaking of the postwar period, he has written: "The issue for the French was to find a way to possess American prosperity and economic power and yet avoid what appeared to be the accompanying social and cultural costs." In brief, America was both a model and a threat, and those threats came in the form of social conformity, economic savagery, and cultural sterility. It is tempting to suggest that little has changed to this day. The marginality of American intellectual life, McDonald's, and Euro Disney; Hollywood blockbusters; the fundamentalist Right; an illiterate President Bush: these are just some of the examples of the horror of America routinely referred to and commented upon. To this can now be added the iniquities of economic neoliberalism (anathema in statist France) and the abuse of military power (an affront to French *grandeur*).

Yet America still has the power to fascinate as well as to charm. In 2005 the philosopher Bernard-Henri Lévy set out to retrace the footsteps of Alexis de Tocqueville in America. His ambition was to confront "the concrete body and face of America today" and to contrast this with "the anti-American phantasmagoria" sweeping across Europe "as never before." The result was *American Vertigo*, a travelogue recounting Lévy's yearlong stay in the United States. The face of America he saw was at times flattering, at times unfavorable, sometimes even

---

86. Richard Kuisel, *Seducing the French: The Dilemma of Americanization* (Berkeley and Los Angeles: University of California Press, 1993), 3.

disappointing and despairing, but it was not the imaginary America of "Manichaeanism, essentialism, and the reign of clichés." Indeed, his view was that anti-Americanism had become "the most powerful 'magnet of the worst' for all the abandoned theories, all those little dark stars fallen from doctrinaire galaxies, all that scattered debris, the directionless iron filings in search of a new pole."[87] One can only speculate on what Tocqueville, the prophet of American liberty and democracy, would have made of this sorry state of affairs.

87. Bernard-Henri Lévy, *American Vertigo: On the Road from Newport to Guantanamo* (London: Gibson Square, 2006), 286, 285.

PART FOUR

BRITISH VIEWS OF AMERICA

8

⁂

FROM ARISTOCRATIC *POLITESSE* TO DEMOCRATIC CIVILITY, OR, WHAT MRS. FRANCES TROLLOPE *DIDN'T* SEE IN AMERICA

Richard Boyd

MRS. FRANCES TROLLOPE AS TOCQUEVILLEAN OBSERVER

Alexis de Tocqueville's *Democracy in America* is renowned for its subtle analysis of democracy. Although the advent of democracy warrants a kind of "religious terror," and Tocqueville laments American democracy's lack of aristocratic honor, aesthetic taste, and cultural refinement, he nonetheless celebrates the ways in which democracy leads to a generalized compassion, transparency, and easy spontaneity too readily obscured by the rigid conventions of an aristocratic society.[1] By way of contrast, Mrs. Frances Trollope, affectionately known to her friends as "Fanny," finds nothing redeeming whatsoever in American democracy. Her voyage to America in 1827 to establish a dry goods emporium in Cincinnati was an unmitigated disappointment, both personally and financially. And yet her visit, like Tocqueville's and Beaumont's of only a few years later, culminated in a successful book analyzing American society. Trollope's *Domestic Manners of the Americans* was a best seller in England and the United States upon its appearance in March of 1832.[2] Its antirepublican thesis and colorful examples of the abysmal

---

1. Alexis de Tocqueville, *Democracy in America*, ed. Harvey Mansfield and Delba Winthrop (Chicago: University of Chicago Press, 2000), 1:6; 2:535–39, 544–45, 562–63.

2. All references are to Donald Smalley's excellent critical edition of *Domestic Manners of the Americans*, ed. Smalley (New York: Knopf, 1949).

manners of the Americans are well known and frequently cited by social historians. However, the book has generated remarkably little scholarly attention from political theorists. Indeed, it is often dismissed as a more extreme expression of Tocqueville's aristocratic critique of American democracy—albeit without his penetrating analysis of the relationship between American society and its system of government.

I want to resist the temptation to read Trollope's book as nothing more or less than an embittered and condescending precursor to Tocqueville's *Democracy in America*. Through an analysis of Trollope's richly detailed account of her life and travels in America, this chapter will underscore important differences between their visions of American democracy. Where Tocqueville appreciates the redeeming features of democratic manners and morals, especially the kind of easy spontaneity and democratic equality with which Americans treat one another, Trollope sees only "vulgarity," "grossness," "familiarity," "presumptuousness," and a "universal deficiency in good manners and graceful demeanour."[3] However, her work seems to rival or even exceed Tocqueville's celebrated *Democracy* in its direct and sustained consideration of American manners. For better or worse, her emphasis is not, like Tocqueville's, on how Americans' civic habits and political institutions suit them for self-government and function to "make democracy work" in the narrowly political sense. Rather, her reactionary loathing of everything American and republican shows a deep appreciation of how everyday manners—or the lack thereof—function to signify and generate democracy in the looser sense of a society of social equals who experience democracy in their private as well as public capacities. Her work ironically manages to capture better than Tocqueville's the sense in which America's democratic norms of civility serve to communicate a sense of the equality and intrinsic dignity of all people. That is to say: there is a connection not just between the social and political, as both Trollope and Tocqueville recognize, but also between the formal aspects of manners and the substantive dimensions of morality they signify.

Following the lead of the political theorist Judith Shklar and her seminal treatment of the "ordinary vices" of a democracy, I begin with the assumption that political theory must address "the common ills we inflict upon one another every day."[4] While taking issue with Mrs. Trollope's criticisms of America and underscoring the "ordinary virtues" of democratic society, this chapter also addresses one of the great puzzles of the intellectual history of liberalism. Namely, how is it that eighteenth-century notions of "civility" and "manners" could be trans-

---

3. Trollope, *Domestic Manners*, 99, 137, 156.
4. Judith Shklar, *Ordinary Vices* (Cambridge, Mass.: Belknap, 1984), 1.

formed in less than a half century from a democratic ideal of easy spontaneity, inclusion, and mutual respect in the treatment of others to the exclusionary idea of *politesse* as the distinguishing mark of the courtly classes?[5] The genealogy of civility from its democratic origins in the eighteenth-century writings of Smith and Hume to its exclusionary permutations in the nineteenth century is conterminous with the rise of democracy itself. Trollope's stark critique of American democracy allows us to distinguish these two commonly conflated synonyms for "manners"—namely, civility and politeness—and to determine why the latter assumed such noxious and exclusionary formulations only in the wake of modern democracy.

MANNERS AND MORALS: CIVILITY VERSUS POLITENESS

One distinguishing feature of nineteenth-century political thought is the idea that there is a connection between the social and the political. Tocqueville, J. S. Mill, and others insisted that democracy was best understood as a "social condition" rather than in its narrowly institutional permutations as a system of majority rule. Notwithstanding their functional appreciation of how democratic manners are intertwined with a nation's political institutions, they seem to have grasped only imperfectly that there is also an intrinsic moral and political dimension to everyday social relationships.[6] Shklar made this thesis famous in her work *Ordinary Vices,* exploring the political significance of everyday vices such as hypocrisy, condescension, and snobbery whose moral valence is patently antidemocratic. "Snobbery," she notes in particular, "is impervious to the rules of democracy," even while democratic norms "condemn it as an obnoxious violation of the public ethos."[7] Even so, social and political theorists have been slow to build on Shklar's fundamental insight into the relationship between manners and morals. Those like Norbert Elias who have taken most seriously the political dimensions of manners, politeness, and civility have generally been transfixed by their undemocratic or exclusionary dimensions.[8] This is understandable, for courtly ideas of politeness served as sharp and derisive tools of social exclusion, allowing the upper classes to claim social prerogatives and frustrating the social mobility of those determined to rise up by talent and ambition alone.[9] Nonetheless, focusing

5. On this question, see especially Mark Kingwell, "Politics and the Polite Society in the Scottish Enlightenment," *Historical Reflections/Réflexions Historiques* 19 (1993): 363–87.

6. This despite the fact that the term *moeurs* seems to suggest this dual sense of sociological *habitus* as well as morality.

7. Shklar, *Ordinary Vices,* 87–88.

8. Norbert Elias, *The Civilizing Process* (Oxford: Blackwell, 2000).

9. I have previously explored this problem in Richard Boyd, "*Politesse* and Public Opinion in Stendhal's *Red and Black*," *European Journal of Political Theory* 4 (Fall 2005): 367–92.

only on the undemocratic face of manners risks overlooking how the "ordinary virtues" of a democratic society, with its quintessential "virtue of civility," can serve as ways of signifying and reproducing democratic equality.[10]

That is to say that there are crucial differences between the democratic "manners" or civility Trollope encounters in America and the aristocratic standards of politeness against which she judges them—a distinction that has escaped critics like Elias, John Keane, and others.[11] Moreover, the view that manners are simply elite inventions, instruments of social control, manipulation, and exclusion, tends to overlook their intrinsic value as well as their potential for communicating democratic virtues of inclusion, respect, and dignity. Trollope's difficulties in America—both in terms of her revulsion to its democratic manners and her icy reception by its citizens—stem at least in part from a fundamental misunderstanding of this sort. Upon closer examination we will see that her indignation about the barbarous state of republican manners in America stems not from the fact that Americans lack "manners" altogether—as she sometimes alleges—but rather from her own disappointed expectations about aristocratic politeness.

Any analysis of Mrs. Trollope as representative of aristocratic or courtly standards of politeness must begin by conceding that it would be misleading to describe her as an aristocrat.[12] Wife of a lawyer whose practice had deteriorated through neglect and whose attempt to reinvent himself as a gentleman farmer was an equal disappointment, Trollope found herself teetering on the edge of bankruptcy. After failing to receive an inheritance from an uncle that would have relieved her family's financial woes, in 1827 Trollope and her husband settled on a plan to establish a glorified department store in the western United States. When the outlandish structure she built to house her grand "Bazaar" in Cincinnati, Ohio, led to yet another failure, she returned to England to write *Domestic Manners of the Americans,* which was published in March of 1832 to popular and critical acclaim.[13] Despite her fascinations with mercantile success, throughout

10. More general and sympathetic accounts of civility as a democratic virtue are Edward Shils, *The Virtue of Civility and other Essays* (Indianapolis: Liberty Press, 1997); and Mark Kingwell, *A Civil Tongue: Justice, Dialogue, and the Politics of Pluralism* (University Park: Pennsylvania State University Press, 1995).

11. See, for example, John Keane's recent criticisms of "civility" as necessarily "conservative" and "repressive," in *Civil Society: Old Images, New Visions* (Stanford: Stanford University Press, 1998). For a much subtler account of the transformation, especially in the first half of the seventeenth century, see Anna Bryson, *From Courtesy to Civility: Changing Codes of Conduct in Early Modern England* (Oxford: Clarendon, 1998).

12. It is quite possible that Tocqueville has Trollope in mind with the following passage from *Democracy in America,* 2:580, "The English amuse themselves very much at the expense of American manners, and what is particular about this is that most of those who draw such a comical picture for us belong to the English middle classes, to whom this same picture is very applicable. So these pitiless detractors ordinarily present an example of what they find fault with in the United States; they do not perceive that they are making fun of themselves, to the great delight of the aristocracy in their country."

13. Some of the best and most comprehensive treatments of Frances Trollope's life and literary

the book one is as struck by her sense of being an apostle of the values of an aristocratic culture as by her palpable insecurity about her place—as a member of the downwardly mobile gentry—within such a society. In any event, her rhetorical appeals to "gallantry," "good breeding," "true refinement," and "gentlemanliness" have more in common with the courtly and aristocratic classes than with the kind of democratic civility, mutual deference, sociability, and easy spontaneity she encounters among republican citizens. The enthusiastic reception of her work in Britain by Tory critics of the Reform Bills of the 1830s—and the scathing denunciation of it in Whig publications like the *Edinburgh Review*—seems a further testament to this affinity.[14]

Trollope was appalled by the "total and universal want of manners" in America.[15] Although she professes not "to decide whether man is better or worse off for requiring refinement in the manners and customs of the society that surrounds him," she clearly sides with Edmund Burke and other conservatives in defending the importance of manners as "that polish which removes the coarser and rougher parts of our nature."[16] As I have suggested above, however, her description of such a "total and universal want" of manners belies the fact that the "manners" she encounters in the United States are in fact clearly defined and ever present. It is not that Americans lack a coherent system of "manners," Trollope just disapproves of the forms they take. Although cast in a strongly negative light, her description of American manners brings to mind the disposition of "civility" featured so conspicuously in the eighteenth-century writings of Hume, Smith, Ferguson, and other defenders of a commercial society. In contrast to the courtly standards of politeness whose exclusionary aspects were so conspicuous, the virtues of civility are those of a commercial, middle-class, pluralistic, and ultimately democratic society whose motivating value is equality.[17] The juxtaposition between these two different systems of manners—democratic civility and aristocratic politeness—is what gives Trollope's account of American morals its

---

career are Donald Smalley, introduction to *Domestic Manners of the Americans;* Pamela Neville-Sington, *Fanny Trollope: The Life and Adventures of a Clever Woman* (London: Viking, 1997); Johanna Johnston, *The Life, Manners, and Travels of Fanny Trollope: A Biography* (New York: Hawthorn Books, 1978); Teresa Ransom, *Fanny Trollope: A Remarkable Life* (New York: St. Martin's, 1995); and Helen Heineman, *Frances Trollope* (Boston: Twayne, 1984).

14. For the political context and reception of Trollope's book in 1832, see especially Neville-Sington, *Fanny Trollope*, 168–70; Johnston, *Life, Manners, and Travels*, 126–27.

15. Trollope, *Domestic Manners*, 45.

16. Trollope, *Domestic Manners*, 46.

17. I have made this argument about the democratic and inclusionary dimensions of eighteenth-century understandings of civility at greater length in Richard Boyd, "The Value of Civility?" *Urban Studies* 43 (May 2006): 1–17, and "Manners and Morals: David Hume on Commerce, Civility and the Social Construction of Difference," in Margaret Schabas and Carl Wennerlind, eds., *David Hume's Political Economy* (London: Routledge, 2007).

perceptiveness and critical edge, allowing us to examine more directly the social and political significance of both.

Her treatment also raises historical questions about the transition from one to another. Tocqueville is not the only thinker to cast the rise of democratic equality as destined to replace an outmoded aristocratic society. And yet despite its "providential" or "fated" character, this process of democratization is far from complete even in Tocqueville's time.[18] Mid-eighteenth-century Scottish fascinations with civility and middle-class manners had been transformed by the early nineteenth century into notions of politeness whose exclusionary implications are well known, and by the late nineteenth century even the United States had begun to develop standards of middle-class propriety and civility over and against the ostensible "rudeness" of immigrants and other denizens of the lower classes.[19] Trollope's invocations of courtly manners and politeness are significant because they seem to represent the last gasp of aristocratic standards—even to the point of caricature—in the face of their replacement by the more egalitarian and relaxed standards of a democratic, commercial nation like America.

DEMOCRATIC TRANSPARENCY AND ARISTOCRATIC DISTANCE

One of Trollope's most consistent grievances about America is its lack of privacy. Whether she is traveling by steamboat or coach, or eating meals in common in the various inns—all of which she pronounces unlivable—she is confronted by a society where familiarity and publicity are the norm. As much as American liberalism indulges itself with the idea of privacy, Trollope discovers much to her chagrin that democratic norms demand a certain degree of transparency. There is a general suspicion if not antipathy to those like Trollope who want to be left alone, to eat or enjoy her tea in her own room, to guard her own personal affairs from the prying and importunate questions of those she meets. From the point of view of her republican hosts, this desire to remain aloof or reserved is interpreted, perhaps correctly, as reflective of a pretended sense of superiority.

In fairness, taking her meals in private is at least in part a reaction to what she experiences as:

18. Tocqueville, *Democracy in America*, 1:6–7. For a complementary and brilliant exploration of how the contested ideal of democratic equality plays itself out in the literature of nineteenth-century France, see Mona Ozouf, *Les Aveux du Roman: Le XIXe Siècle entre Ancien Régime et Révolution* (Paris: Fayard, 2001).

19. See especially, John F. Kasson, *Rudeness and Civility: Manners in Nineteenth-Century Urban America* (New York: Hill & Wang, 2000).

the total want of all the usual courtesies of the table, the voracious rapidity with which the viands were seized and devoured, the strange uncouth phrases and pronunciation; the loathsome spitting, from the contamination of which it was absolutely impossible to protect our dresses; the frightful manner of feeding with knives, till the whole blade seemed to enter into the mouth; and the still more frightful manner of cleaning the teeth afterwards with a pocket knife.[20]

Such a scene would be unappetizing enough for anyone. But her quest for privacy is interpreted (not incorrectly) by innkeepers and other travelers as a signal that she thinks herself better than others. She demands special privileges for herself and her family. " 'Then, madam,' " an innkeeper declares, " 'I cannot accommodate you on these terms; we have no family tea-drinkings here, and you must live either with me or my wife, or not at all in my house.' "[21]

Maybe because of its longstanding connection with the exacting privations of classical republicanism, eating meals in common has always symbolized good republican citizenship. Common meals deny any individual the opportunity to savor what others are denied, and the shared experience of doing something so intimate and ritually symbolic as eating in the presence of others is expected to generate common bonds between republican citizens.[22] And yet as Trollope correctly notes, the paradox of American republicanism is that despite their public nature and physical proximity, American meals take place in almost complete silence, as though the peculiar strand of modern republicanism seeks to balance the privacy and interiority upon which liberalism depends with the democratic expectation that no one withdraw into personal isolation.[23] Americans eat meals in common not because they enjoy them, apparently, but because they are expected to do so, and to demur, as Mrs. Trollope repeatedly does, is to hazard scandal or earning the resentment of one's fellow travelers.

There are undoubtedly inflections of social class to many of Mrs. Trollope's complaints. The necessities and vagaries of travel have long been responsible for flinging different social groups into proximity with one another. But rather than being consigned to travel and eat in shared public space by virtue of her inability to pay for something better, she is shocked to discover that the "decent dignity of a private conveyance" was not even "deemed necessary for the President of the United States."[24]

20. Trollope, *Domestic Manners*, 18–19.
21. Trollope, *Domestic Manners*, 37.
22. Albert Hirschman, *Crossing Boundaries: Selected Writings* (New York: Zone Books, 1998), chap. 1.
23. Trollope, *Domestic Manners*, 25, 47.
24. Trollope, *Domestic Manners*, 142.

Above and beyond the leveling and disordering effects of travel, even the so-called "private" life of domesticity in the United States seems liable to invasion: "[T]he point where this republican equality was the most distressing was in the long and frequent visitations that it produced. No one dreams of fastening a door in Western America; I was told that it would be considered as an affront by the whole neighbourhood. I was thus exposed to perpetual, and the most vexatious interruptions from people whom I had often never seen, and whose names still oftener were unknown to me."[25] Locked doors and private conveyances may go some distance toward blunting the perfect transparency expected among democratic citizens. However, above and beyond norms applying to physical space, one of the most significant ways in which cultures preserve distance is through forms of verbal address. Physical proximity need not in and of itself lead to moral proximity, but in a democratic society like the United States, Trollope discovers, the battle lines are drawn at the level of language itself. The "violent intimacy" and "uncouth advances" of Trollope's "poor neighbours" consist not only of unannounced visits to her home but in their "extraordinary familiarity" of addressing her children "by their Christian names, excepting when [they] substituted the word 'honey,'" a "familiarity of address" that was "universal throughout all ranks in the United States."[26]

Democratic forms of address not only transgress the line between public and private she seeks rigidly to maintain—as when she is addressed by a complete stranger by her first name, or described as "the English old woman"—but also serve to blur distinctions of breeding and birth. "Generals," "Majors," "Governors," and "Judges" are ubiquitous appellations among the seedy riverboat gamblers who populate American steamboats, thus degrading the entire aristocratic notion of titles as reserved to the eminent and worthy.[27] Virtually any miserable soul will be described as a "gentleman" or a "lady." Americans, she complains, see no incongruity in speaking of " 'the lady over the way what takes in washing,' or as 'that there lady, out by the Gulley, what is making dip-candles.' "[28] If a scrubwoman or a candle maker is entitled to be treated as a lady, then what can true gentility consist of? While Mr. Trollope was generally referred to as " 'the old man,' " a whole procession of "draymen, butchers' boys, and the labourers on the canal were invariably denominated " 'them gentlemen.' "[29] Forms of address that seek to communicate, generate, or preserve difference—whether they be European titles of birth, significations of superior eminence or good

25. Trollope, *Domestic Manners*, 100.
26. Trollope, *Domestic Manners*, 99–100.
27. Trollope, *Domestic Manners*, 18.
28. Trollope, *Domestic Manners*, 100.
29. Trollope, *Domestic Manners*, 100.

breeding, specialized authority, or the general respect one owes to strangers—are confounded by their ironic application everywhere and nowhere, without any regard for the naturally higher and lower elements of society. In the case of American English, the language itself serves as an instrument of democratic leveling. This is not surprising given that English—unlike French, Spanish, or other Romance languages—is not intrinsically expressive of the distinction between familiarity and formality, between the *tu* and the *vous*. And yet in Mrs. Trollope's aristocratic world these conventions have somehow been contrived and upheld despite the fact that rebellious language conspires against them.

Another thing that Trollope finds objectionable is the constant stream of intensely personal questions that Americans boldly venture to complete strangers. The line between what is public and what ought to remain decently private is constructed differently in a republican society than in aristocratic England. This transgression of boundaries runs in the opposite direction as well, as another visitor in 1827, Mrs. Basil Hall, laments the tendency of Americans to make themselves and their private lives the endless subject of conversation. "The most disagreeable part of the manners of the Americans," Mrs. Hall complains, "is that you are called upon to admire and be surprised to such a degree that by the time I came home, I was perfectly worn out. The very question shows their deficiency, for what can be more ill-bred than to ask anyone what they think of yourself."[30] In both his novels and his *American Notes,* Charles Dickens records a similar tendency on the part of Americans to demand that both their public institutions and private possessions remain constant subjects of discussion and admiration.[31]

Not only does democratic language confound public and private but it denies the distinction between higher and lower elements. The existence of poverty and ill-breeding troubles Mrs. Trollope less than "the useless meeting of incongruities that prevails all over the Union"—that is, when the rigidly maintained boundaries between the upper and lower classes to which she is accustomed are transgressed.[32] "You are not startled," she notes (although she clearly is), "by a

30. Margaret Hunter Hall, *The Aristocratic Journey, Being the Outspoken Letters of Mrs. Basil Hall Written During a Fourteen Months' Sojourn in America 1827–1828* (New York: G. P. Putnam's, 1931).

31. See, for example, Charles Dickens, *The Life and Adventures of Martin Chuzzlewit* (London: Penguin, 1999), esp. chap. 16. Interestingly, the radical Dickens ends up being just as offended by the Americans as the more conservative Trollope. Despite his intention to admire the United States, Dickens wrote home in 1842 that "I *am* disappointed. This is not the Republic I came to see. This is not the Republic of my imagination." Cited in Neville-Sington, *Fanny Trollope,* 307.

32. Trollope, *Domestic Manners,* 425. This "useless meeting of incongruities" is not confined to public life. Mrs. Basil Hall bemoans the "motley company" they are forced to endure even at private dinner parties, with "senators, lawyers, actors, editors of newspapers, one of them a Jew, all placed indiscriminately at table and all joining equally in the conversation" (Hall, *The Aristocratic Journey,* 75–76).

man reeking of work and whiskey approaching to take your hand." That customary sense of deference or "air of respect, elsewhere assumed by tradesmen, is
wanting."[33] Even the "common courtesies of salutation are abridged, as if every
one was afraid of compromising his dignity by being too condescending."
Although she laments rather than celebrates this tendency, Trollope manages to
put her finger on two important aspects of the communicative relationship
between manners and morals. First, as she correctly notes, being overly deferent,
ingratiating, or obsequious clearly does represent a "compromise" of one's dignity that democratic peoples are reluctant to make. Their reluctance to do so
even in the ordinary and seemingly trivial interactions of everyday life demonstrates both the passionate love they have of their dignity, as well as the fact that
everyday interactions in a civil society are deeply laden with moral overtones.
"All this is trifling," Mrs. Trollope notes, "but human life is made up of trifles."[34]
Consequently, she concludes, such trifles "may be quite as well graceful as not."
However, defenders of democratic civility like Thomas Hobbes and David
Hume argued that these "trifles" of human sociability are only pleasurable when
they take place on terms of "mutual deference" and equal respect; that is, when
respect and human dignity are communicated in both directions rather than only
one.[35] These illustrious social graces of deference and condescension, affording
what Edmund Burke calls the "decent drapery" of polite society, must be distinguished from that bare and seemingly unaesthetic veneer of "civility," which it
is "all you can do . . . to enforce" in a democratic society like America.[36]

AGAINST THE TOCQUEVILLEAN GRAIN: REPRODUCING
INEQUALITY IN THE MIDST OF EQUALITY

Manners may reflect underlying political values, and thus Mrs. Trollope's more
fundamental complaint is that the American doctrine "all men are born free and
equal" is nothing more than a "phrase of mischievous sophistry."[37] If taken literally, as ignoring natural inequalities of talent, intelligence, or beauty, then certainly the doctrine of democratic equality rests on a patent falsehood. Some are
obviously more beautiful, intelligent, or talented than others—not to speak of

33. Trollope, *Domestic Manners*, 425.
34. Trollope, *Domestic Manners*, 425.
35. See, for example, David Hume, "Of the Rise and Progress of the Arts and Sciences," and "Of
the Middle Station of Life" in *Essays: Moral, Political, and Literary,* ed. Eugene Miller (Indianapolis:
Liberty Press, 1985), 126–27, 546–48.
36. Edmund Burke, *Reflections on the Revolution in France,* ed. J. G. A. Pocock (Indianapolis: Hackett, 1985), 67; Trollope, *Domestic Manners,* 426.
37. Trollope, *Domestic Manners,* 71.

conventional distinctions brought about by birth, breeding, and acculturation. As Henry James surmised, "Nature and industry keep producing differences as fast as constitutions keep proclaiming equality, and there are always, at the best, in any really liberal scheme or human view, more conscious inaptitudes to convince of their privilege than conscious possibilities to remind of their limits."[38] Mrs. Trollope's attack on the doctrine of democratic equality reveals, first and foremost, her misunderstanding that this doctrine refers mainly to the civic or political equality secured by the American Constitution. In Jefferson's own formulation the doctrine that "the mass of mankind has not been born with saddles on their backs, nor a favored few booted and spurred, ready to ride them legitimately, by the grace of God" was fully compatible with his belief in a natural aristocracy of talent and genius that must be "raked from the rubbish annually."[39]

At an even more fundamental level, however, equality in America implies that even natural geniuses like Benjamin Franklin, maybe the greatest American proponent of democratic norms of humility and civility, must conform themselves in the "little private incidents" to democratic "rules of prudence in ordinary affairs." As Franklin's friend and correspondent Benjamin Vaughan notes, "[w]hen we see how cruel statesmen and warriors can be to the humble race, and how absurd distinguished men can be to their acquaintance, it will be instructive to observe the instances multiply of pacific acquiescing manners; and to find how compatible it is to be great and *domestic;* enviable and yet *good-humored.*"[40] Thus not only does the doctrine of democratic equality afford a kind of compensatory civic equality, in the sphere of politics every citizen is the equal of any other, no matter how wealthy, famous, or estimable. It also precludes the sort of social pretension that would insist that native inequalities like beauty, genius, or talent—or even acquired virtues like politeness, refinement, or culture—entitle one to deference in other spheres of life where these qualities are irrelevant.

By way of contrast, Trollope clearly assumes that eminence in some quality— good breeding, high birth, or eminence of learning—should translate into special privileges that have no necessary relationship to this particular quality or excellence. She cites with horror the case of the German Duke of Saxe-Weimar's stagecoach ride during his travels in America. This man of ostensibly "unaffected and amiable manners" is outraged when, after having tried to engage a "monopoly on the vehicle" for himself and his luggage, he must share the carriage with

---

38. Henry James, *The American Scene* (New York: St. Martin's, 1987), 233–34.

39. Jefferson, *Writings,* ed. Merrill Peterson (New York: Library of America, 1984), 1517, 272–74, 1304–10. Trollope simply disregards this dimension of Jefferson's political theory, focusing instead on his hypocrisy and his dalliance with a slave mistress. Trollope, *Domestic Manners,* 71–73, 316–17.

40. Benjamin Franklin, *The Autobiography and Other Writings* (New York: Penguin, 1986), 81.

another passenger who has had the temerity to "secure his seat by payment of the customary charges."[41] When the duke protests this indignity and threatens to report the stagecoach driver to the governor, he learns "his first lesson of republicanism" by being beaten savagely and thrown back into the carriage next to the other traveler. Rather than an object lesson about the vices of putting on airs, Trollope regards "this brutal history" as not only "distasteful to the travelled and polished few," but also the very "*possibility* of such a scene to be a national degradation."

Trollope really thinks that the duke deserves a larger share of the stagecoach because of his title and obvious eminence in good breeding. Seen through the lens of democratic equality, however, this expectation smacks of an odious kind of aristocratic presumption. It is this sense of presumption—rather than the inequality itself—that generates that "dislike which every trace of gentlemanly feeling is sure to create among the ordinary class of Americans."[42] While the duke's qualities may be every bit as admirable as Trollope imagines them to be, this does not entitle him to more room on the stagecoach than other paying customers. The notion that some deserve a greater share of public space or some other public good is revolting not just because of the material inequities involved. Actions like cutting in line or taking up two seats on the train provoke reactions all out of proportion to the actual wrong because of the inegalitarian messages they send to others. Owning a private coach may be tolerated or even admired in a democratic society, but taking up additional seats on a public coach represents an unconscionable act of presumption. The broader problem is to be explained by the American inability to recognize and defer to others. "The American people," she complains, "have no more idea of what constitutes the difference between this 'Prince of a five acre patch,' and themselves, than a dray-horse has of estimating the points of the elegant victor of the race-course."[43] Although the democratic response that "a horse is a horse" may have the defect of denying the superior qualities of the latter, the fact remains that in everyday democratic life these qualities ought not to translate into greater civic or public benefits.[44] Nor do they automatically demand a deference, recognition, or respect from others that they are, for whatever reason, unwilling to offer freely and voluntarily.

Trollope's otherwise antidemocratic narrative seems to be redeemed by her

41. Trollope, *Domestic Manners*, 305.
42. Trollope, *Domestic Manners*, 308.
43. Trollope, *Domestic Manners*, 309.
44. Trollope, *Domestic Manners*, 309. This is, substantially, Michael Walzer's argument about the importance of "blocked exchanges" in *Spheres of Justice: A Defense of Pluralism and Equality* (New York: Basic Books, 1983), 10–20, 95–128.

deft criticism of the peculiar institution of slavery. Like Tocqueville, Beaumont, and other European visitors of the era she is struck by its injustice as well as its pernicious moral effects on slave and slave owner alike.[45] In the case of an accidental poisoning of a slave child in a house where she is visiting, she is horrified by the grotesque indifference of the young white girls of the house to the predicament of the child: "the idea of really sympathizing in the sufferings of a slave, appeared to them as absurd as weeping over a calf that had been slaughtered by the butcher."[46] " 'My!' " one of the young ladies of the house exclaims, " 'If Mrs. Trollope has not taken her in her lap and wiped her nasty mouth! Why I would not have touched her mouth for two hundred dollars!' "[47] However, one of the ironies is that Trollope seems incapable of generating a similar degree of empathy for the lower classes who hold analogous domestic positions in the North, and her criticism of slavery focuses largely on its distorting effects on the deference of the lower orders of American society: "I am very far from intending to advocate the system of slavery; I conceive it to be essentially wrong; but so far as my observation has extended I think its influence is far less injurious to the manners and morals of the people than the fallacious ideas of equality, which are so fondly cherished by the working classes of the white population in America."[48] Despite slavery's abomination, "its effect will appear less injurious to the country than the false, futile, and preposterous tone assumed by the white population when compelled by necessity to sell their labour in domestic service." According to Trollope, the existence of slavery alone "renders the idea of domestic service shameful." If only the blight of slavery were removed, "the gradation of ranks INEVITABLE in the progress of all society would take place naturally, and of necessity, leaving tranquility and leisure for the progress of refinement."[49] This and this alone might bring "civilization" and "order" to the United States.[50]

Some of her greatest transgressions against democratic equality take place in her scornful treatment of young domestic girls who, feeling the social awkwardness of their position, aspire to the same dignity as their employers and who bitterly resist being degraded by the labor they happen to perform. "It is more than petty treason to the Republic," she complains, "to call a free citizen a *servant*. The whole class of young women, whose bread depends upon their labour, are taught to believe that the most abject poverty is preferable to domestic ser-

---

45. The injustice and hypocrisy of slavery is a major theme in her subsequent "American novels," especially *The Life and Adventures of Jonathan Jefferson Whitlaw: Or Scenes on the Mississippi* (London: Bentley, 1836).

46. Trollope, *Domestic Manners*, 248.

47. Trollope, *Domestic Manners*, 248.

48. Trollope, *Domestic Manners*, 186.

49. Trollope, *Domestic Manners*, 186n.

50. Trollope, *Domestic Manners*, 186n.

vice."[51] After alienating a series of young girls with her overbearing demands that they know their place, Trollope finds that no American girls will work for her regardless of the wages she offers. Her rapid succession of domestics shares one common conceit. "The horror of domestic service, which the reality of slavery, and the fable of equality, have generated, excludes the young women from that sure and most comfortable resource of decent English girls."[52] They value their dignity more than Mrs. Trollope's money, a principle whose aristocratic over-tones she ought to respect but whose democratic permutation she emphatically resists when the value being bought and sold is not aristocratic honor but a dem-ocratic dignity to which all persons are entitled. All of this gets attributed to a "sore, angry, ever wakeful pride" on the part of these "poor wretches."[53] Their "good feelings were soured, and [their] gentleness turned to morbid sensitive-ness, by having heard a thousand and a thousand times that [a domestic] was as good as any other lady, that all men were equal, and women too, and that it was a sin and a shame for a free-born American to be treated like a servant."[54] Not surprisingly, whole series of hired "help" resist Trollope's efforts to break their pride by compelling them to eat in the kitchen separately from the rest of the family; urging them to dress in a manner more befitting their inferior position rather than having the "bad taste" to attend church on Sunday dressed exactly like their mistress; or otherwise disabusing them of the idea that a better life awaits them after their temporary job passes.[55]

She fundamentally misunderstands the complaints of her "servants," whom she would prefer to think of as "peasants." What affronts the democratic dignity of the lower classes is not any likeness to the condition of black chattel slaves so much as the degrading distinctions between themselves and their employers introduced by the nature of the work. The psychological sticking point is not the fact of being treated like a domestic slave. Trollope's hired girls know that however miserable their condition, they are superior to slaves. What rubs them the wrong way is being treated by another white person like a European peasant or serf, doomed by birth or social position to occupy permanently a subordinate station in life. This explains the emphasis these domestics place on the *temporary* nature of their employment.[56] What Trollope dismisses as immaturity, irresolu-tion, and fecklessness is their aspiration to rise to a better social position. Trollope may be correct that their subsequent luckless marriages and unhappy careers are

51. Trollope, *Domestic Manners*, 52.
52. Trollope, *Domestic Manners*, 118.
53. Trollope, *Domestic Manners*, 53.
54. Trollope, *Domestic Manners*, 54.
55. Trollope, *Domestic Manners*, 54n.1.
56. Cf. Tocqueville, *Democracy in America*, 2:549.

often objectively more oppressive than their jobs as domestic servants. However, this cannot erase the dignity that comes from having chosen them voluntarily. As Tocqueville notes, the courage of American women in subjecting themselves to the tyranny of the patriarchal family makes them worthy of claiming a share of honor otherwise denied them in an aristocratic society.[57]

In passages such as these, where Trollope struggles so mightily under adverse conditions to maintain her social status, one suspects that her obsession with authority, hierarchy, culture, breeding, and birth stems from her tenuous social position. Even living in a peasant cottage on the outskirts of Cincinnati, she can still fancy herself—unlike her peasant neighbors—to be a person of culture and means whose socioeconomic position has deteriorated. Grasping at hierarchies that have been gradually subverted in America by the rising tide of democratic equality heralded by Tocqueville, Trollope is threatened with being absorbed into the midst of the very lower orders she holds in such contempt. Her family's shrinking fortunes and failed business mean that her condition is one of economic uncertainty and even, in the last months of her voyage, dependence on the good will of others.

All of this suggests that the reproduction of courtly manners, politeness, culture, and urbanity in the nineteenth century might plausibly be interpreted as a reaction to the very democratic leveling Tocqueville laments. In the case of the upper classes whose ranks are being invaded by the rising orders of a democratic society, politeness and culture are distinctions that can be invoked as ways of maintaining traditional standards of inequality and deference. Conversely, for the downwardly mobile like Mrs. Trollope, these empty forms and conventions of a courtly society are the last vestiges of aristocratic pretensions to which she clings in an effort to distinguish herself from the great level middle of a democratic society.

Describing a particularly wretched family in her village, Trollope alludes to an "air of *indecent* poverty" that presumably marks the family for special opprobrium.[58] This poverty is less "indecent" because of the squalor that accompanies it than for the refusal of the family so afflicted to personify the kind of deference and shame Trollope expects from them. Residents of this village whom Trollope describes as the "peasants of the United States" refuse to be designated as such.[59] They refuse to accept the "alms-giving" of the Trollopes with proper deference, always insisting, much to her chagrin, that they will pay something for the hand-me-down clothes or perform some reciprocal labor in return for the milk they

---

57. Tocqueville, *Democracy in America*, 2:566–67.
58. Trollope, *Domestic Manners*, 121.
59. Trollope, *Domestic Manners*, 116.

"borrow."[60] She duly notes—but seems unmoved by the fact—that they accept her charity "in a form that shewed their dignity and freedom."[61] Moreover, the industry and ingenuity by which they attempt to raise themselves from their misery are rejected as the "hard, dry calculating" of the "Jew," which Trollope regards with an "involuntary disgust."[62] Even in the lone admirable case where the industry and self-reliance of the woodcutter have allowed him to create a comfortable existence for his family, Trollope remains dubious that "the wood-cutter's son will rank with any other members of congress, not of courtesy, but of right, and the idea that his origin is a disadvantage, will never occur to the imagination of the most exalted of his fellow citizens."[63]

Democratic equality implies that "any man's son may become the equal of any other man's son," and she acknowledges that "the consciousness of this is certainly a spur to exertions." Nonetheless, her broader complaint is that "it is also a spur to that coarse familiarity, untempered by any shadow of respect, which is assumed by the grossest and the lowest in their intercourse with the highest and most refined." Although the "theory of equality may be very daintily dis-cussed by English gentlemen in a London dining-room, when the servant, hav-ing placed a fresh bottle of cool wine on the table, respectfully shuts the door," it is abhorrent "when it presents itself in the shape of a hard, greasy paw, and is claimed in accents that breathe less of freedom than of onions and whiskey."[64] In this respect, at least, Trollope proves a keener observer of the nuances and social dynamics of democratic equality than Tocqueville. Or at least her own social insecurity and aristocratic pretensions lead her to be more attuned to the coun-tercurrents and backwaters of aristocratic pretension that run against the powerful democratic currents Tocqueville fathoms in American political culture. Like Trollope, Tocqueville is struck by the way in which traditional forms of defer-ence and authority are lacking in democratic America. And surely he laments the potential costs of this in the lack of higher learning, aristocratic honor, and cul-tural refinement in the United States. And yet he seems unaware that aristocratic pretension and efforts to reproduce inequality on new grounds will be a perpet-ual struggle, and not just in the case of would-be aristocratic interlopers like Trollope.

In one of her rare "democratic" moments, Mrs. Trollope affects surprise that

---

60. Trollope, *Domestic Manners*, 119–20.

61. Trollope, *Domestic Manners*, 119.

62. Trollope, *Domestic Manners*, 123–24. Disturbing affinities between anti-Americanism and anti-Semitism have been discussed by Andrei Markovits, *European Anti-Americanism (and Anti-Semitism): Ever Present though Always Denied*, Working Series Paper 108 (Cambridge, Mass.: Minda de Gunzburg Center for European Studies, Harvard University, 2004).

63. Trollope, *Domestic Manners*, 121.

64. Trollope, *Domestic Manners*, 121.

while "recognizing in almost every full-dressed *beau*" to pass her at a society ball the very same merchants and shopkeepers with whom she is accustomed to doing business, she is dismayed not to find "among the many very beautiful girls . . . one more beautiful still, with whose lovely face I had been particularly struck at the school examination." Inquiring about her conspicuous absence, she is told that "'you do not yet understand our aristocracy . . . the family of Miss C are mechanics.'" Unlike the other equally prosperous families in attendance, her father "'assists in making the articles he sells; the others call themselves merchants.'"[65] This instance of snobbery strikes her as false not so much because of the natural excellence of beauty and grace unjustly excluded, but rather because of the minute distinctions upon which these invidious distinctions are premised. What is more ridiculous: a gang of shopkeepers and merchants putting on society airs; or that such an unpolished bunch would actually have the audacity to slight someone because her family performs a trade?

Perhaps the sole exception to the general resentment of hierarchy and authority in America falls to the clergy: "Where equality of rank is affectedly acknowledged by the rich, and clamourously claimed by the poor, distinction and preeminence are allowed to the clergy only."[66] There are pockets or spheres within everyday democratic life where moral hierarchy and authority are maintained. And yet even in this case, where one might expect approval for the legitimate moral ascendancy of the higher over the lower elements of American society, Trollope faults the specious ascendancy of revivalist ministers over the women of American society and the "insane or hypocritical zeal" of the revivals she witnesses.[67] "It is impossible," she notes, "in witnessing all these unseemly vagaries, not to recognize the advantages of an established church as a sort of headquarters for quiet unpresuming Christians."[68] Nothing short of an established church can ensure that the "wisdom and experience of the most venerated among the people" gain the ascendancy, thereby "produc[ing] a decorum in manners and language often found wanting" when religion is "placed in the hands of every tinker and tailor who chooses to claim a share in it."[69]

Democratic equality such as Tocqueville describes may indeed function to pull down or level out excellence. People have a dispassionate love of liberty, but they have an insatiable passion for equality, and this may just as easily consist of bringing others down as in exerting oneself to rise up to the middle.[70] How-

---

65. Trollope, *Domestic Manners*, 154–55.
66. Trollope, *Domestic Manners*, 75.
67. Trollope, *Domestic Manners*, 110.
68. Trollope, *Domestic Manners*, 108.
69. Trollope, *Domestic Manners*, 109–11.
70. Tocqueville, *Democracy in America*, 2:479–82.

ever, this ardent love of equality vis-à-vis those who are above does not prevent others from trying to instantiate some new grounds of distinction or inequality to make themselves stand out from the crowd. In his seminal 1840 essay "The Laboring Classes," Orestes Brownson keenly notes that "the middle class is always a firm champion of equality, when it concerns humbling a class above it; but it is its inveterate foe, when it concerns elevating a class below it."[71] In comments applying equally well to Tocqueville and Trollope, Henry James similarly observes: "So beset" is the "'European' mind on the question of 'differences' and the practicality of precautions for maintaining these" that it tends to overlook the fact that "discriminations are produced by the mere working of the machine."[72] Or as Tocqueville himself qualifies: the surface of American society is "covered with a democratic finish, beneath which from time to time one sees the old [and new] colors of aristocracy showing through."[73]

THE GENEALOGY OF CIVILITY AND POLITENESS

Although she insists throughout the book that there is an essential connection between manners and morals, Mrs. Trollope concedes the variability and subjectivity of manners. What counts as politeness or moral decency in one context may be radically different in another: "I could not but ask myself if virtue were a plant, thriving under one form in one country, and flourishing under a different one in another? If these Western Americans are right, then how dreadfully wrong are we! It is really a very puzzling subject."[74] Hardly a day passes when Trollope doesn't find her "conceptions of right and wrong utterly confounded."[75] In the case of a "young German gentleman of perfectly good manners" who made the mistake of uttering the word "corset" in mixed company, the Americans evince an "affected precision of manner" as opposed to "real delicacy."[76] Especially in matters having to do with sexuality, the exceeding stringency of American manners represents a kind of "ultra refinement" that covers over a deeper "consciousness of grossness" like an ungracefully adjusted veil.[77] The superficial modesty of Americans on certain matters belies a deeper immodesty and a "strong propensity to consider everything as wrong to which they were not accustomed."[78]

71. Orestes Brownson, "The Laboring Classes," *Boston Quarterly Review* (July 1840).
72. James, *The American Scene*, 233.
73. Tocqueville, *Democracy in America*, 1:45.
74. Trollope, *Domestic Manners*, 135.
75. Trollope, *Domestic Manners*, 136.
76. Trollope, *Domestic Manners*, 136.
77. Trollope, *Domestic Manners*, 137.
78. Trollope, *Domestic Manners*, 138.

If Trollope is correct—that standards of politeness vary widely from place to place—then it seems difficult if not impossible to map social habits onto the moral values (inequality, equality, recognition, and so forth) they embody. Thus, it is not a matter of trying to distinguish *true* delicacy, *true* politeness, or *true* chivalry from their imperfect and degraded republican analogues in the new world. Rather, the issue seems to be one of examining the kinds of values these systems of manners communicate and signify; that is to say, how they are understood and experienced by others. By now it should be clear that the system of gentility and politeness Trollope lionizes is intended to communicate a sense of superiority; functions explicitly to maintain and replicate traditional hierarchies and authorities; serves as an invidious tool for blocking social mobility; and regards any trace of democratic familiarity, civility, or transparency as a gross indiscretion.

Ironically, however, in the genealogical terms outlined by Friedrich Nietzsche, these aristocratic standards of politeness—notwithstanding their obvious links to principles of hierarchy and inequality—seem to have more in common with the slave morality of *ressentiment* than with the active and affirmative morality of the masters.[79] Why should this be the case? First, because courtly or gentlemanly standards of politeness are life-negating; they frustrate or deny the impulses, desires, and energies of those who subscribe to them.[80] This is effectively the grounds by which the aristocratic/courtly mode of valuation condemns the working-class energy, ambition, and ferocious martial and sexual energies of the lower orders. Second and maybe most important, these canons of politeness are largely other-directed: more focused on generating invidious comparisons between themselves and the impolite or unmannerly than with consciously affirming the virtues and energies of the courtly or polite classes. These categories gain their strength from their relational nature; it is important to hold these qualities mainly because other people lack them. The shame, self-consciousness, and exclusion generated by the deficit of these qualities in others accounts for their power and tenacity.

In contrast, and whatever their other shortcomings from a Nietzschean standpoint, the moral standards of democratic civility have the virtue of actively and affirmatively communicating a sense of moral equality. Although the practices of civility may be generative of a sense of human equality that looks enfeebling from a strict Nietzschean vantage, this kind of democratic equality also represents an affirmation of and excitement toward human potential. It serves to gener-

---

79. Nietzsche, *On the Genealogy of Morals,* ed. Walter Kaufmann (New York: Vintage, 1989), esp. First Essay, sections 10 and 11:36–43; section 16:52–54.

80. On this point, see especially Stendhal, *Memoirs of Egotism,* ed. Matthew Josephson (New York: Lear, 1949), 93, 122, 161–62, 172, 184, 196, 227–29.

ate—as Trollope herself complains—a sense of lower-class energy and working-class ambition, which accounts for the enormous material progress, social advancement, and general agitation of American society. Tocqueville, too, speaks of the "equality of conditions" in America as being the "generative fact" or "mother thought" from which all other facts derive.[81] Notwithstanding the undeniable tendency of democratic equality toward a *ressentiment* that seeks to pull the excellent and successful down to a middling level, as Tocqueville complains, the democratic conceit that no one is better than any other can also serve as a taut bowstring to propel others into the lead.[82]

Conceding the ambivalence of traditional codes of aristocratic honor or chivalry, Mrs. Trollope does "not lament the decadence of knight errantry, nor wish to exchange the protection of the laws for that of the doughtiest champion who ever set lance in rest." She would readily acknowledge what Tocqueville calls the "blind and barbaric fury" and "turbulent virtues" with which traditional codes of aristocratic honor were inextricably linked.[83] She insists, however, that "the better part of chivalry," a kind of "knightly sensitiveness of honourable feeling" that "still mixes with gentle blood in every part of Europe," represents the "best antidote to the petty soul-degrading transactions of every-day life."[84] The problem with her argument is that stripped of the kind of martial virtues and ferocious love of honor with which it was traditionally associated, the "gentle blood" she extols lacks the energy and ambition she finds in American society. Admittedly, as Tocqueville also notes, the objects of democratic ambitions may be less heroic than the monumental chivalrous undertakings of earlier ages.[85] However, they are also more universally accessible and conducive to the dignity of all citizens. Indeed, democratic civility seems to combine the life-affirming and motivating energies of traditional aristocratic honor with the democratic emphasis on peacefulness, tranquility, and human dignity.

Democratic civility has the further advantage of allowing us to affirm the merits and estimable qualities of others without simultaneously suggesting any inferiority on our own part. The kind of "mutual deference" extolled by Hume, Smith, and other eighteenth-century partisans of civility has the consequence of encouraging mutual respect and affirmation.[86] Civility, as I have suggested above, rests not only on the axial democratic value of equality, but it also seems conducive to another core democratic virtue of authenticity. As Rousseau, Wollstone-

81. Tocqueville, *Democracy in America*, 1:3, 14.
82. Tocqueville, *Democracy in America*, 1:50–52.
83. Tocqueville, *Democracy in America*, 2:594.
84. Trollope, *Domestic Manners*, 257.
85. Tocqueville, *Democracy in America*, 2:599–604.
86. See Boyd, "Manners and Morals," and "The Value of Civility?"

craft, Stendhal, and a host of other critics have complained, politeness or courtly manners are too often feigned or affected.[87] What is most striking is their stultifying stiffness and opacity. For if they were indeed natural, spontaneous, and heartfelt, why would it prove so difficult to fathom them, and thus, wouldn't they be equally accessible to all people? By way of contrast, civility seems to thrive in a democracy precisely because of what Tocqueville described as the ascendancy of the natural in democratic society.[88] With the passing of those conventional distinctions clung to so desperately by Trollope, democratic citizens apprehend intuitively what they share in common with one another and the pleasures of human interaction in terms of equality. They perceive this because of the transparency of democratic souls. This leads to the kind of sincerity of democratic citizens observed by Trollope. The Americans she encounters may often say things that are grossly inappropriate or even offensive—one thinks of the "greasy fellow" who crudely accosts President Jackson about his recently deceased wife[89]—but this is a consequence of the fact that they say precisely what they think, for better or worse, and consequently mean precisely what they say. What she describes as a "brutal familiarity," "forwardness," or "importunateness" is simply another way of describing the democratic virtues of authenticity and sincerity.[90]

CONCLUSION

We have seen that Mrs. Trollope's withering critique of American society is both more comprehensive and limited than Tocqueville's. From the very beginning of her book Trollope protests that she is not interested, as was Tocqueville, in America's political institutions. She offers nothing analogous to the hundreds of pages and dozens of chapters Tocqueville devotes to political and quasi-political subjects like administrative decentralization, local liberties, jury trials, inheritance

---

87. Rousseau, *Discourse on the Origins of Inequality*, ed. Roger Masters (New York: St. Martin's, 1964), 144, 149–50, 155–57, 174–75, 179–80, 195–96, 222–23; Mary Wollstonecraft, *A Vindication of the Rights of Women* (New York: Norton, 1988), 3–4, 55, 144–50; Stendhal, *The Red and the Black* (New York: Norton, 1969).

88. Tocqueville, *Democracy in America*, 2:538–39, 544–45, 561–63, 580–81.

89. Trollope, *Domestic Manners*, 145.

90. Trollope, *Domestic Manners*, 145. Mrs. Basil Hall, however, has a very different reaction. While acknowledging the "perfect civility" with which she and her husband are "answered by all ranks," she nonetheless complains that Americans often "torment [her] with civility." She denies that "altho' we complain of want of polish and refinement there must be a great pleasure in feeling that all the Americans express and do for us is at least sincere." Mrs. Hall discovers, to the contrary, that "even in the simplest forms of courtesy there is an insincerity that is very disagreeable." Her American acquaintances are all "smiles and smoothness" while insulting her behind her back. See *The Aristocratic Journey*, 27–28, 263–64.

laws, political parties, civic associations, and so forth. Nonetheless, her book does raise questions about the virtues and vices of republican government, albeit through the lens of ordinary life. On the one hand, her conclusions reinforce Tocqueville's complaints about the difficulty of cultivating the arts, refinement, and high culture in a democratic and commercial society. Among her book's most famous passages are its descriptions of the abysmal behavior of Americans at the theater. What ought to be reserved as a sanctum of high culture ends up defiled by the dirty boots and incessant tobacco-spitting of the patrons. However, Trollope goes well beyond Tocqueville's thesis about the difficulty of achieving a cultivated class in America. The more provocative claim is that this lowering of the highest elements of a democratic society is in no way compensated—as Tocqueville thinks it might be—by a corresponding improvement of the lower orders. Indeed her criticism of American manners focuses disproportionately on the lower and middling ranks in a way that Tocqueville's does not. Regardless of the mediocrity of the upper strata of American society—a fact she simply takes for granted in a republic—democracy's most deleterious effects are on the lower classes. Unguided, disorderly, and lacking even the most basic moral decorum, the presumptuous and uncouth behavior of its lower classes casts a barbarous republican shadow over all of American society.

I have tried to suggest that Mrs. Trollope is both right and wrong about the moral valence of manners in American society. She is brilliantly correct in her notion that manners are morally and politically salient in something other than a crudely functional sense. Manners are the primary medium through which citizens communicate deference, respect, and recognition to one another in everyday life. Arguably even more than the political institutions Tocqueville highlights, civil society and private life are the real locations in American society where democratic equality gets enacted and reproduced. Her complaints about the subversive and disordering effects of democratic manners on everything from language, public space, and privacy to the theater and domestic life unwittingly testify to their importance as potential sites of democratic equality—challenging critics like Norbert Elias and others who have seen manners as nothing more than elite constructions contrived to uphold social hierarchies. Despite her perceptive insights into the moral dimensions of manners, however, Mrs. Trollope is substantively wrong. That is to say, viewed only through the lens of aristocratic *politesse,* her characterization of American manners ignores the potentially ennobling virtues of civility, democratic equality, dignity, and mutual respect.

Looking ahead to the late nineteenth century and beyond, the first question one might pose is whether Trollope is correct in her long-term assessment of American manners. Like Trollope, Tocqueville complained that American society lacked a class sufficiently powerful to forge a system of authoritative manners.[91] Indeed, precisely because of the American impatience with authority and its democratic resentment of anything smacking of aristocratic presumption, efforts by elites to enforce codes of politeness or mannerliness have often been mocked and resisted. What Tocqueville and Trollope failed to foresee, however, is that as the nineteenth century unfolded and America became more preponderantly and self-consciously middle class, this dominant segment of American society began to preoccupy itself with defining proper manners and moral standards. As John F. Kasson and others have recently demonstrated, upper-middle-class elites struggled to construct standards of mannerliness, propriety, and civility and to deploy them as weapons of invidious exclusion against the waves of immigrants from northern and then southern Europe that swept over America's shores in the latter half of the nineteenth century.[92]

Rather than a rhetorical bludgeon hurled back at the United States from across the Atlantic by European critics, the "rudeness" of certain segments of the American population became a cause for concern—as well as an explicit goal of public policy—for many of America's own elites and social planners. From Frederick Law Olmsted and the "City Beautiful" movement to the "civilizing mission" of the late nineteenth-century World's Fairs and their "exhibitionary culture," middle-class manners became explicit subjects of concern and tutelage.[93] Earlier notions that the inherent superiority of American democracy was to be found in its native, untutored authenticity gave way to the conviction that Americanness had to be taught. The naturalness and spontaneity that Trollope and Tocqueville identified became debilities that needed to be remedied by inculcating proper, respectable, and orderly middle-class manners.

These efforts at civilization targeted the rude and uncivilized masses of Europe that were arriving on America's doorstep in ever-increasing numbers from the 1850s onward.[94] No longer were Americans paralyzed with self-consciousness by a sense of European superiority and the inscrutability of European manners. Instead, that abundant confidence in the superiority of all things American

91. Tocqueville, *Democracy in America*, 2:579.

92. Kasson, *Rudeness and Civility*. On the invention of middle-class culture more generally, see Alan Trachtenberg, *The Incorporation of America: Culture and Society in the Gilded Age* (New York: Hill & Wang, 1982); and Stuart M. Blumin, *The Emergence of the Middle Class: Social Experience in the American City, 1760–1900* (Cambridge: Cambridge University Press, 1989).

93. See especially, Frederick Law Olmsted, *Civilizing American Cities: Writings on City Landscapes* (Cambridge: MIT Press, 1971); James Gilbert, *Perfect Cities: Chicago's Utopias of 1893* (Chicago: University of Chicago Press, 1991); Robert Rydell, *All the World's a Fair: Visions of Empire at American International Expositions, 1876–1916* (Chicago: University of Chicago Press, 1984); and Tony Bennett, "The Exhibitionary Complex," in *Culture/Power/History: A Reader in Contemporary Social Theory*, ed. Nicholas B. Dirks, Geoff Eley, and Sherry B. Ortner (Princeton: Princeton University Press, 1994).

94. For an excellent history of American immigration history and the concerns these waves of immigrants set off in elites, see Aristide Zolberg, *A Nation by Design: Immigration Policy in the Fashioning of America* (Cambridge: Harvard University Press, 2006).

observed by Tocqueville and Trollope became a justification for tutoring the rude and uneducated wretches of Europe. Whereas the European emphasis on manners tended to be inward-oriented, focused on cultivating an aristocratic code of politeness and gentility to distinguish the upper orders from transgressive democratic elements of their own societies, in the American case the invention of politeness and civility was much more transparently xenophobic and directed against outsiders. American ideals of manners, civility, and domesticity were geared toward the exclusion (or rehabilitation) of "strangers in the land," interlopers across the geographical and cultural borders of a new nation rather than transgressors of any rigidly maintained socioeconomic or class borders, as in the European case.[95]

As we have seen, Trollope's analysis is striking in its resemblance to the writings of Tocqueville, Charles Dickens, Henry James, and other contemporaneous nineteenth-century observers of America, but her arguments have a deeper contemporary resonance as well. Indeed, in one of those strange paradoxes of intellectual history, many of Trollope's original "aristocratic" complaints about American culture have become part and parcel of a contemporary anti-Americanism whose intellectual center of gravity is normally considered far left of center. Despite her aristocratic sensibilities, Trollope presages some of the most common criticisms of the United States by the contemporary European Left. Notwithstanding America's commitments to the governing ideals of democratic equality and an easy spontaneity among democratic citizens, critics have often focused (like Trollope) on America's barbaric pugilism, its obsession with money making, its intolerance of other ways of life, and its unwillingness to acknowledge how its principles of liberty and equality are often violated in practice. On these points the Left and Right seem curiously to converge.

There are different levels to these contemporary complaints, and Trollope's narrative prefigures many of them. First, as Trollope notes in the case of black chattel slavery, America rarely manages to live up to its own heralded principles of liberty, equality, and social mobility. She notes with bitter irony the phenomenon of Americans loudly boasting about universal values of freedom and equality with a slave owner's lash in hand. "It is impossible for any mind of common honesty not to be revolted by the contradictions in their principle and practice." With one hand they are busy "hoisting the cap of liberty, and with the other flogging their slaves." One minute they are "lecturing their mob on the indefeasible rights of man, and the next driving from their homes the children of the soil, whom they have bound themselves to protect by the most solemn trea-

---

95. The phrase is, of course, John Higham's, *Strangers in the Land: Patterns of American Nativism, 1860–1925* (New Brunswick: Rutgers University Press, 1988).

ties."[96] However, her criticism of America's social and political principles is not limited to its alleged hypocrisy or failure to practice what it preaches. Like many of today's more radical critics of the Enlightenment liberalism with which the United States is often associated in the contemporary world, Trollope rejects the underlying principles themselves. In her view, inequality, deference, authority, and hierarchy are natural elements of the human condition. Even if it were practically achievable, the whole notion of democratic equality is a phrase of "mischievous sophistry," wrong-headed as well as politically disruptive.[97]

The vehemence of Trollope's criticisms of America also strikes a remarkably contemporary chord. There is a sense on the part of many European critics—nineteenth century as well as contemporary—that the values of the United States are destined to become those of the rest of the world. America's ideals of democratic equality and liberty are not just laughably misguided. They are infectious and subversive. A wide range of thinkers in the nineteenth century—Trollope, Tocqueville, Friedrich Nietzsche, and even Karl Marx—caught glimpses of Europe's future in America's present.[98] This was particularly the case for aristocratic societies confronting the pressures of democratization already well under way in the United States. Just as the United States is today acknowledged as the locus of economic modernization, globalization, and consumer culture, even in the nineteenth century its European critics recognized America's status as a political vanguard. Their own future—for better, or usually worse—was unfolding in the great republican experiment on the other side of the Atlantic. In this respect, Trollope's bitter denunciation of American values amounts to more than just a truculent and parochial traveler reacting against the alien and unfamiliar. For Trollope, as for many contemporary European critics, the stakes are nothing less than the preservation of their own besieged cultures from the caustic influence of American habits and values. What I have tried to suggest in this chapter, though, is that while European observers like Trollope may be acute critics of some of the shortcomings and pathologies of American culture, they are too quick to dismiss the virtues of civility and democratic equality that are part of the very fiber of American society.

96. Trollope, *Domestic Manners,* 221–22.
97. Trollope, *Domestic Manners,* 71.
98. For a more detailed examination of this phenomenon of projection, see Richard Boyd and Brandon Turner, "Anti-Americanism and the American Personality," in *Anti-Americanism: History, Causes, and Themes,* ed. Brendon O'Connor (Oxford: Greenwood, 2007), 115–37.

9

TYRANNY OF THE MAJORITY OR FATALISM
OF THE MULTITUDE?

Bryce on Democracy in America

Russell L. Hanson

The nineteenth century brought millions of Europeans to the United States, most to live, a few to witness the spectacle of an emerging nation. Some of these sightseers published accounts of their travels, much to the amazement of their countrymen and the chagrin of Americans wounded by the slightest criticism of foreigners. Most of these journals are forgotten, but two stand the test of time and repay close reading today, Alexis de Tocqueville's *Democracy in America* and James Bryce's *The American Commonwealth.*[1]

Tocqueville visited the United States in 1831–32 and published the first volume of *Democracy in America* in 1835; the second volume appeared four years later. *The American Commonwealth* debuted in 1888, after Bryce's third visit to the United States.[2] During the intervening years the country's geographic area dou-

---

1. British travelers to the United States were especially numerous. Allan Nevins, *America through British Eyes* (New York: Oxford University Press, 1948), surveys the impressions of such well-known literary figures as Harriet Martineau, *Society in America* (New York: Saunders and Otley, 1837), and Charles Dickens, *American Notes for General Circulation* (London: Chapman and Hall, 1842). Less well known was Thomas Hamilton, *Men and Manners in America,* 2 vols. (Edinburgh: William Blackwood and Sons, 1833). The Scotsman's acerbic work preceded publication of *Democracy in America* but failed to gain the audience that Tocqueville and Bryce reached, although it broached many of the same themes.

2. Like Tocqueville, Bryce observed the United States for nine months, although Bryce made three separate visits. He visited New England in 1879 and returned to the United States in 1881, crossing the continent and touring the South. After a third sojourn in 1883–84 Bryce wrote *The*

bled, its population quadrupled, and the value of its gross domestic product increased almost a hundredfold. An industrial revolution was rapidly changing the ways people worked, where they lived, and how they died. Equally signifi-cant changes were occurring in politics, where the Union, rent by civil war, was under reconstruction.

Not surprisingly, Bryce's account differed from Tocqueville's earlier report in many respects. In a very real sense, the two men saw different Americas, but the Frenchman and Englishman also saw America differently. By his own admission Tocqueville came to the United States not merely to learn about this country, but to capture the image "of democracy itself, with its inclinations, its character, its prejudices, and its passions, in order to learn what we have to fear or to hope from its progress."[3] The aristocrat's interest in the tendencies of democracy colored all of his observations on American politics, including his fear of tyranni-cal majorities in the New World and his appreciation for social institutions that impede them.

I recall Tocqueville's argument in the next section of my essay, before taking up Bryce's view of the American commonwealth. A member of Parliament, Bryce was not seeking ways of pacifying the majority or reforming the mixed government of his homeland. Instead he stressed the strong resemblance between British and American political institutions in their operation, a likeness Bryce traced to their common English ancestry. Precisely because he viewed the United States as the offspring of his native land, Bryce was inclined to minimize the risk of majoritarian tyranny in the United States, and this he surely did, as I show in the third section of this chapter.

The real problem in American politics, Bryce insisted, was "the fatalism of the multitude" in large-scale political communities. Widespread fatalism or acquiescence to the majority paved the way for public opinion to be a governing force in the United States, and it also induced unhealthy levels of conformity in the population. I develop Bryce's description of this phenomenon in the fourth section of this paper, and in the fifth section I explain why Bryce, who was critical of American fatalism, nevertheless believed it posed little threat to minor-ity interests or individual liberty in the United States.

Tocquevillians are inclined to see more danger in fatalism of the multitude

---

American Commonwealth, confessing: "When I first visited America eighteen years ago, I brought home a swarm of bold generalizations. Half of them were thrown overboard after a second visit in 1881. Of the half that remained, some were dropped into the Atlantic when I returned across it after a third visit." See James Bryce, The American Commonwealth (1888; repr., London: Macmillan, 1909), 1:4.

3. Alexis de Tocqueville, Democracy in America (1839; repr., New York: Schocken Books, 1961), 1:lxxxii. This is a revised and corrected edition of Henry Reeve's translation, which Bryce knew, though he also read the original in French.

than Bryce did. I close with some remarks along these lines, noting that Bryce's concept of fatalism centered on voluntary submission to the will of a majority. Tocqueville had a more profound understanding of the dynamics of opinion formation; in particular, he acknowledged the power of pressures to conform, which Bryce could not admit, given his emphasis on the racial basis of national character and the Englishness of American politics. As a result, he failed to consider the etiology of soft despotism that is central to the second volume of Tocqueville's *Democracy in America*.

DEMOCRACY AND AMERICA

Alexis de Tocqueville confessed that he wrote *Democracy in America* "under the impression of a kind of religious dread" inspired by the advance of an "irresistible revolution" sweeping Europe and indeed the world. This revolution was thoroughly egalitarian in spirit, and in its wake "divisions which once severed mankind are lowered; property is divided, power is held in common, the light of intelligence spreads, and the capacities of all classes are equally cultivated; the State becomes democratic, and the empire of democracy is slowly and peaceably introduced into the institutions and the manners of the nation."[4]

In an early statement of American exceptionalism, Tocqueville pronounced the leveling process furthest advanced in the United States. As he explained, "The emigrants who fixed themselves on the shores of America in the beginning of the seventeenth century, severed the democratic principle from all the principles which repressed it in the old communities of Europe, and transplanted it unalloyed to the New World. It has there been allowed to spread in perfect freedom, and to put forth its consequences in the laws by influencing the manners of the country." Tocqueville was certain that Europe, including his native France, would sooner or later "arrive, like the Americans, at an almost complete equality of condition," and he came to the United States "to learn what we have to fear or to hope from its progress."[5]

Tocqueville's greatest fear was the omnipotence of a majority in a democratic society. Its power was morally secured by "the notion that there is more intelligence and more wisdom in a great number of men collected together than in a single individual, and that the quantity of legislators is more important than their quality. The theory of equality is in fact applied to the intellect of man," and while minorities hesitate to admit the conclusion, they will ultimately assent to it. Reinforcing this view is "yet another principle, which is, that the interests of

---

4. Tocqueville, *Democracy in America*, 1:lxxii, lxxv.
5. Tocqueville, *Democracy in America*, 1:lxxxi, lxxxii.

the many are to be preferred to those of the few." Together, these ideas conferred on the majority prodigious political power; "no obstacles exist which can impede, or so much as retard its progress, or which can induce it to heed the complaints of those whom it crushes upon its path. This state of things is fatal in itself and dangerous for the future."[6]

The danger to individual liberty and minority interests is clear. "When an individual or a party is wronged in the United States," Tocqueville asked, "to whom can he apply for redress? If to public opinion, public opinion constitutes the majority; if to the legislature, it represents the majority, and implicitly obeys its injunctions; if to the executive power, it is appointed by the majority and remains a passive tool in its hands. The public troops consist of the majority under arms; the jury is the majority invested with the right of hearing judicial cases; and in certain States even the judges are elected by the majority."[7] Hence there was, and is, no relief from tyrannical majorities in a democratic society.

Although Tocqueville found little evidence of majoritarian tyranny in laws of the United States at the time of his visit, he was alarmed by the majority's increasing domination of public opinion.[8] He "found very few men who displayed any of that manly candour, and that masculine independence of opinion which frequently distinguished the Americans in former times, and which constitutes the leading feature in distinguished characters wheresoever they may be found."[9] To the contrary, it seemed "as if all the minds of the Americans were formed upon one model, so accurately do they correspond in their manner of judging. A stranger does, indeed, sometimes meet with Americans who dissent from these rigorous formularies; with men who deplore the defects of the laws, the mutability and the ignorance of democracy; who even go so far as to observe the evil tendencies which impair the national character . . . but no one is there to hear these things besides yourself, and you, to whom these secret reflections are confided, are a stranger and a bird of passage. They are very ready to communicate truths which are useless to you, but they continue to hold a different language in public."[10]

Tocqueville's analysis was shaped as much by his preconceptions about democracy as it was by his observations on American life. Both pointed to the same conclusion, however: tyranny of the majority, operating through public

6. Tocqueville, *Democracy in America*, 1:299, 300, 301.

7. Tocqueville, *Democracy in America*, 1:306.

8. "I do not say that tyrannical abuses frequently occur in America at the present day; but I maintain that no sure barrier is established against them, and that the causes which mitigate the government are to be found in the circumstances and the manners of the country more than in its laws" (Tocqueville, *Democracy in America*, 1:307–8).

9. Tocqueville, *Democracy in America*, 1:314.

10. Tocqueville, *Democracy in America*, 1:314–15.

opinion and law, threatened the future of liberty in the United States. "If ever the free institutions of America are destroyed," Tocqueville warned, it "may be attributed to the unlimited authority of the majority, which may at some future time urge the minorities to desperation, and oblige them to have recourse to physical force. Anarchy will then be the result, but it will have been brought about by despotism."[11]

It is precisely on this point that Bryce leveled his strongest criticism of Tocqueville's characterization of American democracy. By the time of his third visit to the United States Bryce had read Tocqueville's magnum opus and weighed its conclusions. In fact, he conducted a graduate seminar at Johns Hopkins University under the direction of Professor Herbert Baxter Adams; the students included John Dewey, John Franklin Jameson, and Woodrow Wilson.[12] The discussion focused on *Democracy in America,* with Bryce urging his pupils to question the assumptions underpinning Tocqueville's conclusions about democracy in general, and American democracy in particular.[13] Upon completion of the seminar Bryce published an essay comparing "The Predictions of Hamilton and de Tocqueville," anticipating the argument he presented at much greater length in *The American Commonwealth.*[14]

Bryce's principal objection was that Tocqueville's depiction of democracy in America was no longer accurate in 1883–84, and perhaps never had been. Bryce attributed this to the Frenchman's penchant for imputing to America certain weaknesses he believed to be inherent in democracy. Tocqueville also ascribed to democracy features of politics that were merely incidental to America, or so Bryce contended. Thus, Tocqueville offered a treatise on democracy "whose conclusions are illustrated from America, but are founded, not so much on an analysis of American phenomena, as on general and somewhat speculative views of democracy which the circumstances of France had suggested."[15]

To correct the error, Bryce set out to "paint the institutions and people of America as they are, tracing what is peculiar in them not merely to the sovereignty of the masses, but also to the history and traditions of the race, to its fundamental ideas, to its material environment."[16] A far different picture of majority politics in the United States emerged from his broad strokes, as I will now show.

11. Tocqueville, *Democracy in America,* 1:317.
12. See Edmund Ions, *James Bryce and American Democracy,* 1870–1922 (London: Macmillan, 1968); and A. L. Fischer, *James Bryce: Viscount Bryce of Dechmont, O.M.,* 2 vols. (London: Macmillan, 1927).
13. William R. Brock, "The American Commonwealth and the Dilemmas of Democracy," *American Nineteenth Century History* 2, no. 1 (2002): 75–105.
14. James Bryce, "The Predictions of Hamilton and de Tocqueville," *Johns Hopkins Studies in Historical and Political Science* 5th ser., vol. 9 (Baltimore: Johns Hopkins University Press, 1887).
15. Bryce, *American Commonwealth,* 1:4.
16. Bryce, *American Commonwealth,* 1:4.

THE TYRANNY OF THE MAJORITY

Bryce grounded his criticism of Tocqueville on a key definition: the term "tyranny of the majority" denotes "any abuse by the majority of the powers which it enjoys, in free countries under and through the law, and in all countries outside the law." The element of tyranny lies in the "wantonness of the act, a wantonness springing from the insolence which sense of overwhelming power breeds, or in the fact that it is a misuse for one purpose of authority granted for another. It consists not in the form of the act, which may be perfectly legal, but in the spirit and temper it reveals, and in the sense of injustice and oppression which it evokes in the minority." So, for example, a majority is tyrannical "when it decides without hearing the minority, when it suppresses fair and temperate criticism of its own acts, when it insists on restraining men in matters where restraint is not required by the common interest, when it forces men to contribute money to objects which they disapprove, and which the common interest does not demand, when it subjects to social penalties persons who disagree from it in matters not vital to the common welfare."[17]

Tocqueville also associated tyranny with the unjust or arbitrary exercise of power, and he feared it was emerging in the United States. Bryce admitted there was some basis for this concern in 1832: "When Tocqueville saw the United States, the democratic spirit was in the heyday of its youthful strength, flushed with self-confidence, intoxicated with the exuberance of its own freedom. The first generation of statesmen whose authority had restrained the masses, had just quitted the stage. The anarchic teachings of Jefferson had borne fruit. Administration and legislation, hitherto left to the educated classes, had been seized by the rude hands of men of low social position and scanty knowledge. . . . The masses were so persuaded of their immense superiority to all other peoples, past as well as present, that they would listen to nothing but flattery, and their intolerance spread from politics into every other sphere." Consequently, Tocqueville may "have been correct in his description of the facts as he saw them," but "he erred in supposing them essential to a democratic government." As the American nation matured, "it purged away these faults of youth and inexperience, and the stern discipline of the Civil War taught it sobriety, and in giving it something to be really proud of, cleared away the fumes of self-conceit."[18]

---

17. Bryce, *American Commonwealth*, 2:335. Bryce's definition echoes *Federalist 10*, wherein Madison described a faction as "a number of citizens, whether amounting to a majority or minority of the whole, who are united and actuated by some common impulse of passion, or of interest, adverse to the rights of other citizens, or to the permanent and aggregate interests of the community" (*The Federalist, with Letters of "Brutus,"* ed. Terence Ball [New York: Cambridge University Press, 2003], 41).

18. Bryce, *American Commonwealth*, 2:342.

The process of maturation minimized the risk of tyrannical majorities in the United States, which were nowhere in evidence by the latter part of the nineteenth century, or so Bryce claimed. Congress, the likely instrument of majoritarian tyranny, posed little danger to minorities and individuals in the United States, since the Constitution "hedged it round with many positive prohibitions" and "closed some of the avenues by which a majority might proceed to abuse its powers." Of course, Congress did sometimes act unfairly—Bryce admitted that a protective tariff favored one class or set of interests, and for a time the Congress refused to accept Abolitionist petitions and even tried to prevent the mailing of Abolitionist materials. Also "during and after the war in some of its reconstruction measures, the majority, under the pressure of excitement, exercised its powers harshly and unwisely. But such political action is hardly the kind of action to which the charge we are examining applies."[19]

The charge under examination, remember, involves "wanton" acts, meanspirited and ill-tempered legislation that produces a "sense of injustice and oppression" in those who suffer under the laws. Tariffs and the "gag" on antislavery petitions were not wanton acts in Bryce's mind, insofar as they had a legitimate public purpose, the maintenance of the Union. Reconstruction failed the test of wantonness, too; coercive measures certainly produced a sense of injustice and oppression among Southern whites, but this was offset by a newfound sense of justice among ex-slaves, and in any event was difficult to describe as purely self-interested behavior on the part of a Northern majority.

State legislatures were more likely arenas for majoritarian tyranny, but they too "have been surrounded by a host of constitutional limitations which a tyrannical majority would need some skill to evade." Indeed, "one discovers wonderfully little in the State Constitutions now in force of which a minority can complain." With "ample guarantees for free speech, a free press, and the right of public meeting" state legislatures "cannot encroach on the personal liberty of the citizen, nor on the full enjoyment of private property." True, "there are some provisions strictly regulating corporations, and especially railroads and banks, which may perhaps be unwise, and which in limiting the modes of using capital apply rather to the rich than to the masses. But such provisions cannot be called wanton or oppressive."[20]

When it came to state laws, only a handful displayed "a spirit that ignores or tramples on the feelings or rights of a minority" and so qualified as wanton. "The least defensible statutes are perhaps those which California has aimed at the Chinese . . . and those by which some Southern states have endeavored to accen-

---

19. Bryce, *American Commonwealth,* 2:336, 337.
20. Bryce, *American Commonwealth,* 2:337.

tuate the separation between whites and negroes, forbidding them to be taught in the same schools or colleges or to travel in the same cars."[21] Having acknowledged the tyrannical tendency of anti-Chinese measures in the West, Bryce excused them on a technicality: the Chinese were not citizens.[22] Likewise, in his discussion of segregation Bryce limited the problem by localizing it, in much the same way that Tocqueville did in his assessment of the future of the three races in North America.

Seeing little evidence of tyranny in laws, Bryce turned to the most important way in which majorities tyrannize, "by the imposition of purely social penalties, from mere disapproval up to insult, injury, and boycotting." Here Bryce came to a surprising conclusion: "If social persecution exists in the America of today, it is only in a few dark corners. One may travel all over the North and West, mingling with all classes and reading the newspapers, without hearing of it."[23] Bryce attributed the demise of bigotry outside the South to the spread of enlightenment in the postwar period. Habits and methods of free inquiry were widespread, and the "latest results" of European thought circulated more freely in the New World than in the Old.[24] The result was a permanent transformation of American culture, and Bryce thought it unlikely there would be future "attempts to repress either by law or by opinion the free exercise and expression of speculative thought on morals, on religion, and indeed on every matter not within the immediate range of current politics."[25]

Bryce then drew his conclusion: "If the above account be correct, the tyranny of the majority is no longer a blemish on the American system, and the charges brought against democracy from the supposed example of America are groundless. As tyranny is one of those evils which tends to perpetuate itself, those who had been oppressed revenging themselves by becoming oppressors in their turn, the fact that a danger once dreaded has now disappeared is no small evidence of the recuperative forces of the American government, and the healthy tone of the American people."[26] Instead of increasing the risk of majority tyranny, the advance of democracy had lessened or eliminated it, Tocqueville's prediction to the contrary notwithstanding.

---

21. Bryce, *American Commonwealth,* 338.

22. The Burlingame Treaty of 1868 allowed Chinese to emigrate, but denied them citizenship, by the mutual agreement between China and the United States. That is the sense in which Bryce was technically correct, though we find the treaty offensive today.

23. Bryce, *American Commonwealth,* 2:338, 339.

24. Bryce, *American Commonwealth,* 2:342.

25. Bryce, *American Commonwealth,* 2:343. Bryce was wrong about this, but space constraints prevent me from evaluating his (or Tocqueville's) empirical observations, except when they bear on claims about the overall tendencies of American democracy. These theoretical claims are the focus of my essay.

26. Bryce, *American Commonwealth,* 2:343.

THE FATALISM OF THE MULTITUDE

Although he minimized the danger of tyrannical majorities in the United States, Bryce identified a related problem facing the nation. "One feature of thought and sentiment in the United States needs special examination because it has been by most observers either ignored or confounded with a phenomenon which is at bottom quite different. This is a fatalistic attitude of mind, which, since it disposes men to acquiesce in the rule of numbers, has been, when perceived, attributed to or identified with what is commonly called the Tyranny of the Majority."[27]

Anglo-Americans, with their "slender taste for introspection or meditation" and "restless self-reliant energy" were less disposed to fatalism than others, averred Bryce, but even among them certain "conditions of life and politics have bred a sentiment or tendency which seems best described by the name of fatalism."[28] Among the relevant "conditions of life and politics" were rising social and political egalitarianism. Distinctions of rank were rapidly disappearing in the United States, and "many persons in what was previously the humbler class have acquired possession of property." Political leveling was underway, too; every male citizen "enjoys the same right of electing the representatives and officials, the same right of himself becoming a representative or an official."[29] The movement for women's suffrage was bound to extend political equality still further, as the irresistible revolution espied by Tocqueville continued to unfold.

The twin processes of social and political leveling were Bryce's nod in the direction of Tocqueville's linkage of the "rough equality of conditions" and democracy. Bryce identified a third condition that was the basis for distinguishing between the fatalism of the multitude and the tyranny of the majority, however. In America leveling was taking "place in an enormously large and populous country, where the governing voters are counted by so many millions that each individual feels himself a mere drop in the ocean, the influence which he can exert privately, whether by his personal gifts or by his wealth, being confined to the small circle of his town or neighbourhood."[30] In this respect, the American commonwealth of the late nineteenth century was not just a bigger version of the United States in 1832, it was a different kind of political community altogether.

Just how different became clear in Bryce's discussion of the status of majority opinion in large-scale communities. "Where complete political equality is strengthened and perfected by complete social equality, where the will of the majority is absolute, unquestioned, always invoked to decide every question, and

27. Bryce, *American Commonwealth*, 2:344.
28. Bryce, *American Commonwealth*, 2:344.
29. Bryce, *American Commonwealth*, 2:345.
30. Bryce, *American Commonwealth*, 2:346.

where the numbers which decide are so vast that one comes to regard them as one regards the largely working forces of nature, we may expect to find certain feelings and beliefs dominant in the minds of men." One of these beliefs, Bryce noted, was that the majority must prevail. "All free government rests on this belief, for there is no other way of working free government. To obey the majority is, therefore, both a necessity and a duty, a duty because the alternative would be ruin and the breaking up of laws."[31]

"Out of this dogma," he argued, "there grows up another which is less distinctly admitted, and indeed held rather implicitly than consciously, that the majority is right. And out of both of these there grows again the feeling, still less consciously held, but not less truly operative, that it is vain to oppose or censure the majority." The connections among these beliefs are not logical, but psychological, according to Bryce. "A conscientious citizen feels that he ought to obey the determination of the majority, and naturally prefers to think that which he obeys to be right." A mild dissenter "finds it easier to comply with and adopt the view of the majority than to hold out against it." A person with strong convictions may resist the majority but will not continue the protest in the face of rising opprobrium.[32]

The tendency toward fatalism is especially pronounced in large and expanding democracies. In small communities a person might discount the opinion of a majority, knowing that his neighbors are acting out of self-interest instead of a regard for the public good. The wisdom of a majority in a state of moderate size might be questioned on similar grounds. Though not personally acquainted with all the members of a majority, an individual possesses enough information to explain their motivation or imagine their object. "But when the theatre stretches itself to a continent . . . the wings of imagination droop, and the huge voting mass ceases to be thought of as merely so many individual human beings no wiser or better than one's own neighbours. The phenomenon seems to pass into the category of the phenomena of nature, governed by far-reaching and inexorable laws whose character science has only imperfectly ascertained, and which she can use only by obeying."[33]

The belief that human affairs are governed by impersonal forces is what Bryce termed fatalism of the multitude. It must be distinguished from the tyranny of the majority because "fatalism does not imply any compulsion exerted by the majority at all. It may rather seem to soften and make less odious such an exercise of power, may even dispense with that exercise, because it disposes a minority to submit without the need of a command, to spontaneously renounce its own view

31. Bryce, *American Commonwealth*, 2:346.
32. Bryce, *American Commonwealth*, 2:347.
33. Bryce, *American Commonwealth*, 2:348.

and fall in with the view which the majority has expressed. In the fatalism of the multitude there is neither legal nor moral compulsion; there is merely a loss of resisting power, a diminished sense of personal responsibility, and of the duty to battle for one's own opinions, such as has been bred in some peoples by the belief in an overmastering fate."[34]

It was inevitable that fatalism of the multitude would take hold in a nation as large as the United States and be embraced by its citizens. Anticipating Erich Fromm's analysis in *Escape from Freedom* (1941), Bryce saw that for most people obedience was "sweeter than independence." The sweetness came with the realization that "what the individual loses as an individual he seems in a measure to regain as one of the multitude. If the individual is not strong, he is at any rate as strong as anyone else. His will counts for as much as any other," and no less.[35]

There is an obvious connection between Bryce's view of fatalism of the multitude and his conclusion that tyrannical majorities had disappeared from the American political scene. On Bryce's reckoning, the actions of a majority cannot be "tyrannical" if minorities endorse the majority's right to rule and acquiesce in its decisions. The prevalent fatalism of the multitude was not tyranny because the submission was willing. Of course, this assumes that acquiescence by minorities or individuals is unforced or voluntary. To redeem that claim Bryce tried to show that minorities deferred to American majorities, whose liberal instincts inclined them toward moderation and tolerance. I now proceed to show how this argument works, and where it breaks down.

PUBLIC OPINION

It might seem that fatalism of the multitude, operating through public opinion, reintroduces the possibility of tyrannical majorities. By virtue of its size the majority will dominate elections, and lawmakers chosen by the majority will then pursue public policies in accordance with its wishes, ignoring the preferences and possibly even the interests of minorities. Acquiescence, or worse, resignation, by minorities in the face of a wanton majority does not make it any less oppressive, however.

Bryce addressed this challenge on two levels. He first catalogued the many obstacles that must be overcome before any majority can exercise power through national or state laws. Some of the obstacles were constitutional and had to do with checks and balances. Others were of a practical nature and applied to opinion as well as laws. In a large, diverse nation there may not be a majority prefer-

34. Bryce, *American Commonwealth*, 2:349.
35. Bryce, *American Commonwealth*, 2:353, 352.

ence on specific policy issues, or if there is, it might be difficult for that majority to recognize its numerical superiority and act on it.[36] Madison made similar points in *Federalist 10,* where he prescribed the "extended republic" as a cure for the mischief of faction, and *Federalist 51,* which introduced the "auxiliary precaution" of separated powers.[37] Taking all of these obstacles into account, Bryce concluded that American public opinion "moves slowly, and, as a rule, temperately, in the field of national affairs," although he conceded that it is "sometimes hasty and reckless in State affairs."[38]

"Hasty and reckless" actions by state legislatures were regrettable, but did not rise to the level of wanton behavior. Bryce explained the absence of wanton behavior by the centrist outlook of Americans. They were not inclined toward radical causes; at bottom Americans were moderate in orientation, or as Louis Hartz later suggested, bourgeois in aspiration.[39] Consequently, American majorities posed little threat to minorities, and importantly for Bryce's argument, minorities understood this. That is why "hasty and reckless" actions did not lead to expressions of outrage on the part of those harmed by the offending laws or sanctions.

How did Bryce account for the moderation of American majorities? In a word, publicity. Compared to Europe, or even Jacksonian America, the United States of the late nineteenth century was a more open society. American public opinion was "fresh, keen, and full of sunlight, like that of the American cities, and this sunlight kills many of those noxious germs which are hatched where politicians congregate."[40] Public exposure of "selfishness, injustice, cruelty, tricks, and jobs of all sorts" was enough to defeat the petty schemes of political and economic elites, and it was half the battle in curing "serious evils" and "rankling sores" of the body politic.[41]

More fundamentally, the vigorous exchange of ideas and viewpoints kept the public well informed and its opinion sound. Bryce conceded that the multitude needs "a succession of men like the prophets of Israel to rouse the people out of their self-complacency, to refresh their moral ideals, to remind them that the life is more than meat, and the body more than raiment, and that to whom much is given of them shall much also be required." Although America had no prophets of this order, she fortunately possessed two classes of men who perform a similar

36. Katherine A. Bradshaw, "The Misunderstood Public Opinion of James Bryce," *Journalism History* 28, no. 1 (2002): 16–26.
37. *The Federalist:* 45, 252.
38. Bryce, *American Commonwealth,* 2:358.
39. Louis Hartz, *The Liberal Tradition in America: An interpretation of American Political Thought since the Revolution,* 2nd ed. (San Diego: Harcourt Brace, 1991).
40. Bryce, *American Commonwealth,* 2:364.
41. Bryce, *American Commonwealth,* 2:364.

function. "These are the instructed critics who exert a growing influence on opinion through the higher newspapers, and by literature generally, and the philanthropic reformers who tell more directly upon the multitude, particularly through the churches. Both classes combined may not as yet be doing all that is needed. But the significant point is that their influence represents not an ebbing, but a flowing tide. If the evils they combat exist on a larger scale than in past times, they, too, are more active and more courageous in rousing and reprehending their fellow countrymen."[42]

The "genius of universal publicity" was particularly evident in American political campaigns, waged so vigorously in the press, on the square, and at public debates between candidates. In the process of evaluating candidates and comparing their proposals, citizens acquired enough political intelligence to choose leaders with views similar to their own. In that sense, elections provided the occasion for political learning, while the actual lessons were conveyed on the long campaign road leading to the polling both. Without the campaign, American elections would be like those in Europe, where the educational value of the vote was slight because campaigns were far less issue oriented.[43]

Bryce went on to explain how frequent political campaigns engaged Americans' attention, trained them in citizenship, and gave each citizen a strong sense of political responsibility. "Sensible that his eye ought to be always fixed on the conduct of affairs, he grows accustomed to read and judge, not indeed profoundly, sometimes erroneously, usually under party influences, but yet with a feeling that the judgment is his own. He has a sense of ownership in the government, and therewith a kind of independence of manner as well as of mind very different from the demissness of the humbler classes of the Old World. And the consciousness of responsibility which goes along with this laudable pride, brings forth the peaceable fruits of moderation."[44] The entire analysis recalls Tocqueville's account of jury duty, insofar as it stressed the mutually reinforcing influence of political institutions and social mores.[45]

Yet Bryce did not confine the enlightenment of American public opinion to the election cycle. "Opinion is at work at other times also, and has other methods of declaring itself. It secures full discussion of issues of policy and of the

42. Bryce, *American Commonwealth*, 2:362.
43. Bryce, *American Commonwealth*, 2:364, 366.
44. Bryce, *American Commonwealth*, 2:366.
45. The analysis also anticipated key points made by later advocates of participatory democracy, and more recently, deliberative democrats, who stress the formative role of political engagement at the local level. Familiar examples of the former include Carole Pateman, *Participation and Democratic Theory* (New York: Cambridge University Press, 1976), and Benjamin R. Barber, *Strong Democracy: Participatory Politics for a New Age* (Berkeley and Los Angeles: University of California Press, 2004). Deliberative democrats are well represented by Amy Guttman and Dennis Thompson, *Why Deliberative Democracy* (Princeton: Princeton University Press, 2004).

characters of men. It suffers nothing to be concealed. It listens patiently to all the arguments that are addressed to it. Eloquence, education, wisdom, the authority derived from experience and high character, tell upon it in the long run, and have, perhaps not always their due influence, but yet a great and growing influence. Thus a democracy governing itself through a constantly active public opinion, and not solely by its intermittent mechanism of elections, tends to become patient, tolerant, reasonable, and is more likely to be unembittered and unvexed by class divisions."[46]

Class rule, and rule by the worst class, was the specific form of tyranny feared by critics—sympathetic or otherwise—of democracy. The putative absence of class divisions was therefore crucial evidence for Bryce's claim about the moderation of public opinion in the United States. Although the poor were a majority, they refrained from imposing the whole burden of taxation on the rich, or otherwise undermining property rights. Redistribution was only suggested by utopians far out of the mainstream; there was no socialism in the United States, though nothing in the machinery of government "could do more than delay it for a time, did the masses desire it. What prevents it is the honesty and common sense of the citizens generally, who are convinced that the interests of all classes are substantially the same, and that justice is the highest of those interests."[47]

The successful reintegration of rebellious states after a bloody civil war was another important example of the moderation of American opinion, North and South. "When the restoration of self-government, following upon the liberation of the Confederate prisoners and the amnesty, had shown the magnanimity of the North, its clemency, its wish to forget and forgive, its assumption that both sides would shake hands and do their best for their common country, the hearts of the Southern men were conquered. Opinion went round. Frankly, one might almost say cheerfully, it recognized the inevitable. It stopped those outrages on the Negroes which the law had been unable to repress. It began to regain 'touch' of, it has now almost fused itself with, the opinion of the North and West," or so Bryce sanguinely (and quite prematurely) concluded.[48]

Importantly for Bryce, "No one Southern leader or group can be credited with this: it was the general sentiment of the people that brought it about. Still less do the Northern politicians deserve the praise of the peace-makers, for many among them tried for political purposes to fan or to rekindle the flame of suspicion in the North. It was the opinion of the North generally, more liberal than its guides, which dictated not merely forgiveness, but the restoration of equal civic rights."[49]

46. Bryce, *American Commonwealth,* 2:365.
47. Bryce, *American Commonwealth,* 2:369.
48. Bryce, *American Commonwealth,* 2:372.
49. Bryce, *American Commonwealth,* 2:372–73.

Though the restoration was incomplete in the South, further progress could be expected, thought Bryce. Partisans were still reckless, "but the mass of the people lends itself less to acrid partisanship than it did in the time of Jackson, or in those first days of the Republic which were so long looked back to as a sort of heroic age. Public opinion grows more temperate, more mellow, and assuredly more tolerant. Its very strength disposes it to bear with opposition or remonstrance. It respects itself too much to wish to silence any voice."[50]

The last assertion was patently false, and Bryce's characterization of class harmony and Southern whites' good will toward Reconstruction were transparent fabrications meant to bolster his view of American majorities. In Bryce's reading these majorities were temperate, mellow, and tolerant—and becoming more enlightened with the passage of time. They posed no threat to minorities and in fact served as an important check upon political leaders who pursued wanton policies for personal or partisan gain.[51] Thus, Bryce's assessment of American democracy and its prospects was diametrically opposed to Tocqueville's skepticism about majorities' commitment to liberty and justice for all.

The explanation for this is not that Bryce observed a radically different America in the late nineteenth century, but that he brought an English perspective to the United States. Tocqueville saw America through the eyes of an aristocrat seeking lessons for France in America. The Liberal MP wanted to show what Americans had learned from Britain, and tyranny was certainly not the achievement he had in mind or wanted to celebrate. The global triumph of English manners was his subject, not the irresistible spread of *démocratie*.

FATALISM AND SOFT DESPOTISM

Bryce certainly overestimated American majorities' self-restraint, but he correctly identified other limits on their ability to rule tyrannically. He understood the political diversity of the United States and the concomitant difficulty of forming a majority in an extensive federal republic, a Madisonian lesson largely lost on

---

50. Bryce, *American Commonwealth*, 2:374.

51. Bryce was certain that American politicians were inferior to political leaders in other countries, and this was one of the principal themes of *The American Commonwealth*. His explanation was straightforward: politics was relatively unimportant in the United States, where many critical decisions were deemed "private," though they had enormous public consequences. The reverse was true in Europe, where important issues were, or soon became, matters of state. Bryce contended that a nation's best men are drawn to its most important positions, for that is where the path of greatness leads. Thus, European nations had great statesmen, and Americans had great industrialists and business men. The difference in public leadership was substantial and aggravated by the democratization of governmental offices and their control by political parties.

Tocqueville.[52] As a member of the British Parliament, Bryce appreciated the effectiveness of "checks and balances" in limiting legislatures, especially at the national level, which Tocqueville underestimated.[53] Finally, Bryce rightly noted that elites, not masses, were responsible for some of the most egregious offenses against liberty in the New World. On these points *The American Commonwealth* offered a plausible rebuttal to the first volume of *Democracy in America* and its warning against tyrannical majorities.

Bryce was much less successful in discounting other forms of democratic despotism featured in *Democracy in America*'s second volume, however.[54] There Tocqueville predicted the culmination of the democratic revolution in a "nanny State" controlling its quiescent population through an extensive bureaucracy. This administrative despotism had deep affinities with the fatalism of the multitude, insofar as both assumed a passive citizenry. Yet Bryce saw no great threat to liberty in a phenomenon that profoundly troubled Tocqueville. The different estimates of the prospects for freedom are striking, especially since Tocqueville and Bryce described the emergence of mass society in similar terms. Both men saw the same thing but evaluated it differently. Why?

The answer lies in Tocqueville's warning against a rising commercial spirit in the United States, which eroded institutions that encourage citizens to understand personal interests in relation to the well-being of their community.[55] Egoism was displacing self-interest "rightly understood," and internal restraints on behavior were weakening as happiness and human fulfillment came to be defined primarily in terms of economic success.[56] Tocqueville feared the process would eventuate in a society comprising an "innumerable multitude of men all equal

52. To cure the mischief of faction Madison proposed extending the republic: "Extend the sphere and you take in a greater variety of parties and interests; you make it less probable that a majority of the whole will have a common motive to invade the rights of other citizens; or if such a common motive exists, it will be more difficult for all who feel it to discover their own strength and to act in unison with each other. . . . In the extent and proper structure of the Union, therefore, we behold a republican remedy for the diseases most incident to republican government" (*The Federalist*, 45, 46).

53. Lord Acton repeated the charge that Tocqueville never understood the federal constitution, and recalled the *Nation*'s characterization of *Democracy in America* as a "brilliant, superficial, and attractive" book. See Lord John Action, review of *The American Commonwealth*, by James Bryce, *English Historical Review* 4, no. 14 (1889): 389.

54. Schleifer surveys the "gallery of despotisms" that Tocqueville presented as possible outcomes of the democratic revolution. See James Schleifer, *The Making of Tocqueville's Democracy in America* (1980; repr., Indianapolis: Liberty Fund, 2000), 221–37.

55. On this point Tocqueville's concern deepened with the passage of time. See Aurelian Craiutu and Jeremy Jennings, "The Third *Democracy*: Tocqueville's Views of America after 1840," *American Political Science Review* 98, no. 3 (2004): 391–404.

56. The understanding that a regard for others is in one's own interest "produces no great acts of self-sacrifice . . . but it disciplines a number of citizens in habits of regularity, temperance, moderation, foresight, self-command; and, if it does not lead men straight to virtue by the will, it gradually draws them in that direction by their habits" (Tocqueville, *Democracy in America*, 2:147). As such, self-interest—rightly understood—was a useful check on intemperate behaviors associated with democracy.

and alike, incessantly endeavoring to procure the petty and paltry pleasures with which they glut their lives. Each of them, living apart, is as a stranger to the fate of all the rest,—his children and his private friends constitute to him the whole of mankind; as for the rest of his fellow-citizens, he is close to them, but he sees them not,—he touches them, but he feels them not; he exists but in himself and for himself alone; and if his kindred still remain to him, he may be said at any rate to have lost his country."[57]

A comprehensive bureaucracy presides over this anomic society, managing its affairs and regulating its members. "Above this race of men stands an immense and tutelary power, which takes upon itself alone to secure their gratifications, and to watch over their fate. That power is absolute, minute, regular, provident, and mild. It would be like the authority of a parent if, like that authority, its object was to prepare men for manhood; but it seeks on the contrary to keep them in perpetual childhood: it is well content that the people should rejoice, provided they think of nothing but rejoicing."[58]

In this scenario, the tyranny of the majority gives way to a "soft despotism" that remains invisible to those living under it. They do not experience the minute regulation of everyday life as a form of tyranny. To the contrary, "every man allows himself to be put in leading-strings, because he sees that it is not a person or a class of persons, but the people at large that holds the end of his chain."[59] For this reason, too, the imposition of regulations does not drive men to resistance; rather "it crosses them at every turn, till they are led to surrender the exercise of their will."[60] The power of the democratic state is then complete in the minds of its citizens.

Tocqueville's account of individuals surrendering their will to a popular sovereign anticipates Bryce's later description of fatalism of the multitude. Bryce did not admire the result of this process of centralization, but he saw little harm in it. Tocqueville, on the other hand, emphasized the forfeiture of liberty associated with administrative despotism, which, though mild, "compresses, enervates, extinguishes, and stupefies a people, till each nation is reduced to be nothing better than a flock of timid and industrious animals, of which the government is the shepherd." The fact that this government was chosen by the people was no consolation to Tocqueville, since it was "difficult to conceive how men who have entirely given up the habit of self-government should succeed in making a proper choice of those by whom they are to be governed; and no one will ever

57. Tocqueville, *Democracy in America*, 2:380.
58. Tocqueville, *Democracy in America*, 2:381.
59. Tocqueville, *Democracy in America*, 2:382.
60. Tocqueville, *Democracy in America*, 2:383.

believe that a liberal, wise and energetic government can spring from the suffrages of a subservient people."[61]

Bryce, too, believed that a people's character determined the quality of its government, but he did not equate good character with the predominance of aristocratic virtues, as Tocqueville did. Neither did he regard bourgeois character as inevitably coarse and inferior, as critics of democracy did. Bryce impatiently dismissed these aristocratic "prejudices" and baleful predictions based upon them: "All things considered, I doubt whether democracy tends to discourage originality, subtlety, refinement, in thought and in expression, whether literary or artistic. . . . Art and literature have before now been base and vulgar under absolute monarchies and under oligarchies. One of the most polished and aristocratic societies in Europe has for two centuries been that of Vienna; yet what society could have been intellectually duller or less productive? Venice was almost the only famous Italian city that contributed nothing to the literature of the Middle Ages and the Renaissance."[62]

Emphasizing the point, Bryce insisted that American democracy "marks the highest level, not only of material well-being, but of intelligence and happiness, which the race has yet attained." No Pollyanna, he admitted that there was ample room for improvement but insisted there was good reason to expect further progress. "As the intellectual proficiency and speculative play of mind which are now confined to a comparatively small class become more generally diffused, as the pressure of effort towards material success is relaxed, as the number of men devoted to science, art, and learning increases, so will the dominance of what may be called the business mind decline, and with a richer variety of knowledge, tastes, and pursuits, there will come also a larger crop of marked individualities, and of divergent intellectual types."[63] Consequently, there would be no withdrawal from civic life in the United States; Americans would not "lose their country" to administrative despotism.

To buttress this confident prediction, Bryce praised the reliable character of the American people, which he attributed to their English background. "No people except the choicest children of England, long trained by the practice of local self-government at home and in the colonies before their revolt, could have succeeded half so well" as the Americans in governing themselves on the North American continent.[64] There "a small race, of the same speech and faith, has spread itself out over a vast area, and has hitherto been strong enough to impose its own type, not only on the Dutch and other early settlers of the Middle States,

61. Tocqueville, *Democracy in America*, 2:381 and 384.
62. Bryce, *American Commonwealth*, 2:763.
63. Bryce, *American Commonwealth*, 2:872, 828.
64. Bryce, *American Commonwealth*, 2:586.

but on the immigrant masses who began to arrive in the middle of this cen-tury."[65] The declining proportion of this race in a population swelled by the immigration of "backward races from Central Europe" was a cause of concern for Bryce, but in the end he expressed confidence in "the amazing solvent power which the American institutions, habits, and ideas exercise upon newcomers of all races."[66] Even a small proportion of Anglo-Saxons was sufficient for maintain-ing it, or so it seemed to Bryce.

Informing Bryce's conclusion was a view of national character as the deter-mining factor in a country's progress, or lack thereof. This was a common assumption among historians of Bryce's generation, and not only in Britain.[67] What was distinctive about Bryce's expression, though, was the conviction that his own English "race" was particularly well suited to democratic politics. Woodrow Wilson noted this in a review of *The American Commonwealth,* where he agreed with Bryce that the deportment of the English race was generally conservative, independent in spirit, and thoroughly pragmatic in outlook.[68] Con-sequently, he held that English political institutions developed slowly in response to changing circumstances, not by means of revolutions and social theories that inspire them. With respect to democracy, Wilson merely restated his former teacher's opinion in claiming that apart from the Swiss, "The English alone have approached popular institutions through habit. All other races have rushed pre-maturely into them through impatience with habit: have adopted democracy, instead of cultivating it."[69]

The English race was not confined to the British Isles, of course. Present and former colonies were stocked with English settlers, with the largest concentra-tions in North America. Writing against the intellectual backdrop of evolutionary theory, Bryce regarded Anglo-Americans as a strain of the English race. To the extent that American political institutions differed from the mixed government of England, it was the result of environmental differences between old world and new. The same race or character, living in different circumstances, was bound to develop different institutions.[70] Such innovations did not signal any fundamental difference in national character, however, for a people's race was fixed. In fact, it was what made a people distinctive and their history unique, in his way of think-

65. Bryce, *American Commonwealth,* 2:826.

66. Bryce, *American Commonwealth,* 2:861.

67. Alan Lessof, "Progress before Modernization: Foreign Interpretations of American Develop-ment in James Bryce's Generation," *American Nineteenth Century History* 1, no. 2 (2000): 69–97.

68. Woodrow Wilson, review of *The American Commonwealth,* by James Bryce, *Political Science Quarterly* 4, no. 1 (1889): 153–69.

69. Wilson, review, 169.

70. Graham Maddox, "James Bryce: Englishness and Federalism in America and Australia," *Publius: The Journal of Federalism* 34, no. 1 (2004): 53–69.

ing. Thus, the Americans were "the choicest children of England, long trained by the practice of local self-government," even after they obtained independence from the parent country.[71]

In fact, Bryce used the Englishness of the Americans to qualify his analysis of the fatalism of the multitude. Like the English, Americans were not prone to fatalism, he claimed, but the circumstances of their existence were extreme. The sheer size of their political community and the continental extent of its territory were the impetus for fatalism in the multitude. Thus, circumstances overcame the natural English resistance to fatalism in the United States, but only partially, and then only temporarily. In the end, the true character of England's "choicest children" won out, and it would secure the American commonwealth against administrative despotism in the future. And that in turn meant anxieties in Britain over the democratization of English politics in the later part of the nineteenth century were misplaced. If Englishness was the key to success, the mother country would surely fare as well as her "choicest children" in the age of democracy, or better.[72]

AMERICAN VIEWS, FOREIGN EYES

Tocqueville offered his own assessment of the English "race" in his apocryphal discussion of the future of three races in North America. At the conclusion of *Democracy in America*'s first volume he noted how easily French explorers, trappers, and traders adopted Indian ways in Canada and the Old Northwest. The same was true of the French in Louisiana, where the marriage of French men to black women produced a Creole culture. The English, by contrast, not only retained their original identity, they separated themselves from other races, subjugating them in the process.[73] Thus, Tocqueville recognized many of the same

71. Bryce conceded that the spirit of 1776 was revolutionary, but insisted that the enduring spirit of 1787 was "in the main an English spirit, which desired to walk in the old paths of precedent, which thought of government as a means of maintaining order and securing to everyone his rights, rather than as a great ideal power, capable of guiding and developing a nation's life" (Bryce, *American Commonwealth*, 1:307).

72. Abraham S. Eisenstadt, "Bryce's America and Tocqueville's," in *Reconsidering Tocqueville's "Democracy in America,"* ed. Abraham S. Eisenstadt, (New Brunswick: Rutgers University Press, 1988), 229–73.

73. Quoting one of his sources, Tocqueville reports that North American "savages . . . brought into contact with us have not become French, and the French who have lived among them are changed into savages, affecting to dress and live like them." Tocqueville went on to note that "the Englishman, on the contrary, continuing obstinately attached to the customs and the most insignificant habits of his forefathers, has remained in the midst of the American solitudes just what he was in the bosom of European cities; he would not allow of any communication with savages whom he despised, and avoided with care the union of his race with theirs. Thus, while the French exercised no salutary influence over the Indians, the English have always remained alien from them" (*Democracy in America*, 1:411n.3).

durable qualities that Bryce attributed to the English race and its "choicest children" in the North America.[74]

Tocqueville did not attribute the qualities of the English people and their "choicest children" to national character, however. Had he done so, the only viable conclusion of his visit to America would be that France had nothing to learn about democracy from America, except that it should become English. As a political proposition, this was completely unacceptable and even ridiculous. The idea makes no sense analytically either, since a wholesale transformation of the French character, or any people's basic character, was unimaginable. National character held no explanatory value for Tocqueville, given his intellectual ambition and political aspirations.

Thus, Tocqueville abandoned race-based explanations of democracy in America, as Schleifer convincingly shows.[75] Instead, Tocqueville concluded that the character of a people was socially formed, not genetically fixed. Indeed, that is why he stressed the importance of educating democrats to be good citizens. The moderation so essential to the preservation of liberty in democratic societies was by Tocqueville's reckoning a product of religious instruction, sustained involvement in civic associations, and the routine fulfillment of political responsibilities, including jury duty. Americans were blessed with an abundance of institutions that promoted respect for liberty, and this was the primary restraint on tyranny of the majority for Tocqueville. The same result could be achieved in France, Tocqueville hoped, if equivalent institutions could be established there, enlightening the citizenry so that the inevitable transition to democracy would be peaceful.

The notion that a people's character is shaped by social institutions held little attraction for Bryce. If anyone could learn to be a good democrat, there was nothing distinctive about the English model of politics and its New World variations. On the other hand, if the democratic temperament was a racial characteristic, the achievements of England and her progeny were extraordinary, as was their role in spreading democracy around the globe. That is why Bryce stressed the essential unity of Britain and America, and why it was so important for him to cast the Americans as the "choicest children" of England. They demonstrated the adaptability, and ultimately the superiority, of the English model of politics.

The American Commonwealth is full of intimations to this effect, but the political

---

74. Even so, Bryce observed that Tocqueville "has not grasped, as perhaps no one but an Englishman or an American can grasp, the truth that the American people is the English people, modified in some directions by the circumstances of its colonial life and its more popular government, but in essentials the same. Hence much which is merely English appears to Tocqueville to be American or democratic" (Bryce, "Predictions of Hamilton and de Tocqueville," 21).

75. Schleifer, *The Making of Tocqueville's Democracy in America*, 82–96.

project is most clearly revealed in Bryce's 1898 essay for *The Atlantic*. There he placed the American case in global perspective: "Although there are five great world powers, there are only four great world races; for one of the races has embodied itself in two powers, and has built up the North American republic and the oceanic empire of Britain. There has indeed been a large infusion of other elements into the population of the United States, but those elements are mostly drawn from the same sources, Teutonic and Celtic, which form the population of the British Isles, and all have been, or are being, moulded into the same normal American type. That type differs less from the normal British type than the Englishman of Hampshire differs from the Scotchman of Fife or the Irishman of Galway; and the differences which separate the average Englishman and the average American are as nothing in comparison with those which separate either of them from members of any of the other great races."[76]

The essential unity of Britain and the United States was undoubtedly news to Americans who thought of the nations as rivals in the world. Seeking to dispel this notion, Bryce assured American readers that Britain was not jealous of Americans' growing wealth, power, and population. To the contrary, the British people (or most of them, anyway) regarded these achievements with something approaching parental pride. They "thought of the two countries as partners and fellow workers in securing the ascendancy of the language, the free institutions, the ideas, which they themselves cherish, and with whose power and progress they believe the future welfare of humanity to be involved."[77] Thus, the example of democracy that Tocqueville saw in America became the exemplar of democracy in Bryce's celebration of the English race and its "choicest children."

The special relationship between the United States and Britain was not just a rhetorical invention of Bryce; it was also a matter of policy. He served as one of the most popular British ambassadors to the United States between 1907 and 1913. Bryce had good rapport with Theodore Roosevelt, who preferred his book to Tocqueville's.[78] In 1912 the British ambassador witnessed the election of

76. James Bryce, "The Essential Unity of Britain and America," *Atlantic Monthly* 82 (1898): 24. Bryce nominated France, Russia, Germany, England, and the United States as the five great powers with global ambitions.

77. Bryce, "The Essential Unity," 24.

78. In a January 6, 1889, letter to Bryce, Roosevelt offered this congratulation: "You must by this time be tired of hearing your book compared to De Tocqueville's; yet you must allow me one brief allusion to the two together. When I looked over the proofs you sent me I ranked your book and his together; now that I see your book as a whole I feel that the comparison did it great injustice. It has all of Tocqueville's really great merits; and has not got, as his book has, two or three serious and damaging faults. No one can help admiring the depth of your insight into our peculiar conditions, and the absolute fairness of your criticisms. Of course there are one or two minor points on which I disagree with you; but I think the fact that you give a good view of all sides is rather funnily shown by the way in which each man who refuses to see any but one side quotes your book as supporting his" (in Fisher, *James Bryce*, 1:235).

Woodrow Wilson, his former student and another fan of *The American Common-wealth,* to the presidency. It was Wilson who subsequently led the nation into a war to "make the world safe for democracy," and Wilsonian democracy, we have seen, was decidedly Anglo-American in character. After the war Wilson and Bryce worked to establish a League of Nations, which would make peace safe for democracy, too.

By 1921, when Bryce's comparative study of *Modern Democracies* appeared, the "choicest children" were on the way to replacing their mother as the chief stan-dard-bearer of the English model of democracy in the world.[79] Americans embraced this role, particularly after World War II, in a "cold war" with com-munism. The ensuing contest was the bipolar version of the "Great Powers" struggle to achieve global hegemony that Bryce described in 1898. The collapse of communism near the end of the twentieth century reinforced Western, and perhaps especially American, presumptions about the superiority of liberal demo-cratic values, and the Anglo-American institutions thought to embody them.

A similar sense of mission is evident in current American characterizations of the global war on terror as a "clash of civilizations" between Islamofascists and a multinational coalition whose most prominent members include the United States, Britain, and Australia.[80] There is a racial tinge to some of these character-izations, which insinuate that Arab culture is incompatible with Western-style democracy. For the most part, though, Americans believe that liberty is a univer-sal aspiration, and that as the lone superpower on Earth the United States has an interest in promoting democracy, as well as an obligation to do so. How to accomplish that is a matter of contention, to be sure, but that we ought to try is not much debated.

In that sense there is a powerful resonance between Americans' self-under-standing and Bryce's flattering portrait of the American people and their histori-cal importance. Americans may not know Bryce's name, let alone his writings, but they see themselves as an exceptional people. This exceptionalism is no longer described in racial terms, nor is the terminology of national character invoked (though it lurks surprisingly close to the surface of political discourse). Rather, an essentialist notion of American "civilization" underwrites public impressions of the exceptional qualities, accomplishments, and responsibilities of the people who reside on that portion of the North American continent called the United States of America. The defining elements of this civilization are sel-dom identified with any precision, but Americans take its durability and unique-ness for granted in the same way that Bryce embraced the English character of the "choicest children."

79. James Bryce, *Modern Democracies,* 2 vols. (1921; repr., New York: Macmillan, 1927).
80. Samuel P. Huntington, *The Clash of Civilizations* (New York: Free Press, 2002), is the starting

No comparable resonance exists between Americans' self-understanding and Tocqueville's assessment of them, outside the academy at least. Many Americans would vehemently deny being preoccupied with "petty and paltry pleasures that glut their lives"; even more would dismiss Tocqueville's suggestion that they are susceptible to administrative despotism and indeed receptive to it. This does not mean Tocqueville was wrong; as he explained, the nanny state is mild and does not seem despotic to those whom it regulates. By that same argument, however, there is no reason to think that reading *Democracy in America* is enough to revive Americans' interest in liberty and cause them to resist administrative despotism, once it has emerged. They are far more likely to remember the praise Tocqueville gave than the criticism he offered.

It seems that neither Bryce nor Tocqueville by themselves can inspire self-criticism on the part of Americans. One is too close to the Americans, the other too far. In such cases there is value in seeing America through different foreign eyes. Space for reflection can be made by levering outsiders' perspectives against one another, not just against Americans' self-understandings. Precisely because Bryce offered a sympathetic portrait of American democracy, it is useful to criticize him, instead of American democrats, when it comes to analyzing democratic despotism. In that way Tocqueville's criticism of democracy takes hold through Bryce. If Bryce is wrong, so are those who embrace his view of America as an increasingly liberal society with a special responsibility to promote democracy in the world. And if Tocqueville is wrong, the democratic revolution is not irresistible and its future will be decided in clash of civilizations.

---

point for this interpretation of the global war on terror. Huntington credits Bernard Lewis with introducing the phrase "clash of civilizations."

10

⚜

WHAT G. K. CHESTERTON SAW IN AMERICA
The Cosmopolitan Threat from a Patriotic Nation

Patrick J. Deneen

In recent years a rift has opened between European and American sensibilities and philosophies, one that appears to be leading one-time political and philosophical partners to divergent and potentially opposite political trajectories. Numerous books, ranging from the erudite to the popular, contrast an increasingly cosmopolitan and pacifist Europe to a more bellicose and nationalistic (or patriotic) America. Whether posed popularly as the difference between "Venus" and "Mars," or articulated philosophically as a contrast between Kantian cosmopolitanism and Hobbesian realism, the two major Western political units appear increasingly to regard each other as apostates and threats to the future of Western civilization.[1] Never in the two-century relationship between these two Western powers has the philosophical divide seemed vaster.

The divergence between the two political entities centers on questions that broadly converge on the relative merits and necessity of particularity and universality, or expressed more politically, patriotism and cosmopolitanism. Cosmopolitanism—drawing from a liberal tradition informed by Stoicism and Kant—emphasizes the arbitrariness of various human groups and the fundamental shared and equal

---

1. For a more popular treatment on this theme, see Robert Kagan, *Of Paradise and Power: America and Europe in the New World Order* (New York: Knopf, 2003); for a philosophical treatment, see Pierre Manent, *A World beyond Politics? A Defense of the Nation-State* (Princeton: Princeton University Press, 2006).

dignity of all humans, regardless of place and inherited or even chosen commitments. The cosmopolitan perspective—in recent years articulated and defended
by such thinkers as Martha Nussbaum and Kwame Anthony Appiah—views the
multiplicity of cultures on the one hand with sympathy, but not finally as a form
of identity that most essentially defines humanity. Polities are similarly arbitrary
and accidental, and while they constitute a human community to which we
can owe some allegiance, that allegiance is always provisional and not the most
fundamental.[2] As stated by Nussbaum, "we should give our *first allegiance* to no
mere form of government, no temporal power, but to the moral community
made up of all human beings." Our *"fundamental allegiance"* should be directed
to "the world community of justice and reason."[3] Such cosmopolitan proponents
call for greater international cooperation or the ultimate dissolution of nation-
states in favor of ever-larger global entities, even the idea of a world state of a
global federation of states governed by a single transnational entity.

By contrast, critics of this view defend a more particularistic, culture-bound,
nation-based form of politics that best comports with the reality of the human
condition. Such thinkers insist that politics necessarily involves commitments and
loyalties that are by nature limited to a particular people in a specific location.
Such thinkers acknowledge that such commitments can lead to dangerous
extremes, but nevertheless insist that only by means of such loyalties can a people
be sufficiently motivated to embrace a conception of common good. Further,
such thinkers insist that such devotions are by nature limited—humans are incapable of a general love for all humanity. They hold to a "fallen" or imperfect
view of human nature, and thereby mistrust any effort to consolidate all power
to a single global agent. They regard cosmopolitanism as resting on a false conception of human nature, an effort to expunge politics at once born of common
and longstanding allegiance and disagreement alike, and replace it with a more
abstract set of conceptual civic (and legal) relationships, as well as rule by bureaucracy and legal institutions. Thinkers like Pierre Manent, Roger Scruton, and
Jeremy Rabkin have criticized the effort to supplant national political structures
with transnational legal regimes as ill-conceived efforts to "cure" the excesses of
particularity that will in fact give rise to a worse disease—rule by liberal elites and
potential world despotism.[4]

Today, Europe increasingly embodies this liberal cosmopolitan aspiration,

---

2. Martha C. Nussbaum et al., *For Love of Country: Debating the Limits of Patriotism,* ed. Joshua
Cohen (Boston: Beacon Press, 1996); Anthony Kwame Appiah, *Cosmopolitanism: Ethics in a World of
Strangers* (New York: W. W. Norton, 2006).

3. Nussbaum, *For Love of Country,* 7–8 (emphasis mine).

4. See Pierre Manent, *A World beyond Politics?;* Roger Scruton, *A Political Philosophy* (New York:
Continuum Books, 2006); Jeremy Rabkin, *Law without Nations?* (Princeton: Princeton University
Press, 2005).

while America defends patriotic and national commitments. What is striking about the current alignment is the evident reversal that has taken place: not long ago, the United States was regarded as the nation that embodied a universalistic creed, and Europe was defined as a patchwork of often incompatible and diverse cultures. Progressives regarded the American commitment to "natural rights"— the philosophy articulated in the American Declaration of Independence that *all* men are created equal and endowed with certain rights—as a promising avenue by which to overcome localist parochialism, whereas conservatives were inclined to suspect that such a creed might ultimately undermine local and even national commitments.[5] In short, America was thought for many to embody precisely an orientation toward a cosmopolitan and universalistic philosophy, while Europe seemed defined by traditionalist and inescapably particularistic history, culture, and nationhood.

The grounds for this reversal merit further study and exploration (and certainly have much to do with America's leading military role preceding and during the cold war and Europe's horrific experience of two world wars), but in the light of the current divisions, it is informative to recall that the apparent divergences between America and Europe were opposite to the current view. One visitor to the United States—the Englishman G. K. Chesterton—was particularly fascinated by the creedal aspect of the American regime, famously concluding that the universalistic creed of the Declaration of Independence made America "a nation with the soul of a Church." Nevertheless, Chesterton noted also the strong patriotism of the Americans, and in an essay he wrote following his 1922 journey to America—aptly entitled *What I Saw in America*—Chesterton explored the apparent tension at the heart of America's universalistic creed and its strong sense of nationhood. As a conservative Englishman (*not* a self-identified European), Chesterton should have been arguably disposed to view the creedal aspect of the American regime with deep misgiving. Yet, he saw aspects of the American articulation of that creed that suggested inherent limits to its expansion, and thus perceived how America's political commitments would restrain tendencies to philosophic universalism. In that tension he saw one of the great conflicts within the human soul itself, and regarded America's own efforts to negotiate that tension as a likely harbinger of the fate of the political world and the soul of modern man. It was a tension that concerned Chesterton throughout his career, beginning with his first novel, *The Napoleon of Notting Hill,* and given more theoretical reflection in his book *What I Saw in America.*

5. See Carl Becker, *The Declaration of Independence: A Study in the History of Ideas* (New York: Harcourt, Brace and Company, 1922), and *The Heavenly City of the Eighteenth Century Philosophers* (New Haven: Yale University Press, 1932); more recently, see David Armitage, *The Declaration of Independence: A Global History* (Cambridge: Harvard University Press, 2007).

CHESTERTON'S MISTRUST OF UNIVERSALISM

To my knowledge, there are two prophetic novels set in the year 1984: the more famous *1984,* by George Orwell, and G. K. Chesterton's first published work, *The Napoleon of Notting Hill,* published in 1904. Of the two, Orwell's was more accurate in describing his contemporary situation if prophetically less realistic. His description of the "Big Brother" state as a totalitarian, war-making entity might strike some as an accurate description of present reality in some quarters of the world, but in the main his book reads more as an imaginative projection of twentieth-century totalitarianisms that were otherwise defeated in the years 1945 and 1989.

Chesterton's youthful novel, by contrast, while it appears at first glance prophetically inaccurate as well as irrelevant to his contemporary situation, arguably centers on the main issues that animate many contemporary debates over the respective places of patriotism and cosmopolitanism in contemporary society. While seemingly anachronistic in its portrayal of a 1984 in which battles would be fought with swords and halberds, on horseback, and in brightly colored uniforms with flowing capes, the central animating conflict of the novel—between the globalizing tendency of modern states and particularly market-based economics on the one hand, and localism based on emotional and more modest economic ties on the other—nevertheless is arguably more at the heart of issues in contemporary political theory than fears of the impending rule of Big Brother.

In his novel Chesterton describes a future in which most small nations have been absorbed into larger national entities; internally, differences between particular communities, towns, and historic sections are rapidly being dissipated. Both internationally and domestically, diversity is being expunged in favor of cosmopolitan uniformity. The cosmopolitan spokesmen of the novel—almost invariably businessmen—represent the party of progress against otherwise nostalgic and even reactionary defenders of particularity. Chesterton himself acknowledged that the idea for the novel—in which these two forces fight each other in a set of ferocious and even medieval-style battles—came from his own appreciation from the local peculiarities of the London neighborhood of Notting Hill. As he wrote of his reaction:

> It came to me in a flash when I was walking down a certain street in Notting Hill. There was a row of shops. At one end was a public-house; somewhere at the farther end I rather think there was a church. And on the way there was a grocer's, there was a second-hand bookshop, there was an old curiosity shop where they sold, among other things, arms. There was, in fact, shops supplying all the spiritual and bodily needs of man.

And all at once I realized how completely lost this bit of Notting Hill was in the modern world. It was asked to be interested in the endowment of a library in Kamschatka by an American millionaire, or a war between an oil trust and another oil trust in Papua, or the splendid merger of all the grocery interests in Europe and America or the struggles between the brewers and the Prohibitionists to give us worse beer or less beer.

In all these world-shaking events this little bit of Notting Hill was of no account. And that seemed idiotic. For this bit of Notting Hill was of supreme importance.

In the same instant I saw that my Progressive friends were more bent than any on destroying Notting Hill. Shaw and Wells and the rest of them were interested only in the world-shaking and world-making events. When they said, "Every day in every way better and better," they meant every day bigger and bigger—in every way. . . .

In that half-second of time, gazing with rapt admiration at the row of little shops, nobly flanked by a small pub and a small church, I discovered that not only was I against the plutocrats, I was against the idealists. In the comparatively crystalline air of that romantic village I heard the clear call of the trumpet. And, once for all, I drew my sword—purchased in the old curiosity shop—in defence of Notting Hill.[6]

In the novel that was inspired by this episode, Chesterton portrayed a future London in which an idealistic young man—Adam Wayne—embraces a king's off-the-cuff fantasy about a London that is checkered by neighborhoods with definitive borders, traditions, flags, and standards. The king is reproached by a group of businessmen who are in the midst of plans to pave a major thoroughfare through the city of London, including a section through Pump Street in the middle of Notting Hill. Wayne persuades some of the shopkeepers in Notting Hill to resist the construction, and in response the businessmen raise troops (appropriately, mercenary troops who are paid handsomely for their services). The "brute powers of modernity" (NH, 17) attack Notting Hill with superior numbers, but are rebuffed in several battles due to the superior fighting acumen, the patriotism, and the outright trickery of the warriors of Notting Hill.

While the defense of Notting Hill is ultimately overwhelmed (but not before a number of significant victories), it is only when the businessmen assume the same form of localist patriotism that made its defense successful in the first instance. Chesterton appears to imply that the only way to defeat such localism

6. G[ilbert] K[eith] Chesterton, cited in Martin Gardner, "Introduction to the Dover Edition," in The Napoleon of Notting Hill (New York: Dover Publications, Inc., 1991). Subsequent citations from Notting Hill will be cited as NH.

is by more of the same, and that, in the end, the bloodless theoretical love of humanity and economically driven forms of cosmopolitanism will both fall before the stronger bonds and greater willingness of self-sacrifice that is born of patriotism and the more intimate connection born from local settings, whether neighborhood or small nations (*NH*, 130, 147).

Nevertheless, an undercurrent of doubt about the prospects of local self-governance against the tide of cosmopolitan dominion seems at the same time to pervade Chesterton's novel. Ironically, Notting Hill is only defeated when—having initially conquered its cosmopolitan enemies—it begins itself to encroach on the rights and privileges of the other neighborhoods that it had explicitly promised to protect and defend in the terms of surrender that had been tendered (*NH*, book 5, chap. 1: "The Empire of Notting Hill"). Chesterton appears to imply that even the most ardent patriot or nationalist will inevitably give in to the craving for empire eventually. It was perhaps not a coincidence that the book was entitled *The Napoleon of Notting Hill,* not only because of the military acumen of Adam Wayne, but the inevitable temptations of victorious nations toward extending their power outward and threatening the local forms that they initially rallied to protect (*NH*, 144). Further, while it might be possible for a neighborhood of London to resist the mercenary armies of a few businessmen, the novel opens with a scene in which the former president of Nicaragua laments the demise of his nation at the hands of the far superior armies of the United States. The former president—while lamenting the absorption of his country into the American empire—acknowledges that "the whole tendency of the world of to-day is against Nicaragua and against me" (*NH*, 18). While he defends the "idea" of Nicaragua, he admits that the "Yankee and German and the brute powers of modernity have trampled it with hoofs of oxen" (*NH*, 17).

In the end Chesterton appears to insinuate that the cosmopolitan impulse—which he regards as a hubristic impulse to impose standardization and a monoculture upon the desirable diversity of human life—is sown deeply within the human soul (as it is eventually manifested even in the robustly patriotic Notting Hill'ers), but that such cosmopolitanism is finally insubstantial against the more concrete reality of existing human devotions and commitments.[7] As Adam

7. On cosmopolitanism as "monoculture," see the conversation between the ex-president of Nicaragua and his progressive English interlocutors, during which the former president demonstrates the falsity of British claims that "a great cosmopolitan civilization . . . shall include all the talents of all the absorbed people" (*NH*, 18). In response, the ex-president asks, "Do you really mean to say that at the moment when the Esquimaux has learnt to vote for a County Council, you will have learnt to spear a walrus?" (*NH*, 18–19). See also G. K. Chesterton, "The Patriotic Idea," in *The Collected Works of G. K. Chesterton* (San Francisco: Ignatius Press, 2001), 20:595–619. See especially 601–2, in which he describes imperialism as a form of "opportunist cosmopolitanism" that seeks "the opportunity of effacing a distinction, of pulling down a flag, of destroying a nationality." Subsequent citations from "The Patriotic Idea" will be cited as *PI*.

Wayne declares toward the end of the novel, "Do you not see that it is the glory of our achievement that we have infected other cities with the idealism of Notting Hill . . . ? Notting Hill is right; it has always been right. It has moulded itself on its own ultimatum. Because it is a nation it has created itself" (*NH*, 147–48). That cosmopolitan impulse, he implies, can only assert itself through the brute power of modern force and warfare, a necessary partner of the mild seductions of a globalizing commerce. For this reason, Chesterton at times seemed sanguine that, in the face of such obvious and heavy-handed tactics, the patriot and nationalist would maintain the advantage of a defensive posture aided by guerilla tactics that would succeed against the ignorant and clumsy machines of modern warfare. And, given the evidence from the American Revolution to the Vietnam War, it seems to that extent that Chesterton may have been correct in thinking that such a defensive localist and nationalist posture would indeed maintain advantages even against superior forces.

However, while maintaining anxieties about the trajectories of "the brute powers of modernity" and even the "terrible futility" of the defense of local privileges (*NH*, 17, 130), Chesterton appeared perhaps surprisingly optimistic about the capacity of local arrangements not only to resist—if necessary—forceful encroachments of greater cosmopolitan powers, but as well to maintain *internally* their identities against the milder if possibly more insinuating temptations of global (and often, therefore, standardizing) commerce, popular culture, and the accompanying freedom of opportunity that might lead people to a sense of discontent with the parochialism of their localities.

What of those pleasant and insinuating forms of commerce, commended by such thinkers as Constant and Montesquieu to "soften" the militaristic impulses that Chesterton appears to suggest rear their heads nonetheless? Does Chesterton willfully ignore the possibility and attractions of commerce as a *force for good* in undermining the repressive features of localism and the narrowing qualities of parochialism?

The nonviolent attractions of globalizing commerce would have been well known to Chesterton. One of the more powerful analyses of the insinuation of modern commerce was well known, having appeared in no less a source than the *Communist Manifesto* of Marx and Engels:

> The bourgeoisie, wherever it has got the upper hand, has put an end to all feudal, patriarchal, idyllic relations. It has pitilessly torn asunder the motley feudal ties that bound man to his "natural superiors," and has left no other nexus between people than naked self-interest, than callous "cash payment." It has drowned out the most heavenly ecstacies of religious fervor, of chivalrous enthusiasm, of philistine sentimentalism, in the icy water of egotistical

calculation. It has resolved personal worth into exchange value, and in place of the numberless indefeasible chartered freedoms, has set up that single, unconscionable freedom—Free Trade. In one word, for exploitation, veiled by religious and political illusions, it has substituted naked, shameless, direct, brutal exploitation. . . .

The bourgeoisie, by the rapid improvement of all instruments of production, by the immensely facilitated means of communication, draws all, even the most barbarian, nations into civilization. The cheap prices of commodities are the heavy artillery with which it forces the barbarians' intensely obstinate hatred of foreigners to capitulate. It compels all nations, on pain of extinction, to adopt the bourgeois mode of production; it compels them to introduce what it calls civilization into their midst, i.e., to become bourgeois themselves. In one word, it creates a world after its own image.[8]

Marx and Engels describe a modernizing process that subtly insinuates itself in and throughout existing cultures, extinguishing local ways in the wake of the seductions of the openness, liberty, and comfort. While benefiting the "bourgeoisie" (whom Chesterton aptly portrays in the novel as the group seeking to construct the major thoroughfare through Notting Hill) at the expense of the "proletariat," nevertheless the liberating "fetters" of modernity are gladly and freely self-imposed by local cultures, which thereby lose their distinctiveness in the process. The ease and comfort that modern markets afford no longer need heavy artillery, much less swords and halberds: low prices have proven much more effective in their conquest of localities.

Much contemporary evidence suggests that Marx was correct in his assessment of the powerful homogenizing force of markets. By way of one anecdotal example, consider the very local shop atmosphere so beloved by Chesterton in his evaluation of the natural and perhaps inextinguishable attractions of Notting Hill. Recently an article appeared in the *New York Times* that described the specter of homogenization haunting small villages akin to Notting Hill throughout England. The article, about Stratford-on-Avon, related:

To survive the approach to the home where William Shakespeare was born, a striking timber-frame house in the center of this bustling town, it would be wise to bid adieu to all bucolic notions of quaint old England and ready oneself for the onslaught of globalization.

A visitor must march past Country Casuals, Boots pharmacy, Next, and

---

8. Karl Marx and Friedrich Engels, *The Communist Manifesto* (1848), in *The Marx-Engels Reader,* ed. Robert C. Tucker, 2nd ed. (New York: W. W. Norton & Company, 1972), 475, 477.

Marks & Spencer, and pass Accessorize, HMV, Whittard and of course, the dueling coffee shops, Starbucks and Costa Coffee. If it were not for Shakespeare's dwelling and a few notable old houses, this town—with row upon row of British chain stores—would scarcely be different from any other in Britain these days. Most butcher shops and hardware stores have closed. So have the family clothing shops, the fishmongers and a long list of other independent businesses.

"If someone blindfolded you, put you in a helicopter and set you down in a town somewhere in England, you wouldn't be able to tell where you are anymore," said Jim Hyslop, 55, who lives just outside Stratford. The chain stores, he said, "change the character of a place."

In the past five years, chain stores owned by corporations and out-of-town megastores similar to Wal-Mart (one of them, Asda, is, in fact, owned by Wal-Mart), have come to dominate many British towns and cities, creating a palpable sense of homogeneity from Kent all the way to Cumbria, and drawing striking parallels to America.

Many of the main shopping thoroughfares, so-called "high streets," now traffic in sameness: ubiquitous cellphone shops (Orange, Vodafone, O2); the familiar coffee chains (Starbucks, Caffe Nero and Costa Coffee); the typical clothing stores (Gap, Next, Warehouse); and the cookie-cutter restaurants (Cafe Rouge, ASK, Pizza Express). Neighborhood greengrocers are also on the way out, replaced by chain minisupermarkets, most notably Tesco, a company that has become one of the world's top retailers.

"In the case of Britain, and especially England, there is a huge sense of identity investment in the image of towns and cities, and the notion that this sort of bland, gradual effacement of character is taking place has taxed people at a deep level," said Andrew Simms, policy director for the New Economic Foundation, an independent economic research organization that published a report in August called "Clone Town Britain."[9]

Given Chesterton's apparent sanguinity about the capacity of localities not only to rebuff the forces of modern cosmopolitanism by force, but largely to be able to resist such encroachments by dint of the collective will and desire to protect local customs and traditions, in spite of even his apparent admission that these such "progressive" forces seemed to embody the spirit of the age, from where did Chesterton suppose such powers of resistance would arise? Was he insufficiently cognizant of the threat from modernizing forces under which tradi-

9. Lizette Alvarez, "To Be a 'Clone Town,' or Not: That Is the Question," *New York Times,* November 1, 2004, A4.

tional societies existed, or did he believe that a locus of resistance could be identified? Which was more "real" in Chesterton's view—the sentiments that animated the resistance of Notting Hill against the construction of a modern thoroughfare, or the progressive dreams that seemed to drive modern history and put small nations like Nicaragua in peril? Does, finally, Chesterton resist an easy choice between either, and if so, on what grounds?

On the one hand, Chesterton viewed these two aspects of the globalizing tendency of modernity—the imperial and the commercial—in terms that were not mutually exclusive. By portraying how easily the businessmen were transformed into warriors, Chesterton sought to imply the close relationship between commerce's and imperialism's hostile expansionist and imperializing tendencies. The pleasant attraction of "softening" commerce, insinuating itself through the free choice of untold numbers of consumers, undermining the militarism of past ages of honor and warfare, and evaporating all borders, local and national, is in fact premised on a deeper presupposition of the use of violence against those "backward" defenders of localism. The proposed thoroughfare, directed through the heart of Notting Hill, is to expand the ease and convenience of any and all travelers, wholly oblivious to the local forms of life that were obliterated in the construction of the highway. The businessmen have succeeded in securing permission to construct this road through the legal authorities of the kingdom. Hardly noticeable is the observation that the legal authorities stand to back *by force* the expansion of this road. It is due to Adam Wayne's forceful resistance to this incursion into Notting Hill—not through the legal system, but armed with the most visceral and personal forms of weaponry—that the implied force underlying the construction of the highway is revealed. The use of the "romantic" weaponry of the Middle Ages brings home that the unleashed violence cannot finally be sanitized by legal writs or even the impersonal distance of modern armaments: violence, then and now, involves a brutal physical attack by one person upon another. Beneath the business suits of the highway planners are invisible suits of armor.

More fundamentally, Chesterton believed that the impulse to defend one's locality against the encroachments of modern universalizing tendencies—the combined forces of aggressive militarism and materialistic commerce—was inexpungeable, even if increasingly under duress. Adam Wayne's defense of Notting Hill is representative of a permanent human response in defense of one's own. For the remainder of this chapter, I will argue that Chesterton's own inclination to believe in the superiority of the natural attractions of locality, so much so that he rejected the prospect of an easy victory for cosmopolitanism, nevertheless was complicated and chastened by what he saw as inescapably mixed sources that revealed that humans acted simultaneously on behalf of both forces. Neither the love of one's own or the abstract love of humanity was inextinguishable by his understanding of the human condition. And, in spite of the apparent optimism that is projected in *The Napoleon of Notting Hill,* while Chesterton believed himself to be resisting otherwise dominant trajectories in modernity, he nevertheless believed that an inescapable part of the human experience involved the fundamental "localism" of human ties.[10] Finally, I argue, this supposition rested on a fundamentally theological understanding of human beings. One sees his views of this inextricable mixture, and its theological sources, in his assessment of that greatest modernizing force that the world has ever known, the United States of America, and in particular in his 1922 travel essay, *What I Saw in America.*

A NATION WITH THE SOUL OF A CHURCH

Chesterton's *What I Saw in America* contains one of the most oft-quoted and almost invariably misunderstood lines that attempts to describe the essence of America. In his first chapter, entitled "What Is America?" Chesterton famously described America as "the nation with the soul of a Church."[11] Without knowing anything of Chesterton's wider meaning, many people who know only the quote have assumed that the words mean that America is a deeply religious nation.[12] Chesterton does, in fact, conclude that America is a religious nation (though not in terms as strong as Tocqueville in *Democracy in America*), but this is not the core meaning of the famous line. Rather, in its context, Chesterton is speaking of "America's creed." He begins with the charming story of his entry

10. The fundamental things apply, Chesterton asserts. As stated by Adam Wayne, "Notting Hill . . . is a rise or ground of the common earth, on which men have built houses to live, in which they are born, fall in love, pray, marry, and die" (*NH*, 58). Perhaps one sees the strength of Chesterton's assumptions even in the previously quoted article from the *New York Times,* which concludes that " 'Clone towns,' though, as the report calls them, are beginning to encounter resistance as people question whether Britain should emulate America or follow Continental Europe, which is trying hard to preserve its uniqueness. In France and Poland, for example, local authorities can veto the construction of large supermarkets. Local governments here are starting to push for economic incentives to guarantee a greater variety of shops. One town, Ludlow, has joined an Italian movement called Cittaslow, which embraces the 'slow town' concept and promotes the benefits of eating locally grown produce" (Alvarez, *New York Times,* A4).

11. G. K. Chesterton, *What I Saw in America,* in *The Collected Works of G. K. Chesterton* (San Francisco: Ignatius Press, 1990), 21:45. Subsequent citations from *What I Saw in America* are cited as *WA.*

12. Numerous examples might be given. The following example is representative: "G. K. Chesterton's famous description of the United States as 'a nation with the soul of a Church' was never more apt than during the 2000 presidential campaign. Religion was in the limelight from the moment that George W. Bush named Jesus as his favorite political philosopher to the day when Joseph Lieberman joined the Democratic ticket, quoting the Book of Chronicles. . . . The pervasive religiosity of the campaign helped produce one of the closest and most controversial elections in history" (James L. Guth, Lyman A. Kellstedt, John C. Green, and Corwin E. Smidt, "America Fifty/Fifty," *First Things* 116 [October 2001]: 19).

into the United States, when, confronted by customs officers on the docks in New York City, he is asked a series of questions, among which is whether he intends to overthrow the government of the United States of America (he thinks, but wisely does not say aloud, that he should prefer to answer that question at the *end* of his visit rather than at the beginning) (*WA*, 39). Chesterton viewed this "inquisitorial" tendency with both amusement and bemusement, as well thinking it as revelatory of the nature of the American psyche. In contrast to the Americans, Europeans do not evince such anxiety about their identity: "England is English as France is French or Ireland is Irish; the great mass of men taking certain national traditions for granted. Now this gives us a very much easier task. We have not got an inquisition because we do not have a creed; but it is arguable that we do not have a creed, because we have got a character" (*WA*, 43–44). Americans base their identity more or less wholly on a shared set of *beliefs* in contrast to the European's various identities in the form of traditions and practices.

The "characterlessness" of creedal Americans is particularly noteworthy in that it has no inherent limitations: America's creed can be accepted by anyone, regardless of tradition, race, or background. "That creed is set forth with dogmatic and even theological lucidity in the Declaration of Independence. . . . It enunciates that all men are equal in their claim to justice, that governments exist to give them justice, and that their authority is for that reason just" (*WA*, 41). What struck Chesterton especially about the American creed was its universalism: "The chief mark of the Declaration of Independence . . . is the thing called abstraction or academic logic. And the theory or thought is the very last thing to which English people are accustomed, either by their social structure or their traditional teaching. It is the theory of equality. It is the pure classic conception that no man must aspire to be anything more than a citizen, and that no man should endure to be anything less" (*WA*, 48).

One might easily conclude that Chesterton—not only as an Englishman, but as a patriot and nationalist—would have viewed any such creedal identity, one that is universal in breadth and nonexclusionary in its application, as sharing the very cosmopolitan and globalizing features that he otherwise abhorred. Yet, perhaps curiously, Chesterton did not conclude that America's creedal identity necessarily had these universalizing tendencies. In one of his inimitable turns of phrase, he captured his sense of the American creed's dual nature: "Now a creed is at once the broadest and the narrowest thing in the world. In its nature it is as broad as its scheme for a brotherhood of all men. In its nature it is limited by its definition of the nature of all men" (*WA*, 42). If America's creed had universalistic implications, its universalism assumed a humanity that was itself not configured for political universalism. Inherent in its creed was a central assumption of the persistence of nations. Thus, Chesterton argued that the creedal identity resulted in a strenuously nationalistic and patriotic people. The idea behind the American creed, he averred, "was not internationalism; on the contrary, it is decidedly nationalism. The Americans are very patriotic, and wish to make their new citizens patriotic Americans. But it is the idea of making a new nation literally out of any old nation that comes along. In a word, what is unique is not America but what is called Americanisation" (*WA*, 47).

The American creed, as set forth in the Declaration of Independence, remains one firmly rooted within national structures. While equal rights of "life, liberty, and the pursuit of happiness" have universal scope—"all men" being endowed with these and other certain rights—those rights, as articulated in the declaration, can only be secured by "governments instituted among men." Thus, by his reading of America's founding document, as well as through his encounter with fervent American patriotism, Chesterton concluded that America had achieved a curious if simultaneous universal and national character: "the experiment of a democracy of diverse races . . . has been compared to a melting pot. But even that metaphor implies that the pot itself is of a certain shape and a certain substance; a pretty solid substance. The melting pot must not melt. . . . America invites all men to become citizens; but it implies the dogma that there is such a thing as citizenship" (*WA*, 42).

Chesterton contended that America could not simply be understood as a nation formed out of the whole cloth of Enlightenment philosophy.[13] While there could be no denying that America's founding philosophy was grounded in the rationalism of the Enlightenment, Chesterton detected nevertheless a mixed lineage, and in particular an older substratum that underlay the apparently new philosophy of modernity.[14] "The real quality of America is much more subtle and complex than this; and is mixed not only of good and bad, and rational and mystical, but also of old and new. That is what makes the task of tracing the true proportions of American life so interesting and so impossible" (*WA*, 182). For Chesterton, America was a palimpsest, a "new" world founded on the tenets of liberal self-interest and the rights of man, which overlay but could not entirely obscure the self-sacrificing devotion to "public things" that for which he lauds the Stoics and Romans (*WA*, 185–86). These positive affirmations of public devotions, in his view, "redeemed the dreary negations of the eighteenth century" (*WA*, 186). In America, Chesterton believed he discerned an "old-world

---

13. As such, he would have disagreed with the argument of Sidney E. Mead, who understood Chesterton's phrase "the nation with the soul of a Church" in exactly the opposite meaning of many, namely, that America's creed was wholly based upon the rationalism of Enlightenment philosophy (Sidney Earl Mead, *The Nation with the Soul of a Church* [New York: Harpers, 1975]).

14. For instance, Chesterton recognizes the Deistic background of America at *WA*, 185.

atmosphere of the new world," but he worried that the republican ideal might increasingly "lie in ruins" (*WA*, 187).

Nevertheless, Chesterton could not deny that America's success at assimilation of cultures might easily be expanded outward in a cosmopolitan direction. He saw the strains within the universalist rights tradition and the republican tradition of democratic self-rule, and perhaps one does not overstate the case by suggesting that his essay *What I Saw in America* is an interior monologue in which Chesterton debates which tendency is likely to prevail, not only in and through America, but in modernity more widely. In two areas in particular, Chesterton saw a threat arising from America's cosmopolitan tendencies: in the area of commerce and the expansion of an American-style assimilationist nation-state to international dimensions. And in each case, recognizing the dangers, he denied that its realization was not to be feared. Again, the grounds for this confidence need greater explication.

First, Chesterton entertained the idea that America's economic dynamism and the tendencies of free-market capitalism toward uniformity would result in an assault on localism—and in particular, he at least supposed and feared, in English villages. His sense of the American economy's tendency toward standardization is captured in his early chapter entitled "A Meditation in a New York Hotel," in which he contrasts the English inn to the American hotel.[15] In a description that should be as strikingly familiar to the frequent traveler in the twenty-first century as it was when Chesterton penned it in 1922, he wrote that "broadly speaking, there is only one hotel in America" (*WA*, 52). The layout of this "one hotel" is identical everywhere, "among the red blooms of the warm spring wood of Nebraska, or whitened with Canadian snows near the eternal noise of Niagara" (*WA*, 52–53):

If the passage outside your bedroom door, or the hallway as it is called, contains, let us say, a small table with a green vase and a stuffed flamingo, or some trifle of the sort, you may be perfectly certain that there is exactly the same table, vase, and flamingo on every one of the thirty-two landings of that towering habitation. This is where it differs most perhaps from the crooking landings and unexpected levels of the old English inns, even when they called themselves hotels. To me there was something weird, like a magic multiplication, in the exquisite sameness of these suites. (*WA*, 53)

15. For further discussion of the general theme of this chapter, see Robert Royal's introduction to volume 20 of *G. K. Chesterton: The Collected Works*, entitled "Introduction: Hotels Are not Inns: G. K. Chesterton in America," 15–34.

While he did not explicitly analyze the grounds for this tendency toward uniformity, it is perhaps not uncoincidental that later in the same chapter he notes the "homelessness" of Americans, their penchant toward motion, activity, kaleidoscopic movement (*WA*, 58)—akin to what Tocqueville described as the American predilection to "restlessness." Such predictability of lodgings, dining, shopping, and leisure activity is not surprising for a restless people, Chesterton appears to imply. Such grounds for homogenization only strengthen the existing imperative of free-market capitalism toward economies of scale and standardization, not only comporting with sound economic reasons, but with the desires of the consumers as well.

Chesterton, in fact, fundamentally denies the existence of economies of scale, and further dismisses the prospect of widening international standardization, in a subsequent chapter entitled "Is the Atlantic Narrowing?" He writes that "America can give nothing to London but those multiple modern shops, of which it has too many already. I know that many entertain the innocent illusion that big shops are more efficient than small ones; but that is only because the big combinations have the monopoly of advertisement as well as trade" (*WA*, 198–99). Chesterton downplays the possible influence of advertising on the psyches of consumers—a considerable and somewhat uncharacteristic oversight, it would seem—and subsequently even dismisses what he regards as only apparent advantages of efficiencies of scale: "A big shop, considered as a place to shop in, is simply a village of small shops roofed in to keep out the light and air; and in which none of the shopkeepers are really responsible for their shops" (*WA*, 199). In essence, Chesterton does not credit that any human contrivance can be stretched past a certain scale and actually *be* what it otherwise claims. Human organizations, whether economical, political, religious, or otherwise, must always be based upon the reality of locality. A huge shopping mall is but a collection of shops.

The second threat emanating from the potential tendency of American universalism—the possibility of a global state—Chesterton similarly regarded as an ephemeral and unrealizable extension of the reality of the nation to unachievable proportions. In the context of his discussion of America, Chesterton revealingly writes of his longstanding suspicion of the idea of the world state. For his nemeses H. G. Wells and G. B. Shaw, America represented the realization of liberal democracy on an unseen scale, and thus invariably suggested to them the possibility of extending the idea of a federated republic to greater proportions until a world state could be achieved. For Wells, "the World State is to be the United States of the World" (*WA*, 214). Chesterton credited that such an entity—unlike a giant shopping mall—might be created, but only at the expense of the elimination of all human diversity, thereby rendering politics, including democracy, superfluous.[16] Chesterton believed that government on such a scale could only be run—if at all—from the center, and thus would result in the elimination of localism and necessarily give rise to a small ruling elite, what Chesterton called "the aristocracy of globe-trotters" (anticipating what Christopher Lasch would later call "the revolt of the elites"). "What the same town counsillors would be like if they were ruling all their fellow creatures from the North Pole or the New Jerusalem, is a vision of Oriental despotism" (*WA*, 214). In Chesterton's view, echoing a longstanding supposition of classical political philosophy, "internationalism is in any case hostile to democracy" (*WA*, 215). Democracy is necessarily rooted in local self-governance, and rests on the willingness to allow the flourishing of diversity, of parochialism, and of imperfection in politics. "The only purely popular government is local, and founded on local knowledge. The citizens can rule the city because they know the city" (*WA*, 216). His "democratic faith" was not vested in the possibility of realizing people's perfectible potential or eliminating politics from governance, nor did it rest on an idea of physical or moral progress or upon the fruits of technological advances, but rather rested upon a more humble belief that people, even if doing things badly, ought to do so for themselves: "[Democracy is] a thing analogous to writing one's own love-letters or blowing one's own nose. These things we want a man to do for himself, even if he does them badly. . . . In short, the democratic faith is this: that the most terribly important things must be left to ordinary men themselves—the mating of the sexes, the rearing of the young, the laws of the state.[17] This is democracy; and in this I have always believed."[18]

The "world state," like the shopping mall, was most fundamentally an illusion, albeit a supremely dangerous one. While based upon a vision of universal (or, in Kantian terms, cosmopolitan) peace, its hostility to local forms of self-governance and various forms of parochialism would likely take the form of outright physical suppression of those forms of life (and Chesterton allows the analogy of the defeat of the southern states in the American Civil War to be extended to the trajectory of the world state, thereby suggesting that Mr. Wells must accept the prospect of "a Civil War of Europe" [*WA*, 220]). He concludes that "universal peace would only be a reality if the World State were not a fiction" (*WA*, 215). Chesterton held that extension the civilized way of life of

16. In this sense, Chesterton's critique shares a remarkable affinity with the critique by Aristotle in antiquity of Plato's efforts to found a polity upon thoroughgoing unity. See Aristotle, *Politics*, book 2.

17. Again, the opposite example of the perfectly just regime—Plato's *Republic*—comes to mind by contrast.

18. G. K. Chesterton, *Orthodoxy* (San Francisco: Ignatius Press, 1980), 52. Subsequent citations from *Orthodoxy* cited as *O*.

(most likely) European powers would simply result in an empire of one form of parochialism, the homogenous but not universal state of Hegel and Kojeve's imagining. To base this illusion on the example of the United States, Chesterton averred, was to fundamentally misunderstand the American regime and its constitution. The United States, in his view—while stretched to the outer limits of nationality—nevertheless remained firmly a nation (*WA*, 221). To extend such a regime further was simply to spread identity too thin, and make such a universal regime untenable, or to replace the natural bonds of citizenship with the imposed bonds of tyranny.

TOWARD A THEOLOGY OF CITIZENSHIP

Chesterton resisted the notion that there was really such a thing as undifferentiated humanity from a human-eye's view. Humanitarians claimed a love of humanity while in fact evincing disgust, condescension, and disdain toward most ordinary human beings. "A strange coldness and unreality hangs about their love for men. If you ask them whether they love humanity they will say, doubtless sincerely, that they do. But if you ask them touching on any of the classes that go to make up humanity, you will find that they hate them all. They hate kings, they hate priests, they hate soldiers, they hate sailors. They distrust men of science, they denounce the middle classes, they despair of working men, but they adore humanity" (*PI*, 596). Cosmopolitanism was, for him, "a psychological impossibility": cosmopolitanism was a belief in "unreality," against the "reality" of nations and the actual bonds that animated humans (*PI*, 603, 605, 607). Chesterton did not deny that humans longed for the infinite and the transcendent; he found that longing among the most praiseworthy of human desires and aspirations. But he believed such longing to be improperly directed to the political sphere; rather, he maintained that such longing reflected, at base, the aspiration to know the divine. Humans seeking the God's-eye view of humanity assumed a stature and insight that was unavailable to them; rather, if there was the possibility of "seeing" to the universal, it was only through the particular: "real universality is to be reached . . . by convincing ourselves that we are in the best possible relation with our immediate surroundings. The man who loves his own children is much more universal, is much more fully in the general order, than the man who dandles the hippopotamus or puts the young crocodile in a perambulator. . . . A man who loves humanity and ignores patriotism is ignoring humanity" (*PI*, 597).

The human world is one of particularity, concrete affections, and limits: choices must be made between particulars, to the exclusion of others. Cosmopolitanism—another word for imperialism, in Chesterton's view—harbors the illusion that no choices must be made. To be everywhere and love everyone is to be nowhere and love no one: "If you go to Rome, you sacrifice a rich suggestive life in Wimbledon. . . . The moment you step into a world of facts, you step into a world of limits" (*O, 45*). Cosmopolitans cling to the belief that life in the world can be configured without preliminary commitments, limiting parochialism, or unchosen loyalties. "The assumption of it is that a man criticizes this world as if he were house-hunting, as if he were being shown over a new suite of apartments. . . . But no man is in that position. A man belongs to this world before he begins to ask if it is nice to belong in it. He has fought for the flag, and often won heroic victories for the flag long before he has ever enlisted. To put shortly what seems to be the essential matter, he has a loyalty long before he has an admiration" (*O, 71–72*). Cosmopolitans evinced a preliminary dislike for the world, its reality, its messiness and incompleteness. Those working for the "unreality" of the world state exhibited a form of modern Gnosticism with its hatred of the created universe and its aspiration for an alternative reality when the present world might pass away. The difference was that modern Gnostics like Wells and Shaw saw the new kingdom unfolding politically on Earth through the transformative efforts of humans alone.

At the same time, Chesterton did not argue for the inherent perfection of what was "given" and on behalf of an accompanying sense of complacency: while he was not a pessimist, neither was he a Candide-like optimist who believed that we lived in the best of all possible worlds (*O, 71*). For instance, he was the first to recognize the limits and drawbacks of the human reality of parochialism. Yet, against the "unreality" of cosmopolitanism, and particularly the fervency with which it was pursued in the modern age, he endorsed localism, patriotism, and nationalism in the face of what he regarded as the deeper dangers and even evils emanating from abstract universalism:

> The danger of small communities is narrowness, but their advantage is reality. Now, at any specific stage in the world's history we ought to ask ourselves whether humanity is in greater danger from the narrow arrogance of small people, or from the phantasmal delusions of empires. That is the question which confronts the European of to-day, and the answer is not very difficult. It is idle to tell him that nationalism is sometimes an evil in the confusion of a heptarchy, when the fact that stares him in the face that the modern evils arise from remoteness, from unreality, from the circulation of wealth far from its producers, from the waging of wars far from the seat of action, from the wild use of statistics, from the crude use of names, from the investor and the theorist, and the absentee landlord. (*PI, 614*)

More dangerous than the "narrow arrogance of small people"—which he acknowledged to be a danger—were the efforts to dissipate or extirpate local forms of life in the name of abstract principles or love of humanity (*PI*, 614). Chesterton believed that such efforts would ultimately undermine whatever benefits might be secured by overcoming parochialism, since whatever vitality and devotion larger cosmopolitan entities might achieve had their source in preliminary loyalties. It was the blindness of cosmopolitans to that source—their ignorance that within the very word *cosmopolitan* was the root word *polites*, meaning "citizen"—that doomed not only their own project, but threatened to extinguish the "reality" upon which human relations are based.

Chesterton believed that one could not rest content with the imperfect conditions of "reality," but before reform should be undertaken, a preliminary "cosmic oath of allegiance" has to be declared (*O*, 77). Chesterton's Christianity and his eventual conversion to Roman Catholicism were based on his understanding of the fundamental alienation of humanity from existence, the fact that "we do not fit in this world" (*O*, 85). Yet, the world is our reality—along with the limits that accompany reality—and that, opposed to the transformational reforming instincts of moderns to make the world anew, Chesterton asserted that first this impulse must be chastened by an appreciation for, and even love of, that created reality. In short, he argued, we "need to hate the world enough to change it, but love it enough to think it worth changing" (*O*, 77). "Acceptance" of reality therefore precedes the impulse toward transformation: "this need for a first loyalty to things, and then for a ruinous reform of things" (*O*, 79).[19] Christianity, as

19. On the contrast between the "accepting" and "transformative" impulses, see William F. May, President's Council on Bioethics discussion of "The Birth-Mark" by Nathaniel Hawthorne, at http://bioethicsprint.bioethics.gov/transcripts/jan02/jansession2intro.html. This distinction was called to my attention by Michael J. Sandel, "The Case against Perfection," *Atlantic Monthly* (April 2004): 51–62. These discussions center on the ethical issues raised by the possibility of human biological perfectibility by means of genetic manipulation; May and Sandel both object on grounds that this enterprise is driven by the hubristic attempt to overcome the gift of "givenness" by means of complete human mastery over nature. As expressed by May, speaking here of the love of parents for children:

Attachment becomes too quietistic if it slackens into mere acceptance of the child as he is. Love must will the well-being and not merely the being of the other. But attachment lapses into a Gnostic revulsion against the world, if, in the name of well-being, it recoils from the child as it is. Ambitious parents, especially in a meritarian society tend one-sidedly to emphasize the parental role of transforming love. We fiercely demand performance, accomplishments, and results. Sometimes, we behave like the ancient Gnostics who despised the given world, who wrote off the very birth of the world as a catastrophe. We increasingly define and seize upon our children as products to be perfected, flaws to be overcome. And to that degree, we implicitly define ourselves as flawed manufacturers. Implicit in the rejection of the child is self-rejection. We view ourselves as flawed manufacturers rather than imperfect recipients of a gift. Parents find it difficult to maintain an equilibrium between the two sides of love. Accepting love, without transforming love, slides into indulgence and finally neglect. Transforming love, without accepting love, badgers and finally rejects.

Chesterton understood it, does not seek to remake the world uniformly in the image of human desire for order, but accepts diversity and manyness as part of a larger overarching plan. Christianity (as, before him, Tocqueville also expressed) resists pantheism and "accepts" the manyness of "reality" as the only means and avenue by which we can contemplate the universal order that lies behind it: in contrast to pantheism,

> Christianity is on the side of humanity and liberty and love. Love desires personality; therefore love desires division. It is the instinct of Christianity to be glad that God has broken the universe into little pieces, because they are living pieces. It is her instinct to say 'little children love each other' rather than to tell one large person to love himself. . . . All modern philosophies are chains which connect and fetter; Christianity is a sword that separates and frees. (O, 139)

It is this theological understanding of humankind, of the "reality" of human diversity, of the temptation toward the "unreality" of modern dogmas of the brotherhood of all humankind that underlie Chesterton's often conflicted analysis of the United States in *What I Saw in America*. On the one hand, he saw a nation-state, one firmly inspired by patriotism and particularity; on the other hand, he observed a creedal nation that might have tendencies toward the "unreality" of cosmopolitanism. The strength of the latter as it existed in America was, in his view, based on a firm devotion to the former. Much like Tocqueville, he viewed America as pointing the way toward "the future of democracy," but he saw that future clouded by the challenge that modern democracy's tendencies toward political pantheism and international cosmopolitanism posed to itself: "democracy is a very serious problem for democrats" (*WA*, 254).[20] In Chesterton's eyes, democracy and Christianity shared similar worldviews, and with the rise of religious doubt, he believed, one could expect to see a concomitant rise in overconfidence in the human ability to "cure" the excesses and deficiencies of localism and even to overcome the limits of human senses and sinfulness. He saw a potential future in which nations and loyalties were expunged, to be replaced instead by increasing reliance on experts and elites, bureaucratic structures, a growing divide between the rich and poor, and the triumph of abstraction over "reality" (*WA*, 257–63). What Chesterton "saw in America" was a possible future that caused him enough anxiety to write confidently that it would not come to pass. His confidence was born generally out of a belief that the reality of the human

---

20. The concluding chapter of *What I Saw in America* is entitled "The Future of Democracy."

condition would assert itself against the unreality of the cosmopolitan philosophy, and, in the particular case of America, that its own cognizance that "the melting pot must not melt" would provide an internal limit upon the expansionist tendencies of its universalistic creed. If America is "a nation with the soul of a Church," then certainly Chesterton meant to point out that even with a universalistic creed, a church has a definite physical form and structure, and it is a communion of particular people, even as its members aspire to know the universal, above all, the divine.

For this reason, Chesterton might not be surprised to discover that, some eighty-five years after his visit to the United States, America now stands ardently in defense of patriotism and the particularity of nations. Contemporary philosopher Roger Scruton has suggested that "it is a difficult question to answer" and "little short of a paradox" that the United States, "a state formed by federation, constitution and conscious political choice should now be among the strongest defenders of national sovereignty."[21] Chesterton's analysis of America goes some distance to explaining why America' defense of nation is not as surprising or paradoxical as might seem the case. If Chesterton's analysis helps address this seeming paradox, surely Chesterton would be puzzled why it is the case that the Europe he knew—composed of Englishmen, French and Irishmen, among many others—would now increasingly repudiate the centrality of those ancient loyalties. To return to his own continent now would be for Chesterton surely like a journey to a foreign land.

21. Scruton, *A Political Philosophy*, 25.

CONCLUSION

"America" Between Past and Future

Jeffrey C. Isaac

A century separates us from the last of the reflections profiled in this volume. A century that came to be called by many, following Henry Luce's famous (and infamous) 1941 *Life* magazine article, "the American century." Whether with rancor or relish, it is impossible to deny that the twentieth century was a century dominated by the global ascendancy of the United States of America from a continental nation-state of the Western hemisphere to what Raymond Aron called "an imperial republic" with truly global reach.[1] In this sense at least the twentieth can well be viewed as an "American century."

This does not mean that the *telos* of the century was "America." The outcome of the two world wars and the cold war (a third "world war" fought no doubt by other means) was hardly preordained. Simply to name the three conflicts above—each of which signifies a constellation of troubling events and crises—is to underscore the complex and contingent character of America's ascendancy to what political scientists call "unipolar" hegemony. And, writing from still early in the succeeding century, it is obvious that, post-1989 euphoria notwithstanding, the world at the "end of history" is no more "America" than it was "in the beginning" (as John Locke famously denoted America in the late seventeenth century). The debacle in current-day Iraq is merely the most vivid illustration of this.

---

1. Raymond Aron, *The Imperial Republic: The United States and the World, 1945–1973* (Boston: Little, Brown and Company, 1974).

The authors profiled above—Berkeley, Jacquemont, Beaumont, Trollope, and the rest—reflected on emergent American tendencies, and symbolic hopes and fears, associated with the United States as an evolving nation first coming into its own, within its own territory, and in the broader world that would eventually become its stage. This volume makes clear that the tendencies discerned were complex, and the hopes and anxieties expressed were numerous and by no means coincident. Further, while it is tempting, looking backward, to read these reflections as forecasts and evaluations of "America" as a dominant power, the truth is that in the eighteenth and nineteenth and even early twentieth centuries the United States may have been a symbolically distinct and perhaps even "special" or at least "exceptional" place, but in the end it was merely another emergent nation-state, with its own inferiority complexes, centripetal forces, and civil wars. America, in short, was very much an uncertain work in progress, and the reflections offered by our intellectuals were rather tentative and hypothetical, at least with regard to their anticipatory and predictive power.

Nonetheless, the tropes discussed in this volume's pages—America as virgin space or "new world," America as egalitarian utopia (or dystopia), America as pragmatic or crude or anti-ideological—still resonate powerfully for European commentators who continue to focus on and perhaps even to obsess about the meanings or indeed the supposedly single *meaning* of "America." The spate of contemporary essays and books on the themes of "America" and "anti-Americanism" makes this clear; and whether one turns from Jean Baudrillard's famous 1986 essay *America* to Bernard-Henri Lévy's more recent *American Vertigo: Traveling America in the Footsteps of Tocqueville* or Andrei Markovits's *Uncouth Nation: Why Europe Dislikes America* (see below), one finds iterations of the basic idea that "America" possesses a surplus symbolic value, as it were, far in excess of its mundane existence.[2]

Even today, when the United States unquestionably consumes a grossly disproportionate share of the world's energy, possesses so many of the world's weapons of destruction, and exerts such an obvious cultural influence, there is an exaggerated character to much of this symbolic discourse about "America," "pro-Americanism," and "anti-Americanism." Binary thinking is hardly a monopoly of this topic, and having recently said goodbye to a "century of total war" (again, Raymond Aron), we know too much about how easy it is to get caught up in it.[3] All the same, it is impossible today to reflect intelligently on

2. See Jean Baudrillard, *America* (London: Verso, 1989); Bernard-Henri Lévy, *American Vertigo: Traveling America in the Footsteps of Tocqueville* (New York: Random House, 2006); and Andrei S. Markovits, *Uncouth Nation: Why Europe Dislikes America* (Princeton: Princeton University Press, 2007). See also Paul Berman, "The Anti-Anti-Americans," *New Republic*, November 28, 2005.

3. Raymond Aron, *The Century of Total War* (New York: Doubleday, 1954).

"America through European eyes" with an eye to the future, and to avoid this powerful rhetorical preoccupation. For it is pervasive. This is no doubt a complicated matter, condensing a variety of tendencies in American self-understanding, U.S. foreign policy, the distinctively belligerent personalities of George W. Bush and Donald Rumsfeld, long-term European cultural tendencies, and current discursive contests between different visions of "Europe" (for there is also a burgeoning and lively cottage industry of essays and books on the meaning of Europe, its borders, its cultural legacies, and so forth, quite obviously stimulated in large part by the territorial and symbolic expansion of the European Union). But it seems clear that at present there are powerful tendencies toward the crystallization of two competing "European visions" of America: a self-styled "pro-American" view, rooted in Tocqueville and associated by American neoconservative intellectuals with the "New Europe," that is, the newly "Westernized" and thus "Europeanized" formerly "Eastern bloc" East Europeans; and what is sometimes referred to as a new "anti-Americanism" associated with the "Old Europe," that is, the core nations of the original post–World War II Atlantic Alliance, especially France, Germany, Italy, and Spain. These categories are of course constructs, indeed *gross* and politically loaded oversimplifications. But a certain polarization regarding America in European intellectual and public opinion is not hard to discern.

And it is in this context that I am called upon to offer some concluding reflections regarding the theme of our volume. Two such reflections have already been adumbrated—that our situation today is radically different from that of our "long dead" historical commentators, and that in this new geopolitical situation many European and American eyes turned toward "America" have become rather glazed over. In this situation one very useful contribution of a resolutely historical and *historiographical* volume such as ours is to force readers to brace themselves, step back, attempt to enter the mind frames of Tocqueville, Bryce, Chesterton et alia, and recall that the European rhetoric of "America" has a history, and that at one time at least it lacked the agitation of the current moment. Another useful contribution is to prompt readers to ask themselves a question that is not a focus so much as a subtext of our volume: the question of how things got the way they are, whether we are stuck in these discursive patterns, and what alternative trajectories for the future present themselves.

It is in this historical and that is to say *critical* spirit that I offer some concluding reflections on "America through European eyes." In doing so, I take my lead from an excellent new volume edited by the distinguished political scientists Peter Katzenstein and Robert Keohane, *Anti-Americanisms in World Politics,* and especially from the editors' important introductory essay.[4] Katzenstein and Keohane insist that it is wise to approach the topic of "America" and "anti-Americanism" with great care, and to soberly disaggregate and disentangle various phenomena often conventionally but misleadingly lumped together under the rubric of "anti-Americanism." Most important, they distinguish between criticism of what America *is* and what America *does,* and in doing so they underscore the extent to which much current symbolic contention about "America" can best be understood as a response to American foreign policies of questionable benefit to people in other parts of the world, who are thus rather understandably averse to such policies. Upon reflection, this is a rather commonsense suggestion. And yet it is striking how much it diverges from so much of the public and intellectual rhetoric about the topic.

To be sure, the *is/does* distinction is somewhat conceptually imprecise, since all social action takes place in a symbolic universe that is already pre-interpreted, and there is no "doing" that is not also a way of "being." To this extent, all talk about "America," from the very beginning, has condensed understandings of the "empirical" and the "symbolic," what Americans *do* and what America and Americans *are.* Nonetheless, however imprecise, the distinction highlights that these signifiers—"America," "anti-American"—are complex and often misleading, for they cover things that are *different* and have different causes and consequences, however much they may be related. I believe that Katzenstein and Keohane are correct that much, and probably most, current controversy about "America" is fueled by and centered on what America does rather than what it is, in some symbolic or existential sense, the claims of President George W. Bush notwithstanding ("they hate us for who we are"). To say this is not to downplay the significance of deeply rooted antipathy toward America as a nation-state, a society, and a culture—what sometimes goes by the label "anti-Americanism"—in some quarters. Nor is it to foreclose the kind of empirical and policy discussion and debate that Katzenstein and Keohane explicitly seek to promote. To the contrary, it is to insist that contemporary political conflicts about "America" need to be understood in political rather than simply semiotic or aesthetic terms, and that, like all political conflicts, these conflicts have historically specific determinants that cannot simply be read off of grand narratives of the past.

PROBLEMATIZING "AMERICA"

While it is essential to approach the topics of "America" and "anti-Americanism" with care, part of such care requires us to appreciate the extent to which

4. Peter J. Katzenstein and Robert O. Keohane, eds., *Anti-Americanisms in World Politics* (Ithaca: Cornell University Press, 2006).

"America" *is* such a rhetorically and politically loaded signifier. From the work of theorists such as Michel Foucault and Edward Said we know that all social identities are discursively constituted and socially constructed.[5] And from the work of Benedict Anderson we know that national identities condense distinctive visions of "imaginary community."[6] Armed with these insights, it is still tempting to suppose that however much collective identities are constructs, at least the places to which they correspond have some extradiscursive reality. But if we take seriously the constructivist insight, we can see that the discursive constitution of identity is also a constitution of time and space itself. Contemporary theorists thus speak about "symbolic geography," the historical process whereby territories and spaces become marked, bounded, and invested with meanings.[7] Maria Todorova, for example, has brilliantly shown how "the Balkans" has changed over time, both in its historical referents and its symbolic significance; recourse to the trope of "balkanization" is simply one sign of the ways that what is presumptively a place-name has become much more than that.[8] Similarly, we know that "Europe" (as opposed to "Asia," "the East," "the Orient") has always been as much a myth as it has been a distinct place in the material world (to even speak of a "place on a map" is to make clear the discursive and semiotic character of such spaces).[9] We are well aware that in modern times such place-names are much more than spatial tracking devices, for they inscribe the power to rule and to kill, and they have proven able to evoke extraordinary human passions (think "Palestine" or "Eretz Yisrael" or "Greater Serbia" or "Mother Russia," not to speak of "Deutschland über alles").

Contextualizing in this way, it is possible to appreciate both how typical is talk of "America" (and "pro-America" or "anti-America"), but also how distinctive it is, in ways that relate to the distinctive history of America. Consider the following:

(1) The signifier "America" is distinctively ambiguous regarding its territorial referent. Does it refer to "the United States of America" or to the North American continent or to the land mass "discovered" by the European explorer Amerigo Vespucci that in fact encompasses two linked continents (North America and

5. See Michel Foucault, *The History of Sexuality: An Introduction* (New York: Vintage, 1990), and Edward Said, *Orientalism* (New York: Vintage, 1979).

6. Benedict Anderson, *Imagined Communities: Reflections on the Origins and Spread of Nationalism* (London: Verso, 1991). See also Phillip E. Wegner, *Imaginary Communities: Utopia, the Nation, and the Spatial Histories of Modernity* (Berkeley and Los Angeles: University of California Press, 2002).

7. See Sorin Antohi, "Habits of Mind: Europe's Post-1989 Symbolic Geographies," in *Between Past and Future: The Revolutions of 1989 and Their Aftermath*, ed. Sorin Antohi and Vladimir Tismaneanu, 61–78 (Budapest: Central European University Press, 2000).

8. Maria Todorova, *Imagining the Balkans* (New York: Oxford University Press, 1997).

9. See P. H. Liotta, "Imagining Europe: Symbolic Geography and the Future," *Mediterranean Quarterly* 16, no. 3 (2005): 67–85.

South America)? When we praise or condemn "America" are we doing the same thing as when we praise or condemn "the United States" or "the U.S."? There is some strange semantic slippage here that bespeaks a certain geographic privilege that has come to be claimed, and accorded, the United States as both a nation-state ("the United States") that is *of* America in the sense of being located on the American continent, and an "empire of liberty" ("the United States of America") in the sense that it is purported to represent the essence of America, by virtue of which it claims to speak for and to rule over the continent (one way of reading the famous Monroe Doctrine). Is it possible to imagine an analogue to this? What would it mean, for example, if the Netherlands declared itself "the United Provinces of Europe"? What unique historical conditions would enable such a claim to ever make sense as anything more than a curiosity or a joke? Yet in some sense the United States claims just such a semantic hegemony over the continent "America," and when U.S. policies lead to denunciations of "America" by anti-imperialists, such a hegemony is, ironically, affirmed at the symbolic level at least. At the same time, we are treated to such strange rhetorical possibilities as U.S. newspaper articles on the "anti-Americanism" of Venezuelan President Hugo Chavez, who is most assuredly a Latin *American* political leader who seems to harbor no particular hostility toward the territory that is "America" (and especially the part that currently coincides with the nation-state that is Venezuela), however much he might be averse to the policies or even the very existence of the United States (of America) as a continental hegemon that arrogantly claims to "represent" America as a whole.

(2) This strange semantics of "America" is no doubt related to an equally unusual and interesting semiotics of the nation-state called "The United States (of America)." Choose some random names of nation-states in the world today. "France." "Albania." "Germany." "Namibia." "Peru." Each of these others makes explicit reference to a particular place that is presumed to correspond with some "nation," however "imagined," that resides there. Often the name actually denotes or at least suggests a distinct ethnic basis for this correspondence. But even when not—"Nigeria" or "South Africa"—and even when the specific territorial reference is ambiguous or expansive—"Serbia" or "Israel"—what is referenced is a distinct (if constructed) and substantial place and *not* a political form. Now consider "the United States." The very term bespeaks an absence of "substance," a denial of the forms prevailing at its inception ("monarchy," "empire," "city"), and the articulation of a new and distinctive conception of political association that is *formal,* centered on "consent," and on voluntary *association* itself. I am talking here about the semiotics of national identification only. I am not saying that "the United States" was as "consensual" as its name suggests, only

that its very name bespeaks a novel self-understanding and an undeniably novel form of politics.

(3) This American political self-understanding can also be discerned in a range of formulations that have been descriptively and prescriptively applied to the United States as it developed from a confederation to a constitutional republic to a continental nation-state to a global power: "the New World"; "a City on a Hill"; "Empire of Liberty" or "Asylum of Liberty"; "the New Frontier"; "the Last Best Hope of Freedom." Many of these notions were bound up with the ideology of "Manifest Destiny" that fueled westward expansion in the nineteenth century. Like all ideological formulations, these tropes made sense and expressed certain "truths" about America, which *was* originally a relatively "virginal" land settled, colonized, and modernized by Europeans who did envision it as a "new world," who did in time establish a novel form of republican government ordered by a written constitution, and who did present a counterweight to European imperial hegemonies.[10] This sense was shared by many Europeans as well as many Americans. Whether they liked it or not, there was no denying that the emergent United States was something new, different, and to be reckoned with. When Henry Luce declared the twentieth the "American Century" he was giving voice to already pervasive notions of American power on the rise. For European and American commentators, writing from a no-doubt "Eurocentric" perspective, this rising power was momentous and indeed world historical.

(4) This notion of America's unique "openness" to the future has been observed by some of the most astute recent American cultural critics. Postmodern accounts such as Anne Norton's *Republic of Signs* and Frederick Dolan's *Allegories of America* center in part on the idea that there is something inherently antifoundational and deconstructive about America's historical self-understanding. As Dolan writes, "a persistent feature of claims Americans make about their national political life (a feature they no doubt share with other national communities) . . . [is that it possesses] a privileged spiritual or metaphysical value. At the same time, America's self-allegorization is also self-deconstructing, as reliant on tropes of self-creation and fictionalization as on that of . . . the real as a foundation for a national project. . . . In the historicodiscursive events we know as 'America,' the postmodern problematic assumes the form of a national myth."[11] A similar theme was developed powerfully by Richard Rorty, most notably in

---

10. See Henry Nash Smith, *Virgin Land: The American West as Symbol and Myth* (New York: Vintage, 1950); Frederick Merk, *Manifest Destiny and Mission in American History* (Cambridge: Harvard University Press, 1995); and William Appelman Williams, *Empire as a Way of Life* (London: Oxford University Press, 1982).

11. Frederick M. Dolan, *Allegories of America* (Ithaca: Cornell University Press, 1994). See also Anne Norton, *Republic of Signs* (Chicago: University of Chicago Press, 1993).

his 1998 *Achieving Our Country*. Rorty's words—offered in the spirit of a self-described "postmodern bourgeois liberalism"—mirror the sentiments developed more critically by Norton, and they are worth quoting at length. Both describing and endorsing a perspective attributed to Walt Whitman, he writes: "Because the United States is the first country founded in the hope of a new kind of human fraternity, it would be the place where the promise of the ages would first be realized. Americans would form the vanguard of human history because, as Whitman says, 'the Americans of all nations at any time upon the earth have probably the fullest poetical nature. The United States themselves are essentially the greatest poem.'" Glossing Whitman, he declares that "we are the greatest poem because we put ourselves in the place of God: our essence is our existence, and our existence is in the future."[12]

(5) This distinctively American "being as becoming"—expressed by Rorty, following Whitman, in deliberately metaphorical and provocative terms—has a demographic and cultural foundation in America's unique status as a culturally hybrid "melting pot" of sorts that continues to be perpetually renewed by new waves of immigration. America is hardly the only hybrid society, but there has probably been no other historical society so defined—at the level of constitutional law but also public culture more generally—by human influx, traffic between cultures, and ethnic and cultural cross-fertilization and amalgamation. This makes "America" both a shifting target of observation and commentary and a shifting site of civic identity itself. In her *Democracy and the Foreigner*, Bonnie Honig argues that "foreigners" play a particularly important political and symbolic role in democratic societies because they underscore the deeply contingent and open character of political identities and give the lie to any kind of cultural essentialism. "Foreignness," then, is inherent in political community, and it is something embraced by democratic communities.[13] This is surely true of America, as the historical society par excellence, continually evolving, continually incorporating new peoples and cultures into its cultural fabric, and incorporating legal change into its constitution (at the same time that it has wrestled with ensuing resentments and exclusions, something documented brilliantly by Rogers Smith in his *Civic Ideals*).[14]

This constant change helps us to understand the particular ways that "America" can function discursively as a "floating signifier" with a surplus of meanings. But it puts into question not simply what "America" historically "is,"

12. Richard Rorty, *Achieving Our Country: Leftist Thought in Twentieth Century America* (Cambridge: Harvard University Press, 1998), 22.

13. Bonnie Honig, *Democracy and the Foreigner* (Princeton: Princeton University Press, 2003).

14. Rogers Smith, *Civic Ideals: Conflicting Visions of Citizenship in U.S. History* (New Haven: Yale University Press, 1999).

but what it means, in a deeper sense, to even speak about "America through foreign eyes." For *are* there "foreign eyes" when it comes to "America"? Was Hector St. John de Crèvecoeur a Frenchman or an American when he wrote his *Letters from an American Farmer?* Was Emma Goldman a Russian or an American (or "un-American?") when she agitated for women's rights or protested against imperialism on the streets of New York City? When Leo Strauss, Hannah Arendt, and Herbert Marcuse articulated their respective accounts of the post–World War II world, commenting on American politics and about the character of postwar Europe, were they writing as Germans or as Americans?

Who or what exactly *is* an American as opposed to a European? Now, it is surely possible to say that the writers profiled in our volume were all Europeans who visited America without setting up permanent residence or seeking citizenship status here. And it is equally possible to identify the many American residents and citizens who have never been to Europe or experienced any deeply felt connection to it. Nonetheless, the examples in the preceding paragraph could be multiplied, and doing so would underscore just how much of what is "American" incorporates what is "foreign," in terms of biography, ethnicity, political ideals, and even sense of civic identity. This has always been true. In his brilliant book about the Declaration of Independence, *Inventing America,* Garry Wills indeed points out that the "founding fathers" of the American republic—Franklin, Jefferson, Adams, and so forth—were each more at home in London or Paris than they were in the colonial cities (Philadelphia, Williamsburg, Boston) of their "American" counterparts.[15] From the very beginning, "America" has incorporated Europeans, European values, and *Europeanness.* Is it any wonder, then, that Europeans commenting on America would project their own hopes and fears? For in many ways in gazing at "America" they have indeed been looking in the mirror.

More to the point, perhaps, the profound "foreignness" of America as a space of geographic and social mobility and civic recognition—symbolized by the Statue of Liberty bequeathed to the United States by French republicans, and regarded by many the world over as a symbol of the promise of both "liberty" and "America"—explains why "America" excites such passions for so many who are not Americans and have never really even experienced America. *Pace* Locke, neither at the "beginning" nor ever after has the world *been* America. But since its beginnings America has connected to the world, and "spoken" to the world, in distinctive ways that invite and indeed demand attention.

In a 2004 letter to Richard Rorty, published as "America's Dreaming," the

---

15. Garry Wills, *Inventing America: Jefferson's Declaration of Independence* (New York: Doubleday, 1978).

Iranian scholar and dissident Ramin Jahanbegloo notes not only the geopolitical power of the United States, but also its symbolic power. He writes: "The American dream is the centerpiece of a national intention. . . . But it also has multiple meanings for people elsewhere in the world. To some it represents a chauvinistic cliché, to others a symbol of good life and achievement. Some, meanwhile, believe that the dream has proven to be the most effective tool for the subversion of other cultures. In short, people in many countries have a stake in the American dream. The American dream is not only the dream of the Americans, but the dream of others to become American. From the very beginning, America, the land of freedom, has also been the world's dream: a society built on new foundations, held together not by traditions, but by the idea of a generous and hospitable country open to any experience."[16] Jahanbegloo knows that this is a *dream* rather than a reality, and he acknowledges that it evokes numerous conflicting responses. Nonetheless, writing as an Iranian opposed to his own country's theocratic dictatorship, but also alarmed by the bellicose rhetoric of the Bush administration, he insists on the inspirational and aspirational power of "America," citing Martin Luther King Jr.'s moral idealism as exemplary. Jahanbegloo is no European—though he studied in Paris, taught in European universities, and is steeped in European philosophy. But he too perceives "America" to be a distinctively complex, problematic, and appealing place, space, and identity.

RETHINKING "ANTI-AMERICANISM"

It is hard to ignore the fact that in recent years there has been a heating up of controversy about "America." And there can be no doubt that in many parts of the world "America" excites anger and denunciation and has come to symbolize all that is wrong with the world. It is equally impossible to deny that many "Western" intellectuals—the name of Harold Pinter springs quickest to mind, but many others could easily be named—seem to have joined this chorus of denunciation.[17] At the same time, if my comments above make any sense, then it is perhaps necessary to think a bit harder and more deeply about this. For our understanding of "anti-Americanism" will differ depending on whether we take

16. Ramin Jahanbegloo, "America's Dreaming," *openDemocracy* (September 2004), at http://www.opendemocracy.net/democracy-letterstoamericans/article_2067.jsp.

17. See Harold Pinter's claim that "the crimes of the United States have been systematic, constant, vicious, remorseless, but very few people have actually talked about them," in his December 2005 Nobel Lecture, "Art, Truth, and Politics," at http://nobelprize.org/nobel_prizes/literature/laureates/2005/pinter-lecture. html. On the phenomenon more generally, see Todd Gitlin, "Blaming America First," *Mother Jones* (January/February 2002), at http://gopher.mojones.com/commentary/columns/2002/01/blaming.html.

"America" to be a pretty clear and unproblematic referent or we take it to be a complex and polyvalent one. If the latter, then it is equally complex, and problematic, to consider what it means to be "anti-American."

I would like to bring this volume to a close, and explore this issue in a very general way, by briefly discussing what I take to be the most intellectually and politically cogent recent account of the problem of "anti-Americanism," Andrei Markovits's *Uncouth Nation*. Markovits writes as a Romanian American (indeed as a Romanian Jewish American), and in his preface he explains his own deep connection to Europe and his appreciation of the cultural hybridity of America. His critique of "anti-Americanism" is also rather critical of President Bush and is offered not from the neoconservative right but from the social democratic left. Nonetheless, in his own way he joins the chorus of those who sound the alarm about the upsurge of a virulent "anti-American" passion throughout European public culture. I have no doubt that Markovits is on to something important. But I also think that there is a lack of nuance attached to even his sound of alarm, and that a reflection on the theme of "America through European eyes" might help to clarify this.

For Markovits in fact offers many reflections of his own on this theme, and indeed one way to read his entire book is as an answer to the question "how does America today appear through European eyes?" While I agree with many of Markovits's observations and political arguments, what interests me here is the categorical way in which our topic is treated in his fine book. This comes out most clearly in Markovits's discussion of Jürgen Habermas, the world-famous German political theorist best known for his critique of nationalism and his defense of liberal democratic universalism.

On May 31, 2003, Jürgen Habermas and Jacques Derrida published "February 15, or What Binds Europeans Together: A Plea for a Common Foreign Policy, Beginning in the Core of Europe."[18] The essay, published under the name of two of Europe's most distinguished philosophers, treats the extraordinary trans-European mobilizations against an imminent Iraq War that occurred on February 15, 2003, as a potential watershed in modern history. Habermas and Derrida argue that the historical experiences of modern Europe have generated a distinctive political culture centered around political liberalism and social solidarity, and that this culture ought to be the basis for a new European political identity and foreign policy to counter American hegemony and to contribute to the solution of the world's problems. The piece set off a firestorm of controversy, among Europeans—antiliberals, nationalists but also partisans of Bush's "coalition of the

---

18. Jürgen Habermas and Jacques Derrida, "February 15, or What Binds Europeans Together: A Plea for a Common Foreign Policy, Beginning in the Core of Europe," *Constellations* 10, no. 3 (2003): 291–97.

willing"—opposed to the Habermas-Derrida call for a new European politics, and among Americans, especially on the neoconservative right, against the call for a counter to U.S. hegemony.

Markovits, like many commentators, presents "February 15" as "exhibit A" in his case against European anti-Americanism. He writes that "critical intellectuals like Habermas and Derrida, with an almost mythical-metaphysical sense of urgency on behalf of a '(re)birth' of Europe, have been reverting to culturally arching fabrications about a glaring antagonism between Europe and the United States over the definition of ostensible 'norms' and 'principles' for the United States in the light of the Iraq War . . . [promoting] the feel-good dichotomy of an idealized core Europe and a vilified America." Markovits acknowledges that Habermas has long been known for extolling American ideals and ideas. He nonetheless asserts, in light of "February 15," that "this is now a thing of the past," and that Habermas has taken up the cause of an uncompromising European "offensive" directed against the United States as a "common enemy" of Europe.[19]

This charge tells us something important regarding contemporary polarizations about "America through European eyes" and especially the way a certain kind of infantile leftist anti-imperialism, linked to the denunciation of the United States (and of Israel), has led sober intellectuals of the democratic left such as Markovits to feel isolated and estranged. But this characterization of Habermas as somehow "anti-American" simply cannot be right. There is first the matter of Habermas's words themselves. Markovits doesn't cite denunciations of "America" in the "February 15" letter, and the most reasonable explanation for this is simply that such denunciations are absent there. The essay *does* call for a distinct European foreign policy based on a distinct European identity, and it does argue that such a policy would serve as a necessary counterweight to the strategy of "hegemonic unilateralism" pursued by an arrogant Bush administration. And it denounces the Iraq war as "morally obscene." But while it does, rather deliberately, present an idealized vision of "Europe," it offers no broad denunciation of American values or society.

Indeed, in a September 2002 "Letter to America" appearing in *The Nation*—admittedly published before "February 15"—Habermas explicitly addressed the issue of "anti-Americanism." Asked about U.S.-European relations, he writes:

Many Americans do not yet realize the extent and the character of the growing rejection of, if not resentment against, the policy of the present American Administration throughout Europe, including in Great Britain. The emotional gap may well become deeper than it has ever been since the end of

<hr>

19. Markovits, *Uncouth Nation*, 209, 214, 202

World War II. *For people like me, who always sided with a pro-American left, it is important to draw a visible boundary between criticizing the policy of the American Administration, on one hand, and the muddy stream of anti-American prejudices on the other.* Remembering the period of the Vietnam War, it would be helpful in this respect if the opposition in Europe could relate to, and identify with, a similar movement in this country. Yet compared with 1965, timidity now prevails here. Maybe a kind of systematically distorted communication between the United States and Europe is also in play. . . . we would need, perhaps, a discussion on the respective faults and merits of what we might contrast as "liberal nationalism" and "cosmopolitanism." (emphasis added)[20]

In an interview conducted in 2004—well after "February 15"—Habermas was even more emphatic in distancing himself from anything that reasonably can be called "anti-Americanism." While again criticizing the Bush doctrine, he explicitly credits the foreign policy "idealism" of the United States—mentioning Woodrow Wilson and Franklin Delano Roosevelt, but also George Bush Sr.— for the post–World War II reconstruction and unification of Europe; for the promotion of human rights, international law, and the United Nations; and indeed for its leadership, even in the early years of postcommunism, in supporting a more "cosmopolitan" world order. Writing of George W. Bush, he insists that "one must not imagine that the offensive marginalizing of the United Nations and the cavalier contempt for international law which this administration has allowed itself to be guilty of, represent the expression of some necessary constant of American foreign policy. This administration, whose declared aim, to attend to national interests, has so obviously missed its mark, can be voted out of office. Why should it not be replaced in the coming year by an administration that gives the lie to Kagan?"[21]

The reference to "Kagan" is to Robert Kagan, the American neoconservative well known for having argued that the current geopolitical divide between Europe and America reflected fundamentally different cultural horizons— "Venus" and "Mars"—and that while Europe fancied itself a Kantian cosmopolis, the United States was a "cowboy nation" defined by its pursuit of power in a dangerous world.[22] Habermas adamantly rejects this essentialist counterposition of "Europe" and "America." Indeed, he insists that the Bush "war on terror," how-

---

20. Jürgen Habermas, "Letter to America," *The Nation*, December 16, 2002, at http://www.the nation.com/doc/20021216/habermas.

21. "America and the World: A Conversation with Jürgen Habermas," *Logos: A Journal of Modern Culture and Society* (Summer 2004), at http://www.logosjournal.com/habermas_america.htm.

22. Robert Kagan, *Of Paradise and Power: America and Europe in the New World Order* (New York: Vintage, 2004), and "Cowboy Nation," *New Republic Online*, October 16, 2006, at http://www.car negieendowment.org/publications/index.cfm?fa = view&id = 18796&p rog = zgp&proj = zusr.

ever dangerous in its cavalier dismissal of civil liberties, is more of an aberration than a reflection of America's "cowboy" mentality. Identifying with early American republican civic ideals, he insists that the issue is *not* "Europe" versus "America" but "cosmopolitanism" versus "unilateralism," and that America is the site of democratic ideals to be emulated (even if they have a different cast than similar European ideals) and allies to be engaged. He thus insists that "Anti-Americanism is a danger in Europe itself. In Germany, it has always been associated with the reactionary movements. Thus, it is important for us, as in the time of the Vietnam War, to be able to make common cause, side by side, with an American domestic opposition, against the policy of the American government. If we can relate ourselves to a protest movement inside the United States, the counterproductive reproach leveled against us of anti-Americanism is shown to be empty."[23]

Habermas, seeing *with the eyes of a "European"* (influenced by John Dewey, the American philosopher par excellence who was himself influenced by that most Germanic of German philosophers, G. W. F. Hegel) who acknowledges the contributions of America to human dignity in the twentieth century, and who explicitly draws on American political ideals, surely laments and criticizes the current state of American democracy. But it is hard to see how this represents a repudiation or denunciation of "America" or a call for a political struggle against its ideals, or even a denial of the possibility that the United States, under a different administration, might play a constructive role in the world as a dominant power if not as the *sole* dominant power.

The wrongness of the charge of "anti-Americanism" against the "February 15" manifesto is clearer when one considers that many of Habermas's arguments have been echoed not simply by European intellectuals of the "anti-imperialist" Left—Umberto Eco, Gianni Vattimo, Etienne Balibar, and so forth—but by intellectuals quite public in their general defense of a global struggle against Islamist extremism "led" by the United States, and yet at the same time deeply unsettled by the Bush administration's bellicosity.[24] My own "exhibit B" in this regard is two French writers well known for their "*anti*-anti-Americanism," Bernard-Henri Lévy and Pascal Bruckner.

Bernard-Henri Lévy, in a "Letter to the American Left," also published in *The Nation,* chastises those on the Left who simplistically denounce America, but he also questions why there has not emerged in the United States a politically

23. Habermas, "America and the World."

24. For the interventions by Eco, Vattimo, and numerous others, see Daniel Levy, Max Pensky, and John Torpey, eds., *Old Europe, New Europe, Core Europe: Transatlantic Relations After Iraq* (London: Verso, 2005); see also Etienne Balibar's "Whose Power? Whose Weakness? On Robert Kagan's Critique of European Ideology" *Theory and Event* 6, no. 4 (2003), at http://muse.jhu.edu/journals/theory_&_event/toc/archive.html#6.4.

vibrant Left capable of contesting issues that ought to be contested, including the death penalty, the use of torture as a matter of policy at Abu Ghraib and elsewhere, and the Bush administration's abridgments of civil liberties more generally. He continues:

> And I'm not even talking about Bush. I won't even mention Bush's gross lies about the Iraqi weapons of mass destruction, except for the sake of assembling the conclusive evidence. I know, of course, that you denounce him—but mechanically, I am almost tempted to say ritualistically. And yet the United States nearly impeached Nixon because he had spied on his enemies and lied. They impeached Clinton for a venial lie about inappropriate conduct. How is it, then, that it took so long to draw a parallel between those lies and a lie about which the least you can say is that its consequences were anything but venial? How is it that so few "public intellectuals" have been found, within the confines of this formidable, impetuous American democracy, who can bring up the idea of impeaching George Bush for lying?

This from one of the most widely recognized "anti-anti-Americans" in France, the supposedly most "anti-American" country in Europe.[25]

Similar sentiments are voiced by Pascal Bruckner, another Frenchman who condemns European smugness toward America, but also the *American* political smugness that has helped to bring this forth:

> The brusque style of Washington has managed to antagonize its best friends by means of anachronistic ukases and its treatment of allies as unruly children. Unless it is ready to suffer another defeat, *the United States must abandon its splendid smugness. It needs a strong Europe at its side—a Europe able to support it, but also able to criticize it, give it firm and friendly warnings against its symmetrical temptations of withdrawal and hegemony.* . . . America can no more do without us than we can without America. Despite mutual suspicion, we are condemned to strengthen our ties and to increase transatlantic cooperation. If Europe wishes to have the slightest influence over the rest of the world, it is obliged to establish for itself *a new pan-European democratic structure—an entity that would be unprecedented in its ambitions and political form,* and that derives authority from the voluntary surrender of local and national sovereignty to a higher body. Reason demands that we convert European-American rivalry into emulation between two *blocs that are both close and different from each other.* They both have much to learn from one another about audacity and wisdom:

25. Bernard-Henri Lévy, "A Letter to the American Left," *The Nation*, February 27, 2006, at http://www.thenation.com/doc/20060227/levy.

how to temper American hubris with European moderation and European moderation with American dynamism. It is not a matter of choosing between the New and the Old World, because only *a dialectic* between the two is exciting, the source of fruitful prospects. Europe holds its own cards. *Either it will build a counterforce endowed with credible political and military tools or it will be vassalized,* willingly. In the latter case, an aging and declining Old World will reduce itself to being a luxurious vacation resort, coveted by predators, and always prepared to abdicate its freedom for a little more calm and a little more comfort. [emphasis added][26]

Counterforce. Dialectic. Bruckner is a European who appreciates America's virtues and at the same time extols the distinctive virtues of a Europe that is not America and that insists upon its independence.

My exhibit A is none other than Richard Rorty himself. Rorty is well known for having chastised post-1960s American leftists for their estrangement from America's libertarian traditions and their easy denunciations of American "imperialism" in his book *Achieving Our Country: Leftist Thought in Twentieth Century America.* If in contemporary American public intellectual life one was forced to name a single "anti-anti-American" on the liberal left, it would be hard to think of a better candidate than Rorty, who in style and substance articulated an "American" conception of democracy. Rorty also articulated a distinctively "American" and self-consciously pragmatist critique of the metaphysical system-building of European intellectuals of the Left, of whom one Jürgen Habermas was primus inter pares.

And yet Rorty was from the outset a strong and vocal *supporter* of the Habermas/Derrida "February 15" manifesto. He is worth quoting at length:

Bush's apologists in the American media are likely to dismiss such initiatives as Habermas's and Derrida's as just further examples of the envious and resentful anti-Americanism that is recurrent among European intellectuals. Such a charge would be completely baseless. Both philosophers have profited from their frequent and extended visits to the United States to gain a deep and thorough understanding of America's political and cultural achievements. They are well aware of America's world-historical role as the first of the great constitutional democracies, and also of what America has done for Europe in the years since World War II. They appreciate that it was idealistic Wilsonian internationalism in the United States that led to the creation of the United Nations. They know that the unilateralist arrogance of the Bush administra-

26. Pascal Bruckner, "Europe: Remorse and Exhaustion," *Dissent* (Spring 2003), 11–17.

tion is a contingent misfortune—neither inevitable nor expressive of something deeply embedded, and irredeemable, in American culture and society. Both Europe and America contain many millions of people who see clearly that, despite all that America has done for the cause of human freedom, its assertion of a right to permanent hegemony is a terrible mistake. Americans who realize this need all the help they can get to persuade their fellow citizens that Bush has been taking their country down the wrong path. The solidification of the European Union into a powerful independent force in world affairs would be viewed by that segment of American opinion not as an expression of resentful anti-Americanism but as an entirely appropriate and altogether welcome reaction to the danger that the direction of American foreign policy poses for the world.[27]

Rorty's defense of Habermas, of "Europe," and of the importance of balancing the hegemony of "America" has its own distinctive gloss, related to his long-standing arguments with continental philosophers about Dewey, the concept of truth, democracy, and the sources and contingency of universal values. But Rorty here is articulating critiques of the Bush administration, and its global arrogance, that have been expressed by *many* of the most distinguished members of the U.S. policy "establishment." One thinks of recent books by foreign policy experts Stephen Walt, Joseph Nye, Anatole Lieven, and John Ikenberry on the limits of "hard power" and American unilateralism and the need for some form of global "balancing" (Walt's book is entitled *Taming American Power*).[28] Or the recent writings of Michael Lind, the iconoclastic conservative-turned-centrist liberal, whose 2002 book *Made in Texas: George W. Bush and the Southern Takeover of American Politics* outdoes Michael Moore's film *Bowling for Columbine* in its linking of Bush policy to what neocon Robert Kagan extols as a "cowboy nation."[29] And one should not forget the titles of two new conservative journals of opinion founded explicitly in repudiation of the Bush doctrine of American unilateralism—Patrick Buchanan's *The American Conservative* and Francis Fukuyama's neoconservative apostate *The American Interest*. The "American" character of these journals is quite unmistakable. Much of what one finds there is not far from

27. Richard Rorty, "Humiliation or Solidarity: The Hope for a Common European Foreign Policy," *Dissent* (Fall 2003), 23–26.
28. See Stephen M. Walt, *Taming American Power: The Global Response to U.S. Primacy* (New York: W. W. Norton, 2005); Joseph Nye, *Soft Power: The Means to Success in World Politics* (New York: Public Affairs, 2004); Anatole Lieven, *America Right or Wrong: An Anatomy of American Nationalism* (Oxford: Oxford University Press, 2004); and G. John Ikenberry, *America Unrivalled: The Future of the Balance of Power* (Ithaca: Cornell University Press, 2002).
29. For a broader discussion, see my essay "What John Dewey Learned: A Contemporary Reflection on Intellectual Responsibility," *Hedgehog Review* 9, no. 1 (2007): 17–31.

Habermas in its call for a scaling back of American imperial assertions. It would be hard to consider these texts "anti-American." It would be wiser, I think, to consider them important, necessary, and critical contributions to the ongoing debate about the purposes and effects of American policy, and about the role of the United States in the world more generally—surely a legitimate topic of controversy.[30]

In short, the theme of our book—"America through European eyes"—is very much alive, and it is likely to remain so for a long time to come. But its coloration has changed as times have changed and especially as geography, both symbolic and physical, has changed. We now inhabit a single world that is bound together much more than ever before into complex, interwoven, and in some ways instantaneously reactive networks of power and vulnerability. Our late modern world is characterized by what the sociologist Anthony Giddens has called the extraordinary compression of space and time.[31] There is no America "here" and Europe "there." There is simply the world. And while the world is not "America," America's global reach and influence, and its symbolic power, is felt everywhere, and also questioned and contested everywhere. The boundaries distinguishing "America" from "Europe" (and from "Asia," "Africa," etc.) exist, to be sure, and they will remain sources of contestation. But they are porous, shifting, and problematic. There is no longer in any simple sense "America" as an object of curiosity and fascination, aversion and emulation, nor is there any longer any clear meaning that can be attributed to "American" or "pro-American" or "anti-American" or "un-American." What was once a transatlantic conversation among intellectual elites brought together by travel on the high seas is now a single, interconnected, and cacophonous conversation about the fate of our common world. America, the land of pizza and French fries, is inevitably a topic of concern to all who inhabit our world. There are, to be sure, momentous sources of differentiation, discomfort, and conflict in this world. But these will be better understood—and better resolved in ways that advance human dignity and freedom—when they are detached from overheated rhetoric about "America," whether this be the rhetoric of denunciation or defensiveness.

It seems appropriate to give the last word here to the recently deceased Rorty, who in a 2004 exchange of letters with the Iranian intellectual Ramin Jahanbegloo offered a particularly wise perspective on the question that motivated this volume: "The willingness of the intellectuals of other countries to remind their fellow-citizens of what America once stood for, and might once again come to

30. Michael Lind, *Made in Texas: George W. Bush and the Southern Takeover of American Politics* (New York: Basic Books, 2002).

31. Anthony Giddens, *The Consequences of Modernity* (London: Polity, 1991).

stand for, is very important. Walt Whitman helped convince the world that America was a place in which . . . 'anything can happen and any dream can become reality.' The acclaim with which Whitman's poems were greeted in many different countries showed how widespread was the need to believe that the human future can be made very different from the human past. Reminding the world of what the U.S. managed to accomplish is still a good way to encourage hope that every adult human will, some day, be a free citizen of a democratic, global, political community."[32]

---

32. Richard Rorty, "America's Dreaming," *openDemocracy* (September 2004), at http://www .opendemocracy.net/democracy-letterstoamericans/article_2067.jsp.

Contributors

GUILLAUME ANSART is Associate Professor in the Department of French and Italian at Indiana University, Bloomington. He is the author of *Réflexion utopique et pratique romanesque au siècle des Lumières: Prévost, Rousseau, Sade* (Paris: Minard, 1999). He has published articles on Pascal, Voltaire, Lesage, Prévost, Marivaux, Diderot, and Rousseau. His research interests are in eighteenth-century French literature and philosophy, especially the aesthetics of the novel and political theory. Professor Ansart has also worked on the image of the New World in the literature of the period and has just completed a sequel to his contribution to the present volume dealing with the account of the American Revolution in the *Histoire des deux Indes* and forthcoming in the *Journal of the History of Ideas*. He is currently preparing a translation of Condorcet's writings on the United States for the Penn State University Press.

RICHARD BOYD is Associate Professor in the Department of Government at Georgetown University. His research interests are in social and political theory, with an emphasis on seventeenth- and eighteenth-century political thought, contemporary discussions of civil society, and the liberal tradition in American political thought. In addition to articles and book chapters on Hobbes, Locke, the Scottish Enlightenment, Rousseau, Burke, Tocqueville, Michael Oakeshott, and the economist and social philosopher Frank H. Knight, Boyd is the author of *Uncivil Society: The Perils of Pluralism and the Making of Modern Liberalism* (Lanham, Md.: Lexington Books, 2004). He is currently working on a second book-length project titled "Membership and Belonging: On the Boundaries of Liberal Political Theory."

COSTICA BRADATAN is Assistant Professor of Honors at Texas Tech University, Lubbock, Texas. He was previously Havighurst Post-Doctoral Fellow at Miami University and also taught philosophy and history of ideas at Cornell University. His research interests include history of modern philosophy, Eastern European philosophy, philosophy and literature, philosophy of religion, and history of ideas. Bradatan is the author of *The Other Bishop Berkeley* (New York: Fordham University Press, 2006) and of two other books in Romanian: *O introducere la istoria filosofiei românes ti în secolul XX* (An Introduction to the History of Romanian Philosophy in the 20th Century) (Bucharest: Editura Fundatiei Culturale Române, 2000) and *Jurnalul lui Isaac Bernstein* (Isaac Bernstein's Diary) (Bucharest: Nemira Publishing House, 2001). Bradatan is co-editor of *Janus Head: A Journal of Interdisciplinary Studies in Literature, Continental Philosophy, Phenomenological Psychology, and the Arts* (www .janushead.org), and an online editor for the Intellectual History network (H-Ideas) of the project "H-Net—Humanities and Social Sciences Online," hosted by the Michigan State University (www.h-net.org).

AURELIAN CRAIUTU is Associate Professor in the Department of Political Science at Indiana University, Bloomington. His main research interests are in modern French thought. Craiutu is the author of *Liberalism under Siege: The Political Thought of the French Doctrinaires* (Lanham, Md.: Lexington Books, 2003), winner of a 2004 CHOICE Outstanding Academic

Title Award; *Le Centre introuvable* (Paris: Plon, 2006); *Elogiul libertăţi* (In Praise of Liberty) (Iaş i: Polirom, 1998); and *Elogiul moderaţiei* (In Praise of Moderation) (Iaşi: Polirom, 2006). He also edited *Guizot's History of the Origins of Representative Government in Europe* (Indianapolis: Liberty Fund, 2002), *Tocqueville on America after 1840* (with Jeremy Jennings; Cambridge University Press, 2009), and *Considerations on the Principal Events of the French Revolution* by Madame de Staël (Indianapolis: Liberty Fund, 2008). Professor Craiutu serves as Associate Editor of the *European Journal of Political Theory* and is currently completing a book manuscript examining various faces of moderation in modern political thought.

PATRICK DENEEN is Associate Professor in the Department of Government at Georgetown University, where he holds the Tsakopoulos-Kounalakis Chair of Hellenic Studies. His interests include ancient and modern political philosophy, democratic theory, American political thought, literature and politics, and religion and politics. He is the author of *The Odyssey of Political Theory: The Politics of Departure and Return* (Lanham, Md.: Rowman & Littlefield, 2000), which received one of two Best First Book Prize honorable mentions from APSA's Foundations of Political Theory section. Professor Deneen is also the author of *Democratic Faith* (Princeton: Princeton University Press, 2005) and was the recipient of the APSA 1995 Leo Strauss Award for best dissertation in political philosophy.

RUSSELL HANSON is Professor in the Department of Political Science at Indiana University Bloomington. His primary interest is the historical development of liberalism and its impact on the prospects for democratic politics. He has also investigated the political dynamics of social welfare policy in the American states, as well as questions of equity raised by wide variation in state programs in a federal system. He is currently researching social reform movements in the post–Civil War era, including those with close ties to similar organizations in Great Britain. Professor Hanson teaches courses on American political thought, modern political thought, and state and local politics in the United States. He is the author of *The Democratic Imagination in America* (Princeton: Princeton University Press, 1985) and the co-editor of *Political Innovation and Conceptual Change* (Cambridge: Cambridge University Press, 1989), *Reconsidering the Democratic Public* (University Park: Pennsylvania State University Press, 1993), and *Politics in the American States* (Washington, D.C.: CQ Press, 2007). Professor Hanson's articles have appeared in the *Journal of Politics, American Journal of Political Science,* and *Publius,* among others.

CHRISTINE DUNN HENDERSON is Senior Fellow at Liberty Fund, Inc., in Indianapolis. She completed her undergraduate education at Smith College (A.B. in government and French studies) and received a Ph.D. in political science from Boston College. Prior to joining Liberty Fund, she taught political science at Marshall University. She is contributing editor of *Seers and Judges: American Literature as Political Philosophy* (Lanham, Md.: Rowman & Littlefield, 2002), a collection exploring the connections between politics and literature in a democratic society. She also co-edited (with Mark Yellin) a recent edition of Joseph Addison's writings, *Joseph Addison's "Cato" and Selected Essays* (Indianapolis: Liberty Fund, 2004). Her current areas of research include politics and literature, as well as nineteenth-century liberalism.

JEFFREY C. ISAAC is James H. Rudy Professor; Director of the Indiana Democracy Consortium; and Chair, Department of Political Science, Indiana University, Bloomington. He is the author of *Power and Marxist Theory: A Realist View* (Ithaca: Cornell University Press, 1987), *Arendt, Camus and Modern Rebellion* (New Haven: Yale University Press, 1992), *Democracy in Dark Times* (Ithaca: Cornell University Press, 1998), *The Poverty of Progressivism: The Future of American Democracy in a Time of Liberal Decline* (Lanham, Md.: Rowman & Littlefield, 2003). He has also written extensively on the political thought of anticommunist dissidents (in *Social Research, East European Politics and Societies*) and on the themes of democracy and pragmatism. Professor Isaac is a frequent contributor to *Dissent* magazine, where he writes about ethics and politics and the history and future of the Left. He currently is the Book Review Editor of *Perspectives on Politics*.

JEREMY JENNINGS is Professor of Political Theory at Queen Mary, University of London. He has published extensively on issues relating to the history of political thought in France from the eighteenth century onward, translated and edited G. Sorel's *Reflections on Violence* (Cambridge: Cambridge University Press, 1999) as well as two volumes on the role of intellectuals. Professor Jennings also edited a four-volume collection of essays on socialism as well as a volume entitled *Republicanism in Theory and Practice* (New York: Routledge, 2006). His articles have appeared in many peer-refereed academic journals such as the *American Political Science Review, British Journal of Political Science, Journal of the History of Ideas, The Review of Politics*, the *Historical Journal, European History Quarterly, Journal of Political Ideologies*, and *History of Political Thought*. Jeremy Jennings is one of the founding editors of the *European Journal of Political Theory*, published by Sage, and is presently completing a history of political thought in France (forthcoming with Oxford University Press). In collaboration with Aurelian Craiutu, he has translated and edited a volume containing Tocqueville's writings on America after 1840 (Cambridge University Press, 2009). He was previously a Visiting Fellow at the Columbia University Institute for Scholars, Reid Hall, Paris, and at the Institute for Advanced Study in Bloomington; Visiting Professor at the École des Hautes Études en Sciences Sociales, Paris; and held the Vincent Wright Chair at the Institut d'Études Politiques in Paris.

ALAN M. LEVINE is Associate Professor in the Department of Government, School of Public Affairs, at American University. He is the author of *Sensual Philosophy: Toleration, Skepticism, and Montaigne's Politics of the Self* (Lanham, Md.: Lexington Books, 2001), and editor of *Early Modern Skepticism and the Origins of Toleration* (Lanham, Md.: Lexington Books, 1999). He has published articles and book chapters on Machiavelli, Montaigne, Nietzsche, Chinua Achebe, and European views of America. He is currently working on a book entitled "The Idea of America in European Political Thought: 1492–9/11." Levine is the founder and coordinator of the Washington, D.C., Political Theory Colloquium, has worked for the U.S. Department of State in Dakar, Senegal, and is a regular consultant for the U.S. State Department's International Visitors Leadership Program. He has held fellowships from the National Endowment for the Humanities and at the Hoover Institution at Stanford University, the Institute of United States Studies at the University of London, and the James Madison Program in American Ideals and Institutions at Princeton University.

NICK NESBITT is Senior Lecturer in French and the Centre for Modern Thought at the University of Aberdeen, Scotland. He was previously Associate Professor of French at Miami University of Ohio. His book *Voicing Memory: History and Subjectivity in French Caribbean Literature* was published by the University of Virginia Press in 2003. He has recently published a second book for the University of Virginia Press entitled *The Haitian Revolution and the Radical Enlightenment* (2008). He is currently working with the philosopher Jean-Godefroy Bidima on a study of the history and philosophy of human rights and its relation to global colonialism. He has published articles on such subjects as critical, poststructuralist, and postcolonial theory (Deleuze, Adorno, Heidegger, Fanon, Césaire, etc.), French Caribbean literature, and musicology (Adorno, Deleuze, jazz, West African music).

Index

www.ingramcontent.com/pod-product-compliance
Lightning Source LLC
Chambersburg PA
CBHW021853020426
42334CB00013B/305